T0269776

Praise for
Artur Pawlowski
and *Lions Do Not Bow*

Pastor Artur Pawlowski is a modern-day patriot of the highest order. His service to God and man and his stand against an overreaching and global tyranny permeating societies around the world represent a nobility of courage rarely seen in today's world. His cause is that of every freedom-loving person on the planet. He fights for freedom, not because it is his cause. He fights because freedom is ordained by God. And here on earth, Pastor Pawlowski is among a small group of emissaries standing watch for us all. God bless Artur and his family.

—**Lt. General Michael Flynn,** U.S. Army Lieutenant General, Retired, Former U. S. National Security Advisor, Author

I love Pastor Artur Pawlowski and what he does for Jesus. He took a hit for our Lord. God took me from the lowest place and lifted me up. And it's people like him who had a part in that. St. Paul said, "To live is Christ, to die is gain," and Artur Pawlowski did that because he's a great, great man who exemplifies Jesus on the cross.

—**Jim Caviezel**, American movie and television actor, including in *The Passion of the Christ* series and *Sound of Freedom*

Pastor Pawlowski is an unapologetic "Matthew 5:10" kind of pastor and follower of Christ who will be blessed in this life and the next because of how much punishing persecution he has endured for the cause of Christ!

—**Clay Clark**, Founder of the ReAwaken America Tour, Host of *ThrivetimeShow.com* Podcast, Author

I know that Artur Pawlowski will continue to preach and proclaim the gospel for many years to come. I always enjoy times of fellowship with him and his family. If I ever lived in Calgary, I'd be right there with him!

—**Dr. Franklin Graham**, American evangelist and missionary, President and CEO of the Billy Graham Evangelistic Association (BGEA) and Samaritan's Purse, Author

Every country needs a couple of guys like … Canada's Artur Pawlowski. When I first met him, I said, "This guy is the devil's worst nightmare!" He stands as a symbol of unwavering faith. During COVID, he cast the police out of the church like he was casting out demons. They were going to shut him down, and he shut them down. He's a real hero and an inspiration!

—**Dr. Lance Wallnau**, CEO of Lance Learning Group, Host of *The Lance Wallnau Show*, Author

The courage necessary to stand up for one's faith against a tyrannical government with unlimited power and resources is truly unimaginable. Yet, during the COVID lockdowns, there was one who screamed, "Out of this property, you Nazis. Out!" Those seven words of truth uttered by Artur Pawlowski have since echoed around the globe. He has faced persecution and imprisonment by the Canadian government, which is beyond anything one could think. Incredibly, through his faith and love for Jesus, Artur stands strong, unscathed, and victorious today! *Lions Do Not* Bow is an absolute must-read.

—**Bo Polny**, founder of Gold 2020 Forecast

I have had the honor of getting to know Artur Pawlowski through this prophetic journey. His courage, tenacity, and love for the Lord make his book very compelling to read.

—**Julie Green**, founder of Julie Green Ministries International

LIONS
DO NOT BOW

The Unbreakable Courage
of Canada's Pastor

ARTUR PAWLOWSKI

Harvest Creek
PUBLISHING & DESIGN

A lion does not concern
himself with the opinions of
the sheep.

And lions do not bow
to hyaenas.

Cover and Interior Layout @ 2024 Harvest Creek Publishing and Design www.harvestcreek.net

Ordering Information: Churches, associations, and others can receive special discounts on quantity purchases. For details, please contact the author at the address listed at the back of the book.

Lions Do Not Bow—1st ed.

ISBN: 978-1-961641-19-8

Printed in Canada

CONTENTS

DEDICATION

To my parents, Grace and Józef Pawlowski, who were willing to leave everything behind and emigrate from Poland for a better future for our family. Sacrificing your past, you took me and my brother Dawid to the place—to the future—that God wanted for us in Canada. Thank you, Mom. Thank you, Dad.

To my wife, Marzena (her name means "a dreamer"), who remains committed to the call of God in our lives despite the hardships we have faced during this "Hell on Earth." It was you who had the dream of a husband committed to serving the Living God so many years ago. You fought for that dream with the strength of a lioness and won your prize! Through your unwavering example, you introduced me to the true Living God of love and guided me into His warm embrace. Thank you for giving me the best gift a man can give to another man. Thank you for leading me to Jesus Christ, my Lord and Savior!

To my children, Nathaniel, Gabriel, and Maya-Grace. You have paid a hefty price for what we are doing. There were many instances where you couldn't have or do what other kids had or did. Thank you for being my children. You make me proud, and it is an honor to be your dad. I love you very much.

To my brother Dawid for being my friend. Even after being arrested 12 times, you have stuck with me no matter what. The sword of injustice has hammered you, and yet you have faithfully faced ongoing harassment and shared with me the burden of jail. I extend a heartfelt thank you to Marta, your wife, for tending to your wounds and standing by your decision to go all the way.

ACKNOWLEDGMENTS

Thank you, Street Church members, for praying for me and providing the support we desperately needed in this time of great difficulties! Without all of you, I would not have survived this enormous attack on my life. May God richly bless you for your faithfulness.

I want to express my gratitude to my fellow inmates for opening up about the horrors of being imprisoned and for not compromising their integrity for the "rewards" offered to them by the system.

I want to extend my thanks to the countless American pastors, Patriots, and citizens who have stood by me during this challenging experience. You have graciously received me, offered your homes, and accompanied me throughout. Your patriotism and empathy towards my experiences are deeply appreciated.

A big thank you to my friends from around the globe for not forgetting about me when I was hurting. Thank you for standing in the gap! In the end, I want to thank all the freedom fighters who have fought for what is right. A big thanks to all the political prisoners for their willingness to sacrifice their lives for the future of our children! Bless you!

My wife and I thank the prayer warriors who constantly lifted us up. There were many times when we could palpably feel the Lord covering us through us through your prayers and we knew we were not alone.

Thanks to the Harvest Creek Publishing team, along with all the individuals who helped bring this book to life.

Above all, I express my gratitude to Jesus Christ, my God, my Lord, and my Savior. He has selected an imperfect vessel to demonstrate His perfect will and power, touching the lives of millions worldwide. I am incredibly humbled and grateful to You for saving me and choosing me to proclaim Your name. Once more, I repeat the words I spoke to you many years ago: "Here I am. Send me! I am willing to go."

FOREWORD

USE YOUR IMAGINATION as you picture the following scenarios:

- You're a 6-year-old boy who comes home from school to learn that his dad was just arrested for reading the Bible to a few people in a public park.
- You're in elementary school and are picked up by your grandpa because your dad is in jail, and your mom is busy dealing with the situation.
- You're growing up in a home where, any day and at any time, the police may come to arrest your dad. And not for committing any real crimes but for simply being a Christian pastor in Canada.

This was the reality of my life. Regularly, I would find out my dad received tickets, fines, many court summons, and court orders for doing his job of feeding the homeless and preaching the gospel. Sometimes, Dad was in court more often than he was at home.

Occasionally, I would find out my dad was in jail again because he had been feeding the homeless, or he was praying for people, or even because he was preaching. Before 2020, authorities arrested and threw my father in jail eleven times, fining him more often than one can count. Keep in mind that throughout these 100-plus court cases, he was always found "not guilty." Eleven arrests and over 350 citations or fines, yet not one charge stuck.

This was the reality that I grew up witnessing. Ironically, I became desensitized and accustomed to these situations because they were everyday experiences in my life.

After 2020, when COVID restrictions and mandates began, again, the government stretched out its corrupt hands against my father and our family. Once more, he was arrested five times for:

- Keeping the church doors open
- Officiating a church gathering
- Inciting people to attend church
- Taking part in an illegal gathering
- Failing to wear a mask
- Protesting
- Inciting mischief (by delivering a sermon)

Again, he also received over 40 citations and fines during this time. All the charges, arrests, and penalties were disguised with big legal words. But it boiled down to him doing his job as a pastor and speaking out against government corruption.

Growing up, I witnessed a man who would not bow to a system that told him to bow. I learned from a father who lived out the faith and faced enormous persecution. I never knew what might happen to him when he left for work!

Most young boys grow up respecting and revering law enforcement and the justice system. My dad's mistreatment by the system gave me a distinct and different perspective. Politicians and the media have vilified, slandered, defamed, and discredited him. The court system has ticketed, arrested, and jailed him. There have been attempts on his life. Once, while my mother, father, siblings, and I were in the house, someone lit our garage on fire!

But none of this caused him to waver, even for a moment. Having him as my father, I have always looked up to him with great respect and awe. His faith and personal relationship with the living God is genuine. It was undeniable that the miracles and power of God followed him wherever he went. Because his faith is genuine and he follows Jesus Christ, he has faced persecution like no other. The Bible teaches:

> *If the world hates you, know that it hated Me before it hated you.*
>
> JOHN 15:18 (NKJV)

> *In fact, everyone who wants to live a godly life in Christ Jesus **will be persecuted.***
>
> 2 TIMOTHY 3:12 [EMPHASIS ADDED]

The Bible promises persecution and teaches that we should "rejoice" in it. My father rejoices in suffering and hardship for the cause of Christ.

But that does not mean it has always been easy on him or our family. Actually, it's the complete opposite. It has been very difficult, and the road has often been rough. I didn't have the same childhood experience as most of my friends or classmates. But I always knew that my father was doing what was right in God's eyes and had chosen to follow Him.

My father has articulated and exemplified the Christian faith practically and only time will tell what kind of impact he has had on our society and in shaping Canada and the United States. He is a different kind of pastor. He is one who actually goes and lives out the gospel of Jesus Christ and the book of Acts. The influence that my father has had on Canadians and Americans has been impactful.

I am the son of this book's author—Pastor Artur Pawlowski—and I can tell you that his character is one of integrity, honesty, faith, boldness, and kindness. He has these attributes because of Jesus and the Holy Spirit living within him.

> *"I was naked and you clothed Me; I was sick and you visited Me; I was in prison and you came to Me." Then the righteous will answer Him, saying, "Lord, when did we see You hungry and feed You, or thirsty and give You drink? And when did we see You a stranger and welcome You, or naked and clothe You? And when did we see You sick or in prison and visit You?" And the King will answer them, "Assuredly, I say to you, inasmuch as you did it to one of the least of these My brothers, you did it to Me."*
>
> MATTHEW 25:36-40 (NKJV)

There is no man who exemplifies this verse more than my father, Artur Pawlowski. For over 20 years, he has selflessly fed and provided for the poor of Calgary. He has dedicated himself to ministering and assisting people all around the world.

In my opinion, he is the most persecuted person in Canada and perhaps in all of Canadian history. This book recounts some events that occurred during the COVID Era and his personal experiences in prison. It will shock, astound, and encourage all who read it.

—Nathaniel Pawlowski

PREFACE

THIS BOOK details the author's experiences and events during fifty days in a Canadian prison and the background story of the several years leading up to it. A person's emotional and mental state can suffer from spending hours in solitary confinement daily. But as a follower of Christ, Artur Pawlowski placed his trust in God to bring about the victory.

You, as a reader, will fully embrace the highs and lows of Artur's journey. On most days, he had the mental fortitude to document every small detail meticulously. Yet there were other days when all he could muster up was the strength to pen a public statement informing his supporters to keep the faith.

With nothing but discarded scraps of used paper and a single pencil to journal his experiences, Artur has relied on his memory and recollections from phone calls to family to document his imprisonment. Prepare for the vast array of emotions you'll encounter while reading about the horrific conditions he endured, as well as the miraculous events that resulted from his incarceration.

The Bible says to "gather the pieces that nothing will be lost" (John 6:12). It is abundantly clear that God has used every detail of Artur's situation for good. The entirety of his prison stay has resulted in divine opportunities, such as many conversions to the Christian faith and the replacement of tyrannical leaders within the government. Artur Pawlowski has exemplified to others the importance of standing up against evil and having complete trust in the Lord. May you be blessed as you embark on the author's journey of experiencing God's favor and discovering how it applies to you as well.

INTRODUCTION

THE TAKEDOWN
OF THE "EL CHAPO" OF CANADA

AS I STEPPED OUT of my house, I was completely oblivious to what was about to happen. I welcomed a few friends who had come over and were prepared to leave, waiting patiently for me. While gathering my recording equipment, Bible, and some belongings, I failed to notice the grey van parked in front of our house while making my way to the nearby storehouse. Well, the truth is, I was not looking. There was always someone parked across the street, and I was focused on the task ahead.

We were getting ready to go to the Montana border to stand in solidarity with the truckers who were fighting for our rights. I had just been there the week before and couldn't wait to join my Canadian compatriots once more today. In Coutts, Alberta, entire families, men, women, and children, were keeping the fort and seeking support. They needed words of hope.

Having grown up in hell, behind the Iron Curtain under the Soviets' boots, I knew how they felt and felt compelled to go back there. They needed encouragement to hold the line and stand tall. Once again, I needed to remind them that this task must be accomplished peacefully. A meeting would be necessary to come up with solutions and reach an agreement.

Placing my packed bag near the fence, I went to the storehouse to grab more banners, T-shirts, and hats. As I opened the door, I greeted my brother Dawid, who was already waiting there. My son Nathaniel and my close friend John were also among the team members who had just arrived. As part of the trip, two politicians from Alberta were accompanying us to help with negotiations between the government and protesters. The rest of the convoy would join us outside the city limits. More people had contacted me, ready to join us as well.

Just as I was about to enter the storehouse, several masked officers appeared and approached me quickly. Our eyes met as one officer yelled, "You are under arrest."

Then, behind him, I saw marked police cruisers coming up fast and stopping in the middle of the road. Police officers were approaching from every direction. Watching this felt surreal, like some kind of movie set straight from Hollywood. There were RCMP officers, undercover police, Calgary uniformed police, detectives, anti-terrorists, and a special S.W.A.T. team all present—all there to record my arrest.

It was a sting operation, similar to the takedowns of Escobar, El Chapo, or Al Capone. I turned to John and said, "Start your camera. Record everything!"

I dropped to my knees with my hands behind my back. As they tried to take me, I fell down a few steps. It was crazy and chaotic! It was obvious their motives were propaganda-driven. They had a special police officer with a camera recording everything. Just like on a movie set, the actors were dressed in their props and had all the gadgets necessary for the take.

They wanted to send a message to the public, "You see what we do with those that disagree with us? We crush them! We destroy them! We will use any force necessary to achieve the effect of fear! Do you want to become the next Pawlowski? Be our guest. We will do to you what we are doing to him!"

Why choose to do this in front of my loved ones and community? Blocking the entire street! Why? For the drama. All they had to do was send an email to my lawyers, informing them of the warrant for my arrest and my requirement to surrender. I would have no choice. The show of such a sizeable force was just for that—for a show! It was all a performance, an orchestrated takedown designed to intimidate others.

Welcome to "China-da," a land of lawbreakers in uniforms pretending to be officers of the law. This had nothing to do with justice or the rule of law. I became a political prisoner for daring to challenge a regime that wanted to transform Canada into a replica of Soviet Russia or communist China.

An officer pushed me down the stairs. Laying on the ground, I knew I would be hurt. I could feel their hate. But those were not just officers; they were the agents of evil. They wanted me to pay, to be hurt. My peaceful non-cooperation angered them even more. In their fury, they grabbed me with such force that the handcuffs cut my skin, causing enormous pain. Two months later, I still had the scars to prove it.

Finally, they lifted me up, causing my slippers to come off, and multiple officers escorted me to the police car. I thought, *What a Gong Show! What is going on in our country?* Little did I know, my 16th arrest had granted me a title from the biggest outlet in the country: The Most Persecuted Man in Canada.

CHAPTER ONE

INTERROGATION

[DAY 1]

DURING MY JOURNEY to the police station, I endured several insults and false accusations. They said that I was just an actor playing a role. Can you imagine? For them, it was like some sick, twisted game—a joke of some sort.

People had lost their loved ones. Multitudes had lost their jobs. Children were suffering, and we had the highest suicide statistics in the history of this nation because of the lockdowns and the segregation. And yet they accused me of staging my own arrests for publicity stunts. What sick individuals.

They hadn't lost a penny since this craziness started. While other people were losing their savings, they were getting benefits and bonuses for obeying their masters' totalitarian orders. They were telling me we were "in this together," while they never missed a single paycheck. For the rest of the population, outside of government, there were no secure salaries. But who cared about us? Obviously, they did not care!

People with filled stomachs rarely understand those who have nothing to eat. For me, every life is meaningful because every life matters. I guess I entered the part of the "breaking!" When you have nothing tangible against someone, you invent stuff to put pressure on and create hopelessness in the victim. It was a clear psychological mind game, straight from the Gulags.

When we arrived, someone asked me to step out of the vehicle. I did and was immediately pushed by an officer. I told him not to push me around. He got more aggressive and pushed me even more. Inside the police station, I was surrounded by more officers. Some were Calgary police; others were from the RCMP. While surrounded, an officer started reading some statements to me, but I refused to acknowledge anything they were telling me. They locked me in a room and provided me with a telephone to call my lawyer.

Sometime later, an officer identifying himself as an RCMP detective walked in and wanted to talk. He brought a coffee and took me to a different room upstairs, where I was interrogated for hours. The officer was looking for some answers. I made up my mind to talk to him and let him know the story behind why I do what I do. I don't know if he cared for my story or not, but as a pastor, I always try to share the answer to the "whys" when I can.

In the end, there was nothing to hide. I was unashamed, and to this day, I remain unashamed of my participation in the truck convoy. Seeing over 1,000,000 Canadians coming together under the umbrella of freedom, waving our beloved Canadian flag, made me feel proud of being a Canadian for the first time in a long time. It was a blessing to witness tens of thousands coming together, families with children, young and old, and every color, every race and background, to stand in solidarity with each other against the tyranny.

And it made me realize that we had not yet lost the nation. If there were people like this, there was hope. We could turn the tide around to have our beloved Canada back, strong and free. Why would I deny that I spoke at Coutts? Why hide something that hundreds of thousands of people watched and were encouraged by? Particularly when the officer was satisfied that he "had me," and I knew I could never avoid the consequences of being in Milk River and Coutts. And that I was doomed.

The officer said goodbye, and I was escorted to the Spyhill Detention Centre. It was a place I knew all too well with cold concrete, no mattress, no pillow, and the bright white lights, the type that literally tortured the eyes. Surprisingly, the other officers chose not to handcuff me, and I sat comfortably in the back of the cruiser. I couldn't help but think that if other officers were treating me in this way, there would never be a need for my peaceful, non-cooperation during the arrests. I am not a violent criminal. I am a pastor—granted, one with a big mouth—but nevertheless, a pastor.

Spyhill is definitely not a pleasant place. However, compared to the Remand Centre, it was spotless. Once again, the guards thoroughly checked and stripped me of my belongings before placing me in solitary confinement. It was a concrete cell with a concrete bench. There was a toilet with a sink built with one solid piece. And as always, there was a camera attached to the ceiling, recording every move one makes.

The good thing about being a "re-offender" is that you learn something new every time you are in captivity. Having learned from my previous check-ins, this time, I took two masks with me from the police station and noticed how surprised they were when I asked for them. Artur Pawlowski does not wear a muzzle. Everybody knew that.

Lesson #1: When you are being arrested, grab anything that is offered to you. You never know what might be helpful when you're locked in a solitary cell. There is a tremendous benefit to having masks in such a place. They work beautifully as an eye covering. Put something between the folded masks—a square of toilet paper, for example. This invention can block the painful intensity of the bright lamps. In case you find it difficult to sleep because of the police guards who loudly bang on the doors every 15 minutes, you can find some comfort by using an eye covering as you await your fate.

I must confess that I can quickly become bored. I can't help it. All my life, I have worked very hard. Even when we go on vacation, I always look for a way to go somewhere, to see something, to explore. It is in my nature to do something, anything, to be constantly busy. Sitting and slowly dying is not an option!

However, what is there to do when there is absolutely nothing to do? During my previous visits, I had made a few games to "kill time," but now I did not feel like playing. I felt extremely exhausted. The comfort of laying on concrete only lasts for a few minutes. When the pain sets in, simply move to the side. Then to the other side. Then, from your back to your stomach. Initially, there's a slight improvement, but then the pain returns.

And that's how it goes repeatedly. From the back to the stomach, then to one side, then to another, and somehow, the pain will always find you. Unless you're heavily intoxicated, flopping around like this all night is excruciating. I have seen people so intoxicated that nothing bothered them at all. Like dead men all night long, they would not even move an inch. But for me, after a while, I needed to stand up and walk a little. Circle the cell 20 times. Sit, stand, and walk some more.

For entertainment, you can look out of your cell through a little window. Of course, there is nothing to see there, but you look out anyway. It is just part of the "entertainment package." From time to time, if you are lucky, you will see police guards walking by, checking the cells. And without mercy, they are always banging on each cell door, waking up even those who have nearly died from "old age" and are waiting for justice to come. It was apparent they were inspecting the doors, fearing that an angel might have set some captives free. Miracles happen in police cells!

Finally, after hours of hard work, I was able to break a tiny piece of concrete from the bench that I was sitting on. I considered that a miracle because the walls, floors, and benches are coated with a special rubber paint that prevents those types of occurrences. You have no idea what a resourceful and very determined man can do with a tiny piece of concrete. The sky is the limit!

For example, with a bit of logic and some water dumped on the little concrete pebble, you can soften the "rough edges" to write on the wall. For instance, you could write, "Jesus loves you and died for you." And so, I decided to do just that.

I encountered a bit of resistance from my little rock. It was not as efficient as I needed it to be. So, I shortened the message and simply wrote: "JESUS DIED 4 U," which was short and straight to the point! Plus, I added something special at the end, just from me. As I was drawing this image, I thought of my brother Dawid. He would be very proud of me right now.

When I finished, everything looked perfect. I had also carved a symbol depicting the enduring struggle of the Polish underground resistance! The emblem combines the letters "P" and "W," with the letter P sitting on top of the W, which is in the shape of an anchor.

From time to time, I would look at my piece of "art" and chuckle. *You can lock me up,* I thought, *but Jesus and what I stand for is locked up here with me.* That's one thing they cannot take away from us: who we are and what we represent. Every guard passing by would have to look at it; they might stop for a split second to soak in what I had created.

Eventually, I could call my lawyer and my family. However, instead of discussing the bail conditions in front of the Justice of the Peace, they informed me that we would have to wait until the following day to appear before a judge from Lethbridge. They retook my fingerprints and another picture of me, and then off I went to spend some more hours on concrete.

A nurse examined me, and I requested that he photograph my scarred wrists because I wanted a picture for future proof of my illegal treatment. However, the nurse refused! During the night, an officer asked me to follow him. "You're going to the Remand Centre," he said.

Somehow, I knew they would do everything in their power to keep me in prison as long as they could and hurt me and my family as much as possible. After all, I had steadily been exposing their corruption for the past two years. The Admission Office staff escorted a group of us prisoners to a tank-like room. There, shackles were placed on both of my feet, and my hands were bound with handcuffs.

After that, the "Penguin March" began, and we all made our way to the police van.

IN THE BELLY OF THE BEAST

Walking fast is impossible when your feet are bound with shackles; you can only take small, ridiculous steps. I think that's the purpose. When we arrived at the Remand Centre, I did not know who was more displeased about me being there: the jailers or me. The last time I was there, it was not very pleasurable. However, this time, everything was going a little faster.

"What color underwear?" was the question posed by a female officer. I was utterly clueless about her request.

Taking a gamble, I responded, "Black. I think," not knowing why they were asking this question. Was this, in fact, the correct answer? I assume I passed some sort of test because she marked it down and then moved on to the next person. I'm just glad I didn't say "pink" or "purple."

Then came the strip search for contraband. They were clearly searching for freedom in me, but I managed to hide that precious commodity where they couldn't find it—in my heart and my spirit. Then came a shower, a jumpsuit, and, as a bonus, pink slippers. If this was truly a circus, we were dressed to play our parts as clowns. Following that, I was directed to a holding tank with fellow individuals awaiting the nurse's examination. I suspected the COVID swab was on the menu. After all, it had become quite the tradition for the past two years in this madhouse.

Sitting quietly, I watched in horror as inmates went inside the torture chambers, one after another, and returned holding their noses in visible pain. The audible reactions to this pleasurable experience could be heard with an "ahh" or "ow." Once again, I made a mental promise to myself: *I will never go through this pointless treatment.*

A male nurse poked a man so forcefully during swabbing that it caused a loud pop. He commented he had never seen this swab stick go so deep. Ouch! The inmate came out holding his nose in visible distress.

"God," I said to myself, "have mercy on this victim of such cruelty."

When it came to my turn to go to the chamber of Mengele, an officer escorted me. The nurse looked at me and said, "I am sure you had one of them before, haven't you?"

My reply was swift and straightforward. "No way you're sticking this into my nose! I'm not doing it."

The officer who brought me to the room immediately said, "Of course, we all knew that this was going to happen. He never takes it." Well, I took what he said as a compliment. At least they all knew that I was very predictable.

While the rest of the inmates were escorted to their cells, I remained alone in the holding tank. Eventually, they marched me to the scanning area, where there was a full-body scanner like the ones used at airports. They scanned me twice, front and back. This is when I came to understand that the act of undressing prisoners and searching for last year's snowfall was a way to dehumanize and humiliate them, robbing them of their dignity. It had nothing to do with looking for contraband. It was their way of saying, "We own you here. Forget about your rights. You are ours!"

After the body scan, we went back to the Admission Office, where I received a small pillow sack bundle with something inside. Then, I was escorted to solitary confinement for what they explained was "a

14-day quarantine." Only in 21st-century medical logic do they isolate and separate healthy individuals and lock them up in some of the most unsanitary environments. The cell was absolutely filthy. Clearly, nobody had bothered to clean it after the previous person, but I was too exhausted to care at that point.

My wrists hurt, and my shoulder was in great pain from the arrest. I was beyond tired! As morning approached, I uncovered a toothbrush, toothpaste, towel, bedding, and a blanket in the deceptive white bag they provided. Where is the pillow? I wondered. Well, there was none. I quickly put the bedding on the thin mattress and used the white bag as the perfect place to stuff things in and to use it as a pillow. I brushed my teeth with the most miniature, most ridiculous-looking toothbrush and went to bed.

Within what felt like five minutes, the lights were turned on, and the count started. The officer brought me breakfast, but I only accepted the drink they referred to as "coffee." Suffering has its limits, you know. After adding a mysterious white liquid to the coffee, which was cold, I drank it. There was absolutely no hot water; inside my cell, the water was not working. It was a real downer since I was already severely dehydrated, resulting in a pounding headache.

When you are taken out of your environment into a new space or situation, you feel a little disorientated. You're not familiar with the routine, and your timing is totally off. You don't know the when, the how, or even a sense of time. Confinement comes with a huge learning process.

There was absolutely nothing in my cell. There is very little that you can do in a little box that measures 2.5 meters by 4.5 meters (approximately 7 feet by 12 feet). Under normal circumstances, I would have loved to use this time to exercise. However, gyms were closed to people like us—the "undesirables" and the unvaccinated. I had no choice but to neglect my training. This situation, combined with my wife's cooking, for which she is responsible, resulted in a body weight of 100kg.

Since I planned to fast for a more extended period, I was hesitant to start working out. The last thing I desired was to be caught up in a medical drama with the proverbial Mengeles on the loose with their fake tests and bloody needles, ready to pounce. So, I decided to take it easy.

They had stated that I would be locked in this "oblivion" of a little cell for 23 hours per day. For the other hour—separate from other inmates—I would be allowed to take a shower, make a phone call, and walk in a circle in a common area. The common area was a concrete block with three sets of iron bars preventing me from seeing the sky. All of that was graciously offered to me for that entire hour.

During my one hour of free time, I used the opportunity to call my family and recount to them what was happening to me. All phone calls were monitored and recorded; only 20 minutes were allowed per phone call. So, what was there to say to loved ones during that time?

It felt like déjà vu—as though I was back behind the Iron Curtain. But this time, it was actually in some twisted Canadian and Chinese hybrid place known as "China-da." My wife and son, Nathaniel, encouraged me to stay strong and reminded me of their love and support.

THE BAIL HEARING

From my cell (AT103) I was escorted to a different room with a telephone. I grabbed the receiver, and already on another line were my lawyers, the clerk from the court, and the judge with the Crown Prosecutor. It was evident from the start that the Crown Prosecutor despised me and was very determined to keep me in prison as long as possible. Despite being a law-abiding citizen, it seemed like I was in serious trouble. I had no fear of the law because I knew I didn't break any actual laws.

Everything that was happening to me came from the corrupt politicians who were terrified of my growing popularity. In situations involving severely compromised and corrupt bureaucrats, where the law takes a backseat, what remains are political vendettas used for their personal control. Watch out!

The Crown Prosecutor began, and it was obvious that he was selected to handle this prosecution for special political attention. Steven Johnston was the Deputy Chief Prosecutor of Appeals and Specialized Prosecutions (South) at Alberta Prosecution Service. Here's what he has personally disclosed about himself, according to a website that has since been revised:

> I am responsible for prosecuting large-scale white-collar crime and organized crime cases. These cases include fraud, money laundering as well as criminal organization and homicide cases. I also prosecute corruption-related offenses. In addition to prosecuting cases, I provide legal advice to the police agencies, which our office works closely with, including the Calgary Police Service and the RCMP. I am a lecturer at the Canadian Police College on the Network Investigators Course and the Digital Technology for

Investigators Courses. I have been a National Co-Chair of the Osgoode Hall Technology Law and Evidence Course for the past eight years.

https://polcyb.org/Events/qm_bio/StevenJohnston.html

Wow! I thought. *He is a part of the gang that has been attacking me for the past 17 years. There goes my ability to a fair and unbiased trial!* Johnston portrayed me as an extremely dangerous individual with an ongoing history of breaking the law and as someone who has long evaded justice.

The Calgary Herald reported the details of the court during the bail hearing:

Calgary Street church minister incited protesters to continue border blockade," prosecutor tells the court. The prosecutor said the reference to police and the army indicated "he's not talking about any kind of peaceful protest at that time."

After inciting protesters not to abandon an international border blockade even if it meant arrest, street church minister Artur Pawlowski hopped into his luxury vehicle and drove home to Calgary, a prosecutor charged Wednesday.

Crown lawyer Steven Johnston said Pawlowski should be kept behind bars on three charges, including committing mischief by inciting others to prevent the lawful use of the border crossing.

Johnston told Lethbridge provincial court Judge Erin Olsen that Pawlowski, 48, went to the protest at Coutts, on the U.S.-Alberta border, last Thursday and spoke to a group of protesters.

The prosecutor said Pawlowski's speech, which was video recorded and posted online, was made after organizers had agreed to shut down the blockade and move their protest to Edmonton for the weekend.

But Johnston, who appeared in court via video from the border crossing, said the Calgary minister implored the truckers and others blocking the border crossing to stay.

"Pawlowski told the crowd that millions of people had to die to end the world wars ... to get freedom," Johnston said. "Pawlowski said that there were not enough RCMP officers to deal with them and there was not enough army to deal with them."

The prosecutor said the reference to police and the army indicated "he's not talking about any kind of peaceful protest at that time.

"He's clearly, in the context of his speech, referencing the notion that there would be some sort of violence."

Johnston said despite negotiations to leave, "the mood of the people changed, and [they] decided to stay at the blockade."

During his speech, Pawlowski referred to the blockade as "our Alamo," a comment Johnston called an overt threat to commit violence.

"On the video ... he makes reference to the fact that for freedom to be preserved, in Mr. Pawlowski's view, people must be willing to sacrifice their lives."

But the minister didn't stay to maintain the protest. "Following the speech, from my understanding of the situation, Mr. Pawlowski got into his BMW and drove to Calgary, leaving the protesters behind," Johnston said.

But defense counsel Chad Haggerty, who argued Pawlowski doesn't pose a danger to the public and should be released, said his client was simply exercising his Charter rights to free expression and association when he spoke to the protesters.

And Haggerty said his client was just as likely to be charged with inciting them if he suggested they abandon the blockade and head to Edmonton to protest.

Haggerty said Pawlowski had no more sway over the blockade than anyone else.

"That protest is still going on. It began before Mr. Pawlowski went to Coutts and continued after he left," the lawyer said.

Olsen will decide next week whether Pawlowski will be freed pending trial.

February 9, 2022, Kevin Martin

That's pretty much the summary of what took place during that hearing. It was shocking but not surprising. With those types of people, lies chase lies. Manipulation and misinformation follow them wherever they go. That is just a part of the propaganda. That's what they do as professional liars.

I found it fascinating to witness the judge's apparent bias. She allowed mainstream media during the proceedings; however, she forbade my wife from attending via Zoom. Unbelievable! The intention was for this to be an *open* court where the public could observe. Still, my wife, Marzena, was prohibited from attending.

My lawyer argued that my wife should be allowed to hear what was going to happen to her husband. The judge disagreed. The Crown viciously attacked the integrity of my wife. There were no criminal charges against Marzena, and she has never been involved in any offenses. However, she was portrayed as a potentially dangerous person who could misuse the hearing details to undermine or obstruct justice.

The lawyers went back and forth with the Crown and the Judge. But in the end, Judge Erin Olsen decided my wife would not be allowed to listen to the proceedings. It was acceptable to listen to the Canadian News Broadcaster (CBC) state propaganda, but not my wife. At that moment, it was apparent that this hearing had nothing to do with justice or the rule of law; I was in the hands of Jason Kenney's personal henchman.

Judge Olsen shockingly suggested that since the mainstream media was allowed to cover the hearing, and if interested, my wife could read about it in the papers or watch it on the evening news. Can you believe this mockery of justice? This is precisely what I had been warning Canadians about for the past 17 years. I have seen this movie before and if you do not change the script, it does not end well.

My heart was pounding with disbelief. In desperation, I opened my mouth and told the judge on the record, "And just like during the Soviet era." I was immediately shot down by the judge and admonished to remain quiet; my mic was turned off. I was witnessing a "Show Trial." If you aren't familiar with that term, Show Trials are public trials in which the guilt or innocence of a defendant has already been determined. They publicly conduct Show Trials as a deterrent for other would-be transgressors.

Yet the shocking thing was the proceeding was about my life, and I could not say a word. It felt like everything had already been decided. I was to be punished and hurt. Law and order did not matter. The judgment was made before the trial even began, just like during the Soviet Era behind the Iron Curtain. I had seen this so many times before.

My memory recalled watching these Show Trials in Poland during the communist time on television and reading about them in the propaganda papers. It was a pure scare tactic, which said, "You see what we can do to anyone that dares to oppose us? Pay attention because you might be next!"

According to the judge and the state Crown Prosecutor, I was to be locked in a cage like an extremely dangerous monster. Most of the proceedings were unrelated to the case itself, focusing instead on my ability to raise funds for a capable defense attorney. What did this have to do with anything? No one knew except the villains, of course. It bothered them that the story was getting international attention, and people were chipping in to help with my defense.

That was not what they wanted. They wanted me to be separated without the ability to defend myself. Without a strong defense team, I should be vulnerable, which is an argument straight from China or Russia.

This Crown Prosecutor, Steven Johnston, did such poor research. He mixed up facts and made assumptions about things that were simply not true. He publicly accused me of giving a speech to people and then immediately abandoning them while stepping into my luxury car, a BMW. He was painting a picture and making stuff up to present me as a selfish, wealthy individual who was doing this for money.

If he had done his job, he would find out that the car was not mine. But instead it was an 11-year-old car worth $8000 that belonged to my son, who had spent three months working on a construction site to buy it. Yet, their story was more fitting for a narrative centered around a luxury car and forsaking others. It was a good pitch, and the national media loved it. No one cared to find out the truth. No one called us to verify the State's propaganda. Again, it was a *Gong Show*.

My lawyers presented their arguments about why I should be released on bail. The court took a break, and the Judge announced later that she would reserve her decision for at least a week. The guards escorted me back to my cell, and I realized that I would have to get used to being locked in this place for at least another week.

CHAPTER TWO

THE CAGE

[DAYS 2-4]

A COUPLE HOURS later, the doors of my cell suddenly opened, and a guard came in. The guard was someone from our church that I knew. He had a Bible in his hands, a pen, and a stack of papers. I was so happy to see him. He was like a light in this dark place.

I thanked him very much and did what I always do—I gave him a bear hug. He was surprised and taken aback by my response. However, it happened so fast that there was nothing that he could do. I thanked him again, and he left. I sat at the table and began to document my story. I thought, instead of wasting my life here, at least what I can do is put everything down on paper.

A few hours later, the doors opened again. Two officers informed me I had to leave with them. They did not tell me why or for what purpose. But I was to leave everything behind and follow them to the Admission area.

At first, they confined me in a small metal cage painted green, and I had absolutely no idea what was going on. But they kept me there for an extended period, as I could observe other prisoners being processed. I watched other people being given their coveralls and then taken to the medical room.

It caught my attention that every one of them was given either a Bible or a Koran. When I was last here with Dawid, they informed us they didn't have any Bibles for us. But obviously, that was another lie because there were plenty of Bibles around. An officer came and interrupted my contemplation about this strange observance, taking me back to the scanner. *Strange,* I thought. What was I being scanned for now?

The officer was someone I could tell was no fun! I believe he was the guard who processed me and Dawid during our first stay here. As we were walking back from the screening, we passed the medical room on the left, and on the right were empty tank cells. The officer spoke to another guard: "Put him in a blue one."

So, what was the blue one? The blue one was a metal box, about half the size of the previous green one, where I had just spent many hours. The guard opened the door, and inside was a little bench. When I sat on it, I could not move at all or stretch my legs. Dogs have more room in dog houses than I had in the blue metal box. It was unbelievable!

When the door closed, I felt like they must see me as the most dangerous and violent criminal. That experience would not have been so drastic if the temperature inside the prison was not so high.

I overheard an officer complaining that the air conditioning was broken, and they all felt like they were in the Bahamas. But if they were in the Bahamas, then I was in the Sahara Desert because, honestly, it was so hot!

Suddenly, I had a flashback from the Hollywood movies about the Nazi era and the communists torturing people and keeping them in boxes. How appropriate it was, I thought to myself, to call them "Nazis" and "Gestapo" after all. Certainly, I wasn't on the way to a concentration camp, and they hadn't shot me in the back of the head.

Yet, it felt like they were moving closer to transforming into a full-blown police state. There is this famous song that many people sing: "It's beginning to look a lot like Christmas everywhere you go." Well, now in Canada, "It's beginning to look a lot like Soviet Russia everywhere you go."

I started sweating and feeling strange because of severe dehydration. By opening the top of my coveralls, there was a small amount of relief. I'm not sure how long they kept me there because I kept dozing off and passing out intermittently. It felt like hours had passed when suddenly a guard came with two women who I assumed were nurses.

He opened the door, and the woman asked me how I was feeling. I said, "What do you think? I am locked in a cage like a dog. You have learned well from the Nazis how to treat people." I wanted to say more, but the door got slammed in my face, and the nurses ran away. I could not believe it—they literally got terrified and ran away. The guard said that he didn't appreciate being called a Nazi.

My reply was swift, even though logic kept telling me to keep my mouth shut. Still, I just had to open my mouth. "I am not your dog that you can lock in a cage. I am not a dog!" I yelled.

He looked at me with big, wide eyes staring and mumbled something like, "You cannot yell at the guards!"

"You're not allowed to treat me like a dog then," I replied. The guard turned around and left me in the cage. I told myself, "Now I did it. They are going to keep me here forever."

Due to the absence of water for an extended period and the intense heat within the cage, I was gradually suffocating. Thank God that the guard came back, took me to the washroom, and commanded me to do "the number 2." He watched me use the toilet and then took me to the screening machine for another x-ray.

The female guard at the scanner looked at the computer screen and proclaimed, "He's good." I was then escorted to a normal holding cell with a nice, long, and comfortable bench (relatively speaking!). It was a hard bench, but at least a lot better than the small blue metal box.

I was sitting there, getting processed for my new cell, when I saw the guard from prison and church getting arrested. He was the one who had previously given me some paper and a pen; I had no idea at the time that it would ultimately lead to his arrest. As our eyes met, I could see tremendous fear.

Even though he was simply doing his job, by law, because I had filled out a request for paper and pen, they wanted to break me. And so, in front of me, they arrested him for this "offense." He was suspended for one month and later reinstated after they issued him a "private" apology.

I'm not sure how long they kept me there because time without a watch plays tricks on the human mind. When the door opened again, they took me back to my unit. On the way, I had a good conversation with one guard. He felt terrible about how I was being treated. Apparently, everything was coming from the hire-ups.

LIFE IN THE SLAMMER

Inside my cell, there was a surprise waiting for me. Everything had been flipped upside down, and it was obvious that the prison officials were looking for something. I scanned the cell to determine what was missing. They had taken the Bible, pen, and papers! My other Bible was gone, as well, along with the write-ups I had penned for my story.

A guard entered and informed me I had to collect my remaining possessions because I was being moved to a different cell. With a blanket, coveralls, socks, and underwear in hand, I made my way to a cell as filthy as the one I was being transferred from. The one benefit of the transfer was that this cell had a working tap. Water, at last! I began drinking like a desert traveler who stumbled upon an oasis. "I will live," I said to myself and went to bed.

Getting used to this kind of environment will take a while, I thought. There was this interesting game of lights. Sometimes when they were on, you could dim them out, but sometimes you couldn't. Sometimes the lights were on, and sometimes they were off. I'm sure there must be a flawless explanation for the mystery of why. However, being new to this, I could not figure it out yet. The lights were only part of my immediate problems, which I fixed, ironically, with the help of the guards.

When I was taken to the metal box, the guard instructed me to put on a blue gown. Of course, all of that was for our own benefit to fight the virus. This useless piece of nothing was to protect all of us from the vicious attack of something that was 1000 times smaller than bacteria. This is science according to—who knows? Perhaps the Chinese Party of Canada?

When he offered me the gown, the guard mocked me by saying, "Do you have something against this, as well?" Of course, he was talking about my refusal to wear a mask that explicitly states on its packaging, "NOT EFFECTIVE AGAINST COVID-19."

Why put it on, then? I thought. Because they say so! *No, thank you! I am not playing this communist game.*

I had taken the blue gown, thinking to myself, *I'm going to use this for something else.* I had said it before, and I'll say it again: It was a *Gong Show*: three grown men walking in the empty hallway, wearing silly blue hospital gowns, and pretending that, for whatever crazy reason, this was supposed to protect the world from a deadly pandemic.

Escorted by two masked bandits with rubber gloves, I looked like the main character in this movie. This whole charade had its funny moments. But why am I telling you all of this? Oh yes. It is imperative that when you find yourself in jail and you finally realize that you have minimal access to any resources, you never know what can make your life in the dungeon a bit more comfortable.

If they're giving something to you, take it. It might be a priceless commodity soon. When I was removed from the unfortunate events of the dog cage, they gave me another one of those useless gowns so that we could walk "fully protected" through the empty hallways to my cell. I did not have any container for the used cups and plates, so my first instinct was to take it and throw it into the corner where I was putting my garbage.

Then a thought entered my mind regarding that blue gown: *I can use this!* With no difficulty, I tore it apart and folded it multiple times, using as many layers as I could to block the light. Voila! I had fashioned a bandana, which I then placed on my head. It also made a nice eye mask for sleeping, although the see-through blue thin material allowed light to penetrate through the covering.

How can they scientifically justify that this piece of see-through material can stop anything, never mind a microscopic virus? But "follow the science" is what they were preaching!

I looked around my cell. *Think Artur ... What else can be used for that purpose?* My eyes stopped on the socks. They were black. There was also the black underwear. I smiled, thinking about the female officer's question about my underwear color preferences.

Now, I was wondering if I had said pink or purple and if they would provide me with those preferred colors. Who knows? We live in such strange times they probably would have. They have no problem putting a human being in a confined metal box. But for some reason, the color of your underwear is significant. These days, if not provided, it might be a human rights violation. Who knows? Maybe next time, out of curiosity, I will say "pink" and see what happens.

In the meantime, I had found my solution, and black socks would do. One end of the socks was open. With my pencil, I cut an opening on the other end and slid my handmade bandana through it. After tying it together and pulling it over my eyes, I could not see a thing. Bingo!

I was understandably concerned about the possibility of them charging me an outrageous sum for vandalizing public property. Those people are capable of anything. But at this moment, I cared very little about what they were thinking. I needed to survive this insane attack on my life. I needed to survive another day, and my eye-covering device worked perfectly. That was the most important thing to me right then.

Falling asleep was a struggle, thanks to the constant noise of people screaming, talking, and banging on the metal doors. Obviously, this solitary confinement was not working very well in keeping people sane. From time to time, I could hear the opening and closing of the metal doors that would have awoken even the dead. Concrete and metal carried the sound everywhere. In the cell, there was never darkness. Even when they turned off the bright lights, another light stayed on, so I desperately needed my jailhouse eye covering. Every day was a learning experience, and, as humans, we have this amazing ability to adapt to all circumstances.

Peeking through my little window, I noticed several people gathering in the prison parking lot. This was the protest—a vigil organized by my family and the Church—against the Premier's government, which was imprisoning me and others for our crime of exposing their corruption. I saw the flags, banners, signs, and people carrying all kinds of messages—beautiful individuals who were declaring, "Enough is enough."

Every night, the people assembled, coming together to unite against the tyranny of their own government. I had numerous conversations with different guards about what we were witnessing in our nation. Most of them stated their belief that the entire COVID-19 situation was a total hoax.

But what fascinated me even more was their explanation of why they were willing to participate in this charade. "I have to pay the bills," they would say, or "I have to keep my job." Many of them would agree when I pointed out that masks and gowns were useless. Without hesitation, they would reply, "We know. We're doing what we're told to keep our jobs."

The concept of a nation of goats unquestioningly following orders has never sat well with me. Wasn't that what the Germans claimed during the Nuremberg trials following the mass murder of millions upon millions? "After all, I was just following orders. I did what I was told. I had to obey the command."

Really? You had to? It was beneficial for you to obey the order, and it kept you well-fed and safe. But I wonder if it was worth it for those people in the end to keep their jobs and to give up their principles, moral standards, faith, and ultimately their very own souls?

Was their paycheck so important that they were willing to lose their eternity with God? Well, I was not willing, and I guess that's why I was on one side of the fence, and so many of those officers, guards, Crown Prosecutors, judges, politicians, and reporters were on the other side. Ultimately, history and God will judge us all for what we have done. Everything will be weighed and judged. Rest assured of that.

Time in the slammer can be hard, especially in the first few days. After losing the Bibles and paper to write on, I was very upset. I wanted—actually, I *needed*—to do something, but there was nothing to do. Without my reading glasses, my eyes hurt.

While lying down on the mattress, I reflected on my situation because I needed some sort of boost for my morale. Sitting on the bottom bunk of the bunk bed in my room, I stared up at the top bunk overhead, which was my "ceiling." I grabbed a pencil they had not confiscated, and as a reminder to myself, I wrote on the ceiling above me, "Remember, Jesus loves You! He cares for You! He died so you can have life. There is everlasting Hope! Jesus is that Hope! Pastor Artur Pawlowski was here."

Typically, I refrain from writing on walls or ceilings, but this was an exception, and it made me feel good. I stood up and decided to clean my room. If I was to spend some time in this place, let it be at least clean. Using the remainder of the blue gown as a cloth, I washed the beds, table, and shelves. I washed the walls, windows, sink, and toilet. After washing off the top shelf, I placed toiletries, socks, and underwear on it.

When I was finally permitted to come out, I asked if I could clean the floor of my cell using the broom and mop, and I was allowed to use them. The good part about cleaning the cell was that it was not big. Ten minutes later, I was ready to face whatever was coming at me. I filed a complaint to the director about my treatment. After receiving advice from one of the guards, who did not understand why I was being treated that way, he suggested I file a complaint.

In the evening, there was a knock on the door. Someone walked in with a Bible, cards, and a booklet that read, "God bless you! God bless you!" That really cheered me up. However, because I had not received my glasses, I was still unable to read the Bible. Nevertheless, I was glad to have the word of God in my cell.

Since I was still fasting, to the delight of some inmates, I sent my meals to other cells. Inmates had repeatedly expressed their constant hunger. During my one hour out, I would stop at the windows of their cells, looking for hungry souls. God gave me the ability to hold the fast, so I stuck to it, praying for some breakthrough.

The next day, I was greeted by another angel in uniform. When he looked at me, he said, "God is good! God is good!"

"Yes, He is," I replied.

He asked me if I wanted some more time out of my cell. I said, "Yes." A few hours later, I was given an additional 30 minutes outside the cell. Thanks to him, I was able to talk to Marzena and Nathaniel about what I witnessed early on that day. I could also see the rally staged for my release outside in the parking lot.

I walked over to the cell that had the biggest window, where two inmates were being held. When I came close enough, one of them came to me and said through the door, "Look at this," as he pointed outside at the parking lot. "They are showing you love." It was a very touching moment. Hundreds of people came to stand in solidarity with me. There were again flags, signs, and families with children standing for something very dear to them: Freedom.

After being locked back in my cell, a guard arrived with another Bible, a pen, and paper. There was also a letter from the Director instructing the guards to return my belongings to me. I could finally start putting my story on paper. The cell looked clean, to the best of my ability, with very limited resources. No, it was not possible to remove the glued wallpaper from the walls. I lacked the necessary tools to accomplish that. However, I used my new skill as a "graffiti artist" to cover the swear words I noticed in several places throughout the cell.

Once I felt somewhat content with the cell's appearance, I began writing. My fingers started hurting because I hadn't used a pen or pencil in a long time. Of course, nowadays, it's mostly typing. Every time I finished a page, I took a break to give my fingers a little rest.

As I was deciding what to write next, a young man, a native fella, Colin Bearspaw, stopped at the window of my cell and asked me to come to the door. "Would you like some coffee and milk?" he asked.

Coffee in jail is like gold. I did not even hesitate. "Yes, please," I said. Caffeine was just what I needed for my significant headache. He returned with several bags of Nescafé Classic and some powdered milk, dropped it on the ground, and pushed it under the door inside my cell.

Then came the question, "Do you want some hot water?"

Wait a second, I thought to myself, *how can there be hot water?* The door was shut tightly, and I couldn't open it. The man outside couldn't open it. However, I still said, "Sure."

"Hold on a moment," he shouted from behind the door, then swiftly vanished down the hallway.

Where did he go? I wondered. When he appeared again, he held an empty box of Cheetos that was open from both sides.

Now, I was very curious. What was he going to do now? He flattened the box and started to push one end through a little opening in the metal door. Soon, the green corner of the box appeared on my side of the door. The other half of the box remained on Colin's side.

He said, "Go get your cup." I did.

Then he said, "Catch the water." He began pouring the water from his side, and to my surprise, it started flowing into my side. Gravity did its intended job. The water was unstoppable, and very quickly, my cup was filled with hot liquid.

The coffee we were served didn't taste great, so this ingenious water trick at least kept it hot. Whoever was outside would go and fetch the hot water and deliver it to the inmates through the door. At least now I can understand how inmates use anything and everything to their advantage. You truly use whatever is in front of you under the circumstances.

In the cell in front of mine was a guy from Mexico who had lost his right arm. He was the same fella I was supplying with breakfast every morning because of my fast, which made him a very happy camper. One morning, he stopped by my cell to thank me for the food. He admitted that after I started giving him extra calories every day, he slept without any problems for the first time in weeks.

He also told me that he had experienced a vision about me. He was to tell me that my journey was not over yet. He told me, "You have been faithful for many years, and you are God's prophet." God showed him that I would be very rich like the bankers in Switzerland.

Wow! I thought. How does it happen that God uses the most unlikely individuals to carry out His work in such a powerful way? It was nice to hear some positive words about the future, especially when I was stuck in such a poor, humble hole.

I decided to start sharing public statements, informing people about my inner thoughts, and encouraging them to stay strong. Here is one that I did on the third day:

This is my third day of fasting. I am standing strong. However, the treatment I am receiving has nothing to do with justice! In two days, I have been stripped-searched twice, forced to go to the bathroom with an officer, locked first in one cage, then scanned for contraband, and then locked in a tiny cage, almost suffocating for hours. And searched again for contraband. After all of that, I received a hard bench treatment for hours. Finally, I was taken to my cell. To my surprise, everything was flipped upside down. The Bible that was given to me was confiscated.

They also confiscated my narration write-up to my lawyer. At the same time, I observed other inmates having Korans without a problem. What is happening to me is not justice. It is punishment and abuse of power. I need your help. I am not waiting for sentencing. I have already been sentenced and am serving time in maximum prison in solitary confinement. No trial is needed! I am already punished to the fullest of their abilities. For the past two years, I have been fighting for the rights of Canadians. Now, I need you to start fighting for me and my family.

CHAPTER THREE
PILING UP THE CHARGES

[DAYS 5-7]

THAT SAME DAY at 7:00 p.m. I was supposed to have a meeting with my lawyer. However, as usual, everything was complicated. All my phone conversations, even those with my counselors, were recorded and monitored. My criminal lawyer, who has years of experience, revealed during our previous phone call I was his only client to encounter this situation. He had never experienced something like this before.

My lawyer said that he could hear the echo in the line, and there was absolutely no point in talking or strategizing anything while the very people we were trying to expose were monitoring every word. To ensure confidentiality, we would reschedule our phone call for a face-to-face meeting in a secure environment. So, on this evening, 7:00 p.m. came and went, and no one came to get me for the meeting with my lawyer. For some time, I was denied access to my lawyers and the opportunity to strategize our defense.

Then came the morning of February 14th, my seventh day of not eating, and yet I felt great. As people, we have this amazing ability to get used to almost anything. Every morning looked like the one the day before. The inmates would wake up when the bright lights turned on, and an officer entered to inspect our cells. After that always came breakfast. However, I couldn't confirm whether the food was good or bad. It looked good and definitely did not smell bad. Maybe one day I could testify by tasting it myself.

Just before 8:00 a.m., a guard came to get me for another scheduled meeting, this time with my other lawyer, Sarah Miller. I was led through a large, lengthy corridor and then into another one that led to the visitor area, where people were separated by glass and phones. Sarah was already waiting there for me, so I sat down, grabbed the phone, and looked at her through what appeared to be bulletproof glass.

The voice on the telephone asked me for the ORCA number, which Canadian prisons use to identify inmates in all their paperwork and prison operations. It stands for **O**ffender **R**ecognition and **C**lassification **A**pplication. I entered the number 1483464, and it took a few tries for the phones to work.

We were advised that the conversation would be monitored and recorded. How could this even be legal? I thought that attorney-client discussions were privileged and held in confidence, but I guess a lot has changed in the past few years.

I looked at Sarah and asked, "How do you like my blue jumpsuit?"

"Very nice," she replied.

I lifted my feet, showing her my new pink slippers.

Behind her mask, she smiled and said, "Lovely." Of course, she was not allowed to come in without a face covering. While she waited for her laptop to be brought to the room, we chatted about other things. There were six or seven other dockets to deal with, and several trials were scheduled for the next few weeks.

"Let's start with the Health Act charge," she said. You have been charged with organizing an illegal gathering outside on December 13th and 20th, 2020, and participating in an illegal gathering during the December 20th "Feeding of the Poor" soup kitchen event.

Both of those charges are classified under the Health Act. We spoke about those events for about 30 minutes, and she showed me pictures from the Crown's evidence package. There was absolutely no point in denying my participation in any of the events. On both those days, I provided food for the poor and held a church service. So, I guess I was guilty as charged.

Throughout my meeting with Sarah, we were constantly interrupted by a clicking device—recording equipment, I presume, but it was extremely annoying. The presence of a uniformed guard sitting just a few feet away from Sarah, listening to every word she was saying, didn't help either. During our conversation, I had to hang up multiple times and start all over again. The recording equipment's background noise greatly affected our ability to hear each other.

When we were done with the smaller things, Sarah's computer was brought to the room. She turned it on, but she was not able to open the files. *Well, it is what it is,* I thought.

THE CANADA POST INCIDENT

We discussed additional, more severe accusations, specifically related to an incident at a Shoppers Drug Mart. She wanted to hear the entire story. My troubles with Canada Post started at the end of the winter of 2021. At my usual Canada Post office in Calgary, where I've been purchasing stamps for almost 30 years, I went to send some mail. I patiently waited in line but was denied service for not wearing a face covering when it was my turn to buy stamps.

I explained to the woman at the counter that I had a medical exemption. And that the law was very clear, and I had the right to be served under the exemption. She did not care and still refused service. And she called security and the police.

During my conversation with the security guard who arrived first, a police officer showed up and instructed me to vacate the premises. I did my best to reason with the law enforcer, but he was very determined not to uphold the law. I questioned whether it was acceptable to refuse someone entry to the store based on factors such as race or religion.

We conducted an exchange back and forth about the issue, but I couldn't sway his opinion. "You have to go," he said, and I had no choice. To avoid being arrested, I left the place. I recorded my whole interaction with the manager, the guard, and then the police officer on my telephone. I put it on Facebook and YouTube for the entire world to see that Canada had lost its sanity.

As best as I could, I avoided this place going forward. Being preoccupied with other matters, there was no desire to be bothered by the foolishness and prejudice of a hateful Canada Post manager or the clerk named Dori. However, I visited another Shoppers Drug Mart in a different area of the city on the same day. I was not bothered by anyone, being able to purchase my stamp and leave without a problem. This was also recorded on my phone and published to showcase the difference in treatment from the same company by two different individuals. No one asked me about the mask and the truth is no one really cared.

The simple purchase of a stamp shouldn't have been a big deal. But obviously, for some, it was. I posted it on social media for people to see how crazy everything was becoming and moved on. Months had passed. I even went to the United States and back. Of course, I had no problems at all over there, buying stamps and sending packages and letters without any issues.

Back in Calgary, I was swamped, and my wife was picking up and sending mail. On or around December 17th, 2021, I received a notification from the Canada Post instructing me to pick up registered mail in person at their location. It required that I pick up the document myself, and I didn't think twice about it. I saw the same clerk who had caused me problems before, Dori, behind the counter.

I waited patiently for my turn, but instead of serving me, she went into the back room and locked the door, leaving me puzzled at the counter. *How am I to pick up my registered mail?* I thought to myself. This is getting ridiculous. No one was standing behind me, and I wondered what to do next. Before COVID, this type of behavior would be considered criminal behavior; she would have been charged and fired for what she was doing.

Now, however, the more Nazi-Communist behavior you would implement on others, the more rewards you would receive. In Canada, this type of blatant discrimination was one of the most severe offenses. For years, they have been educating Canadians not to discriminate against people of religion, color, sexual orientation, physical appearance, or for medical reasons. You are also not allowed to discriminate against people with a mental or physical disability and could be charged with an offense by the Criminal Code of Canada and taken before a human rights tribunal.

However, we all had noticed that the law, justice, and regulations meant very little to the tyrants. It was only the mighty COVID that mattered and nothing else. The tyrants took every right, law, and form of protection in Canada away. We had truly become a nation of lawlessness. No more debates! Zero data allowed! No questioning permitted! Asking for proof was strictly prohibited.

As I was standing there waiting for Dori to come out, I felt I was witnessing the greatest segregation since Nazi Germany. Unless Canadians would wake up soon, destruction was imminent. The line grew with more people, but instead of standing in solidarity, they turned against me and started complaining. It was absolutely disgusting. They were not willing to stand up for the truth, for their rights. They all ganged up against me, accusing me of holding up the line. The accusations were coming like somehow all of this was my fault.

They mentioned being busy, needing to leave, and having other commitments. They let me know I should go so they could carry on with their business. I challenged them, trying to explain that this was pure discrimination, that this was simply not okay because I had my rights. But no one cared. They were all selfishly focused on their own desires to do what they had come to do and go back to their comfortable existence.

Canadian society had fallen so far. The only thing people seemed to care about was their own egoistic self-centeredness. No one and nothing outside of themselves mattered anymore. It was about me, myself, and I, three Canadian idols that needed to be worshipped.

In this Nazi-like society, I had officially become the modern-day "dirty Jew," a virus that needed to be removed from their path. I wanted to scream about this injustice and yell that we had witnessed this before and should know better. However, I knew that no one here was even slightly interested in what I had to say. Their only concern was being served and leaving. They didn't care to listen—but were totally lost in their own world.

I decided to go. There was no point in me waiting for the clerk to come out. It was clear that she was aware of her ability to discriminate against me without facing any repercussions, and there was nothing I could do about it. People were getting very upset, and I had no willingness to be escorted or arrested by the police for doing absolutely nothing illegal.

So, I left, to the delight of the people standing in the line. If the matter had simply been about buying a stamp, I would have gone to a different Canada Post location. However, I had come there because I had registered mail, and now I wasn't sure if it was extremely important or how I would retrieve it.

To seek advice, I reached out to a friend who used to be an officer in the Royal Canadian Mounted Police (RCMP) and explained what had transpired. After he watched the video of the incident, he called me and said, "Tomorrow morning, call the police."

My friend had already spoken with them and opened a case number. He told me to provide them with the case number so they could assist me in getting back my letter. Based on his understanding of the law, he believed this was a straightforward theft case—that the Canada Post clerk had broken the Criminal Code of Canada, plain and simple.

So, the next morning, I contacted the police, who told me to go to the Shoppers Drug Mart parking lot and wait for them to arrive. A few hours later, I and my son Nathaniel met with the police in front of the store. Two officers came: a female officer and a male officer who was taller than me by at least a head. The police officer told me that I couldn't enter the Canada Post to get my registered mail but that he would do that for me. So, I handed him my notice, and he went inside. Shortly after, he returned from the store with the manager of the Shoppers Drug Mart.

The officer handed me my mail and then a document that was a trespass notice for Shoppers Drug Mart and that Canada Post location. Can you believe it? The store management had discriminated against me rather than upholding the law. They had stolen my mail, which was considered a criminal offense under federal law.

But instead of punishing the actual wrongdoers, I received a trespass notice as a penalty. Unbelievable! Reluctantly, I had to accept this document, and the person informed me that I was permanently banned from returning to this location.

Apparently, justice had been served. I went back to my car, and the officers left the area, perhaps returning to whatever they were doing an hour earlier: catching mask-less shoppers! The store manager looked thrilled. Finally, a highly dangerous criminal was prohibited from returning to his establishment for shopping. I have no doubt that Dori threw a party at her place and celebrated. Victory for her at last!

Honestly, I was so busy that I hadn't dwelled on this incident much. There were rallies to be held, church meetings to oversee, people to visit, things to complete, and places to be. I enlisted the help of a friend, who was a paralegal, to file a human rights complaint.

Some individuals staged an anti-mask demonstration at the same location a few days later. Police intervened, and I was told some people ended up with tickets. One woman from our church was arrested, and her husband was assaulted by a police officer. He was shoved on the wall even though he had his hands in his pocket. I guess this was the new tactic of Calgary's finest. "If we cannot scare them, we will beat them up."

The paralegal I had hired also took that assault case and filed an official complaint to the professional standard unit. Little did I know that seeking justice would have dire consequences for me weeks later. The act of holding those individuals responsible caused them great unease, leading to a renewed sense of aggression towards me.

WRAPPING UP THE VISIT WITH MY LAWYER

My lawyer and I shifted our focus to the recent trouble, specifically the protest at the Milk River and Coutts border crossing. The evidence was based vaguely on an RCMP officer's testimony. He stated that while I was in the Smuggler's Saloon, he had a conversation outside with some protesters. They communicated to him they were going to leave the area in the morning and go to Edmonton. According to the officer's testimony, they chose Edmonton to stage a protest in the capital city of Alberta.

Apparently, the conversation took place while I was inside talking to the gathered crowd. However, I find it interesting that the Crown Prosecutor would even consider including this man's testimony because, in legal terms, this was hearsay. He couldn't make such a statement unless the people who said it were willing to testify.

However, since law and order were thrown out the window, according to the Crown Prosecutor, this was perfectly justifiable evidence. The officer was essentially saying that it was my speech that changed the mind of the main organizers to stay behind and continue the protests at the Montana-Alberta border. Based on that hearsay, I was charged with three criminal charges:

- Mischief over $5,000.
- Failure to comply with a court order.

And the most appalling of them all:
- Violation of the Critical Infrastructure Defense Act for interrupting the operation of essential infrastructure in a manner that renders it inoperable.

Believe it or not, I had been charged as a terrorist for simply telling people to peacefully stand up for their rights.

We discussed several things, and towards the end of the conversation, three uniformed officers approached my side of the window, like waitstaff in a fancy restaurant with a whole tray of food. Was all of that just for me? How surreal. My attorney and I looked at this theater in disbelief.

Like professional actors in a staged play, they gave me plates of food in front of a puzzled Sarah, declaring, "You see. We're giving him food!"

I grabbed a drink and thanked them for the rest. They knew I was fasting. What purpose was this supposed to accomplish? I was not hiding that I was not eating. I asked the entire world to join me in this fast. So why the theatre? Who knows? My entire stay in their "five-star" facility was filled with unexplainable situations. I guess it was part of the entertainment that always kept me on my toes.

Turning to Sarah, I said, "Did you see that? Wow! What a show."

She replied, "Yes, totally just for the show."

The time was up, but before we parted ways, I gave her my written statements and accounts, including the one that was confiscated before and later returned to me. A sigh of relief filled my heart as the guard took them from my hands and delivered them to her. After signing a few documents, I was escorted back to my cell.

It was good to see my lawyer. It broke the monotony and put my mind to focus on the law and legality of this whole infringement on our rights. The door locked behind me. I grabbed a pen, the next form, and began to write everything that I could remember about our visit. NOTE: I was using forms from jail to write on because there was no notebook or plain paper.

When I was finally let out for one hour, I called my wife, who was with Nathaniel. They informed me about the current situation outside. In the evening, a guard walked in, and, to my surprise, a miracle happened. After a week of waiting, he brought me my reading glasses. It only took a written request four times, verbally telling them countless times, and having my lawyers ask them numerous times, as well. But let's not dwell on the past. Good things do come to those who wait.

The day was not yet over when a young man came to the window during his break to talk to me. "So, you are the preacher that refused to shut down his Church," he started the conversation.

"Yes, I am," I replied.

"Good for you," he continued, "good for you. It is not easy to do what you did."

Just as I sat down, another man came up and yelled through the door, "Preacher." I walked to the window in the door. "I have heard a lot about you," he said. The man had tattoos all over his body. We talked for a few minutes; I shared my story, and then he left. Right before the lights went off, the two men returned to me once more, saying "goodnight" and promising to pray for my quick release.

Their appearance suggested they had just left a gathering of gang members. It was difficult to reconcile their words with the way they looked. I should not have been surprised, given what had happened thus far. More blessings had come to me from the so-called criminals in blue coveralls than from the peace officers dressed in uniforms. Prison is truly a place with many contradictions.

"Pray for us, Bro," said one of them as he disappeared into a hallway. Can you imagine? I always marvel at God's surprise encouragement and, ultimately, who He uses as His messengers.

The protests outside were happening every day for a couple of hours, beginning at 7:00 p.m. The first few days, we could show our solidarity by flipping the lights on and off; however, our lights were soon disabled. It appears they were not keen on the notion of letting the people outside know that we could see them and were standing with them.

From my little window in the door, I could see the cars coming in. Sometimes, I could see the people gathered. If they aligned themselves directly in front of my door, I could see the flags, the speakers, and sometimes my wife or son just before the protest would start.

You could also see the guards and sheriffs driving around, blocking a bigger part of the parking lot. The guards parked their vehicles behind the facility where my cell was. While the inmates in the front of the building watched the vigil and car procession, I found my own entertainment: the parade of guards parking their cars and sneaking back into the facility.

Most of them were not wearing the muzzle; we observed this everywhere we went. The bureaucrats and the officers hated the masks as well and only put them on when they thought that someone was watching. When they thought no one could see them, the muzzle came off. If no one could see them, why play the game? Especially when the cameras were not rolling. Rightly so, because it was as useless as a chain-link fence trying to stop a mosquito from coming in. While watching this, I was thinking to myself, *What hypocrisy! What a lie!*

After a couple of hours, the protesters left, and I remained there, stuck in my cell. The lights got dim, and I was lying on the bed. I thought to myself, *how did this whole thing get to this point?* Still excited and stirred from the events outside, I didn't want to fall asleep yet, and my mind shifted to the beginning.

This was not my first run-in with the law. Many times in the past, I encountered difficulties while trying to feed the poor and preach the gospel. In 2006, the police actually arrested me for simply reading the Bible in a public park. I had won my fights many times with the authorities and knew that our victories were enraging those who thought they were above the law. But this time, it felt different. It felt even more evil and dark.

THE END OF A TEN-YEAR WAR

While lying in my cell that evening, a memory took me back to 2015. I recalled a ten-year war with the city and the Provincial government that ended with a phone call to my lawyer. The city wanted to meet, so my lawyer and I went together to City Hall. During that visit, my heart was pounding.

Over the course of many years, there were more than 100 court cases, along with numerous tickets and citations. We lost many friends and supporters who had abandoned us on the battlefield. I considered the time and resources that were wasted. My children had grown up seeing and listening to the abuse of power, the arrests, and the ongoing harassment by the authorities.

Some of the trials lasted for as long as three weeks at a time. At times, I was no longer sure if I was a lawyer, a criminal, or a clergy. The fight had become part of our lives. The struggle of good versus evil, the struggle between enormous corruption and someone who just wanted to be left alone and to do some good.

Michael Bates, our lawyer, did not know exactly what to expect from the meeting at City Hall that day. We both knew that the city wanted to put the continuous ongoing court proceedings behind them. But we did not know what they wanted to propose. Entering the City Hall, we had mixed feelings.

Initially, Colleen Sinclair, the senior lawyer, welcomed us, followed by Ola Malik, the prosecutor from Calgary. To our surprise, the meeting was cordial. Both Sinclair and Malik were speaking with the highest admiration for me and our ministry, Street Church, held in Calgary.

Our visit continued for about two hours. I received praise for being a good person and for our amazing work with the homeless. Instead of being harassed, charged, or arrested, I should be recognized and "rewarded" for my efforts.

As I was listening to this, I could not believe my ears. Fighting this took an immense amount of time and effort. Several times, I had experienced financial ruin, having to re-mortgage my house just to exist. The city had already sent me a letter saying that if I did not pay the property taxes, they would seize our house. This was ten years of my life.

At times, I couldn't determine if I was more of a pastor or a lawyer because I spent more time in court than in the church. Trial after trial, ticket after ticket, arrest after arrest turned my life into a constant battlefield with the city bureaucrats. I had received tickets for giving free goods and services, feeding the homeless, preaching the gospel, and praying. There had been citations for illegally distributing printed material, which meant handing out Bibles and gospel tracts.

Tickets were given out for "stunting" and feeding the homeless, as these were viewed as distractions to motor drivers. The authorities had also given citations for barbecuing, displaying signs, and, of course, displaying the cross. And most importantly, for preaching!

The list went on: for using amplification, illegally congregating, and improperly using a public park. Anything they could come up with was thrown at me. Sometimes, I would catch them searching through their black book, looking for anything to use against me.

Now, suddenly, I was a good guy to them. And they knew that what I was doing was saving lives. This was a hard pill to swallow. My eyes were getting bigger and bigger as the flow of compliments came from the very people who had hunted me down for the past decade.

When you hear things like this, what do you say? How do you react to them? Well, I did it my way. I said, "It feels like you are giving me a Russian medal." They looked at me, puzzled.

So, I explained, "A medal with a very big pin that goes straight to the man's heart," which made them laugh. I continued, "What about all the money that we had to spend defending ourselves?"

Colleen Sinclair replied, "Regarding the money, there is nothing that we can do."

"What about some kind of press release to let the people know that I am actually not a bad guy?" I persisted. "Is there something coming from City Hall that this war has finally ended?"

"It will not happen either," they added.

The truth is that the bureaucracy has no heart. They see you as just a number, another case, another problem that they must deal with. They got a beating in the court system, and they just wanted to move on.

"Like I said, this sounds like a Russian medal with a big pin straight to the heart," I restated with very mixed feelings. Of course, I was delighted that this craziness was finally over. But after ten years of the government's smear campaigns and the constant attack from the mainstream media, I was at least hoping for some restitution or public closure. The vindication never came.

Unfortunately, no one learned about our meeting at City Hall. It never made it to the papers or the evening news. In the public's eyes, I remained the very well-known troublemaker and lawbreaker I had been portrayed as. A man who refused to follow the rules. The apology never came, and the politicians were never willing to publicly acknowledge that they were in the wrong.

But what did come was the restoration of my permits to do what I was called to do: to feed the poor, preach the gospel, give people hope, and save lives. For that, I was very grateful.

Finally, people stopped bothering me. It was a peculiar feeling not to be constantly dragged to the courts. Every time I saw a police officer or a bylaw officer, I would have that awful feeling of negative emotions rush through my brain. Will there be another ticket? Another harassment? Another court or even an arrest? My heart would pump faster, and I would start looking for a camera, just in case.

Throughout those years, I witnessed police officers lying while under oath in front of the judge. Law officers would falsely create criminal acts without any evidence to implicate me or others in my company, potentially leading to imprisonment or financial penalties. Seeing all that mockery of justice and observing those who should uphold the law and stand for its citizens had turned me into a man with very little trust in the modern-day uniform and the badge.

You could say I had become, in a way, damaged goods. I guess when people kick a dog, pound it with sticks, and constantly throw rocks at it, we cannot expect the creature to be filled with a lot of trust. Removing that from my system would be a long process.

The ministry, however, could finally focus entirely on its mandate without the constant attack from the authorities. A ministry that was focused on saving lives by feeding the poor and restoring hope in people's hearts. Amidst the chaos of the battlefield, I lost track of the hours spent immersed in court documents, meeting with lawyers, and enduring weeks of court hearings as the accused. All for the "horrible crimes" of feeding the poor and holding church services in a park.

Soon after my meeting at city hall, everything normalized. There was more time to prepare for sermons. I dedicated my energy and money to doing what I wanted: serving as the pastor for those who nobody cared for.

Almost a decade of battling with the province's most influential individuals had nearly defeated me. Often, I thought to myself, *if the enemy only knew how close they came to the finish line ... if they knew how close they were to achieving their victory ...* it would have all been over very soon. For many times, I had been just one big push away from finally breaking.

There were times I could not even pay for parking at the courthouse, and my wife had to drop me off. Or I would walk a big part of the way and then take the train home. So many times, I did not know how I was going to pay for utilities and taxes, never mind the legal fees. But God knew the breaking point and did not allow it to come to that. He knew what we could take.

From 2015 to 2020, it was known as the five years of peace. We started to expand the reach of our ministry. I had the privilege of organizing the "March for Jesus" in several countries around the world and in many cities. Street Church also became more organized. We bought specialized containers to keep the hot meals for the homeless warm, and we invested in new barbecues and equipment to make this project more efficient. This five-year period of relative peace allowed us to concentrate on the mission.

CHAPTER FOUR

MORE DAYS IN PRISON BRING MORE OPPORTUNITIES

[DAY 8]

MY EIGHTH DAY started well. The guard walked in and said, "Good morning, Pastor."

"Good morning," I replied.

"How was your sleep?" he asked.

"Good," I said, "under the circumstances."

A few minutes later, the guard returned, asking if I would like to have my time out of the cell, to which I gladly accepted. I called Marzena, and we talked for a few minutes. She told me about a prophecy that had been circulating everywhere about what was happening to me. The prophet said that those who did this to me would be judged themselves and that some of them would die. One day, I would be exonerated and elevated.

There will be justice and victory for my son, Artur Pawlowski, because they used him as an example. Listen, my son, I am exposing their dirty plots against you and vindicating your name. You are another Joseph in this hour. Your life will be changed in one day, and one day is all I need, My son. You will rise higher, never to be taken prisoner again. All who imprisoned you will fall and be imprisoned themselves. Some will die by the Angel of Death. You are being vindicated now, my son, so hold your ground. The Great I AM is coming to deliver you.

Julie Green received this word on February 12, 2022

Tears came to my eyes. I knew God had not forgotten about me. He showed me every day that He was with me. However, hearing this from another human being was very encouraging.

To celebrate, I took a shower—a long one! At first, the water was freezing, but like happy campers do during a much-needed vacation, I gladly jumped in. It took a while for the water to warm up, and when it finally did, I just wanted to stay there because it felt so nice. The water was calming me down. I always loved hot baths, but under the new arrangement, the shower had to do.

Snow covered the world outside. Everything looked so beautiful. When my time was up, I was escorted to my cell. The guard asked, "How are you doing? Standing strong?"

"Yes," I replied. "I'm standing strong!"

He looked at me with intensity, as if trying to determine for himself if I was really okay. Then he said, "Just like Paul when he was in jail. Remember?"

"Yes, I remember," I answered. "Just like Paul!" And the guard locked the door in front of me.

THE BAIL HEARING VERDICT

On Wednesday, the 16th, the bail hearing verdict was announced. A computer was placed in a single room, and there I went to "court," where Judge Erin Olsen presided. She was on a mission to slam me with all kinds of ridiculous accusations. Basically speaking, the judge claimed everything that I did was for popularity, and I had to remain in jail because I posed a risk to public safety. She sided with the Crown Prosecutor, Stephen Johnston, who claimed I was an extremely dangerous individual and needed to remain in prison.

They determined I needed to be in solitary confinement as if I were some kind of terrorist. It was hard to listen to those people's reasoning. The presentation was full of false information, manipulation, and outright lies. I guess, in the end, it made perfect sense. I was in prison because of the fake pandemic that was also being fueled by misinformation, manipulation, and pure lies. The courts were doing the same thing, just following the script.

The entire ordeal would not have been as bad if it had not been for the constant noise coming from a very loud television torturing our senses. That, plus a mixture of yelling and banging on doors coming from different cells. Silence is torture, but so is excessive noise. The occasional screams and loud talking that echoed through the concrete building multiplied the disturbance. It was hard to swallow.

Certain prisoners brought to this unit were going through withdrawal symptoms. For a few days, they didn't even know where they were. For some unknown reason, they felt compelled to make it clear that they were not happy by yelling and screaming. And as I mentioned before, there were the lights with their constant off and on, depending on who was at the switchboard.

It may have been something as simple as new officers coming in during a shift change and adjusting them. Or maybe the guards shut them on or off because of the people protesting outside. Only the prison staff hold the answer to that question. Whatever the case, it was wearing us down.

This was my tenth day of fasting. God blessed me with a feeling that food wasn't even necessary. I was reading my Bible (now I had two), and that day, I was provided with an additional set of glasses. I find it amusing that at the beginning, I could not get a Bible or my glasses and now I had been doubly blessed.

At this time, they had still not given me paper, and I continued my writing on request forms, which were my only source of stationery. I don't understand why it was so difficult to bring a stack of paper from my possessions. My wife had brought some paper to the front desk and left it there. The only thing they needed to do was to go to the front desk, pick it up, and bring it to me. But that never happened.

I certainly wasn't concocting a genius escape plan using paper. It would also have been extremely difficult to dig a tunnel with only a pen and paper. I realized the seemingly insignificant things happening to us in solitary confinement were intentional punishments and a method of breaking us down.

Abstaining from food and reading helped clear both my mind and body. The drawback was that the three daily meals could have been a perfect way to pass the time, especially when you are locked up for 23 hours a day in a small room. But I did not have that luxury. My time was being passed by reading, walking for a few minutes, looking through the window, and writing until my fingers hurt.

To break the pattern from time to time, I would play a game of solitaire with cards that someone gave me. To this day, I don't know who gave them to me. Each day, the process started again until I would be let out to shower, call my wife, walk around the cells, talk to a few inmates, and then go back to the box. It's not a very entertaining process, I can assure you of that.

Day 10 brought some unusual visitors. One guard came to my cell with an officer who had some brass on his shoulders. Apparently, the hire-ups heard I was not eating and wanted to know why. The officer came to find out what was going on. He was a black man with dreads and the silly COVID gown halfway on his uniform.

"Is this true," he asked, "that you're not eating?"

"That's right," I answered. "I am fasting."

"So, this is a religious fast?" the officer replied.

"Yes, it is," I confirmed.

He carefully observed me as if assessing my mental and physical well-being. When he was finished staring at me, he said, "At some point, you will have to be taken to medical or they will come here to check on you."

"I have no problem with that," I replied.

"Okay," he nodded his head.

"I have done it before for 21 days," I said. He stared at me again, then turned around and left me in the cell. I went back to reading while lying on the mattress.

Forty seconds later, the same officer with brass on his shoulders returned with the guard. They opened the door, and the officer asked, "When was the last time you had anything to eat?"

"Monday," I replied.

"Monday?" It looked like he was counting the days in his head.

"But not this Monday," I said. "Monday, two weeks ago."

I could tell he was shocked by my answer. He processed the information and asked, "So, this is not some kind of hunger strike?" He looked straight into my eyes.

"Like I said before, I am fasting."

They took off, and I was left with my thoughts. *I hope they will not try to use force against me to make me break my fast.* I had heard horrible stories from other inmates with similar experiences.

[DAY 11]

Today, I felt no hunger whatsoever. My new friend, Daniel, whom I met in this unit, came by. He had been shot in the leg before his incarceration, and so he walked with a limp. Daniel asked about Christian college because he was seriously considering doing a Bible school and perhaps becoming a preacher. I told him that this was a good opportunity for him to turn his life around.

Worried about his past, he said, "I have done terrible things. And being a pastor is a big responsibility."

"That's true," I said, "it is. However, it is the most rewarding work you can ever do. Changing people and saving lives—there is nothing like it! And remember, Saul was a bloody murderer, and God changed him on the road to Damascus. Later, because of that encounter, he became one of the fiercest Apostles in the Bible and wrote the majority of the New Testament."

My new friend smiled and said, "And God blinded him there, right?"

"Well, yes, he did," I replied. "But sometimes, in order for us to see, we have to be blinded for a time."

Daniel smiled again. He punched the window with his fist in a show of respect and went back to his cell. Every day, inmates would stop by my door to talk. They were like sheep without a shepherd, who just needed some guidance to straighten their path.

Later, I received a letter from Daniel. Here is what he wrote to me:

> Thank you for the food. I really appreciate it. We really respect your cause and send good wishes and prayers. Thanks for bringing God's light to this place. Much needed. If possible, I'd like to stay in touch when you get out. My name is Daniel Arthur Johnson. I need more Christian friends. Trying to turn my life around...If you could, please send some prayers that I succeed. That would be great. Ray could also use some prayers. He's trying to find his path. Anyway, we are here for you. And we are routing for you. Keep your head up.

[DAY 12]

I was still fasting and felt a bit dizzy, but I was holding on. Today was Saturday, and we received clean sheets, jumpsuits, and a towel. I hid an extra one and kept the old bedding, which I turned into something that was pretending to be a pillow. We weren't given pillows, and I have no idea why. We had to create them ourselves using extra items such as socks, underwear, or spare jumpsuits. It was not very comfortable, but at least it was something.

I've always had a hard time sleeping without a pillow. *Now, at least I have something,* I thought, looking at my accomplishment with delight. I would never imagine this pitiful-looking pillow would give a man so much joy.

A man came to my window and asked if I would give him my meal today. The man was starving, and I guess the word had spread around that I was still on a fast and giving my food away. "Sure," I replied.

When the meal came, I sent my tray his way. Later, he sent me some of his coffee. Welcome to jail. It is amazing how the barter system works here. Everything is beneficial. Everything, even trivial things, might be very important. When you have very little, even the little you have is not so little anymore. I looked out, and there he was, waiting for me and thanking me for the meals.

I had prayed that morning to let my enemies go from my heart, to forgive them for the evil they had done to me. Since 2005, they have constantly been trying to harm us. I wanted to let go from my heart all the corrupt politicians like Jason Kenney, Deena Hinshaw, Tyler Shandro, Jason Copping, the police officers, the corrupted judges, and the wicked Crown Prosecutors. I needed to release them to the living God. I felt like God was telling me to let them go.

When you hold bitterness and unforgiveness in your heart, you become a prisoner, a slave to your own unhealthy emotions. When you let them go, God takes over, and you become truly free. It isn't easy to let it go. When a man sees injustice, it is his nature to seek restitution. Perhaps to even take justice into their own hands.

But God is very clear on the matter. He said, "Vengeance is mine; I shall repay." He is asking you and me, "Do you want to look for justice with your limited abilities and resources? Or perhaps leave that all to me and I will make sure that one day every man and woman will get what they deserve. My hands are not too short, and my abilities are not bound by this realm. I am the God of truth, and eventually, the truth will be known. Leave them to me. Let go of anger, bitterness, and unforgiveness. Let me deal with your enemies."

I did just that, and I prayed, "God, into your hands, I submit those people. You deal with them as you please in the name of Jesus Christ of Nazareth. Lord, I want to be free! Peace entered my cell, and even though I was locked up like a common criminal in a horrible box, I started to feel good again.

At 1:00 p.m., they took me to the interview room again to have a telephone conversation with Sarah Miller. We talked about other tickets that I was still facing and the trial that I was to attend on Thursday. We had a conversation for approximately an hour, and then I was escorted back to my cell.

Later that day, I ministered to a 46-year-old Filipino man named Ray. He asked me an interesting question. "What is the difference between Catholicism and Christianity?"

Of course, I said, "This is a very complex issue. However, to make it short, here is a simple explanation." I went on to explain that some denominations tend to control people to scare them into submission to their authority and their organizations. So, in other words, they want to own you and everything you have. They use all forms of manipulation, psychological dependency, and organization to keep people within their ranks.

"Money and power can be obtained by controlling others. The difference is this: Jesus came to set the captives free. People, however, in their fallen nature, want to possess others and use others for their own advantage. When I preach, I do not preach to your wallet; I preach to your soul. I want you to be totally free. Organized religion enslaves people. Jesus sets them free."

I continued to explain to Ray that another significant difference is that organizations love to add "stuff" to the Bible that suits their desires and needs, such as praying to Saints or to Mary, the mother of Jesus. I told him, "The Bible is very clear on the subject. There is only one mediator between God and men, and that is Jesus Christ, our Lord. There is only one, not two or ten. No one, not even a saint or Mary, can mediate between you and God. Just one, Jesus Christ. People add things to the Bible because it makes it easier for them to achieve what they want in total compliance with their own objectives. "

"You see, I decided to stay within the Bible. If you want to be free, read the Bible. Do not blindly believe someone just because he says something, even if he is a pastor, a Bishop, or the Pope himself."

This is what the Lord says:

> Cursed is the one who trusts in man, who draws strength from mere flesh, and whose heart turns away from the Lord.
>
> JEREMIAH 17:5

It turned out that Ray was born Catholic, and at one time, he had been an altar boy. He had continually done terrible things in his life and desperately wanted to change; he said he was "ready to change."

It reminded me of the many individuals who, in the previous eight months, prophesied that I would end up in prison. They understood that I would encounter certain individuals whom God had ordained for me to meet to instill hope in their hearts. My encounters over those past few days had shown that God was beginning to fulfill that prophecy.

My one hour out was very late. I called my wife, took a shower, and then I called her again. My time was almost done as I was passing another cell with three inmates in it. I stopped when someone said, "Preacher."

As I approached their door, two guys came to the window. The one who called out to me said, "When we are out, we want to join your church. We want to become part of your group."

I gave them my number and told them, "Call me when you're out." It was very interesting to see everything unfolding.

Inside a jail, the walls are empty, causing voices to resonate loudly against the metal and concrete. Whenever I was ministering, other inmates heard what I was saying and so the impact was much greater than I thought. Those boys could also see the church vigil, with people singing, preaching, and praying outside every single evening. The prisoners were definitely being impacted from inside and outside at the same time. They wanted to be part of something bigger, a family that sticks together. What an amazing witness God allowed us to experience.

[DAY 13]

After thirteen days of fasting, I started to feel a lot weaker physically but spiritually stronger. I could feel the prayers of the thousands of people around the world who have kept me strong. Sometimes, I could even hear their petitions. People were praying for justice and interceding for my release. There were also prayers and visitations through the door with my new friends like Daniel, Ray, and others, which had become a regular thing. They were ripe for the harvest and willing to change their entire lives.

Daniel told me that it was a "good thing" that he was there. Being in prison forced him to reevaluate his entire life. It made him pause and redirect his attention. He had a change of heart and his desires shifted towards God, and undoubtedly, God was waiting for him. It's a fact that God had been waiting for him for a long time. We are the ones who turn everything into ashes, but God can perfectly take the ashes and mold us into a beautiful new man.

Each day, to the best of my ability, I would make political statements that Nathaniel would record on his phone or jot down to broadcast anywhere he could. They were usually short, and their intention was to inform the public about what was happening to me.

One such statement was:

> Every totalitarian regime acts the same way: controls the media, courts, and police force and arrests opposition. In the dictatorship, tyrants like Kenney arrest political opponents. Evil is always terrified of being exposed and dethroned. One can observe this clearly in China, Russia, North Korea, and Saudi Arabia. The Solidarity Movement of Canada had become a tangible threat against government corruption. The world was watching, and Kenney's corrupted government was trembling.

[DAY 14]

My fourteenth day started early in the morning when the prisoner from across the hallway knocked on my door and said, "Bye-bye, my brother. I'm going out."

I was still lying down on the mattress. I lifted my thumb up and said, "Bye."

Off he went, towards his destiny—a man who had been there locked in solitary confinement, just like me, for weeks. He was a man with an amputated arm who had been arrested and sentenced for dangerous driving, even though he was not the driver. I was informed that the driver was the daughter of a man who was very wealthy. This man, who was an amputee, took the blame and served the time. I was also told that the father paid him a decent amount for that.

My armless comrade was very excited to get out before me, but it felt like I had just lost a friend. A familiar face that I saw every day through the window of my cell. It's very interesting how attached you become to another person when you are facing very similar circumstances. The psychology of it all is fascinating. I guess when you have very little, you get attached to something or someone familiar to you. We had great conversations together.

Now, I was staring at the empty cell, wondering who was going to fill this void. I was able to talk to my lawyer, Sarah, about the upcoming trial. She briefed me with some statements about facts. After we were done, I was taken back to my cell.

Suddenly, I felt the presence of God in my cell. I began praising Him, remembering all those declarations that I had made before. I reaffirmed to myself:

> All the way, Lord. Not my will, but Your will, Lord. Not my plans, but Yours. For Your glory and Your honor. Right now, I am here for a purpose, for a certain reason. I may not know far into the future, but soon I will. Give me the strength to endure it. Fill my heart with courage. I am Yours, and I know that nothing happens without Your bigger plan. You have allowed the enemy to do this to me because You have your purpose for my life. You know all the Whys and Whens.

Today, I had yet another great talk with my new friend, Daniel. We talked about what it means to live with God and the peace that comes with His Spirit. Daniel shared with me that all his life, he was chasing money, and in the end, it never satisfied him. That's what happens to everyone who lives without God. It does not matter how much you have or what titles you possess. If you do not have God, you are poor and miserable.

He shared a little about his life and about always being surrounded by people who wanted him dead. He had been shot at, stabbed, and threatened.

"This is not the life that I want anymore," he said. "How do you know what to do, and how do you find wisdom in life?" he finished.

"Well," I replied, "Read the Bible, and before you open it, pray. Say to God, 'Give me the understanding of what I am about to read.'"

I continued to explain that when you know the Truth, then it is a lot easier to spot the lie. I told Daniel, "Read it, and when you taste the wisdom of God, you will never want to go back to the fake. Taste it for yourself. It is like me trying to describe to you the taste of a steak. I can do my best, but if you have never tasted it yourself, it is just words that mean nothing to you. To truly understand what I am talking about, grab it and chew on it. Only then will you know."

Daniel thanked me and went to take a shower. We had very limited time outside of our cells, and he needed to hurry. But I came to enjoy my opportunities for these mini-sermons, which gave me purpose in the middle of the craziness.

CHAPTER FIVE

ADJUSTING TO PRISON LIFE

[DAY 15]

IT TURNS OUT that during my trial, they piled on five more charges against me. One from June of the previous year, two from December, one from January, and one breach of probation from February 2022. It looked like they were doing everything in their power to keep me here as long as possible, which made it a somber and long day.

"God," I prayed, "they have built a gallows for me. Please help me."

Later in the day, Daniel came by, and I shared what was happening.

He said, "Don't worry. They just want to break you. Do not let them. Just don't let them. What they do to us is inhumane." And then he listed a litany of things that seemed unjust.

- Having only two working phones for so many people to use.
- Spending 23 hours inside the cells.
- Taking showers in places that flood over.
- Not being able to exercise because there is no gym for us.

Daniel continued, "This is not right. But all of this has one purpose: to break us. Do not let them. Some time ago I had a dream," he said. "In the dream, I saw a fire. Then I remembered that gold and silver are purified in the fire. You will come out of this better. Do not allow them to break you!"

Another inmate was listening to the conversation and, referring to me, he said, "He's not a criminal. This place is for criminals. He should not be here. I feel sorry for what they do to him."

The first two weeks had been tough. Everything needed to be adjusted. My body, mind, and spirit had been subjected to something that I had never experienced before. The isolation and being away from my family and friends were difficult. Not being able to do the things I was accustomed to was tough.

All my life, I have been very busy and worked long, hard hours. The inability to do things, meet people, organize things, and go places was very hard on me. I truly felt like a caged lion walking back and forth.

[DAY 16]

The friendly guard returned from his long weekend. I informed him that the treatment we received here, being confined in solitary with only one hour out, violates the Charter of Rights and Freedoms as cruel and unusual punishment. In other words, it was torture. He replied that, apparently, under the Geneva Convention, it was alright.

I responded to him. "Even dogs at the shelters are taken out three or four times a day."

He nodded his head and said, "It is what it is," and walked away.

That morning, I read 1 Chronicles, Chapter 21, which was the story of King David and the Angel of God with his sword out, ready to strike Jerusalem. King David wanted to purchase the threshing floor where the Angel stopped striking people. Instead, there, he wanted to build an altar for the Lord. The owner of the place was willing to give it to the king for free. Not only did the owner plan to give him the place, but he also wanted to provide David with his own oxen and wood for the ritual.

However, David replied, "No. I want to pay you what they are worth. I can't just take something from you and then offer to the Lord a sacrifice that costs me nothing." What a man—what a king!

David was not perfect, but he sought God with all his heart. A sacrifice must cost us something dear to us; there is no other way. Otherwise, it's not a sacrifice.

Is that not one of the biggest problems that we see in our society? We want to give—however, only what is convenient and acceptable to us. We want to pay—but just the minimum and comfortable share of what we have.

If it does not inconvenience us in a bigger way, then we are willing, or if it is too much, then we set the limit. We tell Him, "God, I will give if I receive some incentive back. Perhaps a tax receipt or maybe some other benefits from men. Or some extra blessing from You. I will go if you do this, and I will do it if you answer me."

We live in a society that will go all the way for its own pleasure. However, paying an uncomfortable price for God and his Kingdom—now that is too much of a sacrifice.

While reading this portion of the scripture, tears came to my eyes, and I said, "God, make my time of imprisonment a sweet aroma in your side as my sacrificial offering to You. Take it as Yours. May I burn for Your glory and for Your honor. May it be acceptable to You. Here I am, and I give all to You."

When you do it the right way with clean hands and a pure heart, the Lord will bless your offering with the fire. It will be a fire that purifies everything. We must tell Him, "Lord, let the fire come. Here I am ready to be purified for Your Kingdom."

A few days beforehand, I had seen a wolf through my small window. It was beautiful, white, and massive. My heart was lifted as I watched the creature stroll through the field, even from my cramped cell. The wolf was very cautious, paying attention and looking around. He spotted some sheriffs a few hundred yards away from him moving in his direction and started to run. And just as quickly as he appeared, he was gone.

What a special blessing it was to see him. It was a treat to observe one of the top predators in its natural habitat. He was still free and alive, but for how long only God knew.

I had another virtual court today. However, everything had to be rescheduled because the Crown only provided their video evidence the weekend before. It took them 14 months to prepare it, and we could not cross-examine the witnesses identified in the video. My bail hearing was also canceled because the audio on the laptop provided by the Remand Centre did not work. I was unsure about the next course of action.

Later, I learned from our lawyers that the bail hearing for other charges and breaches was scheduled for March 10, 2022. My day ended, of course, with my now regular conversation with Daniel and a few other inmates. My next-door neighbor, a young lad, came to my window and slid a painting underneath my door that he made for me. That was very special. Every day, God was showing me He had not forgotten me. It was as though He was saying, "I want you to know that I am watching over you."

[DAY 17]

I was supposed to be transferred after 14 days of isolation to a different unit with four to six hours of daytime and access to a gym. Well, that did not happen. I remained in my original cell with neighbors who were interestingly loud, screaming and yelling for hours on end. It felt sometimes that I was locked in the asylum, especially when I saw the guards in their half-fastened, silly, useless gowns and blue masks.

It felt like a madhouse straight from a Hitchcock movie set. I often wondered who was crazier: 1) those who were yelling and screaming, tormented by a withdrawal from some kind of drug, or 2) the so-called "peace" officers pretending that the gowns and masks protected them and others from a microscopic virus. I also pondered if the COVID theater was worth the paycheck.

I tried to write a lot to keep myself occupied to where my fingers would ache. My day would start with reading the word of God, then breakfast. Since I finished my fast, my wife picked it up from there, so I ate and read at the same time. Then came the time to write a page or two, followed by more reading. Since I began eating, I thought it was also time to get in shape. Push-ups and sit-ups were a good start.

The day guard was not bad. He would visit from time to time just to talk. In the end, people are people; it does not matter where they are. On multiple occasions, I had witnessed different guards taking their masks off, particularly when they thought no one was watching, and rightly so. Many of them knew that this was a farce; they just did not want to get caught and pay the consequences for not following useless orders.

One time, a guard told me everyone knew this was all "BS," but they wanted to be smart about it to keep their jobs. What an interesting concept! They all knew it was a lie, but still, they threw me in solitary to keep themselves safe! If all of them had just said "No more," it would have been over. The country would have been free again.

My shaving tools were missing, and it had been three weeks since I last shaved, but my wife thought I looked wiser with a beard. According to that line of thinking, the longer my beard, the wiser I would become. If they did not release me, I would soon look like Moses, ready to part the Red Sea of corruption in our beloved Canada!

That day, a feeling of strength filled my heart, and it made me feel good. The longer they kept me here, the greater the story became in my mind. It felt strange, but I understood that the more they aimed to inflict pain on me, the more blessings would emerge.

I was reading from 2 Chronicles, Chapter 20, where a vast, powerful army came against the people of God. The king turned to the Lord for help, and God responded in verse 15. He said, "Do not be afraid or be discouraged by the power of the enemy's force for the Lord; He will fight on their side." I think that what the Lord wanted was for them to take their positions and watch the Lord rescue them from their enemies. He said that they would not even have to fight. Wow! They were not to be afraid, just to obey and do as they were told.

So, they went marching and began singing to the Lord, and the enemy got so confused that they turned on themselves, completely wiping each other out. When the Israelites came to the battlefield to see, it was all over. The enemy was dead. The Israelites carried the spoils for three days and went to the temple praising the Lord.

My prayer for today was this:

We are not afraid or discouraged by the force of our enemies. We take our position in obedience to you. We sing to you, and we praise you. Please confuse our enemies and let them turn on each other as we watch. Let them wipe each other out. Let us be blessed with the spoils from the wicked. Amen!

Right before the lights went out, this guard showed up with two nurses and asked if I wanted a COVID swab. They asked me if I had changed my mind and if I was willing now to take the test. My thoughts were, *Seriously? I have been here in isolation for 17 days, and now I need a test. Will this insanity ever stop?*

I had been in solitary confinement, having no contact with other prisoners. The guards continually passed by in their silly gowns, all masked up and with rubber gloves. But I had been there almost three weeks, and now they were asking me for a test so they could build up their fake statistics—unbelievable! There was certainly a virus in this prison, but its name was not COVID. Using their own terminology, it was a mental governmental moron-ism (Omicron).

When they came to my cell, offering me this craziness, I could not believe my eyes and my ears. I thought I had witnessed everything by this point. Apparently not. When I looked at those nurses dressed up in useless pieces of material, masked up and gloves on, I had this sudden image popping up in my head that would not shake out of my head. *They look like dumb goats with no brain of their own,* I thought to myself. They were just repeating what they were told. Baa!

Baa! Baa! Repeatedly. Well, we know what happens to goats in the end.

On the outside, things were no better. I learned that one of the biggest crooks had just been appointed to a position of even greater power. Tyler Shandro had been appointed as Alberta's Minister of Justice and Solicitor General. As you remember, that was the man who sent the Gestapo to shut down our churches and places of business while he was Minister of Health. It was truly a shocker, but not a surprise.

Now I had to make a statement. Here is what I said:

To appoint Tyler Shandro as Minister of Justice is one of the biggest sick jokes of the UCP party regime. This is the same guy who was caught red-handed breaking his own mandates and restrictions in the Sky Palace Party. While he was partying with his boss Kenney, drinking whiskey, pastors and protesters were being charged and arrested. Now, in Alberta, we have one of the biggest hypocrisies in a country running the so-called justice system as his personal muscle. We cannot talk about fairness, the notion of innocent until proven guilty, the rule of law, or rights if the very man on the top is as corrupt as Tyler Shandro.

To be the Solicitor General and Minister of Justice, you must have a pure heart and clean hands. Shandro is as dirty as dirty can be. What a mockery of our system. Kenney, appointing this crook, declared to the whole world: We can get away with anything we want, and there is nothing you can do about it. We will always get the carrot, and you will always get the stick.

There is this very old English saying: "The fish stinks from its head." My God, this fish called Kenney is unsalvageable. Not only does it stink, but it is also very poisonous.

[DAY 18]

Every morning, I was blessed with a sunrise. Today, it was particularly beautiful. Through my little window, I saw that the sun was very bright. The entire land, as far as I could see, was covered in snow, like a huge white blanket placed there by God himself. If it was not for the barbed wire and the fence, one might say, "What an amazing view." About 200 yards away from my window was a small forest. I was wondering what was hiding in there. Maybe the hungry trespasser from before, the white wolf?

Now, every day, I could exercise. It was not only keeping me in shape but also making me feel a lot better. Multiple times daily, I looked at the wall write-ups that I had created when they brought me here. "Jesus loves You!" "He cares for You!" Such simple words, but they always penetrate my very inner being. "He died so You can have Life!" "There is everlasting Hope!" I could almost see this truth coming into my body, soul, and spirit. "Jesus, is that Hope!" "There is hope, Artur. Remember that. Do not forget that!"

Initially, I thought those words were going to encourage some other inmates who would be locked here after me. During their 23-hour confinement, they would look up and find solace in a few words of comfort and hope. Even though locked up, they would be injected with a new dose of life for their souls.

It ended up being me, the inmate, getting motivated by those simple yet powerful words every day. It's amazing how everything works. I'm thankful that I had the foresight to put those words up there to empower me during my lowest moments.

Just before I was to be let out for my one-hour break, the guard came announcing that I was being transferred to a different cell. Apparently, this was being done on the Director's orders. I had no idea of my destination or how the new accommodation would appear. After packing my belongings, I was surprised that my "move" was only a few feet across the hallway into a bigger cell with two other inmates.

In just a few minutes of being there, I discovered both fascinating and frightening things. Those two inmates, Benny and Justin, told me that the guards were inciting them and other inmates to beat me, hurt me, and punish me for my stance. The guards were also upset about the everyday protests going on outside the prison walls, which resulted in the prison management forbidding visitors from coming and seeing the other inmates.

By doing this, they were hoping to incite hate and potential violence against me by telling the inmates that all of this was because of me. The prison hardly gave any parking to the protesters, yet they used it as an excuse to deny visits. The abuse of power was appalling. Apparently, inciting violence against a man who is awaiting his day in court was perfectly legal. That is, if it was done by those who aligned themselves with the government regime.

One inmate was directly told to punch me but refused to do so. He informed me that he told the guard, "I will not do any such thing. I'm not going to beat him up because this man has done nothing wrong. And besides, he is a priest or something." Thank you, Jesus. It turned out that the inmates were more decent than the guards.

Tonight, I was also blessed with a treat. A convoy of trucks showed up at the prison, taking up the entire road. It was an absolutely magnificent view. Since I was relocated to this adjacent cell, I had a clear view of all that was happening. I saw my son Nathaniel setting up the speaker system. My wife and brother, Dawid, were also in plain view.

It was an exceptional sight which lifted my spirits high. The truckers came with Canadian flags and signs. People were chanting, "Free Pastor Art! Free Pastor Art!" I heard my brother preach, and then people began to chant again.

More trucks came; some parked directly on the street, and others came straight to the parking lot. It was amazing to see those powerful, massive trucks decked out with signs and patriotic symbols, such as iron horses, representing freedom. Seeing all the people waving and cheering made me thrilled, and, of course, I waved back.

Nathaniel was pointing people to the very window where I stayed. Marzena came closer while Nathaniel recorded her. I presume they were streaming live for the entire world to see what was going on in our beloved Canada. She came closer and closer, speaking to the camera. The event went on for about an hour and a half.

Many police vehicles and correctional officers were running around, unsure of what to do. I kept waving to the people outside. Music was being played, and my wife was addressing the crowd. The inmates were absolutely thrilled, and they all loved it.

One man said, "I have never seen something like this in my entire prison life." It was not his first time in prison; he had been incarcerated for gang-related charges and armed robbery. All the prisoners were visibly touched, and it was a good experience. When all was said and done, that was the core of the whole thing—family, friends, and even inmates in solidarity with each other, standing firm in the face of adversity.

Once the trucks left, this guard came up to me and said, "Those protests are pointless, man. They need to stop ASAP." Wow! That comment solidified my belief in the effectiveness of those protests.

The officials were simply afraid of them. Pressure, pressure, pressure. Praise Jesus!

The day concluded with another surprise. One inmate volunteered to aid the guards in tidying up, resulting in an hour of freedom for everyone. It was the first time since my arrest that I could hang around other inmates. One inmate became teary-eyed after hearing a part of my testimony. They all wanted to change, to break the vicious cycle that had been their life until that moment.

Before they locked us back into our cells, I led one inmate to the Lord. As I prayed with him, he received Jesus Christ as his Lord and Savior. I gave him a bear hug, and he was so grateful. Another prisoner was watching our prayer and wanted the same thing. He came to me and said he would like to pray as well. I led him to the Lord and blessed him. What a glorious day! The entire ordeal was worth it, even if it was only for those two.

[DAY 19]

It was Saturday, and I was missing the church. By now, Nathaniel had opened the church and started preparing the equipment for the service. Soon, people would start coming in, and I wondered who would preach today.

While I was still writing these words, two guards entered my cell. One was the regular uniformed guard, and the other was someone I had never seen before who had brass on his uniform. Unfortunately, they came with bad news.

Last night, the director decided to "punish" me. The guards came on the director's orders to move me back to my old cell and into solitary confinement. The guard, whose last name was Freeman, apologized and agreed that this made little sense. Nevertheless, I was being moved back.

I had a feeling that this was going to occur. Once the trucker's convoy concluded, I informed other inmates of my belief that they would carry out this action. They would move me back so that I could not see the tremendous support that I was receiving. After all, their entire purpose was to break me, to make me suffer, to overwhelm me so I would quit. This had been the story of my life.

After packing the few things that were mine, I moved everything to my old cell. After finishing, I glanced out the window and had just missed the sunrise. Yesterday was a great day. Today, I would face whatever came my way. But no matter what, God would get His glory.

This was my public statement for the day:

I would like to thank you all for your continuous prayers and your support. May God bless you for your kindness and love towards us. Today especially, I want to thank you for the support of the truckers who came to join the ongoing protests at the Remand Prison. Your appearance with your amazing steel horses cheered the inmates up and put a big smile on my face.

Some inmates said that they had never seen something like this before. They were amazed. It created an atmosphere of openness, and when you left, I was able to share part of my testimony with the prisoners. After I prayed with them, two men repented of their sins and gave their lives to Jesus. I pray that many more lives will be transformed while I am here.

Yesterday, there was a party in heaven. Two souls were saved, and you were a big part of that. For that, I thank you! As a punishment, I was moved back to solitary confinement. Obviously, whatever you're doing is working. Hold the line! Do not quit standing up for your rights!

[DAY 20]

I was feeling a lot better because I had a good night's sleep. The mornings were always more bearable than the evenings. I called Adam Soos, a reporter from Rebel News, and gave him an update on my situation at the prison. I had tried to listen to the radio, at least when it was working, to keep up with the world outside.

Today, Canadian politicians were condemning Putin's actions in the Ukraine with their fancy speeches. And yet they were doing similar things in their own country to their own people. It made me sick. They were such liars and hypocrites. After a few minutes, I shut the radio off.

They let us out twice that day; maybe something was changing for the positive. Two hours a day out of the cell was more bearable than just one. I spent more time on the phone, and I had more interactions with the inmates. I was very grateful for that extra time.

Before the guard on duty's shift ended, he came into my cell to apologize for swearing so much. This interaction stemmed from our previous conversation, in which I pointed out his inappropriate language usage. According to him, the cause was the environment. Inmates swear a lot, and after so many years working here, he said he picked up this nasty habit.

Just a few hours prior, when we were in the common area, this man swore and then looked at me and apologized, saying, "I am sorry. I keep forgetting that I am in the company of a clergyman." He assured me he would try to do better.

We must do our best, and God will do the rest. The man wasn't evil; he just needed some direction. I had never seen this guard abusing his power over anyone. He had been highly professional and fair to all.

People like this man always restore hope in my heart for the system. If we only had more people like him, the prison would not just be a place of cruel punishment and abuse of power but a place of rehabilitation. People could see that there is a better way of life, a way not filled with hate, violence, and evil. Who, if not the guards, should show the inmates how to be better men?

Every few days, I kept making public statements. Here is the one that I read to Nathaniel that day:

Keeping me in prison sends a powerful message to the whole world: This is what we do with those we disagree with. If you dare to oppose the abuse of power by the bureaucrats and politicians, you will end up like Pastor Artur Pawlowski in the hole, as a political prisoner sitting in solitary confinement. I am telling you, my friends, that the only way to win against this totalitarian regime is to hold the line and resist their dictatorship. There's no other way.

So, my fellow Canadians. Stay strong! Keep the faith! Honor God! Love yourselves and hold the line. Truth wins in the end. I also find it appalling that the Canadian media is applauding people somewhere out there protesting Putin's regime and, at the same time, condemning Canadian Patriots fighting against very similar abuses right here at home. There is such a sick double standard!

Putin is doing what every dictator does: he takes and waits for a reaction. If people do not oppose his tyranny, he takes some more. Hitler did it, Mussolini did it, and Stalin did it. History is very clear.

First, they infringe on our rights, then on our ability to oppose them. Then, it moves to a total control and police state. I know history and I am not surprised at what is happening in Ukraine. When they first took Crimea, I said, 'This is just the beginning of Putin's expansion. He's following the example of Hitler when he took Austria and Czechoslovakia.' The handwriting has been on the wall for years.

Trudeau, Kenney, and Ford are baby dictators in the making. They took our rights and are waiting for our reactions. Since the opposition was minimal, they took some more. Now, you have political opponents, pastors, and protesters in prison. Bank accounts are frozen. Protesters and reporters have been trampled by horses. People who dared to oppose them have been terrorized and threatened. There is censorship and de-platforming of views not aligned with the current regime.

Nothing is new under the sun. Welcome to the land behind the Iron Curtain, where the wall of communism is getting taller and taller. Welcome to the land of Trudeau and Kenney, the tyrants in the making.

> *I will tolerate no opposition. We recognize only subordination—authority downwards and responsibility upwards.*
> ADOLF HITLER, MAY 1931

I continued to write daily statements, which I read to Nathaniel over the phone. Despite knowing it could harm me, I still wanted the public to hear. We understood that the only choice that we had was to expose the corruption publicly and fight as hard as we could. The story needed to get out. Sitting there, afraid and silent, would accomplish absolutely nothing. Fearlessly, I roared and kept doing so throughout my imprisonment. I refused to roll over and die. Because if I were to go down, I would go down fighting.

CHAPTER SIX

LIONS DO NOT BOW!

[DAY 21]

TODAY, I WITNESSED a commotion going on. I came closer to the door and peeked through the window into the hallway to see what was happening. An officer passed by the door saying, "When I tell you to f***ing sit, b****, then you sit."

This made me sad. The officers have their fancy titles, "Correctional Officers," but what do they correct? It's obvious that this guy was not attempting to correct anything. He was just as bad as the people he was shouting at.

This kind of behavior and language corrects nothing. Furthermore, it intensifies the existing resentment felt by individuals confined here for over 23 hours. People here are depressed, stressed, and have no support. Their daily freedom is limited to just an hour or two, intensifying the drama they experience, making it understandable why sometimes the inmates snap.

I now grasped their situation, particularly since I had become one of them. The guards should always do their best to diffuse a situation, not add fire to the flame. When I talked with the prisoners, every one of them had a hard time understanding why some guards behaved that way. It is not, after all, their place to be the executioners. They were hired to watch over us and facilitate the process. That is what society was paying them for.

Today was another blow in the face by Canada's so-called "justice system." When people are kept in isolation for an extended period without any reason or explanation, eventually, it is going to cause some unnecessary situations. We were confined to our cells for 23 hours on some days. Other times, we were let out for an extra hour.

Why? What was the reasoning? The long hours in solitude and the unpredictable schedule were pure cruelty. Punishment for the sake of punishment.

The common area was completely empty. The officials could have let us out so we could interact with each other, but they were very determined to stick to the one-hour rule. That is exactly why people were snapping.

Today, I witnessed one man have a total breakdown. He was crying and repeating the same thing over and over. "Why?" he asked. "Why do we have to be locked alone in this crazy box for so many hours a day?" He kept repeating this question multiple times.

He continued pleading, "This is not right. We are not animals. This is so wrong!" As tears were coming down his cheeks, he looked at me with a crazy look in his eyes. This man had reached his limit. They had driven him to the verge of insanity. And even now, the question remained: Why?

I agreed with him; this was very wrong. After a straight 28 hours in solitary, I was finally let out. It was not only wrong, but I'm sure it was illegal. It was purely and simply psychological torment. The sad part is that they didn't have to do this, but they were more than happy to do so. If you understand what I'm getting at, they were actually getting away with murder.

Today, one inmate slipped a newspaper under my door. People were protesting Putin's actions all around the world. The double standard of Western democracies was shocking. There was a story in the Calgary Herald about the blogger Raif Badawi, who had been arrested for criticizing countries' clerics.

A horrible thing happened to Badawi. He ended up in jail, and all the mainstream Canadian media were condemning the actions of the Saudi Arabian government. While they focused on criticizing one regime, I and many others were locked up in solitary confinement. We were imprisoned for speaking out against the corrupt Canadian politicians in power.

It was such hypocrisy—a double standard—to be in prison for encouraging people to stand up for their rights and to make those political villains accountable. Just like the politicians, so were their puppets, the bribed media. Without them and the cooperation of the gullible, brainwashed citizens, the tyrants could not have achieved the destruction of so many lives.

> *The receptivity of the masses is very limited; their intelligence is small, but their power of forgetting is enormous. As a consequence of these facts, all effective propaganda must be limited to a very few points and must harp on these in slogans until the last member of*

> *the public understands what you want him to understand by your slogan.*
>
> ADOLF HITLER

[DAY 22]

They let me out of my cell at about 8:00 a.m. I decided to take whatever God gave me, one day at a time. I called my wife and wrote my public statement because I had to keep roaring. Here is what I said:

Corrupt politicians like Jason Kenney and Tyler Shandro thought that by locking me up, they would effectively stop me from roaring against their evil corruption. They said, "We will silence his voice. We will scare him into submission." Well, here I am, locked up but not scared and still roaring. To roar is in our nature. We are lions, and lions do not bow before hyenas. We eat them for breakfast. Lions do not make pacts with vultures. Today, the Kenneys, Shandros, Fords, Trudeaus, and Tams are pillaging, lying, and murdering.

However, the time will come when the eyes of the people will be open, and the real villains will pay for what they have done to our beloved Canada. I am calling for all good men and women to roar for justice with me. The Kenneys can lock up a few, but they cannot lock up millions. I am calling for judges, officers, healthcare workers, teachers, media personalities, restaurant owners, business owners, truckers, and politicians to stand up with the Truth.

Stand up for the people. Defend our rights. Do the right thing. Together, let's push away this great evil that has crept into our land.

With the help of the Almighty, we shall make Canada great, glorious, and free again!

During the day, every inmate, including myself, came together and signed a petition demanding that the prison director allow us some time out of our cells. The petition stated, "If you don't let us out together, like normal human beings, then you're going to have a problem on your hands." (NOTE: The following day, we were allowed to congregate in the common area, so the petition proved successful!)

Later that day, I had a great conversation with another guard who had immigrated to Canada from Slovenia. He saw me during my one-hour time outside the cell, and we talked. It was reassuring to witness that there are still like-minded individuals within this corrupt organization who understand the true purpose of this endeavor. I read today from 1st Kings, Chapter 21 of the sad story about the highest level of corruption coming from those who should protect people, not murder them.

One citizen, Naboth, owned a piece of property that the king wanted. Naboth was not willing to sell it, but that did not stop Ahab and his wife, Jezebel. Evil never stops. Oh, how many times I had preached about this.

Wickedness is like a cancer that spreads around, consuming more and more, yet is never satisfied. It must be cut out. If you don't, it will eventually kill you. That is exactly what was happening in this passage. The cancer, known as Ahab and Jezebel, murdered Naboth. They got what they wanted by eliminating the owner. Ahab acquired the man's possessions, but in the end, he paid a much higher price: his own life.

Today's politicians are robbing and destroying those that they swore to protect. They are gaining more possessions and power for themselves. However, there will come a time when they have to face the consequences of their evil deeds with their own souls.

In Kings 21:19, God sends his prophet Elijah to deliver a message from the Lord to Ahab. It is very interesting that when the evil king sees the man of God, he says to him, "So, my enemy, you have found me at last."

Another interesting point is that one man was working for evil, and another man was working for good. Elijah is not apologetic, dancing around the issue, nor is he doing everything in his power to be politically correct. He was dealing with a bloody murderer that God was not pleased with.

"Yes, I did," Elijah replied to Ahab. "You have managed to do everything the Lord hates. Now, you will be punished." In the ears of the righteous and the good, those words are like sweet honey. The day will come when those pretending to be kings who have killed our loved ones for ages will face justice.

While I was reflecting on this scripture, a young man named Carson came to my window to talk. He was only 21 years old and had already spent two years in prison for dealing drugs. Carson wanted change. Our conversation was amazing, and he plans to go to rehab once he's released. I told him about Teen Challenge, and he promised to check it out.

Carson said that he plans to sever all connections with his old friends once he's released. He confessed that being around them always led him back to prison. But no more! Now, every day, he reads the Bible. He is not going back to his old lifestyle.

"Fantastic," I replied. With God, you cannot lose.

[DAY 23]

When you are in a difficult situation, you always look for hope or for anything that would show something good is coming your way. Every day I would ask Marzena for some words of encouragement, a prophecy perhaps. Below is what my wife read to me from Julie Green's prophecy on March 9, 2022. (Remember, at this time, I had never met Julie Green, yet God was using her to encourage me here in prison.)

Artur Pawlowski, My Glory will fill your cell. I am pouring My peace upon you. My joy will fill your heart. Yes, people will see My Glory on you. I want you to know, my son, I am here to deliver you from that cell. Continue to praise and worship Me. You are coming out by My hand, and they cannot stop this from coming to pass. No judge, no law, no leader can hold that prison door shut when I, the Lord, tell it to open.

Artur, I AM is here for you. I never left you. This time will soon be a memory of what the enemy tried to do, from stopping My Glory to filling you to overflowing and being used in this time as a great and mighty man of valor and a child of the Most High God. But your enemies can't stop My Will from coming to pass. So, stand every day, Artur, and believe Me. You are coming out never to go back there again. Remember, you are My Joseph, going from prison to the palace in one day. The God of the impossible is showing up for you, so believe this day that I always have the final say, saith the Lord of Hosts.

This revelation brought tears to my eyes. The words penetrated my inner being and touched my heart, mind, and soul. It was good to hear that God had not forgotten about me. One day, justice will be done. It was time for some vindication.

Today was "Canteen Day," and I ordered a few things for the coming week. Moreover, I learned that I would be remaining there for an extended period, although we didn't know for how long. The courts were doing everything in their power to hold me here for as long as possible.

My lawyers had not received the documents they were supposed to have received weeks before. Without those transcripts, they could not do anything. Therefore, I had to prepare myself for a longer ride.

The person who brought the canteen order asked me for my inmate (ORCA) number. I stated that I needed to retrieve it from my cell. On my way to my cell, the guard who had been watching us didn't seem pleased with my answer.

He looked at me and said, "You have not memorized it yet? Come on. You're smarter than that."

When I picked up my stuff on the way back, I told him, "I will try never to remember this number. To me, it is a symbol of tyranny, just like the numbers in Auschwitz."

This upset him so much that he followed me. "You are Polish, right?"

"Yes, I am," I answered.

"Then you should know better," he said. "It is very disrespectful to compare Canada to the Nazis."

"Why is that?" I replied. "What is happening now is exactly what was happening in Germany. That's how it started. I grew up in a city where we had a concentration camp. I was born in Poland under communism. Where were you born?"

"In Canada," he said.

"So, how would you know?" I replied.

He quickly finished the conversation, threatening me with some kind of punishment for my views. He was greatly offended. I wanted to say something else, but he looked straight into my eyes and said, "I don't want to hear it," and walked away from my cell.

This is the problem with Westerners; they refuse to listen. They think that freedom grows on trees and stays there forever. Every generation loses bits and pieces of freedom and the third or fourth one must rise up and fight for what was lost. Pure history, my friends.

> *Each activity and each need of the individual will be regulated by the party as the representative of the general good. There will be no license, no free space in which the individual belongs to himself. The decisive factor is that the State, through the Party, is supreme.*
> ADOLF HITLER, 1933

> *Tyranny, it must be remembered, does not arrive all at once—it arrives in installments, and it must be fought off in installments.*
> REX VAN SCHALKWYK

It left me wondering if many Canadians had been indoctrinated and truly believed the lie or if they were just plain stupid based on their responses. The idea that their own government was destroying them and their loved ones had not even crossed their mind. Perhaps, just like the Nazi officers before them, they all thought that the government knew best, and they were strictly to obey orders.

When Adolf Hitler was getting his moment in time, he was viewed as the good guy, a brilliant politician, and was even named *Time Magazine's* "Man of the Year" in 1938. It's important to note that this dictator was democratically elected and that his associates greatly profited from his rule. The Nazis took care of their own.

Comparing what we're witnessing now to the early stages of the Nazis was offensive to their delicate, brainwashed, and ignorant sensibilities. The Bible says it this way:

> *Woe to those who call evil good and good evil, who put darkness for light and light for darkness, who put bitter for sweet and sweet for bitter.*
>
> ISAIAH 5:2

I voiced my complaints to the nurse during their daily visits, expressing my discontent with our treatment and the 23 hours spent in a box, describing it as "unacceptable." What was the reasoning behind lengthy hours of solitary confinement? The guard mentioned that their job was to make sure we were fed and "everything else" was above his pay grade.

So, when the nurse inquired about my well-being, I informed her we were being subjected to torture, and I had strong suspicions about its legality. The nurse promised to "look into the matter." I guess the complaint to her worked because they let us out later that day for an additional hour.

On my call to Marzena, she gave me the bad news that my brother, Dawid, had been arrested earlier that day on a highway. Authorities had staged a check stop and arrested him on some made-up charges, a "breach of probation." The sheriffs were waiting for him on a highway, and when he was coming home from work, they stopped him and announced that he was under arrest. Now, you don't have to be a genius to understand that this had nothing to do with the law. This was a simple persecution of my family.

Here is my public statement for that day regarding the arrest of my brother:

The disgusting arrest of my brother Dawid is another proof of the state's ongoing persecution against our family. It is pure vengeance that has nothing to do with law or justice. Kenney's double standards are absolutely appalling. How can the politicians criticize the actions of the tyrant Putin while, at the same time, they are using these tyrannical tactics to silence the opposition themselves? Shandro and Kenney are using this opportunity to destroy those who have been criticizing their abuse of power for the past two years.

Jailing pastors, protesters, and their family members are exactly the "modus operandi" of the Nazis, communists, and other totalitarian regimes now and in the past. The question I have is this. Are Canadians OK with this? For now, soft communism is a godless system that hates and arrests clergymen.

Today, we are under the gun of state-sanctioned oppression. Today, it is me, my brother Dawid, the truckers, and the freedom-loving patriotic protesters who are in jail. However, if you stand idle and do nothing, history teaches that today it is us; tomorrow it might be you, or your brother, or your sister. Canadians, rise up with us against this tyranny!

[DAY 24]

Today (Thursday), I was let out for a few minutes in the morning. During our call, my wife told me that Dawid had been released on bail the night before. Praise the Lord! This was truly good news.

Dawid is a huge part of the ministry. And while I was imprisoned, it was extremely difficult for my wife to do all the things that needed to be done without his support. One brother in prison was more than enough.

When we got extra time during the day, it allowed me to minister to the inmates. They really needed encouragement, especially in that place of such darkness. There was a desperate need for hope and light. God gave me the opportunity to meet and minister to:

- Gang members
- People who committed armed robberies
- Bank robbers
- Drug traffickers
- Thieves

The diversity in a location like that is comparable to my renowned chili. It has a bit of everything in it, every ingredient and every spice. Sometimes, the spices are so hot that it's hard to listen to their stories. Incidentally, since we're talking about chili, let me share with you how God taught me to cook it.

At the beginning of our food pantry ministry, we served pizzas, barbecues, and, finally, big pots of soups, macaroni, and chili. My wife oversaw it all. However, the more people needed our services, the more food was needed.

The pots were getting bigger and heavier every week. Some were too heavy for my wife to carry, so I decided to step in. Watching her, I had the impression that this would be easy, not a big deal. After all, how difficult would it be to throw some stuff in a pot and let it cook by itself for a while? I thought.

I made a magnificent chili by starting the fire, putting a big pot on it, and throwing everything in. I recollected the ingredients and the things I had noticed in other chilies. It was fun! The work went smoothly, without any problems whatsoever. The ground beef mixed nicely with the carrots, beans, greens, and all kinds of other ingredients.

But after a while, I tasted it. It had no taste at all! I said, "We need to put some spices in." So, I added black pepper and some chili powder while stirring and tasting it. It wasn't bad.

I wanted the whole thing to be super hot and nicely mixed, so I left my culinary creation to simmer for a few hours on the burner. When I came back to check on my masterpiece, the smell was unbearable. Something just was not quite right. I opened the lid and attempted to stir it, but shockingly, the whole bottom of the pot was burned. The taste was awful. *Even dogs would not eat this stuff,* I thought to myself.

Instead of making a good meal for the homeless, I made a burnt sacrifice to the Lord. How sad because so much was destroyed. I had given it my all, and now everything will be wasted, which was incredibly disheartening. As I stared at the pot and meditated on my failure, God spoke to me. "Take a clean pot and do it again, but this time, listen to my instructions." I did, and I waited for the step-by-step recipe instructions from the Lord.

"Now," He continued. "Take the ground beef and throw it into the pot." I did.

"Start the fire," God said. I immediately put the fire under the big pot.

"Now let the meat be cooked just a little bit so it begins to brown. It will give a good flavor to the chili. And then stir it." I kept stirring from time to time until the grease from the beef melted, and the meat got its nice brown color all over.

The Lord continued, "Now take all the ingredients and keep putting them in. From time to time, keep stirring it. When you see that the fire is too big, turn it down a notch." I did everything God told me to do. I put carrots and all kinds of beans, greens, different vegetables, and tomato sauce into the pot.

"Chili," God said, "is like the world that I created. Every ingredient, color, age, background, and nation is unique and necessary in making the final meal. To have a good, healthy church, you need to include everyone willing to be part of my Kingdom. A good Shepherd keeps the fire of my Holy Spirit going. Get the carrots, beans, meats, greens, whites, blacks, yellows, and reds and put them all inside, allowing the flavor of each other's uniqueness to mix in the pot (i.e., the church). A good cook needs to stir it so that comfort, selfishness, self-centeredness, greed, and pride will not create a horrible stink and spoil the meal.

"A good shepherd also puts the spices into the pot to make it more alive and more vibrant. There's nothing worse than a spice-less meal or a lukewarm one. That is why you must stir it to keep mixing the ingredients together and to allow the heat to go through from the bottom all the way to the top. It must penetrate all the way. You keep the fire going, and you keep stirring it. When you keep doing it, it will distribute everything equally to heat the spices and ingredients.

"One more thing that you have to remember is when you stir, do not do it too violently. Because if you do, you will spill some of the chili out. Some people are new, and they need a gentler approach. Keep stirring. Keep the fire, but also be gentle with those that still do not understand or are too fresh in their faith."

After being given these excellent instructions, I kept the pot going for a few hours. The mixture inside the pot started boiling, and the smell was incredible. When I was stirring everything inside, I noticed that all the things that I had put in melted together. I could still see them and when I tasted them, I could differentiate the different ingredients. However, an amazing thing happened. Despite being separate items, through heating and stirring, they transformed into an incredible dish.

The final product was so delicious that I couldn't resist having a second bowl. I took the giant pot to the streets. The homeless people tasted it with a little sprinkled cheese on top. It was officially declared and still stands as the "Best Chili in the World."

Every time I have the chance to make "God's Chili," as it is known, the reaction is always the same. People say they have never tasted a better chili than this one. Of course, it is not me. This journey came from the best coach that there is, my Lord and my God.

Remembering the one-on-one lessons on cooking with God, I do my best during my sermons to keep the fire of the Holy Spirit burning. I will always do my best to keep stirring and keep adding the spices that the Lord wants for His own chili (i.e., the church). It should be served hot and without imperfections if it is properly cooked and free from contaminants, bugs, and impurities. Only then can it be presented to others. The world is waiting in anticipation for the manifestation of the Son of God. The world is yearning for a heavenly, spirit-filled, and perfectly seasoned bowl of hot chili. So, Bon appétit.

Just weeks ago, I learned that the individual who closed our businesses, enforced mask mandates on our children, and invaded our places of worship in a manner reminiscent of the Nazis has been appointed as the solicitor general and Minister of Justice in Alberta. Tyler Shandro, the Health Minister of Alberta during the lockdowns, caused devastation to many lives and businesses. It looked like Premier Kenney was well pleased with his achievements because he had appointed him to the highest office in the land of our once-free Alberta.

Now, Shandro had been given the power, just like Haman in the story of Esther, to pillage and destroy those who exposed him and opposed him for the crimes he had committed in 2020 and 2021.

Here is my statement for today:

> While I am locked in solitary confinement for crimes I did not commit, the very people who did this evil to us and committed real atrocities are being rewarded with the highest positions in the land. Sending a message to us all loud and clear that corruption and lies pay in the land of lawlessness and hypocrisy. One law for me and another law for thee has always been the signature of the tyrants.
>
> My prayer is very simple. Oh, how long, Lord, God of justice, will you put up with such a mockery? When will you stand up from your throne and hold them accountable for their crimes? When will people like Jason Kenney, Tyler Shandro, Kaycee Madu, Jason Nixon, and Travis Toews pay for the destruction that they have created and caused? When will the people who openly lied and stole, like Deena Hinshaw, Justin Trudeau, and Teresa Tam, be brought to justice?
>
> Come, Lord Jesus, and bring your truth to this troubled land. Come and have your way with all of us.

CHAPTER SEVEN

MAKING THE MOST OUT OF SOLITARY CONFINEMENT

[DAY 25]

EVERY MORNING, the lights came on, and the guard who was on duty for that day would walk into the cell to check if everything was alright. Perhaps one or a few of the prisoners escaped by digging a tunnel using plastic spoons or plastic knives. I could always tell without even opening my eyes who was on duty that day.

The officer would walk in. I would say, "Good morning," and if he responded and shut off the lights, I knew he was a good guy. If he did not, I knew it could be a rough ride. It was interesting to watch the differences between people who were there to keep the peace and not antagonize inmates, while others came to work filled with their own agenda, trying to pass it on to others just because they could.

It's unfortunate that in every place you visit, there are human beings who have forgotten the true essence of what it means to be human. I looked outside through my little window. The entire world was covered with a blanket of white. Even the barbed wires, now with this snow on top of them, looked more like a Christmas decoration. Normally, they looked very depressing, but now they looked kind of nice. Everything was white: the building, the trees, the fence, and the ground.

All the dirt was blanketed with intense white. It was truly a beautiful view. So, there I was around dangerous criminals. I was being held without a trial and did not know for how long. That was the most difficult thing—not knowing the fixed date for the trial.

Then, out of the blue, an officer walked into my cell and said that I should consider changing religions. Honestly, I was totally puzzled; he had caught me by surprise. Why in the right mind would I change life for death? Real freedom for real, tangible slavery?

I did not expect this from the guard. Was that what was going on here? Were they being paid to pressure people to walk away from faith in the real God? When prisoners were down, depressed, or vulnerable, would they come and offer an easy solution?

Drugs and the Devil. I guess I should not be shocked. The whole system was rotten and corrupted to the core. It is only to be expected that the minions of their master, Satan, sooner or later would come to you and try to enroll you into their cult. Looks like evil was doing overtime. Here is my public statement for Day 25:

Just like the political prisoners before me, my voice has not been silenced, but in fact, it is amplified for the whole world to see and hear that Canada has lost its way and has become a totalitarian regime. Where you do not allow opposition to exist, but instead, you arrest and imprison, without trial, anyone that you fear or disagree with. Kenney is a coward and a tyrant, and those types of weak men are the most dangerous. Their narcissistic and psychopathic tendencies simply do not allow them to sit down with the opposition and talk things out.

No, people like Kenney, Trudeau, and Ford are terrified of being exposed for what they truly are: evil tyrants who have a total disregard for the rights of the citizens and the Rule of Law. They will continue to lie, cheat, and steal as long as the people allow them to.

I say to you, my fellow Canadians, you have the power to stop them. You can say, "No more! Not anymore! Not an inch." Stand up against those wicked people, and let's replace them with good Canadians who love this country and love you. It is time for a change. Evil has ruled for far too long in our beloved Canada. Let's change that together. May God give us the strength and the power to be able to do that. Be blessed, and stay strong!

[DAY 26]

Another week had passed. We were still waiting for the court disclosures and transcripts. Sitting there, in solitary confinement in limbo, was the hardest, not knowing how long this was going to go on for. That day, Marzena was preaching about Esther, Mordecai, and Haman. It is such a good story. At that time, for me, the gallows were still standing. The Hamans in the land were being rewarded, and the real lovers of this country were waiting for execution.

The day before, I had another great talk with the boys. One said, "When I get out, I'm going to join your church and I am bringing my whole family with me."

I was doing my best to use the time there wisely. I read a lot and contemplated a lot. I wrote and prayed. The claws of wickedness had a solid grip on my life, and at that moment, only God could free me from their hands. I knew that he had my back covered.

In 1 Samuel, I read the story of Hannah and her prayer. It greatly encouraged me. She prayed, "You make me strong and happy, Lord. You rescued me. Now, I can be glad and laugh at my enemies. No other God is like you. We are safer with you than on a high mountain. I can tell those proud people, 'Stop your boasting!' Nothing is hidden from the Lord, and he judges what we do..." And in verse 9 she continues, "You protect your loyal people, but evil people will be silenced in darkness" (1 Samuel 2:1 NCV).

The guards came to do their thorough upside-down search, which was very unsettling and such an infringement of our privacy. I lost some of my socks and my beloved pillow, which had been a faithful servant for the past few weeks. I called it "Stuffy" because it was literally stuffed with extra blue diving suit coveralls, a towel, and an extra blanket. That pillow was hard, but it was also comfortable under the circumstances, of course.

When they let me out, I learned that only the "special ones" received the blessing of the search. And I was one of them. Again, I do not know what they were looking for. The most dangerous thing that I had—the truth—I always kept deep inside of me. That contraband was safely stored in my heart, soul, mind, and spirit and was something that they couldn't search for or take away.

Someone must have been praying very hard because they let me out of the cell at a precise time. My wife was just finishing the story of Haman being hanged on his own gallows—the one that he had built for Mordecai. My buddy Ray saw me standing right by the telephone, waiting for him to finish his conversation, when he suddenly hung up and gave me the phone. Just wow! He looked at me and said, "You can have your call now. I'll call later."

God wanted me to address the Church straight from my dungeon. When I called Marzena, she put me on the speakers, and I heard an enormous crowd cheering and blowing shofars. How amazing! I was able to share a mini-sermon with the church. It felt so good to be able to talk to the parishioners.

I thanked them for standing with us and for all the letters I had received. I shared about the life of a pastor locked in Remand and encouraged them to stand strong. "One day, everyone will receive what's due to them. God will judge the living and the dead." I told them. It was a great experience to be able to preach to the church again, especially under the circumstances. I bet the enemy didn't expect that.

In the evening, I asked the inmates to gather around and pray with me. A good number came and joined us around the tables. Someone said, "This is exactly what we need."

A young man, 21 years old, was so moved that he said my words were sticking in his brain. I really needed to hear that. Thank you, Jesus, for yet another fantastic opportunity to spread your hope in this hopeless environment. Lord, to you all the glory and honor.

The young man's parents owned a big farming business and raised cows and other animals. God gave me a revelation about his life and how much his parents hurt because of his actions. "I am a father of a 21-year-old son as well," I told him. I could feel their pain, so I shared the gospel with him,

And in the end, he said, "I need to go to a good treatment centre to become clean again."

I replied, "Go back to your parents. Work hard. Be a blessing to them. With God, you can do it."

"I will," he assured me.

What a Saturday! What an opportunity to be the light in the darkness. This was a good day. I studied my Bible, did my exercises, read some more, prayed some more, preached at the church, and ministered to the prisoners. It was a busy day indeed, and I couldn't help but think, *"I will need a vacation when I come out of this 'all-inclusive' resort!"*

Later, I saw my family coming in. They were in our red van with its now famous write-up on the side of the van, "Jesus is Coming Back." Through the window, I saw my wife coming out. My brother Dawid and his wife Marta were there as well. I could see them unloading the speakers for the day's music and preaching.

A few minutes later, I saw Nathaniel arriving in his car. Then, about ten minutes later, I saw my father's car. I watched them walking around, putting up speakers and the stands. Larry was already singing, but I could not hear him or the music.

However, I could see people already dancing and clapping. It was wonderful to see so many people coming to support us. A guard came to me, upset and angry. He gave me a look and complained from behind his mask, "You should tell them they're protesting in the wrong spot."

The mask mandates were already lifted. However, the prison administration demanded that everyone still wear them (so much for democracy and freedom)! The officer continued, "It would be better to do it at the Court House. It would get the media's attention."

This guard was completely missing the point. Those people were here in support of me. They were united in love and solidarity against what was happening to our family. This wasn't designed for media attention; the media knew what was going on and had chosen to align themselves against the people of the land instead of standing with them and for them. The media had become so corrupt that none of us even wanted to look in their direction.

A few hours later, everything was over. All the people, including my family, went home, which made me extremely sad. I had to stay there still without a date for court or a bail hearing—stuck, locked in limbo, all alone in my seven-by-twelve-foot cell. I guess seeing them out there, walking and talking with each other and other people, made me miss them even more.

Just before going to sleep, I realized that I lost something else during the special search of my humble accommodations. They took the covering that I had made from the gown and the black socks that I used to cover my eyes. The lights can be brutal, and the covering allowed me to sleep. When I went to bed, I looked for it everywhere, but it was gone. Another casualty of war. The lights were so bright that I thought to myself, "You would have to be blind to be able to sleep in such an environment."

I read again, hoping that at some point, they would shut off the lights so we could sleep. While reading, someone passed by my cell, and there was a banging on the door. It happened multiple times and was quite annoying, to tell the truth, especially in a place where every noise is magnified by the bare concrete walls and the metal doors.

Finally, I stood up to investigate, but I did not expect what I saw. The person who was making all this noise was a blind man carrying his walking stick. Every time he passed next to my cell, his stick made an annoying bang on the metal door.

I could not believe it. What did a blind man do to end up in this asylum? This was one mystery that I vowed to investigate during my time out of the hole the next day. I've witnessed many things, but this particular experience caught my attention and is a story worth exploring.

As I stood at the door trying to see this person responsible for the banging noises, someone from another cell yelled, "Do you see it now?" The man with the stick just walked past my door again, wearing big black glasses, and then disappeared into the hallway.

I thought to myself, *"Now I am stuck here with a bunch of bank robbers, drug addicts, gun offenders, and thieves. And to top it up, we have a blind man and the pastor. Just wonderful."* I grabbed a pair of black socks and tied them together, putting them on my head to cover my eyes. Now, I was also blind. I couldn't see anything, and I conked out.

[DAY 27]

Today, I studied the Book of Samuel. During his time, the enemy was also very strong. People were terrified, and many were crying. Just like today, families were devastated. Evil was stealing and robbing left and right. Just like then, today, it feels that people do not have anyone to look up to. No one to rescue them. No one to speak and stand up on their behalf.

Then, in 1 Samuel, Chapter 11 is this story: King Nahash of Ammon decides to come with his army and surround the town of Jabesh in Gilead. The force is big and too powerful for the Israelites. People are afraid, and they cry out. Saul hears about it, and the Spirit of the Lord takes control of Saul and makes him furious against the enemy. He gathers the army and becomes the voice of the Lord. He shows how to stand up and fight for what is rightfully yours. The land today needs courageous men and women to lead the way. This is not the time for retreat but to advance, to move forward.

I needed to share this with everyone, so when they let me out of my cell, I called home and asked Nathaniel to record my statement.

One month ago, I was literally kidnapped from my house. Police and RCMP have locked me up in solitary confinement as a warning to everyone else, "Don't you dare oppose our corruption. Don't you dare to speak against our tyranny unless you want to become another Pastor Artur Pawlowski in the hole.

However, my fellow Patriots, this is not the time for retreat. This is not the time to stand back. This is the time to advance, to move forward, to take back what is rightfully ours—what belongs to you and to your children—freedom. The Kenneys and Trudeaus think that they have the power to scare you, to control you, to force you into submission. However, the truth is that they only have that power if you give it to them. Don't!

You are nobody's slave. You will be free if you choose to be free. That is not up to villains like Shandro or Kenney. This is up to you— you, the thousands of lovers of this country. You hold your destiny in the palm of your hands. So, stay strong. Be courageous. Look into the eyes of the children and say to them, "You, my children, are our Canadian heritage. You are worth fighting for!"

So, even though I am locked up like a common criminal, I have not lost my faith. I know that one day, justice will prevail. The truth will come out, and the villains will be judged. Until then, I stand strong, and I pray for you and for my beloved nation that God's will is accomplished. If my chains can contribute at least a little towards that victory, then I am greatly humbled that God has chosen me to be able to be part of that ultimate goal. Do not lose hope, for we know that in the end, we win.

The boys and I had another great prayer session. Afterward, I went to see the blind man. They told me he doesn't have eyes. Can you believe that? I brought him some hot water. He's in his 30s, but I still do not know what he did to deserve to be here.

A new guy joined our prayer group. He was there for armed robbery. After we prayed with our heads down, he said, "That actually felt really good. I could use that."

Praise Jesus! He was touching the hearts of people. I finished my day with a passage from 1 Samuel 14:20. Lord, let the enemy become so confused that they would turn on each other.

[DAY 28]

Last night was a tough night. Someone was arguing with a guard for a very long time, and the words were bouncing through the walls. The prison refused my request for earplugs, and sometimes, it was challenging to fall asleep with all this noise around.

I was glad when I woke up in the morning. That meant that I finally managed to fall into oblivion. I drank my cold, instant coffee. Hot water for the coffee only comes when there is a friendly guard. But no such luck today.

I was fascinated by the Bible and savoring the chapters—not rushing them, just taking my time. It's incredible how those stories never got old—every time I read them, there was something new to discover, and that excited me.

It's like hunting. When I go to the forest or to the mountains, I never know what I might see—the beauty and majesty of the mountains, the mystery of the forest, the animals that, if you are careful and quiet, you might encounter. This makes every moment priceless. I love it.

The Bible is also like that for me. At every corner, there is something new and thrilling. If you pay attention, you might see something fascinating. In the story of Samuel, there is this brief statement that many have missed. I believe that many Christians have an incorrect view of God and who He is. Most people believe He's all about kindness, mercy, forgiveness, love, and grace.

He's so much more than that. Hs is also wrath, vengeance, and holiness. He gets upset and angry. If He's a perfect judge, then His righteousness demands fairness, justice, and punishment for evil. Rebellion requires consequences. Wickedness must be confronted.

So many have missed that. They have created God after their own desire, a Jesus made in their own image, like an idol formed based on their own limited fleshly understanding. A hippie Jesus with two fingers stretched in the victory sign, long hair, and a long beard, saying with a smile: "Peace, brother."

I do not see that image within the Word of God. It says: "For I am the Lord, I change not" (Malachi 3:6 Old Testament). And it also teaches us that "Jesus Christ is the same yesterday, today, and forever" (Hebrews 13:8 New Testament). God is the God of the New Testament, but He is also the God of the Old. Once, the Lord said to me that there is only one Word, one Book, and one Testament that He left with us.

When you read the whole thing, it's like a love letter describing His nature. It shows you who He really is and what He wants from us. You do not really know Him if you only take the Old Testament, and you do not know Him if you only take the New Testament. The entire Bible talks about what He wants for our future.

In 1 Samuel, Chapter 16, verse 4, Samuel comes to a town. When people see him, they are terrified. Why? Because a man of God shows up. They know in their hearts that they are not perfect. All have sinned and fallen short of God's glory. They know that when God sends a prophet, He means business.

It was time to make things right. A prophet meant accountability. So, when Samuel showed up, they did not know if this visit was for correction, punishment, to make things right, or for a blessing.

So, the people of the town asked, "Is this a friendly visit? Are you coming in peace?" Imagine the understanding of those people. Samuel represented God's justice and holiness. The people knew they were lacking. We have lost that in our fast-paced, self-focused society that thinks God is only a means to an end, believing you can treat Him as you want without eventually paying the consequences for your actions. What a man has sewn is what he will also reap.

When I talked to the inmates, everyone had a date and an appointment with the judge. They were counting the days. Every day was one day closer to an answer, one day closer to their freedom.

But it was like torture not knowing what would happen next and not being able to cross off the days on a calendar to show that I was getting closer rather than further away. They had robbed me of that. The authorities deliberately did not give us the documents needed for judicial review, which was a form of punishment. They wanted me to be stuck here, not knowing what was going to happen to me or when this craziness was going to be over. They wanted me to think that this could go on forever. It was part of their plan to break me.

Time went by slower, with very little to do. A person who has been busy all his life has a hard time adjusting to not doing much. Outside of the barbed wires, time is your biggest enemy. You can never satisfy that beast. He is always hungry. He never has enough. Time slips through your fingers. You're chasing it, but to no avail.

Behind bars in the cell, time also becomes your enemy. It drags its feet and stares at you with its sneer. You want it to go away, but like a torturer, he takes his time with you. Slice by slice, this enemy cuts you to pieces.

When it is done with you, you wish you could just close your eyes and fall asleep forever. But when you finally open your eyes, you realize that nothing has changed. You know that you must walk through this valley of the shadow of death and endure it. There is simply no other way. Oh time, why do you have to be so fast out there and so slow in here? I guess you are cruel to us all.

On this day, I looked outside through my little window, and the snow was half gone. The wind was strong, attacking the trees mercilessly. I thought about the wolf and wondered what had happened to him. His beautiful white fur was still vivid in my mind. I haven't seen him again, and it's unlikely I ever will. He was gone, and I was still there. He was searching and hunting. I was waiting and watching the world pass by from a cell.

I could see a Canadian flag off in the distance. How did I miss that? It was puzzling because, after nearly a month, I was just now noticing the Canadian flag flapping through the wind. Perhaps the wind was never strong enough for me to notice it from far away. The red and white colors were violently being tossed from left to right. Many days before, I saw some men working on something. Maybe they were working on this flagpole? I do not know.

It didn't matter, anyway. The Canadian flag was supposed to symbolize purity, with the white and red reminding us of the brave people who sacrificed their lives for a better future. The men of old had a dream of a nation where a person could work hard and achieve something. They could be free and happy.

Then, consider the maple leaf placed in the middle of the flag, which symbolizes the healing of the nation. My God, how far have we fallen from that original plan? We're not healing anyone. We are even sicker than the countries that we claim to be helping. God, we need healing. This country needs healing. Come, Lord, and cut this cancer out.

[DAY 29]

It was another rough night. The inmates were talking loudly for what seemed like forever, and I could not sleep. Earplugs were not allowed (*I guess they could be used as some sort of dangerous weapon!*), so I tried other things. However, nothing worked effectively.

If you are caught in their system, you have to suffer. By then, that was plain and simple. So, we were suffering—plain and simple. The inmates kept telling me that is how they break you. They want to humiliate you and embarrass you. That is why you can't even use a bathroom in privacy. They can look and come anytime they want. It is part of the design.

In the common area, I read the Remand Centre's write-up. Here is what it proudly said, "This is a Correctional Facility and subject to monitoring and recording" and so on. The part that caught my attention was the title. "This is a Correctional Facility." Huh?

If that was the case, we were all doomed. For over a month now, I have observed no attempt to correct *anything* or *anyone*. Just to reiterate, nothing was being done with the prisoners at all. There were no activities nor the ability to complete any work. There was no counseling, not even from clergy coming daily to say a few words. There was NOTHING! They had people locked up like cattle for almost the entire day. If they came out, there wouldn't be much time to do anything, anyway.

The first thing an inmate does when given the opportunity is grab the phone to call family, friends, lawyers, etc. Then, they will take a shower. Once he's finished, he has to go back to his tiny cell for another 24 hours. In the few minutes in between, I often observed them talking about their crimes. They would share their expertise and experience on "how to" and "with whom."

This was all they knew—the life of a criminal. Instead of feeling remorse for their evil deeds, they just hyped each other up to commit more crimes and compete to be the baddest gangster. When I got out and had my little opportunities to talk to them, I did my best to change their focus from evil to good. However, a few minutes a day was certainly not enough to accomplish that in everyone.

Do not kid yourself; this correction facility was not correcting anything. By design and by the way it was being run, it encouraged people to keep sticking together in what they knew—a lifestyle of crime. One day, they will walk out of this place, and instead of being better citizens, they will be even more hardened, bitter, wounded, and hateful criminals. They will be better equipped and more connected than before. It saddens me that all of this is done with our taxes to "benefit our society and protect our loved ones."

The day before, we had very little time to talk, but we managed to sit at the table and pray. I prayed with a bank robber, a man accused of human trafficking, and also with a tremendous athlete—a basketball player who got a scholarship and traveled the world playing tournaments.

His problems started when he took prescription drugs for his injuries and eventually shifted to heavy illegal substances. It was good to pray and share with him. If I had more time, I would have been able to have a bigger impact. If only we had more time, which, at this moment, the guards were not willing to give. I planned to write to the director and see what he had to say.

I was reading the story of Ziklag, the city that was given to David by the Philistine King Achish. When David was away, the enemy attacked Ziklag and burned it to the ground. They took away the women, children, and everything that they had. When David and his men came back, and he saw the burned-out ruins and learned that their families had been taken captive, they cried. They cried until they were too weak to cry anymore.

David was a mighty and brave warrior. His men were tough, well-trained soldiers who fought in many battles. They had faced many difficulties before, yet when they faced personal tragedy, they cried. When I was growing up, I remember being taught that real men never cry! You do not show your emotions. Do not bleed in front of others. The world is like an ocean, and when the sharks smell your blood (i.e., your weakness), you will be done for. Those sharks will finish you off.

But I was beginning to understand how totally wrong this teaching was. When bad things happen, cry! Cry to the Lord! Give your tears to Him as an offering to God. Let go of your emotions. God changed my stony heart for a heart of flesh. I am very grateful to Him that when I am overwhelmed with difficulties, I can cry. Tears of a man are so freeing, so cleansing when they are being shed for love, the cause of truth and righteousness.

Even Jesus Christ, the strongest person who ever walked the earth, shed tears. Now I know that there is a time to laugh and a time to cry. Do not be ashamed of your tears when they are shed for a good cause.

After shedding some tears, David pumped himself up with the Lord's help, sought His guidance, and went to get back what was taken from him. He won a great battle and got what was his and more. A humble warrior of God who is soft enough to cry is the one who is the strongest of all and wins in the end. There is a scripture that says:

> *A broken and a contrite heart, O God, You will not despise.*
>
> PSALM 51:17

Being humble and broken means relying on God, not people. That's what He wants—a total surrender.

My friendly neighbor and ex-bank robber, Daniel, came to talk. They didn't let me out, so we chatted through the door. My friend was looking for some advice.

"The Crown wants six years, almost the maximum sentence for what I have done," he said. Daniel was debating whether to take that deal or choose from a few other options. He wanted to know if he should: 1) plead "guilty," 2) take the deal that was not a deal at all, or 3) fight it in court.

What kept replaying in my head were Daniel's own words, which he had said to me countless times. "It's a new start. Put the old behind … have a clean slate."

So, I said to him, "Do a total surrender. Go before the court and acknowledge the responsibility for what you have done. Face the judge and share your story with him. Tell him how sorry you are and that you are changing." Daniel had already finished several courses and was ready to start college here in jail by correspondence.

I said, "Share that with the judge and throw yourself into the hands of God. Let Him decide what is next for your life. Total surrender. No more games. Everything or nothing." He took the advice and went to call his lawyer. Daniel came back to share with me that he was going to face the music. And he felt liberated and fresh. Now, God would have the final say. He went back to his cell feeling happy.

I looked at my wrist. Remarkably, a month later, I still had a scar on my right wrist. This last arrest was very rough. I was making my point, and they wanted to make their own. I ended up with this scar.

Today marks one month in jail, and it was also "Women's Day." But the romantic dinner and flowers would have to wait. Instead, I was again able to pray with most of the prisoners. Others were watching and later came to me asking for prayers. They said it helps them; they feel better after it. Nathaniel was outside the prison, playing songs and speaking to the people who showed up for the daily protest.

An inmate came to me saying, "I hear them chanting 'Free Pastor Art!" He looked at me and continued. "It feels so good. It makes me feel human again." His entire body, including a sizeable portion of his face, was covered in tattoos. He looked into my eyes, put his fist on his chest, and said it again. "It is good to see such love." Wow! I asked the Lord to touch them all, including the guards. *One soul at a time, Lord. Save them all.*

CHAPTER EIGHT
THIRTY DAYS IN

[DAY 30]

I WAS TOLD I'd have to appear before the court for my other charges: Shoppers Drug Mart, the protest at the minister's house, and breach of probation. I wasn't sure what else, and I didn't know what God had in store for me. No matter what, my life belongs to Him.

The longer I stayed here, the more dirt would be exposed, but I needed to be there to see what He wanted me to see—to experience the pain of those that many didn't care for. Canadian corruption was coming to light.

That morning, I made a statement for the Ohio legislature. Nathaniel told me that the Ohio House of Representatives had introduced a resolution asking that Canada be placed on a persecution watch list because religious liberties were being threatened. That was a big deal! There was a possibility that the persecution and prosecution of Christians in Canada might be heard by the Congressional Committee, and that would be very powerful. It would put a spotlight on this whole craziness.

This is what my friend Cindy from America (she planned a tour for me last year) sent to the American politicians:

THE PERSECUTION OF PASTOR ARTUR PAWLOWSKI IN HIS CHURCH.

It all started in 2005 when the government declared that feeding the poor in public, preaching the gospel, congregating, and giving away Bibles and municipal laws prohibited gospel materials. They cited many of them, for example, giving free goods and services, distribution of printed material, and illegal gatherings in public spaces. Illegal signage when we had our banners, "Jesus is King" and "Jesus Loves You."

For feeding the homeless, we received over 300 tickets and court summons from 2005 to 2015. According to them, tables for food were illegal, barbecues were illegal, and placing material on the ground, like the cross, was also illegal. We were charged with stunting and distracting motor vehicles when we fed the poor. Law Services, the police, or both monitored and harassed almost every service that we conducted.

This resulted in over 100 court cases, some conducted for as long as three weeks. In 2006, I became the first clergyman in modern Canadian history to be arrested and criminally charged for reading the Bible in a public park. A number of charges were placed on me. From 2005 to 2015, I was arrested a dozen times for crimes related to preaching the Bible, congregating in parks, or feeding the poor.

At times, I had to fight dozens of city and provincial attorneys and sometimes the Solicitor General himself with all his crown prosecutors. I was forced to re-mortgage my house seven times so I could survive such an enormous attack on our rights and freedoms.

In 2015, we won. After the victory, the politicians and their lawyers left us alone for a few years. Our church feeds thousands of homeless and less fortunate people, including the working poor and single parents with kids, every month. We provide our services without any government assistance. Not one tax dollar comes to us from the government's coffers. All the work is done by volunteers, and the food is donated by good people in Alberta.

For exposing government corruption and speaking about what was happening to me, I have been slandered by the government and media. I have become the voice for the poor and for freedom, which they are desperately afraid of.

In 2020, the attack on our peaceful church, which houses and feeds so many less fortunate, was hammered with a new viciousness and force. In April 2020, I became the first person to receive a "Covid" ticket for feeding the poor. I was told that soup kitchens were now outlawed. From 2020 to 2022, our church was harassed and fined on a regular basis, with over forty tickets, multiple trials, and five arrests in just a matter of a few months. All were done by S.W.A.T.-style operations, some in the middle of the highway.

I have been charged alongside others for the crimes of: 1) Inciting people to come to church, 2) Officiating an illegal gathering or Church service, and 3) Participation in an illegal gathering, all for feeding the poor, as well as holding supposedly "illegal" church gatherings.

During our church services, we had anywhere from half a dozen officers at once. During our Christmas celebration, for which I received fifteen more tickets, we had over 100 police officers, the gang suppression unit with 52 police cars, and a special team of officers with video cameras harassing and intimidating our parishioners. The Chief of Police himself also came.

In April 2021 and again in May, our church was invaded contrary to the Criminal Code of Canada, Section 176. Eventually, for kicking the armed officers out of the church, I was charged and arrested. Right now, I am facing criminal charges for refusing to shut down our church, for conducting church services, for doing protests, and for feeding the poor. I also face contempt of court, a compelled speech ruling, financial hardship, and huge penalties. I'm writing this from solitary confinement with no court date after they denied my bail.

All of this is happening to me and our church, contrary to the Criminal Code and the Canadian Charter of Rights and Freedoms. Christianity is under a heavy attack, and the government has declared that churches are non-essential. Therefore, we have lost our protection.

As a result, about seventy churches experienced vandalism, and some were burned down in 2021. Abortion clinics, liquor stores, marijuana shops, Costco, Walmart, and Ikea have more protection than a Christian pastor who feeds thousands of the most vulnerable people in our society.

I am presently in prison because I dared to give a speech to support the truckers who did their best to stand up for our liberties. From 2005 to 2022, sixteen arrests, over 100 court hearings, over 340 tickets, three court injunctions, two contempt of court charges, and a compelled speech forced me to repeat the government's lies regarding the COVID narrative, which I refuse to do. So, I need your help. Canada needs a good shaking.

I was supposed to see my lawyer, but for the past three weeks, they've been doing everything in their power to prevent our meeting. I am in the claws of a very evil and corrupt system. This morning, I was informed that my lawyer had been calling every day and was trying to come and see me so we could discuss the cases.

However, every day, they put her on hold for an hour, and no one talked. It was a total blockage. They had been successfully preventing my ability to defend myself for a month. How are you to fight with such lawlessness where the rule of law does not exist?

Some powerful people with influence have broken every law in the name of the law. I asked the Lord to bring justice to this case.

> *Our Lord and our God, you are my mighty rock, my fortress, my protector. You are the rock where I am safe. You are my shield, my powerful weapon and my place of shelter.*
>
> 2 SAMUEL 22:2-3

> *Your way is perfect, Lord, and your Word is correct. You are a shield for those who run to you for help. You alone are God! Only you are a mighty rock.*
>
> 2 SAMUEL 22:31-32

> *You protected me from violent enemies, and you made me much greater than all of them.*
>
> 2 SAMUEL 22:49

Today was a hard day for me. It was a flashback to a very difficult time in my life. And being here in prison caused my imagination to process overtime. In the end, I was very stressed and walked back and forth in my cell. When I got to make my phone call, the guys all gathered around me by the door and said a prayer for *me*! It was a very touching moment. I kept walking back and forth, thinking, *Lord, how much longer is this going to last?*

I couldn't calm down, so I stood by the window and stared at the Canadian flag fluttering in the distance. I came to this country for freedom, peace, and a better tomorrow. But here I was, locked up like some kind of dangerous animal. My mind shifted, and I remembered the last few years—all the things that led up to this moment. *Why is this happening to me?*

Sitting in this cell all alone for 23 hours a day, you couldn't help but think or ponder the memories of how this whole craziness unfolded. Oh, how I thought I would be left alone to the business of life. *How did I get to this point?*

The constant bombardment of information and the constant demand to do and to go had moved me into a never-ending perpetual machine that refused to slow down. Being locked up made me shut down temporarily like a tired roller coaster slowing down. My mind catapulted back to a few years before our world completely changed.

CHAPTER NINE

A FLASHBACK TO THE EVENTS BEFORE MY IMPRISONMENT

PLEASE ALLOW ME to shift focus from detailing prison life to explaining the events that led to my imprisonment. I remember it like it was yesterday. Deep down, I had a hunch that peace wouldn't last much longer. It never does. In the Bible, Solomon reminds us of the universal truth that there is a time for peace and a time for war.

I never enjoyed fighting. Training myself, yes. But fighting with another human being, no. Deep on the inside, I am a man of peace, and I prefer quiet. I've always liked food and gatherings and being around people to talk and laugh with them. And after we close the doors, there is once again peace in the comfort of my home.

Unfortunately, people will always be the same, and history shows that when you succeed, haters will come knocking. The quiet time is usually when the villains are licking their wounds or plotting another attack.

Remember, evil never stops. The previous few years had been incredible. I had regained my focus after walking through a trying time of a couple of years before. We traveled to awesome places and did some fascinating mission trips. Also, the Street Church was flourishing, not just in Calgary but in over forty cities around the world. My finances were still lacking. I was still driving a 20-year-old pickup truck I got when I was still in business. However, the strain of the constant courts, fines, and lawyer fees was behind us. Not much was coming; however, not a lot was going out.

The Street Church ministry required about ten thousand dollars a month. I would constantly re-mortgage my house to make ends meet. And yet, I was not super stressed about it. God was healing me from all the past wounds. I remember when He told me, "I want you to start another church," and I was like, "No way!" I had been the pastor of a church in a building before. And I didn't want to do it again!

People who were used to comfort were awful, always complaining about something and never satisfied. I said, "Lord, I am not a typical shepherd. Please allow me to be on the streets. Let me feed the poor. I am okay with that. Let me preach a simple message of salvation. Let me just do what I do now. Please."

However, God was unwavering. "I want you to start another church."

He was repeating His command, and I continued giving him excuses: "I am busy. I am traveling. We organize so many things. The marches for Jesus. The festivals. The Crusades. The missions."

In the end, I threw out my best argument: "I do not have the money. And Lord, by the way, there are over 500 churches in this city, and over half of them are empty. Why do you need another one?"

There was also one more problem. No one was willing to rent a facility to me. They were all terrified of associating themselves with what we do, and they feared losing their charitable tax status. For two years, I was dodging His command. For two years, I was busy with the things I had on my plate. I knew that I was disobeying his orders, and eventually, one day, a heavy spanking came. We completely ran out of all our money, and we had to re-mortgage my house yet again. We were plummeting. And even though I knew I was disobeying God, I just could not find within myself the strength to "cross the Red Sea."

All my life, I have been very stubborn; it took a spanking to get me moving. I do not blame God for the chastising because He is always right. Humans are flawed and weak. We only see things that are right in front of us. It is very difficult for us to see through the eyes of the faith. I thought I could not do it. He said to do it, and that should have been enough for me. So, I finally gave in to God and began looking for a place.

However, the moment people recognized me, the owner would say "No." We checked out various ads, but every time things seemed hopeful, they shut the door on me right away until one day when I met an ex-Singaporean special forces member who had turned pastor. His name was Sam. He listened to my struggles and said, "If you want, you can rent from us at no cost for one year. It is not a huge place, but it will be perfect for you at the beginning."

So we made the arrangements and started having our weekly church meeting on Saturdays because we were doing services on the streets on Sundays. I figured things would be moving fast with all those people asking me to start a church in a building. But that was not the case.

I'd often find myself preaching to an empty room. When I was debating with the Almighty about this endeavor, I asked him what he wanted me to call this new church. Here is what He said: "I want you to call it the 'Cave of Adullam." It will be the fortress where many men and women of valor will be trained. Many mighty warriors of mine will come out of this place."

People have these amazing names for their churches, but "the cave?" Seriously? And not just any cave. It will be the Cave of Adullam that most cannot even pronounce properly. Plus, lots of people won't even get it. Some will probably think that this is some kind of Arabic Centre. However, I did not argue with God. I knew better now. The *spanking* had done its job.

We were on the edge of our seats for the first few meetings about how God was going to do it. How many people would He bring? But weeks came and went, turning into months.

When the first year was over, with only a handful attending, I started to question myself. *"Did I actually hear from God? Did He really tell me to start this church? What is going on?"* I literally asked Him, "Where are you, Lord?"

People were coming and then disappearing, never to be seen again. I'd spend hours and hours getting my sermons just right, sometimes even two or three days a week. And then to only deliver it to ten people sitting throughout an empty auditorium. It felt like I was preaching to empty chairs. A year later, we were nowhere closer to a breakthrough. The finances were still not coming either. And now we have to start paying rent.

We prayed and kept seeking God. But still no answer and no people. That second year was the hardest. I had very mixed feelings and would say, "God, why do we even bother to set up the equipment and spend days preparing sermons? For what? A few people and half of them my own family! What is even the point of paying for the facility? We can do the same thing at my house." We had previously conducted a home church for eight years; we could do it again.

I tried to reason with God, but there was no answer. When I talked to Marzena about the whole situation, I was frustrated and quite often angry. Before the sermons, I would look out the church window expectant to see people coming in. During those two years, I was ready to quit, not able to function like that.

One day, I told God, "Obviously, you have picked the wrong person for this task. People dislike me and don't want to hear me preach. Even those that came initially eventually ran away and did not return. Lord, I'm telling you—you have the wrong man."

Sometimes, on our way to church, I would tell my wife, "If people do not come this week, then this is my last sermon." And then the next week would roll around, and I'd still show up and get ready for the next sermon. On one front, those two years were hard; on the other, I would get a special favor from the city and get permits for church services in our own City Hall, right beside the hall chambers.

Every three months, we would conduct a special gathering. We would bring the Cross and the Ten Commandments as a reminder of how far the city has fallen from God. We would bring a sound system, speakers, mics, piano, and guitars, and the city provided a podium with the city crest on it, as well as the chairs.

So, every few months in the heart of the beast, the light was shining. Behold, hundreds of people would come to participate in this gathering. We could blow the shofars, play music, sing songs, and dance. The words that were delivered were strong and precise.

From the invited speakers, Calgary was asked to turn back to God or else. I invited several speakers to declare what God put in their hearts. People were crying and interceding for the city. In the corporate prayers, some went to their knees, asking God to forgive the sins of the city. We stood in the gap for the rest of the population.

Even though other churches were invited, they simply weren't interested in coming. I was repeatedly told that they had their own activities. Coming to the city hall was something that they were not interested in doing. One after another, they rejected what I believe to be an invitation from God himself. When I looked from the perspective of time, knowing what I know now, I was certain God was giving them a chance to repent and come and cry for the nation. However, most of the leaders were not interested. Only a handful came from our own little circle.

The people themselves responded and came ready to fight against the darkness in their land. The so-called "shepherds of the city" refused to come. But the remnant came, and we had a historic time. Mainstream media would do a hate campaign against us, pressuring the politicians, asking, "Why are the Christians allowed to come and have a church service inside City Hall?"

They trashed us in the media. The judgment, the shaking, the purification, the separation was coming. It felt like God stood from His throne and said, "It is time to remind the people that they control very little, and their insults directed towards me will not be tolerated forever."

This was the place where we were meant to be. That was exactly where God would be honored. Not in a place where nobody could see it, but right here in the beating heart of the city.

I was beginning to realize that if people started honoring God the way He deserves, this land would be the closest thing that we could call "Paradise." It would be a land flowing with milk and honey. Right here in public, prayers should be offered. Here, the name above every other name should be lifted high. From this place, the rest of the people would be blessed.

When the head is healthy, the body will heal itself. When the heart is right, everything else shall follow. However, at this moment, that was not the case; in fact, it was quite the opposite. The Muslim mayor, with his secular wicked counselors, hated the God of the Bible. He wanted nothing to do with it.

They even removed prayer from the chambers, replacing the Lord's prayer with a prayer for natives. They totally swapped worshiping the living God for worshiping the creation. You can poke God for a season, but sooner or later, He will say, "Enough." And He did!

THE COVID LIE

About two years before the "big lie (COVID)," the Lord told me that we were about to see the greatest separation during my lifetime between sheep and goats and between sheep and wolves. Of course, at that time, I had no idea what was coming. But I shared a sermon about the differences between these creatures. And how sheep will go to His right hand and goats to His left.

Around three or four months before the craziness started, God gave me a vision of a chain-link fence, which somehow, I knew, represented the whole world. Many people were sitting on the fence, enjoying their lives and the view. They had no interest in jumping to either side; but instead remained "on the fence."

Then I saw two powerful hands, representing the hands of God, shaking the fence violently with huge force. People were falling to either side and when the shaking was done, there was no one left on the fence itself. I heard God's voice say, "When I'm done shaking the

fence, everyone will have to make a decision: either Me or the devil."
The vision ended, and low and behold, the year 2020 arrived!

In March 2020, I received a letter from the Parks and Bylaw
Department informing me that I was to stop feeding the poor
because we were in the middle of a global pandemic. So I replied: "If
we are indeed in the middle of a global threat, our services are
needed more than ever!"

In the beginning, we tried everything to accommodate their
suggestions. My brother Dawid walked the lines of those waiting for
food to ensure that people were safe. Food in sealed containers was
handed out by volunteers, and people quickly grabbed them and
moved on. The volunteers stayed behind the tables, and there was
absolutely no scientific way that anybody was being endangered.

It did not matter what we did. Our efforts were never good enough
for the government agencies. The media joined the government in a
unified attack on our soup kitchen, demanding that it should be
closed down. This whole thing did not make any sense. If we were
truly in a crisis, then what did they think was going to happen to
thousands of homeless people and others facing homelessness?

Closing down shelters and soup kitchens and denying people
access to the necessities of life will result in people turning to crime
to obtain them. People will get those essentials because they need to
eat; they just won't do it the legal way.

After a few weeks of monkeying around with the authorities, I
received the final letter. Our permits were revoked, and we were told
that from now on, everything we did would be deemed "illegal." I
wasted no time in appealing this decision to the mayor's office,
Premier Jason Kenney's office, and every member of his cabinet's
office. No one cared to respond to me; no one cared.

We decided that we had to keep on going and do what was right. The soup kitchen had to remain open. It was treacherously cold that winter. Other ministries were already shut down. Where were those thousands of people roaming the streets supposed to go to get the necessities for survival? The group included individuals who were homeless, mentally challenged, addicts, poor families, and people sleeping in bushes and under bridges. I repeatedly told the authorities that we were saving lives. We kept feeding the poor, and the authorities kept threatening us.

One day at the beginning of April 2020, more than ten officers, along with the Health Inspector and Bylaw Services, showed up at Street Church. I noticed them an hour earlier, sitting in their cars, waiting. As we began loading the truck after feeding the people, we were suddenly surrounded from all directions. An aggressive officer forcefully pushed a parishioner, commanding him to maintain a six-foot distance while simultaneously moving towards him and pushing him away with his hand on the parishioner's chest. It was weird.

The Bylaw came with the police, and one could tell they were not there to talk—they were there to punish us. I wore winter camo clothes that day because it was around -25 degrees Celsius. The operation's leader arrived with a $1200 fine, warning us of more if we continued aiding the impoverished. I faced the threat of arrest and millions of dollars in tickets.

So we finished packing and left. Once I got home, I wasted no time reaching out to a journalist friend to see if he would want to cover this story. He was! By doing so, I became *Rebel News*' first client in their "Fight the Fines" initiative.

The day after, I received a call informing me that the police chief had held a press conference discussing the incident. Apparently, I was the first Canadian to receive this type of citation—a COVID-19 ticket. *Rebel News* covered the story, which quickly went viral, with people sending donations to provide me with a lawyer.

The Democracy Fund was created soon after due to numerous instances of unconstitutional tickets and police harassment. More abuse of power ensued. Ironically, in the end, my ticket was withdrawn. The regime was furious. The Crown Prosecutor did not want the evidence to come to the courts since the incident had been recorded on camera and had captured the police officer assaulting a partitioner.

The fight continued. Every time we went out to feed the poor, we were surrounded by numerous people monitoring our every move. The number of resources that the city was willing to waste to prevent a peaceful ministry from feeding the poor was truly shocking.

We started a Call to Action, telling other ministries and Christians to rise up. We organized another "Call to Repentance." Canada's spiritual decay was evident in the absence of clergy. After all, everyone said we were a good country with good morals and always doing what was right. But only around 40 people answered this call.

Here are a few things that I told the people gathered:

Everywhere we look, we see unconstitutional and unreasonable Restrictions. Power-hungry politicians are using this difficult time to advance their own agendas. The Abuse of power is visible all around the country. While politicians are giving themselves a raise, Millions have lost their jobs, and hundreds of thousands are suicidal and depressed! Canada is in distress!

Double standards are willfully and deliberately implemented in our cities! Some people are treated with special privileges, while the rest of us suffer! The average man has no representation! No one fights for him and his family! Christians and places of worship are those bullies' primary targets!

This country feels more and more like Germany under Hitler, where the Jews and normal-thinking Germans were treated as second-class citizens. Arrested and fined and later sent to concentration camps!

Martin Luther King Jr. once said that the hottest place in Hell is reserved for those who remain neutral in times of great moral conflict. Once again, politicians have drugged us in the middle of such a conflict! They have betrayed the very people who elected them.

We have no choice but to stand up before it is too late. The evil in the country can only be defeated when we are on our knees. We have to humble ourselves before the One and Only Living God and ask Him for forgiveness.

As a nation, we have done terrible things. Murder of children, homosexual perversion, greed, selfishness. We have a lot to confess to God. We have to raise our voices against the lawbreakers in Canada. The politicians decided to abuse their powers against the very people who elected them to protect them from corruption.

Today, they have become corrupted. The elected officials, with the help of Police and so-called Peace Officers, are breaking the law by passing legislation that directly targets citizens of Canada. We have seen this before. Stalin did it, Hitler did it, and we can see it clearly today in the Middle East and in communist countries around the world.

Will we, Canadians, stay idly and watch those thugs take our God and state-given rights? Will we do nothing?

Have we forgotten the rights that our forefathers won? Let me remind you of a few of them!

Our Canadian CHARTER OF RIGHTS AND FREEDOMS states:

- Whereas Canada is founded upon principles that recognize the supremacy of God and the rule of law.

- God first, everything else follows! Fundamental freedoms!

Everyone in Canada is free to practice any religion or no religion at all. We are also free to express religious beliefs through prayer or by wearing religious clothing, for example. However, the Charter also ensures that others have the right to express their religious beliefs in public.

- We're free to think our own thoughts, speak our minds, listen to the views of others, and express our opinions in creative ways.

-We're also free to meet with anyone we wish and participate in peaceful demonstrations. This includes the right to protest against a government action or institution.

- The Charter protects everyone against unreasonable laws that could lead to imprisonment or harm their physical safety. Everyone should be treated the same under the law and is entitled to the same benefits provided by laws or government policies.

Now, in this time of crisis, we need more than ever the Almighty's protection and guidance! We need His wisdom and His divine counsel!

Will you stand up and fight for your land? Will you humble yourself before the Living God?

> *If my people, who are called by my name, will humble themselves and pray and seek my face and turn from their wicked ways, then I will hear from heaven, and will forgive their sin and will heal their land.*
>
> 2 CHRONICLES 7:14

In this time of great shaking, let's go to our knees and ask our Amazing God for an outpouring of His Holy Spirit! Now, more than ever, we need His Truth, Power, and Boldness!

Every few months, we would call the church to stand up and be counted. We held meetings, gatherings, rallies, and Jericho Marches. Month after month, we did our best to awaken the Church. Now, looking back, I am confident that God was waiting for the church to rise up—to be the Light, because more and more darkness was covering the land. The Church was removing itself from any public significance instead of staying relevant.

Evil completely took over our nation during this time. Masks, six feet apart, restrictions, and threats from the government paralyzed our society. Public gatherings were no longer allowed; neither were church services. Singing became illegal. Coffee with your extended family was prohibited and could land you in jail. Dinners with your parents were outlawed. It was absolute craziness.

Circumstances like this continued for months. Marijuana stores, liquor stores, and abortion clinics were open throughout the whole time. Big box stores operated at full capacity without a problem. But now, we began to see other churches taking a stand. The tide had turned. According to the government, you could go shopping, and the virus was inept, but coming to attend a worship service made it super dangerous. By now, anyone who had eyes and a brain could see and understand clearly what was going on: double standards all over. Crooked judges were selectively shutting businesses down; arrests and imprisonments were increasing daily.

Someone had to tell the public about what was really happening. So, we joined the Yellow Vest Movement, an organization advocating for Alberta's own Constitution. There were just a handful of us; most of the time, we had 10 to 15 people. But we kept going to the streets and informing people about their rights. We encouraged them week after week to stand up and say "No" to the tyrant.

The Calgary police were always with us whenever we went out, our most "faithful listeners." I have to confess that they were extremely focused and dedicated, never leaving our side, no matter where we went. All of it was pure tactics of intimidation and harassment.

Of course, there were the regular threats of tickets. The full regime was getting comfortable in our beloved Canada. Then came May 2020, when the Muslim mayor, with his evil counselors, decided to outlaw a portion of the Bible. The passage refers to homosexuality.

His own homosexuality made it a personal vendetta. I called upon pastors and clergy to unite at the City Hall to show our strength of unified Christianity. We would show up and tell the evil rulers that we would not submit to this illegal infringement of our rights because it was unacceptable.

Sadly, not even one clergyman showed up. There was no opposition. Apparently, a few individuals decided to have a phone call and discuss their disagreements via Zoom. I chose to deliver a speech that was carefully monitored by seven attentive police officers.

The law was very clear. No one was allowed to try to convert or even counsel someone who was struggling with their sexual identity. It didn't matter if they were seeking counsel or asking for help. Anyone who would talk to them without affirming their confusion was guilty under this new law. And it didn't matter if they were adults or minors. The penalty for counseling was $10,000. But I had chosen to follow the Bible rather than the corrupt, perverted politicians.

CHAPTER TEN

A DETERMINATION TO PRESS ON

CONTINUING WITH my recollection of the events that led to my imprisonment, I can say that we maintained our weekly meetings throughout 2020, both indoors and outdoors. When Passover came, it was the most anointed celebration we had ever witnessed. We held the event right in front of city hall, and dozens showed up. We sang and had the Lord's Supper together; it was a very special moment.

Not even one police officer, by law or security, came to harass us. It was just us and God. We reminded ourselves of what He did on the cross. However, we all knew in our hearts that the judgment was set. The moment had come for this society to face the repercussions of its wicked deeds.

Summer 2020 flew by between organizing the "Call to Repentance" and dealing with the police. Over 90% of the churches in Canada had completely closed or moved their services entirely to Zoom. Because of this, more and more people would show up at our Saturday meetings.

We began a food distribution campaign, bringing in truckloads of cheeses, meats, dry food, chips—you name it. It took hours to divide everything and then distribute it to the struggling families and seniors in impoverished neighborhoods. The parishioners who brought the food also prayed with every family who received it. This program grew and grew over time and the testimonies that were coming in were extraordinary. And the more we gave away, the more that was coming back to us.

After hearing about the closure and struggles of the native reserves, we extended our support by delivering food to them as well. The Tsuut'ina, Blackfoot, and Stoney Nakoda nations received God's blessing through this food delivery program. They opened their homes to us, guided us through their surroundings, and joined us in prayer with the hope that a few would find solace in the Lord. There were tears of happiness and stories of hardship and pain. No matter how hard the enemy was hitting us, God was encouraging us even more giving us those stories of miracles.

Another blessing during the summer of 2020 was the ability to travel back to Poland. We traveled and ministered in a number of cities, and the kids were able to see the real beauty of the old country. It was a deep and emotional experience as Marzena was able to visit places from her childhood.

During our visit, I was invited to speak at a local church, pastored by a dear friend, Ryszard Krzywy, who we hadn't seen in years. He is a true prophet of God, and I was touched that he was willing to share his pulpit with me. The service was packed—standing room only—with more waiting outside. In the middle of his sermon, Ryszard paused and delivered this word:

You have paid a great price, and you did not deny your God. The first prophecy (in 1999) said that you would lose much, and now I tell you, the devil will have to repay it all. Remember that the blessings are for you and your house. For the church and ministry, I will give you from a different source.

But what I am giving you now is a reward for your service. This is not pity. This is a reward. You will not lose what you have in heaven. You are now accomplishing a breakthrough. Even though I do not fully understand what I am explaining to you, you are breaking through and going further.

You are climbing to a higher level, going deeper, gaining new power and a new dimension, being tested, and being a man with integrity. Many times, you were attacked, and many times, you saw alternative paths, but you always took the right course.

This is a time when you will reach higher and deeper. This is a time when I will repay you, pressed down and running over. This is a time when your heart will be given new gifts. New perspective. The spiritual realm will be open to you. Words that you will speak will be words of power and precision. They won't be general. It will be something that is right on target. Demons will tremble before you.

But that does not mean they will not attack you. Start this intense time. Sometimes, you are tired, but I tell you, I will not let you rest. Because there is a lot of wild strength in you. That is what I need. I have called and anointed you. You have come to this place, but you are leading others to the same place.

You are a mentor, like an apostle who subdues the land. You have the kingdom of God in your heart, not just something small for yourself. Son, wherever you look far and wide, you will see what to do.

You won't have to get a special message from the Lord; it is already in your heart. In your heart, there is a spring, and it will never stop running.

After the prophecy was delivered, I teared up as I felt God's presence. It was my turn to share what God had put on my heart. After I spoke for a while, Marzena also shared about her childhood there. It was a profound service.

We also visited Warsaw, Poland's capital. Because of "Jesus' Week," there were festivals of preaching and Christian concerts throughout the city. These activities ended, as they do every year, with a March for Jesus.

What a great time it was! We reconnected with old friends and made new friends. Some so many amazing people were compassionate for Jesus. We visited castles and historical sites and got reacquainted with family members. It was wonderful. Mission accomplished. God was so good. And now, it was time to return to Canada to work and fight for our God-given rights.

Fall and winter back in Canada were spent organizing events and rallies in Edmonton, the capital of Alberta. That was ground zero for the legislature. There, we prayed for the leaders and anointed the ground with oil. Although the police and sheriffs constantly monitored the events, they never interfered. We prayed that God would forgive our land of sins and bring repentance into the hearts of people.

CHRISTMAS IS CANCELED

As Christmas 2020 approached, we held another festival for the poor. However, Canadian government officials went on television and declared that they were "canceling Christmas." No one would be allowed to gather; there would be no family dinners. Officers would monitor driveways to see if there were extra cars. Tickets would be issued. You couldn't even have someone over for coffee if they weren't already living with you.

Amongst all of this craziness, I had only one thought: *Who do they think they are?* Canceling Christmas? Just a few weeks before, they were on television telling children to have a great Halloween. What had changed? These people truly hated Christ.

So I decided to go on television, as well. I told those villains that they could not cancel Christmas—and that I was canceling THEM! I invited people to the biggest Christmas celebration in the land. My friends and entire family came, and we had the biggest dinner that we could fix. I also took pictures and sent them everywhere.

We also prepared a generous Christmas for the poor. For weeks, we prepared and stored food in advance. Some of Alberta's finest steaks (triple A) were marinated before the festivities and then grilled on barbecue pits and grills at the event. Hundreds of gifts were brought. We also assembled the biggest choir possible, and the carols sung were heavenly. (The nation had been previously told that singing was prohibited by law, that we would collapse and die if we sang.)

Thousands of happy people filled the Plaza. The celebration continued for hours, and hundreds of homeless people received food and gifts. They were treated like royalty; after all, they had been created in the image of God.

Of course, we were also surrounded by the unfriendly faces of the Bylaw Services and police. Over 120 officers stood watch, including a special S.W.A.T. team with telescopic cameras, taking pictures and recording us by video. Even the chief of police showed up, with over fifty police cars and twenty officers on bicycles.

They were all there for one purpose: to intimidate, disrupt, and ticket us "bad guys" for the horrible crime of organizing a Christmas celebration for the most vulnerable people in our community. The officers were harassing our parishioners, and I wondered if they were proud of what they were doing.

I chose to intervene and reminded them that this was a religious gathering, and the people there were in our congregants. In fact, the police were breaking the law. They backed off for a little while. I also talked with the chief of police. As I approached him, his face was completely covered. I asked him why he was handing out ticket after ticket, hoping that we would stop. I urged him to stop harassing us and let us take care of the needy in the city.

His eyes grew bigger and bigger, and he didn't know what to say. His face was covered completely, so I couldn't read his expression. Which was ridiculous—the top law official in our city, standing there dressed like a bandit working for Al Capone. If it weren't real, it would have made for good standup comedy.

At the end of the celebration, hundreds, if not thousands, had been fed, and it was truly a great Christmas. My Christmas gift was 15 more tickets for my "crime" of cheering people up on the biggest holiday of the year! As they say, "No good deed goes unpunished."

The following month (January), the Calgary police and bylaws officers knocked on my door with a summons to appear in court for participating in an illegal event of giving food to people. There were

15 offenses in all. Of course, these visits to the house were a regular occurrence, and the tickets were stacking up.

What surprised me about these visits was the high-level ranks of the officers who came to my door. Sometimes, detectives in plain clothes, who made over $200,000 a year, would knock on my door to deliver a $50 ticket. What a waste of taxpayer money for them to bring a bylaw infraction ticket to my home. Many times, you could see the shame in their eyes because their being there was all for intimidation. They would return to their unmarked cars without talking to me.

THE CHINESE HEALTH INSPECTOR

Very early in 2021, I arrived at our church in the Cave of Adullam when I noticed the usual gathering of police vehicles surrounding the perimeter. Today, however, their cars were blocking the entrance to the parking lot in an attempt to intimidate people from coming. The police were also talking to our associate pastor, and as I walked up, a Chinese man got out of a car parked next to the police vehicle.

The man identified himself as the "Health Inspector" and told us that they wanted access to the church to inspect the facility during our worship service. Of course, I replied, "Absolutely not. You will not come to intimidate and harass the people while they worship God. Are you insane?"

With a heavy accent, he repeated numerous times that he wanted to come observe the service to ensure we were following COVID protocols. It was a game they were playing; we are the good guys, and we just want to make certain everyone is safe. I told them to visit the local warehouse store, where the sign said a limit of 475 people was allowed but where hundreds of people were congregating. Then I turned to the inspector, and while pointing to the highway, I said, "Get off of our property. Go. And do not come back!" The man promptly left.

Later in the day, I got a call from the man who had arranged for us to use the building where we held The Cave. He told me that we couldn't come back to his church anymore. "What happened?" I asked (expecting that perhaps the church had caught on fire or had been vandalized after we left for the day).

It turns out that officials were threatening him with a $10,000 fine if he continued to rent the building to us. He said that he couldn't afford a fight with the authorities. This man had previously been with the Special Forces while serving in the military. A part of his testimony was about being bullied while in the Army yet standing tall.

Despite my begging for him to join *our* special forces and fight against these bullies, his mind was made up. He would not risk his reputation for our church. We went back and forth as I explained that it would take time for us to find another place to gather for services.

Ultimately, he agreed to give us three weeks before we had to vacate the building. But that was it—we no longer had a place to gather and worship God. And knowing that I was often on the news, others might be hesitant to rent to us. It turns out that for several months before, my wife had a "feeling" that something like this might happen. And she had been looking for churches that were for sale or rent.

She had found one for sale, but the cost was out of our reach. Our associate pastor called and said, "I had an urge to look for another church today, and this one came up." It was the SAME ONE that Marzena had found.

The owner was from Haiti and was looking for someone to rent the building on Sundays. It wasn't long before we had signed an agreement and were preparing for the move. This church was a free-standing building four times bigger than the last place (which was on the second floor). My first thought was, *Lord, how am I going to fill this building?* But it wasn't long before we were asking, "Where are we going to put all of these people?"

Sure enough, after just a few weeks in our new building, the Health Inspector showed up again. This time, he walked around with a camera and took pictures of all the women and children there. Naturally, this infuriated the men who followed him to his car and gave him a hard time. It's one thing to intimidate a man, but when women and children are involved, that's another story.

AN EASTER SERVICE THAT FOREVER CHANGED MY LIFE

For about a month, we had been preparing ourselves for the Passover and Easter festival of 2021. We wanted to make that celebration special. Some had fasted for weeks, and many had dedicated themselves to prayer because we believed that it was going to be a powerful Easter. I came to the church as always, two hours early before the service began, and started setting up the lights, Cross, and cameras. There were a few people gathered, and the choir practiced while people were praying in the Auditorium.

Someone called out to me, causing me to turn and witness something beyond belief. I stopped and stared for a couple of seconds. It took me a little while to process what was happening. Right in the auditorium by the stairs was a masked woman accompanied by uniformed officers, along with a few other plain-clothed officers. I paused briefly. Despite my repeated warnings, they were trespassing after I had explicitly told them not to enter. I went to where my phone was charging, grabbed it, and began recording.

Our experience with the authorities over the years had not been very positive. Through trial after trial, we learned that the police, bylaws, and government bureaucrats had absolutely no problem lying to the judges or fabricating reports and incidents that never actually happened. In other words, they had no problem lying if it helped them achieve their goals or cover their own skin.

Having learned from experiences, I understood the importance of recording every interaction with them. As I moved toward them, the only thing that I was able to say was, "GET OUT!" However, they did not move. I kept walking towards the intruders and firmly said again: "Please get out. Get out of this property. Immediately get out."

The woman did not move. However, I noticed the confusion in her eyes. "Get out of this property immediately!" I said, raising my voice. There were six of them, all masked up. The woman wanted to say something, but I just kept telling her, "Out. I do not want to hear anything. Out of this property immediately."

She took a step back to the stairs and kept trying to say something. "I do not want to hear a word. OUT! OUT! Out of this property immediately! Until you come back with a warrant." The men accompanying her were on the steps, and some were at the bottom by the entry door. "Out!" I repeated it even louder. She constantly kept trying to engage in conversation with me, but I would have none of it. The officers remained quiet.

The words "Out! Get out!" kept coming from my mouth. "Out of this property! Immediately out! Immediately go out and don't come back!" I couldn't hear what she was saying, but she was speaking. I had no interest whatsoever in engaging in a debate or discussion with those individuals.

She said something, but I interjected. "Don't. I don't want to talk to you. Not a word. Out of this property. Out of this property. Immediately out!" Step by step, they retreated. Yet again, she tried to interrupt me and say something. I sharply cut her off, "I don't care what you have to say! Out! Out! Out of this property, you Nazis!"

By now, she was halfway down the stairs, and the officers were slowly inching towards the door with every word: "Out! Out! The Gestapo is not allowed here! Immediately! The Gestapo is not allowed! Out!" They needed to go. Evil had entered the sanctuary, and I had to cleanse it out.

The woman took another step back, still trying to engage me in a conversation. "Do you understand English?! Get out of this property!" The irony lies in the fact that I am an immigrant who speaks broken English. And yet, with my accent, I was asking these Canadians if they could understand English!

"Go! Go! Go and don't come back without a warrant. Out Nazi! Out! Out! Do you understand? Nazis are not welcome here. Out! And don't come back without a warrant. Do not come back without a warrant. Do you understand that?"

I continued: "You're not welcome here. Nazis are not welcome here. The Gestapo is not welcome here. Do not come back, you Nazi psychopaths. Unbelievable. Sick, evil people. Intimidating people in a church during Passover. You Gestapo, Nazi, communist fascists. Don't you dare come back here!"

The police, peace officers, and the woman finally left the church and drove away slowly. It took me repeatedly telling them to leave over 30 times! As they were walking away, I noticed that the woman was wearing jackboots just like the Nazis of old, which left me shocked and angry.

I turned to address the camera and gave a few of my thoughts. "Can you imagine those psychopaths? Passover is the holiest Christian festival in the year, and they came to intimidate Christians. During the holiest festival—how unbelievable! What is wrong with those sick psychopaths?"

Although the whole interaction lasted only about five minutes, it left me feeling exhausted. It felt as if I had just battled against a powerful army attempting to conquer our territory. I went back into the church, where the musicians, singers, and people were praying. Who did they consider themselves to be?

Unbelievable! I uploaded the video of the entire exchange on my Facebook page with little thought. I had to prepare myself to deliver the Passover and Easter sermon. Interestingly, for that day, I had prepared a sermon about Pharoah and Moses' demand to "Let my people go!"

The service proceeded without further interruptions. We prayed for people and had a great time that day. I turned off my phone during the service, and when I switched it back on, I couldn't believe what I saw. The short video capturing my interaction with the authorities had gone viral, reaching millions globally. The story circulated repeatedly, and by Monday, the video became the most-watched worldwide during that weekend. My phone never stopped ringing or receiving text messages. The biggest news outlets around the world were talking about this story.

Initially, I was completely clueless about the situation. Why was this garnering so much attention? I had done what any pastor would do. And this was certainly not my first run-in with the corrupt authorities or the first video I had posted of this nature.

It turned out that those few words became a symbol of resistance for the people. I started receiving invitations for interviews worldwide. Every day for over a month, I would do an average of 10-15 interviews. It was crazy!

By that point, it had been nearly a year of people being shut down, locked down, forced to comply, scared, threatened, and intimidated. Fear covered the world like a blanket, and people did not know what to do. Lost in despair and facing wickedness, they were at a loss until a small video started circulating. The video was a beacon of hope.

People finally saw how to deal with the jackboot of tyranny. And the answer was so simple: just tell them to "get out" and "don't come back." This is how you stand up against tyranny with a firm voice and an unyielding stance, not giving them an inch—not even a fraction of an inch.

Somehow, a wave of hope entered people's hearts. They thought, *"If this Polish immigrant can do that, so can we. If he stood up, so can we."* Like a spiritual awakening, many were shaken from the enchantment of that blanket of fear.

This definitely became one of the most intense times in my life. I was on hundreds of shows from around the world. In the blink of an eye, I went from unknown to internet famous. The video gained one billion views across all social media platforms.

I recalled a moment many years before when God spoke to me and said, "Do not despise small beginnings because they are actually huge." I always considered this a contradictory statement until later in my walk with Him. Building something magnificent requires a lot of work, including digging a big foundation, adding iron and rebar, and pouring tons of concrete.

Day after day, I gave interviews, doing my best to encourage people to stand up. I shared my story, hoping that this would empower others to resist the evil we had been witnessing for the past 12 months.

The response was phenomenal. People were contacting me from all over the world. They sent letters and Thank You cards. I had never seen such an awakening in my entire life. I was contacted by individuals of various religious affiliations, including Jews, Muslims, Catholics, Protestants, and even atheists.

The message was loud and clear. "Thank you for speaking out loud about what we were all thinking. Thank you for your courage and boldness. It has given us hope. You are an inspiration. You showed us how to resist this tyranny."

At times, I thought it must be a dream and that at any moment, I would wake up to find out that this wasn't real. It was incredible to be able to impact so many lives in such a short period. There were countless conversations, prayers, and statements. People were coming to the Lord at every turn.

So many contacted me, saying that even though they are atheists, they were inspired to go back to church because of what I did. Others would say, "If you serve God like this, I want to serve a God like this as well." Doctors, lawyers, soldiers, and workers, by the thousands, sent words of gratitude and prayers. Some people claimed they had abandoned their faith, but because of my stance, faith returned to their lives.

The interim period provided a brief respite, but my intuition told me that the authorities would not allow this to go unaddressed. As expected, they quickly returned with a vengeance. The lady wearing her Nazi jackboots, along with the assistance of a S.W.A.T. team, showed up at the church door. They were all masked up, as well.

She handed me a piece of paper, and as I read it, she talked incessantly, interrupting me repeatedly. She wouldn't even let me finish reading the document, which was a court order signed by Judge David Gates. I told her that I would give the document to my lawyers and let them figure things out. I turned around and went back into the church, leaving them behind. They would not be allowed to enter.

Later, my attorney informed me that the order was to allow anyone to enter the church... or else. It gave them the power to bring anyone they wanted into the church. That's the reason for the arrival of the Inspector, accompanied by the anti-terrorist police unit. I had been preaching for about a half hour when they showed up again.

Peter, the Associate Pastor, stopped them at the door. "You're not allowed to come in and interrupt a church service," he told them. They departed but returned within minutes. Peter stood his ground. As the inspector tried to come in with the assistance of the S.W.A.T. team, he stood between them and would not allow them to enter. Eventually, they left, but not for long.

THE PERSECUTION CONTINUES

In Alberta, another church took a stand. It was a bigger church called Grace Life in Edmonton. The pastor of that church said "No" to closing his building and continued operating as usual. First, just a few officers showed up with a health inspector at his church. Then, week by week, the harassment intensified. Eventually, he was arrested, and the church was seized by the government. Over a hundred police officers showed up against peaceful Christians.

They locked the doors and put not one but three fences around the property to keep people away. When the pastor was still in prison, I went to visit his church to show solidarity with the family and congregation. There were about 600 people gathered. The police were parked outside, monitoring and taking pictures. We organized a protest for him at the courthouse in Edmonton. We had multiple speakers, we sang hymns, and we sang the national anthem.

The police were there but did not bother us at all. A few days later, the pastor was released from prison. During that time, a few pastors stood up publicly against tyranny: Pastor Hildebrandt from Ontario, Pastor Tobias from Manitoba, Pastor Art Lucier from British Columbia, and Laura Lynn Tyler Thompson. The Church in the Vine from Edmonton, as well as one or two more churches from Calgary, also took a stand.

It's likely that some people opposed the evil but chose to stay silent and hidden. As a whole, not many were willing to face the beast and say no. Those who were vocal were hammered without mercy. The regime was cracking down. Churches were forcefully shut down while Walmart, Ikea, and Costco could have hundreds of people without a problem.

Laura Lynn contacted me and invited me to help organize a church service on the steps of the Vancouver Supreme Court in British Columbia. What a fantastic idea, I thought, and so I agreed. We flew there and set everything up on the steps. People came with banners and signs and we all stood our ground. Right in front of the watchful eyes of the police and sheriffs, the word of God was preached, and testimonies were shared. We prayed and anointed the ground.

OUR FAMOUS ARREST ON THE HIGHWAY

In May 2021, Alberta Health Services (AHS) recruited Senior Judge John Rooke, aka "the crook," to help them gain total power over the entire population, resulting in the erosion of individual liberties. Judge Rooke and others privately met with AHS, off camera, without creating records or notifying citizens, and issued ex parté orders. Judge Rooke's order went after a few well-known individuals like Chris Scott, a cafe owner who had refused to shut down his restaurant. The order included a clause called "John and Jane Doe," which meant that every single one of the 4.5 million Albertans had to comply. Essentially, anyone who refused could be arrested and imprisoned.

Armed with this totalitarian edict, straight from a Nazi Germany playbook, a S.W.A.T. team, along with regular uniformed police officers, visited our church. In previous weeks, hundreds of people had been displaying signs of support outside the church. On this day, the church was packed, and so the media did what they were best at: they lied as much as they could.

Now, with billions of dollars given to them by the liberal government, the media had free range and zero accountability. No lie was too big for them. Like a pack of hyenas, they jumped to discredit the validity of our resistance. All major news outlets, including CBC, CTV, Global News, National Post, Herald, and Sun, shamelessly promoted the government's lie without question.

As I was getting ready for church, I observed a significant police presence gathering outside through the window. During the service, people worshipped and prayed. Just as I began to deliver my sermon, someone yelled from the back, "Gestapo is here!" When the doors flung open, I feared being arrested while speaking. When I glanced at the men in the front rows, I observed something remarkable. Emptying their pockets, the men gave their wives their wallets, keys, and phones. These courageous individuals were getting ready to be arrested alongside their pastor. *That is what courage looks like,* I thought to myself.

Interestingly, they never arrested me there, and it wasn't until later on that I discovered what had happened. When the Anti-Terrorist Police Unit opened the church door and saw hundreds of people with standing room only, they realized it would be a disaster for them. So, instead of arresting me, they dropped something on the ground and left. I carried on with my sermon, oblivious to the events unfolding at the church entrance.

It was a relief when someone yelled from the back, "The Gestapo just left!" My thoughts were, *I guess I won't be dragged from the pulpit today* and the service finished without any further incident. At the end of the service, after the usual visiting and clearing of the sanctuary, we prepared to head home. My family had already gone, so only my brother, our friend Dave, and I were left to close up.

While driving home, I suddenly saw police lights flashing behind us. They stopped us in the middle of the highway. It was the same S.W.A.T. team who had come to the church earlier; multiple vehicles of officers accompanied them. One officer went to the driver's side and another to my side. Dave was behind the wheel while my brother Dawid sat in the back. Dave opened the window, and the officer looked straight at me and said, "You are under arrest." Then the officer turned to Dawid and said the same to him: "You are also under arrest. Step out of the vehicle."

We were arrested for the injunction, known as the "Rooke Order," despite not being mentioned in it. As I stepped out onto the busy highway, I was already recording on my phone, so I handed my phone to Dave to continue. As cars raced past, the rain made it seem like Heaven was weeping for the state of our broken justice system.

Leading up to this day, I had felt that, eventually, I was going to be arrested again. God had shown me in a dream that it was going to happen; I just did not know *how* it would happen. I reassured myself that when the time came, they would have to do it "Nazi-style" and drag me away.

As I went to my knees, I saw Dawid coming out of the car. I put my hands behind my head and waited for the officers to take me in. With their angry eyes, masks, and dark uniforms, they resembled gangsters. They handcuffed my hands behind my back and started to drag me down the highway to their police cars. My brother was experiencing a similar scene. He was handcuffed, and three officers carried him as well. They carried him face down, with an officer gripping his left arm and another gripping his right arm while a third officer held both of his legs.

While being pulled by two officers with my hands restrained behind my back, all I could think about was my suit getting ruined as they dragged me across the muddy road. My shoes were completely destroyed, as well, although I was doing my best to save them. I was stopped by the officers near one of the cruisers, forcibly pinned against the side of the police car, searched, and subjected to physical aggression. The fact that they had to carry me made them furious and so they decided to put me in a van instead of the cruiser.

It turned out to be the shorter version of the van, so there was not much room inside. When they forced me onto the van floor, my head was down, but my legs didn't fit inside and were sticking out. They pushed and pushed very hard, but the space in the van was just too small to lay me in it. Every time they pushed, my head hit the wall. After a few attempts, one officer said to the other. "If he kicks you, we will charge him with assault!"

Picture this scenario: I was lying on the ground, handcuffed, with all my body weight on my wrists and my legs hanging out of the vehicle. Two officers are using all their strength to push my legs in. This would be incredibly amusing if it weren't so excruciatingly painful. I realized that those people would stop at nothing. They were going to lie, just like they did before, to hurt me more.

I made every effort to squeeze my legs into this cramped area and assist them. Eventually, they managed to shut the doors. A few minutes later, the van started to move. I do not know how long the journey lasted, but we stopped. I attempted to assess our location by contorting my body on the ground with my head in one corner and feet in the opposite corner of the ceiling. At the same time, my handcuffed wrists were twisted and pressing against me. Seeing only the tops of the buildings confirmed we were downtown from my vantage point on the floor.

The officers were laughing and apparently having a great time together. A few minutes later, an officer opened the door and read me my rights. I was being charged with multiple offenses, including some criminal. He finished reading, shut the door, and smiled at my unconventional position before leaving. A few other officers peeked through the window to see how I was being transported, and then the van started to move again.

It took a long time to reach the destination. It was far, but also I was in extreme pain, so every minute felt like an hour. The handcuffs were so tight the circulation in my hands was being cut off, and I felt a tingling in my fingers. My entire weight was resting on my wrists, and any movement caused pain.

The small van and my awkward position left me stuck and unable to adjust in order to help ease the pain. The journey lasted over an hour. When we stopped, an officer opened the door, and I recognized the place as the Spyhill Detention Centre. Dawid and I were escorted to the Admission desk. Although I was still handcuffed, at least now I was sitting and not laying down on my wrists.

We were processed and each taken to the search place. While removing my handcuffs, an officer asked me to remove my jacket, tie, shoes, and socks. Then, I was thoroughly searched. My picture was taken, and I was asked to face the wall and not move. One officer was holding my arm on the wall while another searched me. When one side was done, they moved to the other. Once again, an officer held onto my arm while another conducted a search.

When they finished, I was escorted to a solitary cell. The door was opened, and I was told to walk in. The door closed to the sound of a loud metal clang. The cell was built with concrete and concrete blocks. The toilet and sink were made from one solid metal piece. In the middle of the ceiling was a camera recording my every move.

The first few hours were not so bad. The bright lights were the only issue; otherwise, it would have been fine. I walked a little, laid down, sat, and laid down some more. The problem was that you could not sit on cold concrete for very long. Resting didn't provide any relief either. Eventually, your entire body aches. You had to keep switching positions back and forth. Spend a few minutes on your back, then switch to your stomach, and then back to your side.

An officer would come in and bang on the doors every half hour, so I asked for a Bible when one passed by. The request was denied. I was informed that there is not a single bible at the police station. *No wonder we are in this crazy mess. What a Godless society,* I thought.

The doors were opened, and I was taken to the medic, who checked my pulse and asked if there were any problems.

I said, "Yes. Look at my wrists." She did and noticed a deep scar. My wrists were all swollen and cut.

She shrugged her shoulders and said, "Anything else?"

"No" I replied and was then escorted out. While I was there, I had a couple of chances to participate in media interviews by using my phone calls wisely. I talked to *Rebel News*, and I did one with *InfoWars*. I spoke with my wife and then with the lawyer, but at that moment, there was nothing they could do. It was Saturday, and I would have to endure this until Monday.

That was hard. The lights were so bright they blinded my eyes. When you are locked inside a small place without any reference of time, it confuses you. You do not know if it is an hour, ten minutes, or five hours that have passed. There's literally nothing to do to pass the time. I would walk around and then sit again. I tried to fall asleep, but it was impossible.

As I was walking around in my cell, I noticed a loose piece of concrete. It was very small, but I wondered if it was big enough to write on. The floor and the bench were painted gray, and a portion of the wall was painted the same way. The upper part, walls, and ceiling were painted a lighter color. I wondered if the tiny concrete fragment could really leave a mark on the gray wall.

So I decided to give it a shot. Nothing—it was like invisible ink. *How frustrating,* I thought. I was so enthusiastic about doing my own prison graffiti. Then I thought, *wait a minute. When you add a little bit of water, perhaps it will soften the concrete piece, and the cement might become more visible on the surface of the wall.* I put my theory into practice by placing a bit of water on the bench and soaking the piece of concrete in the water to soften it.

A few minutes later, I tried to write again. Voila! The first letter, "J," appeared on the wall. *Years in construction are paying off,* I thought to myself. Laying on the bench, I painted my very own first-ever prison masterpiece. It was a very long process. The rock was small, and the letters were relatively big. I wanted them big for the guards to see them when they came by. Slowly, the work was moving forward. The second letter was done, so I took a break.

My fingers were hurting from holding such a small and awkward writing utensil. I do not know, of course, how long it took me to finish, but I can tell you it felt like a very long time. When I was done, I stood up and walked further away to look at my work of art. My heart was filled with joy after a great achievement, looking at something that I wish everyone on earth could have seen and would understand: JESUS ♥ U.

Perhaps I was being watched, as the doors suddenly opened, and two police officers stared at me and my art in astonishment. Which shocked them more: 1) me writing on their wall or 2) what I had written? The only thing the bewildered officer managed to say was, "You're not allowed to do that!"

I wondered *Why?* And told him that I was bored. And if they would get me a Bible, I wouldn't spend my time writing on the walls!

My dear friends, stand firm
and don't be shaken...

You know that everything you
do for him is worthwhile.
1 Corinthians 15:58

CHAPTER ELEVEN

THE WALLS WERE CLOSING IN

NEEDLESS TO SAY, the Bible never arrived, and by the second day, I had a terrible headache due to a lack of coffee. My body was in full force, demanding its caffeine dose since I drank coffee every morning. My head was exploding, and nothing was helping. Walking around made the headache even more hammering, so I sat down.

After what felt like an eternity later, sometime in the evening, an officer opened the door. Apparently, I was not supposed to be there, and they were supposed to have taken me to the Remand Centre. But for whatever reason, that had not happened. The officer asked if there was anything I would like, so again, I asked for a Bible. He went to look for one. After his return, he mentioned that there was no presence of a Bible anywhere in the building. He questioned whether there was something else I would like.

I said, "Coffee—if you are sincerely asking. I have a terrible headache because I haven't had coffee for a few days now. If you are really asking, I would like some coffee."

He said, "I will see what I can do for you," and left.

Around 20 minutes later, he returned with a coffee and said, "I couldn't get you any. But you can have mine." I thanked him very much and sat down on the bench. The coffee was not particularly anything special; however, at this moment, it tasted like heaven. While I was drinking, taking another sip of this delicious drink, another officer came in. He was shocked that we were still at the police station. He said we should have been transferred to the prison already. He was shocked and assured me that he would investigate this.

Sometime later, the officer brought me a mattress so at least I could sit without feeling constant pain. This was a good man and true to his word. An hour later, in the middle of the night, the officer managed to transfer Dawid and me to the Remand Centre. He was unaware, and understandably so, that this transfer would cause even more significant issues for us.

When we arrived at Remand, escorted by the police, we were greeted by a number of guards. The first thing they commanded was: "Put your masks on."

"We are exempt," I said.

They turned to Dawid and said, "Put your mask on!"

Dawid replied the same thing, "I am exempt."

For a few seconds, there was a visible manifestation of frustration. They did not know what to do. "But you must put your masks on," they proclaimed.

"But we are exempt," I replied again.

More confusion ensued amongst the ranks of the guards. "But everyone here is wearing one!" one of them said.

"Well, they can wear one if they want—but we will not." They went to talk to someone who returned and grilled us some more. For a moment, I thought that they would force the stupid, useless masks on us. Instead, they brought us inside and put each of us in a cell equipped with a sink, toilet, and a bench made of wood or plastic. At least it was not cold sitting on the wooden bench.

To kill time, I thought about some games from my childhood—a soccer game that we used to play nonstop and Tic-Tac-Toe. *But how do you play that alone?* I remembered a game that we played with metal pieces. The idea was to throw a coin towards the edge of a wall, and the one that was the closest won.

I decided to make some games. The only thing that I received from my captors was a square piece of paper. Since there was no toilet paper in the cells, I improvised by using the paper to create balls for a game. Believe it or not, it takes a while to make eight equally round balls. I had to be very careful because I only had one piece of paper and if I did not do it the right way ... well it would be over.! No games for me, just staring at an empty wall that I was not willing to do.

Finally, the moment of truth came, and I had fashioned eight round balls from a portion of the paper. With the remaining paper, I made the goalposts and started my game. "Who will win?" I smiled to myself, "Me? Or me?" In the end, I guess I had the victory in my pocket.

With excitement, I used my index finger to push the ball towards the goal, but it fell apart before it could get there. *What a bummer,* I thought. I really wanted to play. One of the worst things for a person like me is doing nothing, just sitting and wasting time. The paper ball fell apart, so I pulled out another one, but with the same results.

I thought to myself, *if I make them wet, will that bind the material together and make it solid?* I tried with one paper ball, and it bonded nicely. The water caused the paper to stick together, so I pushed the ball again with my finger. The water made it better, but we were not there just yet because, after a few pushes, the ball fell apart again.

Being persistent, I tried again and put some more water on a paper ball. But instead of playing right away, I chose to wait until it dried out. That bonding made the paper a more solid material, making it more durable. And it was flexible and bouncy. Goodness! I had just created my first professional jail soccer ball. Life was good. I shall have my game.

The complete process took hours. Wetting the paper and waiting for it to dry solid must have taken around six hours. But after all, I had all the time in the world. Once the balls were dry, I kicked them and played with my imaginary opponent, having a great time. I used different rules, made different obstacles, and made it more interesting. It was fun!

I brought my homemade soccer game with me when we were transferred to Remand. The cells there were filthy; it looked like someone had peed on the floor. The "bathroom" was disgusting. The walls had not been washed in forever. Stuff was on the ceiling that I would be afraid to touch. The location where we were locked up was directly across from the guards' desk. What separated us was glass all the way across the room we were in. We could see the guards, and they could see us.

The guards wore ineffective, low-cost masks that offered no protection. Additionally, they had to wear a gown over their uniforms whenever they needed to communicate with non-guards. Furthermore, they would wear plastic nylon gloves. But the moment they were done, they would take all that garb off and throw it away, and then the process would be repeated.

While spending countless hours there, we witnessed prisoners touching items and staff without gloves. The phones were being used right in front of us without any disinfectant. The same thing was happening when the new inmates were brought into the room. The new inmates would use the same phone, and then another batch would come.

The sight of the guards in their masks, gloves, and gowns playing this insane game at the circus from a mental asylum left me shaking my head. This was never about keeping people healthy or safe; this is about tyranny and control. So much money was being wasted. The Alberta Health Services argued that these extreme measures were necessary for pandemic containment. And yet the contamination (if we were really in a pandemic) was spreading freely all around. If we were ever in an actual crisis due to a biological deadly weapon or a serious, deadly virus, then we would be done for. We would not survive this as a society.

So, they kept playing their part in this sick, twisted movie, and we were stuck sitting in a room with big windows and no privacy. "Let's play," I told Dawid. He looked puzzled.

"Let's play soccer. And see who is better," I urged.

His eyes grew big with excitement. I pulled those little soccer balls out of my pocket. He laughed when he saw them and said, "Okay."

We set up the goals, one on his end of the bench and another on my end. I don't know how long we played, but we had so much fun. Occasionally, the guards would glance over at us, clearly displeased by our enjoyment. When we got bored with the soccer game, I made little crosses for the Tic-Tac-Toe game. In this holding cell, there was toilet paper, so I had more than enough material for the game. We used the balls and the crosses as the pieces and the goalposts as the squares.

Sometime during our stay, a man came to our cell—a guard. He stared at us from behind his glasses. His voice quivered and cracked as he conveyed that what had occurred to us was not fair. "This is wrong," he kept repeating. Before he left, he promised he would try to help us out and that, at the very least, he would try to get us a mattress. However, his goal was to get us into a unit with a bed.

I watched this man arguing on the phone for hours. It was clear that he was making every effort to convince someone higher in authority to grant us a bed, as we had been without rest or sleep for two days and two nights. He returned, stating that they won't let him provide us with a bed for some unknown reason. He said that he was Catholic, and he couldn't believe what was happening right now.

Then he left and tried again. I watched him very closely as he talked on the phone. He looked like someone who was fighting with his superiors. However, it was to no avail. The higher-ups were very determined not to give us rest. We were to suffer. Period.

In the end, with a sorrowful expression, he informed us that they had declined by saying "No." But he would keep trying, and maybe something would happen. He also mentioned, "You will have to go through a check and change of clothes, and we will at least be ready if something changes." He apologized again for everything and went back to his phone to try again.

Another guard arrived and escorted us to a location where he instructed Dawid and me to undress and wait. The guard took Dawid's clothes and checked for any contraband. After checking Dawid, I was next. After being stripped naked, I was led to a shower. They gave me a towel and a blue jump suit with pink slippers. I handed my regular clothes to another man at the counter. He took them and said Thank you, Pastor."

I was surprised. "You know who I am?" I asked.

"Yes," he said. "God bless you."

"Thank you," I replied, thinking to myself that I guess not all of them were rotten to the core. Once we finished showering and put on our jumpsuits, we were taken to the same dirty cell. I looked at Dawid and started to laugh. With his blue suit and vibrant pink slippers, he resembled a clown ready to amuse his visitors. It was about 4:00 a.m. when our Catholic friend, the night shift supervisor, brought us two mattresses and two small blankets.

There were no pillows. However, we were very grateful for his kindness. Despite the short blankets and lack of pillows, at least we weren't sitting on a hard bench or on concrete in the cold cell. We laid the mattresses on the grimy floor and tried our hardest to drift off, even if only for a few minutes. At 6:00 a.m., the sheriffs came to escort us to the court. First, they started with another search. Surprisingly, they discovered contraband: my soccer balls and goalposts!

The officer removed them, inspected them, and disposed of them in the trash. I angrily said to him, "Why have you done this? This was my property. You had no right to throw that into the garbage. You are a thief, a gangster in uniform. Why did you do that?"

I was upset because it had taken me hours to make those, and without any cause, he just threw them away because he felt like it. He did not like my response and shoved me against the wall with big force and yelled, "Are we going to have a problem with you?!"

I replied, "I have a problem with you! Because you are just a thief pretending to be an officer. A gangster in uniform. Why did you throw my stuff away? Why?"

He roughed me up a little and put handcuffs on my wrists and chains on my legs. Off I went in the penguin march to the Sheriff's van. We traveled to downtown Calgary to the courthouse. Upon our arrival, we were guided down a large corridor to the holding cells adjacent to the court chambers. Everyone was locked in a separate cell. The chains were designed in such a way that when you walked, you could only do tiny little steps. It reminded me of penguins making little steps.

If I attempted a larger step, I would certainly fall and injure myself severely. I spent some time sitting, then decided to start walking around the cell. The chains were making a loud noise, like in the movies when you have the prisoners walking and this specific sound of iron hitting iron. It was loud.

It was quite comical when we were finally allowed to see the judge, and Dawid complained about the annoying noise of someone next door walking in circles with their chains. He said, "I just wanted to punch that person in the nose!"

I looked at him and laughed. "That was me!" I said.

"What?" he exclaimed. "It was *you* walking around, making that noise?"

"Yup," I said. "I could not just sit still and do nothing, so I walked around."

We finally reached our destination—a tiny room with a big glass separator. On the other side was our criminal lawyer. We had a conversation and deliberated on the bail hearing and potential agreements. When we saw the judge, the moment he opened his mouth, I knew that we were not there for justice; we were in big trouble!

This man was already told what to do. He started his talk with this statement, "We are in the middle of a global pandemic. A health crisis. ..." Blah. Blah. Blah. He sounded like a CBC/CNN reporter repeating the government-approved script. His talk had nothing to do with the merits of the case or why we had been arrested.

Everything was about COVID-19. Of course, the judge himself was not even present in the room; we were seeing him via WebEx. He was Heaven knows where—maybe in his bathroom, as far as I knew. We were chained like bloody criminals at the mercy of a judge who turned out to be a former wannabe politician for the liberal party, appointed by the same political party responsible for our suffering. We were doomed. We never stood a chance.

Later on, I found some fascinating information about this individual. He was a judge from Fort MacLeod. Why did we have a judge from another part of the province? I did not know; I only knew that he was to be the judge, the jury, and the executioner. Corrupt politicians preferred to have someone from outside who was willing to carry out their evil deeds. He was not living in the city; no one knew him. What a perfect occasion for the party.

I said to Dawid, "We do not stand a chance with this man. He is a political activist. He talks like them. He believes like them. He is them."

Finally and miraculously, we were released on bail and they packed us up to take us to Remand and wait there for the paperwork. Even though we were released, they still kept us in the cell for an additional seven hours. During that time, we observed more people being brought to the facility. The same thing was happening repeatedly.

The guards pretended to observe the COVID protocols. The inmates did not care but were bullied to comply. The contamination—if there was any—was happening freely between the inmates after every time the gown, gloves, and masks were removed and thrown away. I suppose this charade was occurring everywhere. Taxpayer money was being thrown away, draining billions of dollars by the hour.

Out of nowhere, there was a commotion among the guards. They were looking at the local newspaper and pointing at us. "I guess we made it to the news," I said to Dawid.

Walking around, an officer lifted his hands high while laughing and exclaiming, "Praise the Lord. Praise the Lord."

It was later in our jail stint when we finally found out what was happening in the media. The mainstream propaganda was having a Heyday! They were absolutely thrilled about our arrest. According to them, we had finally gotten what we deserved. There were press conferences about this dramatic middle-of-the-highway arrest, and the politicians and the chief of police were very proud of themselves.

They shared how we had been arrested on multiple charges: Inciting people to participate in an illegal church gathering, participating in an illegal gathering, and officiating an illegal gathering (all because we conducted church). *What had we done to deserve such hate?* We feed thousands of people every month. Free from the use of taxpayer dollars. We gave people hope during one of the most difficult times in Canada's history, and now the government wanted to crush us. Wow—simply wow!

While still in lockup, the guards mocked and laughed at us. Dawid walked over to the window and told them, "One day, you will not be laughing. One day, you will pay for what you have done and pay for this mockery." He was distraught.

I was sad. How had Canada, which was built on the word of God, come to hate him so much? What had He done to them to deserve such a mockery? The officers were laughing and having fun. But I was sitting on a bench, feeling God's sadness. He had sent His Son for them. He gave them life. He gave them such a beautiful land to enjoy. And like spoiled brats, they were taking everything for granted.

They acted as if they were entitled to everything, with no justification. Well, I knew that one day, someone would hold them accountable for everything. I felt sad because the time of reckoning was drawing near. People enjoy eating, drinking, and playing without worrying about the price tag. Here at the table of their lawlessness was the waiter standing with the bill. The bill was so huge that they would never have the means to pay for it.

As I stood up to walk a little, Dawid drew in closer and said, "Artur, what are you going to do?"

I took a step back and said to him, "I do not know. Maybe I have to take a step back and see what God will do." Right after I spoke those words, I heard God's voice in my heart. "That is exactly what I want you to do. Take a step back and let me deal with your enemies." I knew at that moment that I was to go to the United States and warn them about what was happening in Canada. I was to share my story and tell them that if they did not push hard now, they would also be living behind the Iron Curtain, just as we were.

There was a slight problem. I had been invited to come to the States many times, especially in the previous month. However, Marzena firmly opposed that idea. "You are needed here," she would say. "Now we are under attack here, and you have to stay with your people to fend off the wolves." I agreed, but now I had received a drastically different command. I was to go. So, I did what I always do in situations like this one. I prayed, "God, if this is your will, you will make this happen. Talk to Marzena and talk to the Americans. Lord, open the door, and I am willing."

As we awaited the release, I created a new collection of soccer balls, and we played a small game to occupy ourselves. The extensive time it took to produce the paper soccer balls was both a positive and negative aspect. But there was nothing else to do, so I might as well.

OUR RELEASE FINALLY COMES

Finally, they were willing to let us go. The delay was, according to them, because the paper order said "Dawid," not "David." Of course, the proper spelling of my brother's name was Dawid with a "W." Still, they did not believe that, so they went back and forth with the lawyers and the judge verifying what the proper spelling was. It took them seven hours, and finally, they let us go.

We were tired. Some reporters were waiting outside to do an interview with us. Once we finished, our friend from the church drove us to the house. We were trailed by a helicopter and an unmarked police pickup truck until we reached the house. It can be difficult for me to grasp their thought process. Why the helicopter? Why the unmarked police truck with a uniformed officer inside?

What were they thinking we were going to do? Start another church gathering in the middle of the street on our way home? We had not eaten for three days. The nights spent on hard benches and concrete left us completely drained. I wanted to go home, eat something good, and go to bed with a soft pillow. So that's exactly what I did!

The next day, I shared with Marzena what the Lord had told me about taking a step back and about the States. I was expecting her to oppose this idea sharply, just like before. After all, she told me many times that I would not be traveling for a while. I was to stay with her and the church here in Calgary.

Much to my surprise, she confidently stated that God had told her the same thing—that I was to go to the States. She looked at me and said again, "Go."

So, I began making preparations. My intention was to travel with my son Nathaniel for a duration of two, maybe three, weeks. If there was interest in this story, I might stay a few days more. Now, back then, there was no flying whatsoever. No one was allowed to leave the country unless it was an essential service. I stated that spreading the word of God is of the utmost importance. I must confess, I was somewhat concerned. How was I going to cross the border and board the plane with such draconian government restrictions? But, as always, Marzena had total peace about it. "If God is sending you there, you are going to be there. Do not even think about it. Do not worry," she said.

A FEW MORE IRONIES

I got a call from a friend just two days after we were released. He used to be an alderman in Airdrie. He called me and said, "You have to come to the Islamic Centre and see what is going on there. Bring your camera."

So, I did. I went with my wife, and when we arrived, I could not believe what I saw. Thousands of Muslims were congregating together. The Imam was yelling something through the microphone. There were signage, different speakers, and thousands of people. Most were not wearing masks, and no one was keeping their six-foot distance apart.

We recorded everything. I was so upset. Dawid and I had been arrested because we incited people to come to the church and participate in an illegal gathering. And yet, right here, there were ten times more people than in our church, and for some reason, this was all legal. The Rooke Order, which led to our arrest, prohibits any form of gathering. The weight of the hammer fell hardest on the Christians, while the Muslims faced no repercussions for their actions. There was no police harassment, no bylaw officers taking pictures, no health inspectors forcing themselves on the Muslim gathering, and no arrests.

I told Marzena, "What a sham. What hypocrisy. What a lie this whole thing is."

When we filmed the whole gathering, we went back to the car and drove around. The police were distant and did not get involved, just observing. We encountered a friend who approached the officers to inquire about the "illegal gathering" and their plans to address it. They said that they received orders not to interfere.

"There you go," I said to Marzena. "There is one law for Christians and another one for a more privileged, special protected class." In 2020, we witnessed how BLM protests received preferential treatment from the police despite violating restrictions. The churches and the restaurants had to be stopped at all costs for "health reasons" but others more aligned with the government rhetoric were protected.

The same Premier, Jason Kenney, who had said that he would crush us for breaking the restrictions and health mandates, was caught red-handed partying with whiskey in the sky palace in Edmonton with his top ministers. He was breaking the very rules we had been arrested for.

Someone snapped pictures of their hypocrisy, and it became a scandal on the news. No one, not even the waitresses, had masks on, and there was whiskey on the table. There was no social distancing between the Premier and his Health Minister, Tyler Shandro, the Minister of Environment, Jason Nixon, the Minister of Finance, Travis Toews, and others. Again, one law for us and one for the elites, the new masters of the universe.

In a real democracy, these people should be recalled, or if they had any decency, they should resign. However, since we had lost democracy, we had entered a new era—an era of the "pharaohs." The pharaoh could do whatever he wanted, and that is just how the story unfolded. Nothing was done to the lawbreakers (according to their own mandates and restrictions).

Everything was brushed off, and at the same time, we were facing potentially up to four years of imprisonment for breaking the same restrictions that they did. Just two days later, after doing my best to expose the double standards, the unequal application of the law, and the hypocrisy of the very people who were doing this to others, the retaliation came.

A RAGING FIRE AT MY HOME

It was about 11:30 p.m. one evening when my wife noticed some flashing lights outside of our home. Looking through the window, my first thought was that it must be the police who came to arrest me again on some more bogus charges. I quickly got dressed and went out, where I saw a few firetrucks and smoke. The police were also there.

I had no idea what was going on and went to the back alley, thinking that the neighbor's house was on fire. But as I got closer to my shock, I saw that it was not my neighbor's house that was on fire, but the fire was coming from our garage! Someone had tried to burn us alive!

The fire was still raging, and smoke was everywhere. I stood and watched as my possessions went up in smoke. *Who would do such a thing? Who would hate us so much that they would try to burn me, my wife, and three children who were already sleeping? What kind of monster would do this?*

Nathaniel and Marzena came out. It made me sad to watch thousands of dollars go up in flames, but there was nothing I could do. The firefighters did an impressive job and quickly put out the fire, but the smoke was still considerable.

A firefighter chief came to me and said that we were extremely fortunate because, just a few days before, they had dealt with a very similar scenario. Only in that situation, the fire started in the garage and very quickly move through the trees to the house. The whole house had burned down. So, we were very fortunate. The police took a report from me, and when the firefighters left, we remained behind, securing what was not burned down. It was such an intense night.

The next day, an investigator came and looked at the debris to determine how the fire started. It seemed that someone had used our recycling bin, which was filled with paper and cardboard, lit it on fire, and pushed it up to the garage's wooden door. If it was not for a neighbor who saw the fire starting, the whole house would have burned down. It took us a few months to deal with the repairs and the burned stuff from the garage.

A few days after the fire, my daughter Maya and I found ourselves in a store buying a birthday cake for her upcoming celebration. As we were coming out of the store, a man came up and punched me in the face, right in front of my daughter. He wanted to start a fight. I guess the brainwashed people were getting very clear instructions from the mainstream media and the politicians themselves.

But that was not the end of our troubles. The media started a smear campaign against us and the church. They did a series of articles about how "dangerous" we were. They said that because we were not wearing masks and not shutting down the church, we were "terrorizing the neighborhood."

According to them, people were afraid to leave their houses because of us. We were accused of being super spreaders who caused deaths in the province. I was called a "bloody murderer" and compared to Adolf Hitler on social media. They demanded my immediate arrest and a shutdown of the church.

Despite all this, we kept going. Every week, we would be attacked by Antifa, BLM, and homosexual activists. We were subjected to their screams and curses, and occasionally, a young woman would strip and curse at us and the kids outside the church. At times, we would find dog manure all over the church's parking lot.

Another time, there was vandalism; they broke into our church multiple times, stealing our equipment, including cameras and speakers, trying to prevent us from conducting services. Eventually, they tried to burn the church down. But they only managed to burn the children's bus. One day, the parking lot had nails spread out all over the ground.

Ironically, for a few months, the politicians and the media were portraying *us* as villains. Yet, week after week, we were targeted either physically, or our properties or cars were attacked. Nathaniel's car was vandalized. Another volunteer's car was shot at with a high-powered pellet gun. Our windows were smashed on several occasions. However, we stood our ground, and we kept worshiping our God!

For her birthday, Maya asked me to baptize her. My heart melted with excitement, knowing that I could be charged for this "illegal" act of baptizing. But there was no way I could say "No."

The day of Maya's baptism was absolutely beautiful. The sun was shining, and many people came to celebrate that day with my family. In addition to her, I conducted baptisms for several other people. A reporter was filming the event, and it was clear he was deeply moved by the ceremony. Before he left, he turned to me and said, "Next week, would you baptize me?"

"It would be a great honor," I replied. The following Sunday, he was baptized.

Since it was summer, we conducted services outside. One Sunday, I noticed a man sitting in an SUV. I saw he had a big professional telescopic camera and was snapping photos. In my heart, I knew I would be in trouble again.

It turned out that he was working for the *Calgary Herald*, and that very picture was used to charge me criminally and would eventually lead to my next arrest.

CHAPTER TWELVE

A DOOR OPENS: AMERICA HERE WE COME!

BECAUSE OF THE worldwide viral video of the arrest on the highway, I received countless invitations from several news media outlets and continued my daily interviews. I was a guest on a podcast that caught the attention of a woman named Cindy. It turns out that Cindy had felt a strong urge from God to tell the podcast host to invite me and had even sent a text to him about it. This is how our tour to America began to take shape.

I booked our tickets and prepared for the journey. At the airport, we waited in anticipation to check our luggage. When we arrived at the border check, a U. S. Border Patrol Officer looked at us and smiled.

"Why are you going to the United States? What is your purpose there? And why are you traveling now?"

I thought to myself, *If this whole affair is from God, He will make a way where there seems to be no way.*

The officer kept smiling, which to me was strange. My previous experiences with American border patrol agents had not been pleasant. Every time I traveled alone, they would grill me without fail. But this time was different. The agent was polite, smiling, and very interested in us. He might have recognized me from the news, TV, or the press. He wanted to know what I did and why. The officer seemed intrigued as I shared a little of the story of Nathaniel's miraculous survival and healing.

In an instant, the agent said, "Welcome," then smiled and ushered us through with a welcoming gesture. I briefly considered the possibility that he might be an angel. This border guard was unlike any I had encountered before and left a lasting impression on me. We entered the Food Court on the other side and breathed a sigh of relief.

The entire airport was nearly deserted. Everywhere we turned, we encountered writeups stating that only "essential travel" was authorized. Like in the apocalyptic movies, after some horrible event, we were being reminded that something was not right.

Nathaniel said, "The place looks abandoned."

"I know," I replied.

Nathaniel then pointed at a TV screen showing an announcement stating that no one was allowed to travel. He said, "When God wants you somewhere, he will get you there."

The plane we boarded was nearly empty. When we arrived in the U.S., we grabbed our luggage and headed straight to the church. It was a prominent place and somewhat unique, resembling Noah's ark. It had some animals all over the place and looked very nice. As soon as we stepped into the building, I noticed the heavily armed security who looked like the military. Every entrance was guarded, as well as the pulpit on both sides.

The church leader introduced me to a packed house, and I shared my story with the congregation. To my amazement, I received a standing ovation, which was something I wasn't used to. It was nice, although humbling. After years of rejection, it felt good.

We spent some time in the church talking with people. They were telling us how blessed and inspired they were after they saw what we did and what the authorities did to us. I realized again how desperate people were to see an example of courage.

While in that city, we spoke at another church and held a few interviews. A few days later, we flew to Virginia, where we met Cindy for the first time in person. She had been hired to schedule the entire tour. Invitations kept coming from all over the U.S.A.

In Virginia, we came across a small church that truly embodied the essence of an African American civil rights movement church. While interacting with the crowd, we were serenaded by the ancient African American worship. I had a strong impression that I was feeling the same way Martin Luther King Jr. did. It isn't easy to put into words, but I loved it. I loved the setup, the songs, the people, the countryside. And once again, the reception was overwhelming.

People were taking pictures with me like I was some kind of celebrity. I engaged in short interviews with a few reporters. The crowd enthusiastically responded to my preaching with loud "Amens" and "Praise the Lords." They seemed to be thoroughly enjoying the service!

Throughout the tour, I delivered sermons in various American churches and received exceptional respect and honor everywhere we visited. People were crying, sharing their struggles, and everywhere, people were taking pictures with us. It felt bizarre at first. It dawned on me that to those individuals, we were the courageous ones who stood up against tyranny, and they sincerely appreciated our actions.

Soon, we arrived in Washington, DC. First, we went to see the nation's Capital—but only from the outside. The whole building was still fenced off after January 6, 2020. Then, we did some commentary outside the U. S. Supreme Court. Next, we visited Steve Bannon, a captivating man who had once served as an advisor to President Donald Trump of the U.S.A. and now hosted the program *War Room*. During the few segments with Steve, he told me several times that I needed to write a book about this whole experience. (NOTE: *It only took 16 arrests and a lengthy stay in solitary confinement to take Steve's advice and begin the project!*)

From there, we flew to Tampa, Florida, for a large conference organized by Clay Clark. The venue was Pastor Rodney Howard Browne's church. While standing at the front of the church, Cindy gestured towards a man and said he was our host, Clay Clark. After spending some time with him, I realized that Clay was a very kind man with a huge heart!

Rodney's place was impressive—90 acres of private land. There was a large sanctuary, many offices, and other rooms in the facility. The event kicked off with a special dinner called "The Influencer's Dinner." Prominent figures from across the United States who were widely recognized attended the event. They were individuals who took a stand and refused to submit to the modern-day Hamans.

The conference itself lasted for three days and I met so many powerful men and women of God amongst the 10,000 people gathered in attendance. We met doctors, people from the movie industry, scientists, politicians, businesspeople, pastors, and many others. When I spoke, there was again a standing ovation. Everything I was saying resonated with the Americans. They understood the importance of standing up, fighting for our rights, resisting communism and socialism, and opposing Godlessness in their land.

Pastor Rodney proudly gave us a tour of his complex. I have to admit he was a brilliant man—a great Pastor, organizer, and businessman. He seemed strict and firm but also fair and kind.

Each day at the conference, we encountered remarkable individuals - the heroes of America. In the Green Room, we did media every day, and that's where I made connections with people for the trip. They invited me to come to their cities and churches across the U.S.A. to share our story.

During our tour, we spoke in small churches, big churches, private venues, conference halls, rented rooms, and private homes. During that time, we boarded at least 80 flights, rented countless cars, and explored numerous states. Everywhere we went, it was always the same thing—a huge positive reception. We had the chance to visit my friend Paul and his family in Arizona. While there, we had a big meeting—a packed house—with the Patriots.

Arizona is beautiful. But being extremely hot and dry, it was a big difference from Florida. Three weeks turned into six, then into two months, and eventually, I ended up staying there for four months.

Then we headed to Tennessee where I was privileged to preach in Pastor Greg Locke's church. Greg is an incredible man with an amazing ministry. He is a "man of fire" who refused to shut down his church during the pandemic. And because he took that stand, his church had significantly expanded. My speech there was overwhelmingly received; it was an experience I'll never forget. What a blessing it was to be among such a hero of faith.

While Nathaniel and I traveled from state to state, Marzena, Dawid, and the Street Church were holding down the fort back home. They were preparing for the March for Jesus in Calgary. The attacks were always heightened during that time of year, and of course, *this* year was no different. Someone unscrewed the bolts of the front wheel of our pickup truck, which was parked in front of our home. Thank God the driver sensed something wasn't quite right and slowed down a little because the wheel flew off in front of him, and the truck collapsed to the ground.

He later mentioned that if Marzena had been driving on the highway, this event would have resulted in a dangerous head-on collision. Obviously, someone tried to hurt my family or even kill them. The police arrived, surveyed the area, and did something truly bizarre—they asked my wife what she wanted them to do about it.

"Seriously?" she replied. "You do not know what to do? Catch those who want to murder us. First, they wanted to burn us alive, then my husband was attacked coming out of a store, and now this. Do your job!" she finished.

Well, they did not. I suppose their top priority during the pandemic was apprehending unmasked shoppers and shutting down as many churches and soup kitchens as possible. Catching *real* criminals was not a priority for them at the moment. They never contacted us about it again. After they left, Marzena faced the task of determining how to repair the truck, which had suffered significant damage.

When Greg learned about this, he wanted to help. I've never met such a generous and compassionate pastor like him. I hugged Greg and thanked him for his genuine love. The memory of that day and the overwhelming gratitude from a man and a church who barely knew me will never fade.

DISCOVERING MORE ABOUT MY DESTINY

While in the United States, I had a strong sense that our time there was deeply impactful. It felt like it was meant to be for me to be there—to meet those amazing people and get to know them. There was much to learn from them and also to warn them about what was coming their way. I know that my life will be forever intertwined with Americans because I felt at home, and they treated us like family. I also sensed that this was just the beginning of my adventures in the United States.

We encountered another person in New York City who would have a positive impact on our lives. We stepped into the hotel, and my attention was immediately drawn to a group of people conversing in the lobby, with security personnel on either side. It was clear that they were protecting someone of significance. We were asked to come sit at the table, and a pleasant man smiled and asked if I would like a cup of coffee.

I gladly said, "Yes. That would be wonderful!" That man was General Flynn. He struck me as a down-to-earth man with a very humble demeanor. We talked, and I introduced Nathaniel to him. General Flynn is an amazing man—a Patriot who loves his country and a very strong and firm person. He has also suffered much persecution.

His manner of speaking made it clear that he held authority and had a clear vision. Nathaniel and I had a brief interview with him. During this, he expressed his gratitude for the work we had been doing in Canada.

Hours later, we found ourselves in the heart of Times Square, where a press conference featuring a mayoral candidate and General Flynn was being held. We were also asked to join the candidate in visiting an Italian neighborhood. During that time, I had a great opportunity to preach in Manhattan and then in Brooklyn. We then met with our dear friend, Andy, from New Jersey, who had a very popular show for Polish people.

Andy took us to the site of the World Trade Center, where the Twin Towers had once stood. The time we shared exploring the city was exceptionally precious. I was able to meet with hundreds of Polish friends and organize a concert for them; people absolutely loved it.

During my time in the States, there were many memorable occasions. There was the time we went to a monastery in a California valley where the guy who created the Church of Satan, Anton LaVey, owned a ranch. There were some fascinating stories about Mr. LaVey, and a book had even been written about him.

We preached in the middle of a cotton plantation that used to have slaves working in the fields; the plantation still had old barracks. I remember looking at them and thinking, *that's exactly what the government wants to do to us now. They are trying to turn us into modern-day enslaved people, and if we don't wake up, we might end up living in similar barracks ourselves.*

When we were in Washington, DC, we saw the Lincoln Memorial, and I had the chance to stand where Martin Luther King, Jr. delivered his famous "I Have a Dream" speech. The White House left me with a lingering impression that its symbolism of integrity and truthfulness had faded. It had become one that was dark and possibly even evil.

We traveled to Washington State from Portland for several church services and a panel of discussions. In the panel was the Mayor of Squamish, along with a constitutional lawyer, a doctor, another pastor, and myself. It was a very informative evening. During the week, the church building was used as a school—a brilliant idea. In Canada, most of the church buildings during the week were completely empty. But this way it could be utilized as a school. I loved the idea and thought, *I have to remember that!*

In Washington, we visited with a doctor who explained the risks of taking the COVID-19 vaccines and the long-term problems that might develop within a few years. This man was knowledgeable because he had treated over 10,000 COVID-19 patients. He warned us not to take the shots!

TWO DREAMS AND THEIR IMPACT ON ME

During my time in Washington, I met a man named Nathan, who was a prophet of God. When he was younger, Nathan had tried to commit suicide and almost succeeded. From that moment, God gave him an insight into the spiritual realm, and he could see and hear things that others could not. Nathan took me to his parent's home, which was a fantastic log house overlooking the ocean bay. His parents welcomed me with open hearts. His mom was a fabulous cook and prepared a delicious meal. My guest room had its own deck with a breathtaking view.

During the first night at Nathan's parent's house, I had a dream. I usually forget my dreams, but when I do remember, they feel significant. In my dream, I experienced the thrill of diving into a vast and deep ocean. I couldn't perceive how deep or large the water was, but I was equipped with the best diving equipment. My diving suit was also sophisticated, boasting cutting-edge technology.

I plunged deep into the depths, where the darkness was so intense that nothing could be seen beneath me. There was no light except for the one that enveloped me. There was nothing there. There was no one with me and yet I was not afraid at all. In fact, I loved the adventure. When it was time to go up, I came out and spoke with the equipment supervisor. I asked her, "How much does all of the equipment cost?"

She said, "It is very expensive."

"How much?" I insisted on knowing the price.

"It is $10,000," she said.

I thought to myself *that is not expensive at all* and so I told the lady, "I am buying it!"

Nathan informed me in the morning that a group of coyotes arrived at my door and began howling. I was so tired I did not hear a thing. Another dream occurred on the second night. There was a war going on. The enemy was mighty and had overwhelming numbers. In the dream, my very close friend—my best friend— decided that in order to protect us all, he had to leave and fight.

I told him, "The enemy is so strong; you might die."

He replied, "That is what needs to be done. Someone has to go and defend everybody else." He was willing to fight against all odds.

So my friend went to fight with the enemy. He was an incredible fighter, one of the best. He successfully killed all of them, but he also sustained wounds and passed away. When I arrived to see the battlefield, there were countless bodies of the enemy. Corpses of evil warriors were everywhere.

My best friend was lying dead in the middle of the field. I shed tears for the immense loss, aware that he sacrificed everything to save us. His own life was lost, but because of him, we were saved. I was awakened, and that dream ended.

I was puzzled and did not know what those dreams meant. So the following day, I shared about both of them with Nathan and his parents. Here is the interpretation that I received from Nathan:

The first dream was about your willingness to go for the Lord to places and in depths like no other man. You are willing to do it even if it means to do it alone—to go deep, surrounded by great darkness but with the light of God in you. The price tag, even though for others, is too much. It is too expensive. A sacrifice is too huge, but for you, it is actually very affordable. The price to pay to go all the way for the Lord was big, but you were willing. You have no problem paying that price and getting the best that the Lord has for you.

The second dream was also about you. You are your best friend. You are that great warrior who is willing to go and fight for others, sacrificing everything. You bravely fight against the enemy while others hide and are scared. You dying in the end, saving everybody else, does not mean that you're going to die physically. You have to die to yourself. You must sacrifice your own desires in order to win a great victory for others, and you are willing to go all the way.

For you, the price is acceptable, and you are ready to pay it. Be encouraged. God is going to use you to save many people. You are his warrior, and because of your stand, people will become bold and courageous. Because of you, many people around the world will rise up. You are destined to spread courage and love.

I consider the time with Nathan and his family very precious. It was good to be in the house of a prophet.

A TIME OF REST AND AMERICAN PATRIOTISM

Traveling within the States was simple but exhausting. Many times, after a long day of meetings and speaking engagements, we would have to wake up at 3:00 a.m. to rush to the airport, head somewhere else, and repeat the same thing again the following day. Sometimes, we would change planes twice a day. Eventually, this constant rigor wears you down and we were ready for a break. Marzena came with the kids, and we spent a few weeks together enjoying the beautiful Florida hospitality and weather.

Pastor Rodney decided that since the authorities had canceled "Canada Day" in our homeland of Canada, we should come to Florida and hold our own. He told us, "Let's do 'Canada Day' in America." He invited people from all over, and the celebration was live-streamed, and I was asked to share. Participants sang the Canadian national anthem, and we prayed for Canada. Some cried for the nation. I delivered my message, standing in the gap for my country. It was powerful.

I also spoke to the church days later on the 4th of July for America's greatest day of celebration. I thought, *God, this is the most honored day in their calendar. What am I to preach about?*

I felt like God said to me, "Remind them about their heritage and history. Teach them about the foundation of their country," He whispered.

And so I did. Many individuals approached afterward, admitting their previous unawareness about their country. They thanked me for reminding them what the whole thing was all about: the courage of those who believe in God's protection for their homeland and fatherland. I reminded them of the profound significance of being American. Those were patriotic moments: the American flag, the singing, the pride of the people of all races, colors, and backgrounds, united with one dream, as well as the American dream of a nation where, with God, everything was possible. It was a great honor to witness those moments and to be part of that. At least for that time, I could feel like an American and feel free to pursue my dreams.

While in America, I had the opportunity to meet members of Congress, state senators, U.S. senators, and a few mayors, and I was a keynote speaker at the annual Ronald Reagan dinner. There, I met Bill Lee, the 50th governor of Tennessee. Many U.S. politicians were speaking publicly against abortion and acknowledging their faith in Jesus Christ. Without hesitation, they openly professed their faith in God, which was refreshing to me.

It is forbidden for politicians in Canada to mention their faith. Publicly acknowledging their support for Jesus Christ or expressing opposition to homosexuality or abortion could be seen as political suicide, so no one did it. Americans were so different. Their words were like a fresh breeze in the hot summer or like a drop of rain in the middle of a parched land. Everywhere I went, I was so refreshed. Ultimately, I'm unsure who provided more encouragement, me to them or them to me. They were my countrymen, a kindred spirit.

Everywhere we went, I encountered the same favor. At these events, I could deliver sermons, offer prayers, and lead people toward repentance, resulting in numerous individuals sharing their personal experiences of being impacted. I also met Eric Trump, the son of the former President of the United States of America. Eric gave a passionate speech about America, and I could tell that he honored his father. It was a beautiful moment when he spoke, and we got to see the person behind the news headlines.

On that day, I had the opportunity to meet Mike Smith, the author of the documentary *Out of Shadows*. We later met to film some footage, and I ended up spending the day and night at his house with his family. Mike is another great man with a very powerful testimony. He used to work for Hollywood, and he knew all the skeletons hiding in many closets. Now he was free, and Jesus was his movie director. God was preparing him for another powerful assignment.

VICTORY OVER THE ENEMY'S SNARES

People had been inviting me to Portland for more than a month to pray and uplift fellow believers. I was also told that if I dared to come, Antifa was going to kill me. They were sending all kinds of threats. It turns out that Portland is some kind of hub for their evil activities. And one thing they hated the most was a patriotic Christian.

Despite that, our tour was named "Courageous Faith," and we refused to give in to the devil's threats and intimidation, so the event was still confirmed. Upon arrival, we met with some patriots who debriefed us about what was going to happen. Prayer and worship were scheduled to take place at the Battleship Oregon Memorial. However, the police told the event organizers that it would be better if they would move their venue a few hundred yards towards the bridge for safety reasons. The police felt that Antifa might show up and that way, it would be easier for them to protect us. The event organizers agreed.

As we arrived at the new location and prepared the speakers, around 30-40 Antifa members in black attire, armed with weapons and riot shields, unexpectedly appeared from the police's direction. They swiftly moved in the direction of the Christians. The villains were closing the distance when the first flash bomb hit the ground right next to a mother with a stroller with a baby in it. Then, another one very close to where I was standing.

Antifa members were grabbing everything they could. I saw them smashing the speakers; someone took one of the speakers and threw it into the river. We had not come prepared for a fight. There were women around us with young children. The Christian men were dressed in shorts and t-shirts.

Those evil people, dressed in black, completely lost all humanity. They went as far as stealing sandwiches that were intended for the children. Just when I thought things couldn't get worse, the pepper bombs began exploding. I looked towards the police, standing by their cruisers, watching and smiling.

I realized that this Christian event had been a setup for an attack by the police themselves. I could not believe my eyes! The police saw the whole thing. That is why they wanted the organizers to move so far away so the public could not see what was going on. Then it hit me. The powerful pain of the tear gas. The one that chokes you and immediately blinds you.

Someone handed me a gas mask, which I put on. We were moving away from the cloud of gas. I looked around but could not breathe in this thing. Eventually, I took it off and decided to walk without it. A few minutes later, it was all over. The police finally decided to show up.

After I expressed my thoughts, they promptly left. We assembled the leftover items and established ourselves in the exact location we had initially planned to be—at the Battlefield Oregon Memorial. We did what we came to do: pray and worship. I delivered my speech and told them that because those wicked people did what they did, I would come back to Oregon for a few more days.

The people there were impressive; they remained brave and courageous, not shaken by what had happened! A pastor received a direct spray into his eyes and onto his face. Yet an hour later, despite still suffering the aftereffects of pepper spray, he grabbed the mic, and still delivered his sermon. They showed their unwavering allegiance as Patriots and faithful children of God, like lions and lionesses.

KEEPING MY PROMISE TO RETURN

True to my word, I returned to Oregon. Due to an attack by Antifa, I extended my visit there from one hour to four days. The mainstream media consistently portrays Antifa as a peaceful organization fighting against fascism. They are the good guys; Christians and Patriots are the bad guys. There, in Portland, however, they showed their true colors—who they really were.

After the attack, the news of what had happened spread around the world. They were attacking Christians during peaceful prayer and worship time by throwing flash bombs at toddlers and women and stealing food prepared for children. Regardless of your opinions on Christians or Patriots, the viral images clearly showed something was wrong and was pure evil.

Antifa thought that they would scare us into hiding. That we would crawl into a hole and be too scared to come out. Our God is not one of fear but one of power, and this was evident the following day. Sean Feucht, a well-known Christian singer and worship leader, showed up at the very spot of the Antifa incident. Thousands of others showed up, as well, who were praying, worshipping, and lifting up the name of Jesus.

Once again, Antifa showed up, but their presence was rendered ineffective due to the large number of worshippers. They couldn't do anything but stand, filled with hate, as they had to listen to hours of prayers and worship. What the enemy meant for evil, once again, God turned around for good.

This incident gave Christians even more strength, boldness, and power to stand up for their faith. My team decided to conduct a few more indoor and outdoor events in Oregon. The initial gathering was organized to take place outside the Holocaust abortion "clinic" in the capital city of Salem, where prayers would be offered for the unborn victims.

While churches were ordered to close during the pandemic, abortion clinics were considered essential. Health services, mainstream media, and evil politicians could freely endorse and promote the taking of life. But to worship the God who gives life was prohibited. The Antifa members decided to come join us for Rumble #2.

While driving to the destination, we witnessed a haunting sight of hate-filled figures clad in black marching towards the designated gathering point with their weapons and shields. Of course, those cowards were all masked and covered from top to bottom, with only their evil eyes visible. They were humans who had completely lost their humanity.

We found a big gathering of "demons in black" waiting at the clinic when we got there. I noticed that they also had a few medics on standby in the back. I thought to myself that these people came for blood, to hurt people. On our side, we had women, children, and men who did not come to fight with flesh, but they came to fight with the spiritual.

Suddenly, to our side emerged a group of men dressed in body armor, wearing helmets and carrying guns, semi-automatic rifles, and all kinds of other weapons. They were the good guys and had heard about our troubles in Portland; they came to ensure that would not happen here. There were about 30 of them dressed and ready for battle.

These patriotic soldiers moved like military personnel and immediately formed a line between the people in black and the Christians. Every time an Antifa member made their move, the Patriots immediately blocked them. And those Patriots were tough, well-equipped, and ready to fight. When I looked at them, I said to myself, *I would not want to fight with them!* Their eyes showed determination, not fear, as they vowed to protect those who came to worship and pray.

The Antifa members realized what was happening and began to curse and yell at the Christians. We simply turned up the music louder and began to worship our God. The sound was loud, and it overpowered the demons. People fell to their knees and prayed.

It was a powerful moment in the middle of the battlefield, and it greatly confused the villains. They did not know what to do. So, every time they tried to come closer, the Patriots stopped them. I was sure that the Antifa members wouldn't be left unscathed if they dared to try anything because the line of "our guys" was unbreakable.

A leader from the evil gang pointed at me and said, "We want him!" As he extended his hand towards me, his eyes were filled with intense evil and hatred. He yelled again, "We want that one!" And they moved forward, trying to break the line. But they encountered opposition once again. Those evil men wanted me very badly. Yet, they understood that launching a full assault would likely cost them their own lives. Because our guys were ready to go, all the way.

The Patriots told me, "No one touches you today. They will die if they try."

In my sermon, I told them that I did not hate them. Christians pray for people like them, and our God loves them so much that He gave his Son, Jesus Christ, who died on the cross for their evil sins. I said, "Why so much hate? Why do you want to do so much evil? Stop this!

God will forgive you! We love you! We do not hate you! We love the unborn babies that are being murdered in places like this one. God loves everyone and wishes that everyone would come to repentance."

While speaking to them, I made sure to maintain eye contact and noticed my words were making an impact. Initially, they raised their weapons high, but gradually, they began lowering them bit by bit. I knew that the love of God was the most powerful weapon of all, and I was using it like a sword. Others preached at this event, as well. We prayed and worshipped some more.

By the time we finished, Antifa had lost half of its members. They just quit. They took their weapons away and walked back to where they came from. The police were keeping their distance away from all of us, and just like in Portland, they did not interfere. We finished and went home.

An event was planned for the following day in the park by the river. During the day, I did some media interviews and arrived at the park just before the event. We did not know what to expect. Would Antifa show up again? Would they try to attack us again?

When we arrived, a few people were already gathered. The speakers went on, and the worship music hit the park. There was no Antifa. They did not come. We had outlasted them. We stood our ground, and God gave us the victory. Several of us preached, and without any interference, we went home.

Later, I learned that a local high-ranking government official was, in fact, a Satanist and had come earlier that morning to curse the ground. But God was no match for those evil, wicked spells. The Word went forth, and the mission was accomplished.

The next day, we had a meeting with some pastors in a very peculiar place. It was an old bar that had a dark history of being used as a slave-trafficking enterprise. With hidden rooms and passages, it was where young girls were taken and smuggled to other parts of the country. Some time ago, God gave that place to a church that transformed this horrible dungeon into a temple of the Lord. I had a great privilege to share in this place. God was good. A lot of leaders and pastors came to unite by putting their efforts together and fighting in the name of the Lord for their country.

I will always be grateful to the incredible Christians in Oregon who were brave and willing to go all the way. They took me to their homes, blessed me, and fed me. May the Lord repay them mightily for their kindness toward me.

CHAPTER THIRTEEN

MY VISIT TO THE LONE STAR STATE

TEXAS WAS ONE of the last stops of the tour after four months of traveling in this remarkable country. Pastor Ramiro Pena, an advisor to President Trump, invited me to speak at his prophetic conference in Waco, Texas. The conference included Lance Wallnau, an American preacher and evangelical leader, and Chuck Pierce, from Glory of Zion International Ministries.

The Waco venue was big, and I felt a bit anxious speaking to such a large crowd about prophecy. I prayed, "Lord, you brought me here. I ask you to open my mouth and tell those people what you want them to hear. I am your servant. Use me as you please."

The event started with worship and a release into the ministry of one of Pena's spiritual daughters, Anna Khait. We laid hands on her, anointed her, and prophesied into her life. Every one of us said a few words, encouraging Anna to stand strong in the lord. We blessed her and released her in the mighty name of Jesus Christ.

After that, Anna shared her powerful testimony. She told about how God took her from the lifestyle of gambling as a professional poker player and a contestant on the reality show *Survivor* and brought her to Him. Lance also delivered a very important teaching about the Seven Mountains of Influence. Chuck delivered his insights into what was happening in the spiritual and physical realms. Finally, I shared what God had told me about what was happening around the world with this shaking and separating.

During the conference, Lance, Pierce, and Pena delivered a word for me. On September 18, 2021, Chuck Pierce delivered a prophecy to me, conveying the message from the Lord:

> You will be able to be stuck in the grounds that I send you to, and people will learn to rally around what you're saying. I am going to use you as one who stands strong in days ahead and says some things that others I couldn't trust to say. But I trust you, sayeth the Lord to say them. In the midst of you saying them, upheaval will break loose. Get ready. You are headed to a new launching pad this year, and I am getting ready to launch you to become a standard for every nation. And every place I send you to sayeth the Lord.

Lance confirmed what Chuck had said as well. It was definitely one of my highlights to be with those giants of faith and speak from the same podium as them.

Following the conference, Pena took me to meet his friend Gary, who owned a Texas-sized ranch. I must say I loved those people, and they loved me back. I must admit that there was something about this land and its people that I felt a deep spiritual connection to. At that time, I could not describe it, but I knew that my destiny was intertwined with theirs. I could feel that God was connecting everything together.

While in Texas, at Pastor Pena's conference, a woman came to me crying. She handed me a belt and said a man wearing this belt was going to be arrested. Another person during a service said the same thing. A friend former from Barbados prophesied I would be arrested upon arrival. I was told by so many Americans to stay in the States. Not only was I given the opportunity to pastor churches in America, but they also offered me their houses and land.

People told me, "Just stay. You can do the same thing from the U.S.A. We need you here." So many beautiful people cared so much. They wanted me to be safe, and they were offering to bring my whole family, my wife and my kids. How could I abandon everyone else to the mercy of the tyrants in pursuit of safety and comfort?

Deep down, I knew there was only one path for me. Canada was the place where my destiny would be played out amidst rampant corruption and the plight of the oppressed. I prayed to God for wisdom. I gave my last word to the people in America before facing the giants back home.

Once I was done, people rose and approached me individually, offering embraces and assurances of their prayers for me and my family. Hundreds of people came with tears in their eyes and blessed me. It was one of the most moving moments, and I knew that I had a considerable family in the United States of America. I said my goodbyes to so many amazing people. I did my last media interview, and off I went with a looming potential arrest on my mind.

My final speaking engagement in America was in Colorado Springs. The venue was crowded, and while I was there, numerous people informed me about what awaited me when I returned home. Here is what I shared:

> During the time of the Nazis in Germany, there was a man, a pastor, who refused to bow! His name was Dietrich Bonhoeffer. This remarkable theologian who wrote *The Cost of Discipleship* refused to obey the Nazi regime! He was different! During that time, many, instead of fighting evil, joined evil; they joined the Reich Church. The bowl of soup, the silver coin, to them was more precious than the God that they claimed that they were serving!

> Bonhoeffer, however, served Christ—not the Führer, not the Fauchis, Clintons, Obamas, or other tyrants of his time. They were not the head of the Church—God was!

> Bonhoeffer produced a radio address two days after the Nazis officially came to power, defying Hitler and cautioning Germany about the developing cult surrounding the Führer, who he referred to as the Verführer (translated as misleader or seducer).

> Do you know that Bonhoeffer's broadcast was cut off in mid-sentence? Just like today, with the de-platforming and censoring of Google, Facebook, and YouTube. These social media platforms learned from the best—the Nazi Party itself!

> In June 1939, Dietrich Bonhoeffer was invited to the United States and was offered to stay there! He could have remained here, but on June 20, 1939, he made the fateful decision to return to Nazi Germany. Why? Despite intense pressures from his friends to stay in the United States, he wrote these words to his friend:

> > *I must live through this difficult period of our national history with the Christian people of Germany. I will have no right to participate in the reconstruction of Christian life in*

Germany after the war if I do not share the trials of this time with my people...Christians in Germany will face the terrible alternative of either willing the defeat of their nation in order that Christian civilization may survive or willing the victory of their nation and thereby destroying civilization. I know which of these alternatives I must choose, but I cannot make this choice in security. The ultimate test of a moral society is the kind of world that it leaves to its children.

As of now, I am facing three contempt of court orders—for inciting people to come to church! For officiating a church Service and for taking part in an illegal gathering. And then there's the latest—a pending criminal charge—for baptizing my 12-year-old daughter during her birthday in the river against the mandates! I might be arrested straight from the airport, and if they want to be mean, I can be sentenced to six years in prison for my crimes of being Christian!

Like Dietrich Bonhoeffer, I had the opportunity to remain in your beautiful country. A house, a church, and money were offered to me. My friends, like Dietrich Bonhoeffer's friends, were concerned about my safety and said, "STAY!"

Staying here would be the safest and most logical decision! However, *safe* does not necessarily mean right! I, like Bonhoeffer, have to obey my God! Someone has to fight the evil in the land! Canadians are worth fighting for! Canadian kids are worth fighting for! My home is worth fighting for! In the words of Dietrich Bonhoeffer, "One act of obedience is worth a hundred sermons."

If I stay and choose comfort and safety rather than responsibility, obedience, and courage to face the Giants—if I run away from facing Goliath of the land, all those millions that I could inspire and encourage—then all those people who received hope because of my actions and stands will be heartbroken! If I stay, I will become a living lie to everything I believe in and everything I have been speaking about. If I run, others will start running as well! I must face the evil myself! **I must not run!**

> *We are not to simply bandage the wounds of victims beneath the wheels of injustice; we are to drive a spoke into the wheel itself.*
> DIETRICH BONHOEFFER

It is important to provide people with examples that demonstrate the possibility of standing tall. People need shepherds who will not only preach words but act upon them! We are their voices! We represent the millions who are oppressed and attacked around the world! We have to speak and walk the talk! Bonhoeffer also taught us:

> *Silence in the face of evil is itself evil: God will not hold us guiltless. Not to speak is to speak. Not to act is to act.*

I was offered the opportunity to stay in the U.S.A. But how can I stay? This story is no longer about me and my family, but about all those millions looking for hope, boldness, and courage. In the Bible, the Priests led the army of the Lord! Now, we need the priests more than ever. Bring God back to America! I came to the United States with a mission! To warn America! To tell my story! They came for me—rise up my American brothers and sisters, because they are coming for you also!

Being here, I did my best to sound the trumpet and unite the clans! I always wanted to see the body of Christ as one, for people to see and understand that whatever the wicked once did to one of us, they are doing this to all of us! The wicked always attack the forerunners first! We have to stay together as one! One for All and all for One!

I did what every man is called to do! I stood for what I believe in! For my God! For my Family! For my Country and for those generations that will come after us! The generations that will inherit what we have nourished and protected for them! The freedoms that we held precious! All those values that we received from others who walked and fought before us!

We received their dream! A nation where a hardworking man can prosper and provide for his loved ones. A land of the free and the home of the brave. A place on earth where we can worship our God and pursue our happiness. And this land is worth fighting for; this dream is worth standing up for!

Thank you for allowing me to do my mission here. Together, we have accomplished a lot. We preached hard, fought hard, and set many captives free! I have been treated in your home like the son of this land, like one of your own, and for that, I am very grateful! Thank you from the bottom of my heart!

What I am going to take with me in my heart forever is not the places that I have seen, even though they are some of the most beautiful on earth, but the people! You! Your generosity, your kindness, your love! You are the biggest treasure that I will carry in my heart for the rest of my life—a treasure that no chain and no prison cell can take away from me!

Now, I am going back to Canada, and I will keep fighting the evil in the land. I promise you that!

This part of my mission has come to an end. A new one has just begun! Pray for me and for my family! May God's will be done.

> *I have declared to both Jews and Greeks that they must turn to God in repentance and have faith in our Lord Jesus. And now, compelled by the Spirit, I am going to Jerusalem, not knowing what will happen to me there. I only know that in every city the Holy Spirit warns me that prison and hardships are facing me. However, I consider my life worth nothing to me; my only aim is to finish the race and complete the task the Lord Jesus has given me—the task **of testifying** to the good news of God's grace. Therefore, I declare to you today that I am innocent of the blood of any of you. For I have not hesitated to proclaim to you the whole will of God.*
>
> ACTS 20:21-26 [EMPHASIS ADDED]

America, I love you! Pride of Lions, keep Roaring! Eagles, keep flapping your wings! My heart will forever be with you! If it is God's will for me to return to you, I will be here again, Roaring and flying with you!

Until then, May the Lord bless you and keep you; The Lord make His face shine upon you, And be gracious to you; The Lord lift His countenance upon you, And give you peace." (Numbers 6:24-26).

People were surrounding me, crying, praying, and encouraging me. They said that I should stay and bring my family down and that they would take care of me and my family. Hundreds of people were around me, all praying to God. It was so touching I could not help but tear up.

During my tour in the States, my trial was going on at the same time. Due to the COVID protocol, I was not required to appear in person; court was held via Zoom. I had to attend several hearings and listen to the prosecutors' outrageous arguments. I listened to the judge who was appointed by the same judge, John Rooke, who gave the court order basically straight from Soviet Russia that we were charged and arrested under.

When that appointed crooked Judge, Adam Germain, opened his mouth, I knew that this whole thing was going to be a "show trial" and that we did not stand a chance. I knew that this person was already told how to judge us. This was never about justice or the rule of law. This was about a vendetta coming straight from the political arena.

During my time in the States, Marzena mentioned multiple times that the government was furious because I had escaped their claws, and they did not know what to do. There in the States, they could not touch me, and I was getting stronger and stronger and more popular than ever. On the way to Colorado Springs, we had to appear in court. When we were commanded to appear via Zoom on the last day of the trial, the judge asked if we had any final statements. Dawid and I both said, "Yes." I *figured if the verdict was already decided and there was nothing I could do about it, then at least let me make a statement that the whole nation would hear.*

The media were very closely monitoring this trial. Here is what I said from a Tim Horton's coffee shop in the United States of America on the way to another conference. It was ironic that out of all the coffee shops in this little town, the Canadian-based coffeehouse, Tim Horton's, was the only one open. I read my statement to the judge. Here is what I said exactly:

I am here, before this court, as a political prisoner of conscience! The AHS and the politicians have found a new way of penalizing anyone who is opposing their unconstitutional medical Tyranny! They hate the idea that they have been exposed for what they really are. Liars, hypocrites, and cheaters!

I have seen this growing back behind the Iron Curtain under the boots of the Soviets! I have heard from my grandparents about the similar tactics during the time of the Nazis! Persecuting Churches and the clergy! And that is what we are talking about here. Canada has fallen very low! Nelson Mandela said that when a man is denied the right to live the life he believes in, he has no choice but to become an outlaw.

The politicians and the AHS have been embarrassed by the level of hypocrisy and double standards that we have shown to the whole world, and now they are using this court and this judge as their personalized weapon against us, the whistleblowers, who are simply exposing their corruption. We do not have a flu crisis; we have an opioid crisis in Canada! Alcoholism crisis! Record high among the youth suicide crisis! Homelessness crisis! Hopelessness crisis! As a Pastor, I do not just deal with the physical problems but also emotional, spiritual, and mental as well! People in our community are dealing with loneliness, stress, grief, loss, and isolation, and they desperately need their Pastors!

We are and always have been the front-line workers in the time of crisis! Now we are needed more than ever! People need more Church, not less! More prayers, not less! We, the clergy, are essential! Now, the Church is more essential than the corrupted politicians are! How can the politicians say that they care about the health and safety of people if they are imposing rules and are not even bothering to follow them? If they claim these rules are about safety but they violate their own mandates, then it must NOT be about safety - so then what exactly ARE these mandates about?

The politicians who mandated these orders, such as masks, social distancing, and lockdowns, have been caught breaking their own restrictions and should also be found in contempt and held accountable. Because they are not being held to the same standards, it shows to me that this is not about justice and the Rule of Law, but about simple vengeance.

If this were really about health, would those politicians not keep their own mandates? If this was a real emergency, would they be partying at the Sky Palace? If this so-called pandemic was real, are those politicians not putting the public at large and their own colleagues at risk by breaking their own rules?

I am here in this court as a victim of a personal vendetta against a very corrupted and evil, lying and deceiving politician! If I am guilty of a crime, then so it is the Premier of Alberta, Jason Kenney, with a bottle of Jameson Irish whiskey on the patio of the Sky Palace. Breaking their own rules and mandates with Parks Minister and House Leader Jason Nixon. And with the biggest hypocrite of them all, the boss of the AHS that is persecuting us here today, the Health Minister Tyler Shandro, not caring about his own rules, having a good time with the Finance Minister Travis Toews! They also have broken the Rooks order! The Associate Chief Justice John Rooke's order caught them as well! If I am guilty, so are they!

If this court has found us guilty and wants to send us to prison and is refusing at the same time to prosecute those who have subjected us to those mandates and broke them without blinking an eye, then this court is willing to have two sets of laws, one for the corrupted politicians and one for the rest of us! Then this court is also not about justice and the Rule of Law!

I hope that this court is about justice and the Rule of Law, not like those hypocritical politicians with their personal vendetta! If that is the case, then there is, in fact, selective and unjust application of the law and now two sets of laws: one for the corrupted politicians and one for the rest of us citizens. If that is what would happen, then this would be the biggest mockery of the justice system in the modern history of democracy!

What is the government doing for the people that are looking for spiritual guidance? For those millions hurting, hopeless all around us? Do their lives matter? What safety measures are they taking for those people? What are they doing to stop the deaths from drugs and suicides?

Abraham Lincoln said those powerful words: Those who deny freedom to others deserve it, not for themselves. If you sentence me, you will be sentencing yourselves and those hypocrites in Edmonton in the Legislator!

Sure, you can lock us up and throw the key away. But our political imprisonment will shout even louder from prison about this hypocrisy and the mockery of justice! This will be loud and clear that this nation, Canada is no better than China, North Korea, and Russia! The world will see that here in Canada, there are two sets of rules! One for the corrupted politicians and another for the citizens!

If you send us to prison, you must send those Alberta politicians to prison, also! We can even share a cell if that is what you wish! However, if you do not do that, then the whole world will know that there is no justice in Canada anymore!

John F. Kennedy said those powerful words: *The rights of every man are diminished when the rights of one man are threatened.* The corrupted bureaucrats want my apology! They want me to say that I am sorry for doing my job! For saving lives! For feeding thousands of the most vulnerable in our society! For giving hope to the people! Well, here is my answer: Exactly 500 years ago, another man faced a very similar trial, and I was told to apologize; if he would recount, he would be off the hook. His name was Martin Luther! Let me echo today his words as my response to those who seek to hurt me, to hurt the poor, our Church community, and to hurt my family!

I opened the Church for the hurting people looking for help, and I will not apologize for that! I cannot and will not recant anything, for going against my conscience is neither right nor safe. Here I stand; I can do no other, so help me, God. Amen.

The judge was furious. You could tell he was barely holding himself together, and if he could, he would probably shoot me dead. The whole time, he was writing notes, and he looked at me from time to time with pure hatred. This man hated God, he hated the Rule of Law, and he hated me and Dawid. That political judge said his final words and reserved his verdict for a later day.

CHAPTER FOURTEEN

BACK TO CANADA FOR ME

IT WAS TIME to head back to Alberta. I contacted my lawyers before boarding the flight to check for any outstanding warrants; there were none. Before leaving Bowman, Montana, our friend Gary, who owned the plane and was giving me a ride back, informed Customs about our journey. He completed the manifest, and I had to respond to a few inquiries.

Additionally, the authorities questioned whether I had undergone COVID testing, and my response was "No." There was a very long silence on the other side. I believe they were conversing with the higher authorities. They likely concluded that if they insisted on the test, then I might say, "I'm not coming back." The person on the other side was okay with it, but I sensed something was wrong. Everyone traveling to Canada was required to take a COVID test, so why the exception now?

Instead of the usual landing spot for small planes, Gary was directed to take his plane to the Customs building upon landing. Gary suggested that it might be nothing, even though it was strange. My wife, kids, Dawid, and his wife, along with around 100 others, gathered at the usual landing spot to welcome me home after four months away. But now, they were told to stay hundreds of yards away.

We taxied through the entire airport. We crossed several runways before spotting the small Customs office building. Gary parked the plane when suddenly three Customs officers emerged from the building. Gary looked at me and said, "So far, nothing unusual." Gary opened the door and was asked to stay behind. I was instructed to leave everything behind and come out immediately.

I hadn't stepped out of the plane yet when an officer approached me and said, "You are under arrest!"

"What?" I exclaimed.

"There are two warrants for your arrest." One officer stood behind me, another to my right, and a superior officer watched us from 15 yards away.

I was thinking, *Oh, you little devils; that is how you play?* I had previously called to inquire about arrest warrants, and they had found none, but now I suddenly had two! They must have activated them just as I was in the air.

So, I made up my mind not to make things easy for them. I went to my knees with my hands behind my back. Unsure of what to do, the officer near me looked over at his superior, who said, "Go ahead. Arrest him."

While on my knees, I was arrested. However, I didn't want to be pulled along the ground as usual because it was quite far, and I didn't want to damage my dress shoes. So, with my hands cuffed behind my back, I stood up and allowed them to walk me inside the building.

Inside, there was a surprise waiting for me. Calgary's finest were hiding like a bunch of vultures waiting for their next victim. The Calgary police took me under their wings. As I was being informed of the charges, the Customs personnel brought all our bags inside and informed me, "We are going to search everything."

My thoughts were that there was nothing in there but my dirty clothes, a few books, and some souvenirs. So why did they need to search it all? It occurred to me they might have seen videos of people donating money to me and suspected I was smuggling millions into Canada. Unbeknownst to them, all that money went towards covering the tour, hotels, and expenses.

I took a quick look outside to see how my friend Gary was doing. While being escorted away in handcuffs, the commanding officer instructed his colleague to seize Gary's phone because I had asked Gary to film the arrest. Gary did not stop recording and did not give his phone to them. I was informed later on that he was heavily interrogated, both in Canada and the United States.

I was denied the opportunity to embrace my wife or greet my children due to being taken to the police cruiser. The people that came to greet me were kept away hundreds of yards away. When I came out, there were police cars hidden behind the building so that no one would see what was going on. So much secrecy and resources were put into arresting a pastor.

They were taking me to Spyhill Detention Centre, and as we traveled along, I reflected on the past few months and the fact that they had been waiting for months to hurt me. The media were furious, and the politicians had their hands tied because I had "escaped their claws," as Marzena put it. Now I was back, and they could reach me again; now they could hurt me again.

I can still remember the relentless criticism I endured about going to the States, being denounced as a coward and traitor. Some people thought I should remain in jail and decline to sign the bail papers. They believed I wanted to escape the prosecution to save my own skin. It is very interesting that those who were so eager to criticize my decisions were the same people who had never been arrested or jailed before for the cause of Christ.

By this point, I already had over 100 court cases, more than 350 citations, tickets, and summons to court under my belt, and this was my 13th or 14th arrest for the cause of Christ, and yet *I* was the bad guy. It's challenging to comprehend the situation unless you've walked in someone else's shoes. If you don't know the whole story, keep quiet and stay humble. When you serve God, you have to get your orders directly from Him; If you don't, you can end up in big trouble.

People may have their own opinions, but you should follow the instructions from your boss, God almighty. One important lesson I learned early in my Christian life is to never change orders in the middle of the battlefield. When enemies surround you, pressure mounts, and the noise of battle grows deafening; it becomes incredibly tempting to listen to deceptive voices urging you to quit or change your path.

Thousands of different ideas flood you from every direction. Do this. Do that. Don't do that. When faced with confusion, I've made it a habit to return to the most recent command I received from the commander-in-chief.

It is very easy to make a mistake under pressure and to change the Lord's orders, believing that it was Him speaking to you. God is not schizophrenic—when He tells you to do something, do not deviate from it to the left or to the right. Stick to the plan. I did not care what others said or thought; I knew what I heard. God told me to go, and that was good enough for me. I obeyed by going, and God blessed my obedience.

Sitting in my solitary confinement, locked up by the evil rulers, I remembered a similar story of a young man who was told to do a specific task. In 1 Kings, chapter 13, the Lord commanded a man of God to go and to give a condemnation for the shameful acts of King Jeroboam. The young man had been given very specific instructions. He did what he was told to do, but not entirely. After he uttered the words from God, the Lord manifested with incredible power, and then the young man was told to go back to where he came from and not to eat and not to drink in that land.

The king saw the power of God: the altar split in half; the ashes fell to the ground, and his hand was paralyzed. The king wanted to give gifts and food to the prophet of God, but the young man refused. This prophet of God had been given his own instructions, and he left to return to his home.

However, on the way back, another older prophet found the young man sitting under an oak tree and told him that he, too, was a prophet and to come with him. The man said, "The Lord's angels told me to take you to my house and to give you something to eat and drink." The prophet from Judah joined him and had a meal and beverages at his place.

It turns out that the old prophet was lying. The young one disobeyed a direct command, and for that, he died. A lion killed him because of his disobedience. The young man of God was supposed to carry his instructions all the way, not just half the way, and for not doing so, he lost his life.

You see, I don't care who comes to me or what title he or she might have. They can use any tactic they want and say, "Thus says the Lord." If what they're saying contradicts my last assignment—my direct order from my King— then I will not listen. I do not want to end up dead, killed by a lion. Listen to the King's voice and when you obey, you will be victorious, and you will live.

In Spyhill, I was searched again. My belt, jacket, shoes, and all other personal things were taken from me. Another mugshot was taken, and off I went to a solitary cell and the concrete bench, which was all too familiar to me by now. Mentally and spiritually, I was ready for the possibility of being confined for weeks or even months. I had a gut feeling that they were scheming to maintain their oppressive hold on me.

After a while, my bail hearing came up. Much to my surprise, I was let go despite facing many criminal charges. I was charged with 1) participating in and officiating an illegal gathering (i.e., church) and 2) not wearing a mask in public. Outside the jail, I found a group of churchgoers camping. They were willing to stay there all night long if need be.

Some carried shofars, and I informed them that I had heard them blowing from inside my cell. They had a piping hot pizza ready for me, as if they anticipated my arrival. What wonderful people. God, you have blessed me with amazing friends. I went home tired but free at last.

Upon my release, I requested my luggage, but the police were clueless about the whereabouts of my belongings. "Where are my computer and luggage?" I asked.

The officers exchanged glances and responded with, "We have no idea."

"So much for police work," I told them. Finding me on the tarmac at the airport was easy for them, but locating my belongings proved to be too difficult for our finest.

The next day, I went on a quest to find my things. It took me some time, but eventually, I found them in the police storage and went to pick them up. Everything was turned upside down and ransacked. The computer was unlocked, and it appeared that they had gained access. I suppose they were intrigued by what I had hidden. But everything looked like it was all there.

The next few weeks were very busy for me. From morning till late at night, I was occupied with sermon preparation, media interviews, and daily meetings. The rallies were going strong; more and more people were joining our cause.

Then came the day of sentencing. Dawid and I had to confront our sentencing after being found guilty. Adam Germain, that crooked judge, would be delivering the court's sentence via Zoom on Webex. We had planned a rally at the entry of the courthouse while we listened via Webex. Many people with signs and banners were there to show their support.

Dawid and I were listening to the verdict. Like an offended toddler, this fake judge ranted for 45 minutes straight. His words stated nothing about the merits of the case. He was disgusted with my tour to the U.S. He talked about my media interviews and my meetings with the politicians. He mentioned my appearance on Fox News. He kept talking about everything I was doing except for the actual law and the alleged "crime."

Everyone was shocked! No one would ever expect something like this to come from a civilized democracy with an independent justice system. It was wrong, and it was illegal. These days, the judges were acting like kings, so the judgment was binding. The government was so fearful of my trips that it issued a ban on me leaving Alberta.

My own province placed me under house arrest as punishment for being well-treated by the American people. We also had to hand over a sum of $50,000. The money was meant to provide food for the poor and homeless individuals we support. We were obligated to provide payment to the very individuals who committed the initial crime. Much to our astonishment, we were given the punishment of completing 120 hours of community service. It turns out that those cruel individuals didn't consider our 22 years of feeding the poor and saving lives to be enough.

We were instructed to perform community service at a ministry or charity approved by the government. The most shocking part of this so-called judgment was the compelled speech sanction. This man ordered us to give a government-approved script every time we spoke in public.

This is the explanation of the ruling and his statement as taken from *Rebel News*, October 15, 2021:

JUDGE'S OUTRAGEOUS RULING IN PASTOR ARTUR CASE

The official written decision from Justice Adam Germain regarding the case of Pastor Artur Pawlowski has been released. The document puts in writing some the bizarre statements from the judge, including his suggestion that sending Pastor Artur back to jail, as requested by prosecutors representing Alberta Health Services, would "make him a martyr" and the script Pastor Artur is compelled to read any time he speaks against the official government narrative surrounding COVID-19.

Describing Pastor Artur's statements to the court as "taunt[ing] me to imprison him," Justice Germain said that the proposed additional 21 days in jail sought by Alberta Health Services would be a "slap on the wrist that will make him a martyr."

The judge further outlined how Pastor Artur, after being found guilty of contempt, went on a speaking tour in the United States.

According to Justice Germain, Pastor Artur "parlayed his title as a pastor and the fact that he had been arrested for holding a church service into a rally cry that attracted like-minded individuals in the United States who also oppose healthcare measures addressed at combatting COVID-19."

Justice Germain also ordered Pastor Artur to condemn his own words, compelling the pastor to effectively denounce himself any time he makes comments on lockdowns, masks, vaccines or any other pandemic-related topic.

Wrote Justice Germain:

The final term of his probation order will be that when he is exercising his right of free speech and speaking against AHS Health Orders and AHS health recommendations, in a public gathering or public forum (including electronic social media); he must indicate in his communications the following:

I am also aware that the views I am expressing to you on this occasion may not be views held by the majority of medical experts in Alberta. While I may disagree with them, I am obliged to inform you that the majority of medical experts favor social distancing, mask-wearing, and avoiding large crowds to reduce the spread of COVID-19. Most medical experts also support participation in a vaccination program unless for a valid religious or medical reason you cannot be vaccinated. Vaccinations have been shown

The Health Inspector (the woman in the center) and various other officers stormed Pastor Artur's church on Easter before he ordered them to "Get Out!" The video of this incident went viral within hours of being posted on social media.

Dawid Pawlowski (Pastor Artur's brother) speaking to the crowd gathered outside the Remand Centre. Ray is standing just to his left.

The Freedom Convoy displays the Canadian flag.

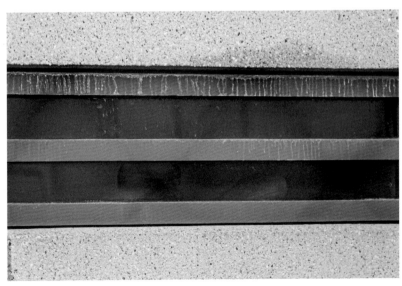

The small sliver of a window at the Remand Centre where Pastor Artur had a distorted view from his cell. Here he is watching the Jericho March, before he was apprehended and taken to the concrete cells.

Pastor Artur being arrested at his home.

Steven Johnston, the Crown Prosecutor.

Dinner with our American friends. The man in the front is Nathan, who hosted Pastor Artur in his home during the tour to America and prophesied over him. Sitting directly behind Nathan are Bo and Sophia Polny.

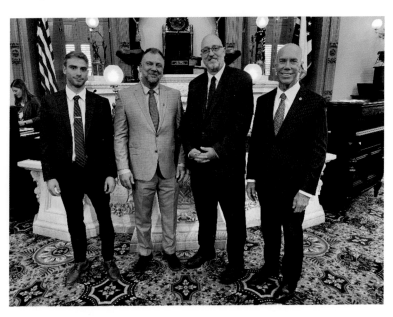

The House floor of the Ohio State House of Representatives where the entire room gave Pastor Artur a standing ovation. Left to right: Nathaniel, Pastor Artur, Ohio State Representative Gary Click (R-Vickery) and Timothy Ginter (Speaker Pro Tempore).

Pastor Artur speaking at the Calgary Rally.

More American friends. Left to right: Chris Green, Marzena, Julie Green, Bo Polny, Pastor Artur, Nathaniel

March for Jesus—Poland

Pastor Artur and Dawid as they are being released from prison; notice they are holding red Bibles which were given to them by the supporters outside. (Remember: The guards refused to give them Bibles while in prison).

Pastor Artur praying at the Calgary Remand Centre.

Dawid (left) and Pastor Artur (center) being arrested on the highway, during the rain.

Ray Friesens and his entire family were present every single day outside of the prison to offer their love and support.

Pastor Artur conducting baptisms in a river in Calgary.

Dawid and Pastor Artur baptize Artur's daughter, Maya Grace, in the river in Calgary.

Pastor Greg Locke was instrumental in securing thousands of people to call and fight. He mobilized these valiant efforts, resulting in what people referred to as the "Artur Pawlowski switchboard."

March for Jesus—Calgary.

Dominion Day, where Pastor Artur delivered a speech in front of the Ottawa Parliament, addressing thousands of people who came to honor that special day.

Positioned in front of one of the multiple signs demonstrating support for Pastor Artur after his highway arrest.

Praying over the grounds of the Alberta Provincial Legislature in a "Call to Repentance" where the ground was anointed.

Dawid being dragged on the highway while being arrested.

Pastor Artur being arrested outside his home.

Inside the Smuggler's Saloon in Coutts, where Pastor Artur delivered a sermon.

Members of the Street Church have been working to feed the homeless and poor three times a week for the past 25 years, as is customary.

Pastor Artur spoke to the national prison during a trip to Barbados.

A high-ranking prison guard, talking with Rob, our Worship Leader. Rob has always been willing to risk his life for our freedom.

With General Michael Flynn and his wife, Lori, at Mar-a-Lago in March 2024.

A crowd gathered outside of the Remand Centre. Pastor Artur's father, Josef, is standing near the fence with his hand raised. This photo was taken at one of the lowest points of Artur's imprisonment, and his wife organized a Jericho March to encourage him.

After the Canadian government officially canceled Christmas, the Street Church held a Christmas celebration. Sadly, this resulted in 15 extra tickets/citations for Pastor Artur!

People coming to offer prayer and support faithfully while Pastor Artur was imprisoned at the Remand Centre.

Pastor Artur's parents, Grace and Josef Pawlowski, celebrating 50 years together.

September 18, 2023, Pastor Artur and Marzena are leaving the courthouse. Because the judge said, "time served," he was leaving as a free man. Someone handed him this stick and told him that God was giving him authority as a Shepherd.

Pastor Artur greets his daughter, Maya Grace, with a big hug shortly after his release from prison.

A warm greeting exchanged between Pastor Artur and his son, Gabriel, after Artur's release from prison.

Pastor Artur with Ezra Levant, a Jewish man and the owner of Rebel News who put the story out. If not for Ezra covering the story, Americans might never have heard about it.

A fist bump with Eric Trump in Miami at a 2023 ReAwaken Tour.

The Pawlowskis, along with Lara and Eric Trump at the ReAwaken Tour in 2023. Eric posted on social media that he considered Pastor Artur's situation in September 2021 as a "true embarrassment to Canada."

A prayer rally being held outside the courthouse in Lethbridge, Alberta as led by Pastor Artur and Marzena.

Nathaniel Pawlowski addresses the European Parliament.

A press conference led by Pastor Artur at the Legislature in Alberta.

Times Square, NYC. Someone prayed and asked God for the ability to let the people know what was happening to Pastor Artur. Suddenly, someone stepped up and donated the funds for this sign to be displayed here!

Even though Canadian officials claimed there were no arrest warrants for Pastor Artur, when he arrived home from America, he was arrested on the airport tarmac.

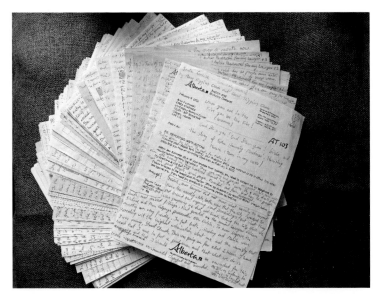

Several times during his imprisonment, Pastor Artur's writing materials were confiscated, along with the daily notes he had recorded. He made use of any available means, such as writing on his prison forms, to record his thoughts and experiences while in custody. A big chunk of them were smuggled out by his lawyers. He received these remaining notes, along with his other belongings, weeks after being released.

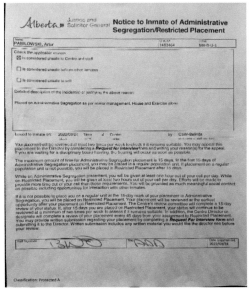

This is the notice used to segregate Pastor Artur into solitary confinement because he was considered "unsafe to Centre and staff."

The Pawlowski Family
(Left to right: Gabriel, Marzena, Pastor Artur, Maya Grace, Nathaniel)

statistically to save lives and to reduce the severity of COVID-19 symptoms.

Discussing any potential violation of Pastor Artur's rights, Justice Germain described pandemic restrictions as "intrusions on personal liberty," but felt that they were not "sacrifices that would offend the Canadian *Charter of Rights and Freedoms* and they are not egregious sacrifices."

Unbelievable! We have seen this in history before. Mao Zedong mandated that those he conquered wear a document around their necks or take the control styles of Saudi Arabia and North Korea. Stalin did it with his famous show trials, where everything was decided before the trial even started.

It did not matter what evidence was provided. The accused by the regime never stood a chance. I remember watching some of them when I was growing up behind the Iron Curtain. I will never forget this one man who was brought to the court in a bed. He was so severely beaten that he could not walk.

At this point in his life, a man who was barely alive was ready to confess to everything. The courts accepted his confession willingly and were satisfied with his explanation of an "accident in jail" where he had somehow slipped and fallen! The courts accepted that as the explanation for the man's bruises, broken teeth, black eyes, and missing fingernails.

The controlling courts have been playing this game for a long time. The East was teaching the West. In the end, they could force a confession out of anyone. Fear and pain were the tactics of the oppressors. It was all a game of illusion. Smokes and screens. Shadows, technicalities, mirrors, and slavery.

> *"The appearance of the law must be upheld—especially when it is being broken."*
> ROSCOE CONKLING

I've seen this well-known saying in action too many times, and it's hard to admit. That is why I love my God so much. He is a just judge, and He hates hypocrisy and corruption. Read what He has to say about crooked judges in Psalms 94:20-22. Proverbs 17:23-28, and Ecclesiastes 3:16-22.

After Justice Germain's remarks, then the sentence came. Unlike any other judge in Canadian history, the judge took action against a private citizen. Here's an excerpt from Rebel News, October 13, 2021, which explains what the judge did.

BIZARRE: JUDGE ORDERS PASTOR ARTUR PAWLOWSKI TO CONDEMN HIMSELF

Justice Adam Germain ordered Pastor Artur Pawlowski to provide the government's narrative to counter any comments the pastor makes about lockdowns, masks, vaccines, or anything else pandemic-related.

Today the judge enforcing Alberta's pandemic lockdown laws sentenced Pastor Artur Pawlowski. His crime? No crime — he simply opened his church during the lockdown.

In a bizarre 40-minute rant, Justice Adam Germain ordered that for the next 18 months, whenever Pastor Artur talks about lockdowns, the pandemic, or vaccines—in tweets, speeches, or media interviews—he must immediately repudiate himself and give the "official" government view condemning himself.

He must argue against himself. He must condemn himself. Or go back to jail.

It's compelled speech, like a Maoist "struggle session" in Communist China. You have to say what the government tells you to say.

(The judge also hit Pastor Artur with $42,000 in fines and another $10,000 for his brother, Dawid.)

Forced speech is unheard of in Canadian law. Even convicted murderers cannot be ordered to apologize for their crimes — and anyway, such a forced apology would be meaningless.

But a convicted pastor must now violate his own conscience and repeat an angry judge's talking points or face prison.

That's the whole point of it: this judge wants Pastor Artur to submit, to acknowledge the government as his master. And if he can't convince Pastor Artur of that voluntarily, he'll force him to say it.

It's like forcing him to kneel. Which the police have already done.

What a disgrace this judge is. Especially to Alberta, whose official motto is "strong and free."

And that's not all. In his 40-minute rant, the judge repeatedly criticized Pastor Artur for talking about civil liberties to the media. He specifically mentioned Pastor Artur's appearance on *Fox News*.

But what does that have to do with allegedly breaking a Canadian law? Nothing. But it has everything to do with politics.

So to stop more media appearances, the judge has ordered Pastor Artur to self-denounce after every public statement.

The judge also raged at Pastor Artur for going on a speaking tour, warning other churches around North America about the threat to civil liberties. So, to stop that, the judge also banned Pastor Artur from leaving the province of Alberta for 18 months.

There is no legal precedent for this; it's completely unconnected to Pastor Artur's alleged lockdown crimes. It's simply a power-mad judge's revenge on Pastor Artur — a blatant attempt to stop him from speaking freely.

This truly is the most absurd, un-Canadian, and clearly illegal court ruling in recent memory. In fact, to find anything like it, one has to look back nearly 90 years to William Aberhart, the former Alberta premier.

Aberhart passed a series of laws called the "*Alberta Press Act*," which forced newspapers to print the government's rebuttal to their own editorials. That laughably illegal law was struck down in 1938 by the Supreme Court, and the *Edmonton Journal*, the newspaper that led the charge against it, won a special Pulitzer Prize for its efforts.

Justice Germain has brought back that illegal law but applied it to just one citizen. Alas, today, the mainstream media are cheering for the censors.

It will probably not surprise you that Justice Adam Germain is a failed Liberal politician who was appointed to the courts by Jean Chretien after he lost his election.

Obviously, Pastor Artur intends to appeal—and obviously, we've got to help him. I just got off the phone with Pastor Artur's top-gun lawyer, Sarah Miller.

We're relieved that Pastor Artur was kept out of jail: Jason Kenney's prosecutors had demanded a 21-day prison term. But Justice Germain is smart enough to know that actually throwing a pastor in prison *again* would have made international headlines *again* — and clearly, that's been on the judge's mind.

But what he's done here — issuing a political self-denunciation order — is just as bad.

Sarah and the rest of Pastor Artur's team are already working on the appeal. I promise to send you a copy of their appeal the moment she files it in court.

I'm glad that Pastor Artur will sleep at home tonight instead of in prison. But the judge's Communist-style sentence must be fought with everything we have.

When the judgment was pronounced, I grabbed the mic and gave a speech outside of that courthouse. "How can I obey such orders?" I made it clear that I would never comply with such cruel and oppressive commands. And if I was to be locked up again, so be it. But they would not win. They could not get away with these draconian orders.

Adhering to those commands would mean admitting their victory and the demise of our democracy. But I knew in my heart that this was not over yet. That we could still fight. That we could push this corruption away.

My brother Dawid spoke after me. He was more direct and precise than me. His less polished attitude came out, and he really wanted the so-called judge to hear his answer. "Judge," he said, "You can shove your order where the sun doesn't shine."

After hearing that, I thought, *we are doomed!* I told the reporters, "That's it, we're going to prison."

But no one came to arrest us that day. A week later, we received the written judgment and were assigned a probation officer. This was a new thing for me, and I did not know what to do, so I called the lawyers to find out our next steps.

I was instructed to hold off until the paperwork came. A probation officer was assigned to us. In our initial discussion, we covered my background, family, and occupation. We were instructed to call back daily for a period of two weeks, which is not out of the ordinary. Then, the real circus sideshow began!

FUTILE ATTEMPTS TO FULFILL THE JUDGE'S ORDERS

First, we were told to look for a charity that would allow us to do the 120 hours of community service work. That was easier said than done. I contacted over a dozen ministries, including the Mustard Seed, Salvation Army, and even the Humane Society; no one would take us in. Some organizations said that they do not take new volunteers because of COVID. Others said that we would need a COVID passport to volunteer. They told me that I needed to be double vaccinated, even to walk dogs and cats!

I called our lawyer. "What do I do?" I asked.

"Well," Sarah replied, "It looks like they have set you up for failure. Keep looking, and we will deal with whatever comes in the courts."

Both Dawid and I kept searching. Finally, we found a ministry called Hope Mission, which was willing to take us in and did not require a communist vaccine passport. We each served for ten hours with them. To my surprise, our probation officer told me and Dawid in the end of November that she would not approve our hours. She was informed that we were engaging in conversations about our ministry on the streets during our designated community hours, and she did not approve.

We entered totally new bully tactics. The Probation Officer also called me during that time and said, "I want to speak with your wife. Give me her telephone number."

I said, "Absolutely not. You are not going to drag my wife and my children into this charade."

She was furious. "You must listen to me!" she yelled. "You must. If I want to talk to your wife, you have to obey me. If not, I will give you a strike."

"Well, you can give me 1000 strikes, but I will not give you my wife's number."

The heated exchange continued: "I will breach you. You will be arrested." She tried to intimidate me.

I said, "No!"

Dawid later informed me that she had also attempted to bully him regarding his wife. Just like me, he stood his ground. One day, my wife came to me and said, "Guess who just called me?"

"Who? I asked.

"Your probation officer."

"What?!" I said. "How did she manage to get your number?"

But then I remembered it would not be too hard. Our numbers were published on our site and not restricted. "What did she want?" I inquired.

"She wanted to talk to me about you, but I said there is nothing to tell her, and I hung up."

"Good for you," I said. I couldn't believe she had the audacity to harass my family members like some sort of sociopath.

Eventually, we found another organization that would take us in. We were required to load and unload food every Tuesday and Friday. Sometimes, it took three hours; sometimes, it took six hours. It went well without any problems, and I completed over 20 hours in December and about 30 hours in January. Before my arrest, I also had six hours in the first week of February.

I was summoned to the probation officer's office one day in December. "You have to wear the mask when you come in, though," she insisted.

"You know I have a medical exemption," I said to her.

She said, "I don't care. When you come in, you have to wear a mask. That is our policy."

"Well, that may be *your* policy, but the law says otherwise. I will not wear a mask."

"Then you will be arrested," she replied.

"If this is the hill you want to die on, then that's fine by me." *What a bully*, I thought to myself. What is wrong with these people? All it takes is a small taste of power over another person for it to corrupt their judgment.

Two weeks later, I walked into her office and was asked to go to a special room, which was divided in half with a table. In the middle was thick glass all the way to the ceiling. My first thought was, *so why do they force people to wear stupid, useless masks on their faces if they have this crazy setup?* It must be a power trip. Most people in this kind of situation are terrified of the probation officers because they could throw them in prison for any little reason. So most just bite their tongues and do their best to endure this abuse of power.

The probation officer walked into the room wearing her mask. She looked at me with disgust when she realized I had no mask on. She sat down, opened her binder, and looked through the file. "I see you paid the fees and penalty," she said.

"Yes, I did," I replied. As you remember, we were ordered to pay the AHS communist party of Alberta a considerable sum of money. We could have chosen to pay them $500 per month, but they insisted on a complete house viewing and inspection of our home and possessions. They wanted to know what we owned, how many vehicles we had, and disclosure of our assets—couches, TVs, chairs, tables, clothes, absolutely everything. At the time, my wife said, "This is total insanity. Absolutely not, no way. I do not want those wicked people snooping in my house and in my bedroom." So we decided to raise the money to pay the fine.

Meanwhile, the judge promptly suspended the compelled speech sanction and travel ban, deeming them unconstitutional. The sentences were temporarily suspended for the Court of Appeal judges to review the case during the appeal process coming in a few months. Now, here in the office with my Probation Officer, she had no idea that this order had been struck down.

As she was looking through my papers, she said, "You know you are not allowed to travel."

"What?" I said. "I am allowed to travel. I just came back from Ontario." She gave me a look like she was staring at a monster.

"Look here—it says you are not allowed to travel."

"I am allowed to travel—"

She interrupted me saying, "But it says here you are not allowed to travel!" It's shocking to discover that someone with authority could imprison me and was playing a twisted game.

I told her, "A few weeks ago, a judge from the court of appeal said that I may travel. Are you not getting updates on your clients?"

"Here, it says you cannot."

"Well then, your paper is wrong. Do your job properly."

She jumped up from her chair. "So, I don't know how to do my job?!"

"Obviously not," I replied. "The appeal judge stayed the order, and you still hold me to it? Do your job."

She sat down, and I could tell she was completely confused. She was lazy and had not done her job. Despite the files not being updated for weeks, she continued to fulfill previous orders. She knew she messed up. She jumped again from her chair behind the thick glass wall and said, "We are done for today."

Right before I departed, I handed her an invitation to our Christmas festival happening soon. She stood up and yelled, "Take your propaganda from here and go before I call the police."

"It is not propaganda; it is an invitation to a Christmas celebration. The only propaganda I see here comes from you." And with that, I left.

Our relationship was fiery. She tried to bully me, and I am sure she got away with it with others, but I would not allow her. I told her that I was not her slave to be treated in such a way. Just over a month later, she sought revenge and confronted me multiple times for various reasons. They were constructing the gallows specifically for me, and it was pretty evident.

CHAPTER FIFTEEN

MY VISIT TO JASON COPPING'S HOUSE

ON JANUARY 1st, 2022, I received a call asking me to participate in a peaceful vigil outside the home of Jason Copping, Alberta's Minister of Health. I was invited to ensure peace as some hot-headed individuals were planning to protest on the Minister's private property. Of course, that was a terrible idea and would only give more excuses for the corrupt, totalitarian regime to crack down even more on the peaceful protests.

Along with my brother, Dawid, and my son, Nathaniel, I decided to attend. After almost two years of lockdowns, mandates, and government infringement on people's rights, many people had become frustrated with politicians hiding behind the computer screens or remaining inside buildings without access to their constituents. So the idea was that if we couldn't see them inside their offices and government buildings, we would try to reason with them outside their homes. The politicians were violating the law without any accountability, and that needed to be addressed.

When we arrived, there was already a group of people gathered about a block away from the Minister's house. We parked the car and joined the group, heading towards Copping's house. The property was in a cul-de-sac neighborhood, with only one way in and one way out. People positioned themselves in front of the house and began to chant the standard slogans. "My body, my choice! No vaccine passports! Leave our children alone!"

You see, Jason Copping was responsible for masking our children and pushing the Communist/Nazi vaccine passport that was absolutely destroying our society physically and economically. In the crowd, some individuals believed it was a great idea to stand on the Minister's front lawn. Of course, that would be against the law, and I told people not to do it. "Do not give those villains anything," I said. "They will use this against us and the movement. The protest/vigil has to be done peacefully and lawfully."

Thank God people listened, and everyone remained on the public road and sidewalk. There was a complete absence of a police presence, which surprised me. When I looked at the house's window, I saw someone peeking through, which confirmed that someone was inside.

A few minutes later, we noticed a police helicopter circling around us. The police helicopter remained with us for another half hour, and the whole protest concluded within about 45 minutes. No police cruisers, no incidents, all peaceful. As we headed back to our parked cars, we saw police vehicles approaching from all sides. First, they blocked one road and then, with a dozen police cruisers, blocked the other end of the street. They later referred to this as a "routine check stop." Every vehicle was stopped and checked for impaired driving.

Can you imagine? A check stop? Seriously? Oh, how low the Police Department had fallen, having to use such tactics. When our turn came to be stopped, Dawid opened the window and asked what they wanted. An officer replied that this was a random check stop and they were looking for impaired drivers.

Dawid started a conversation with an officer, and I stepped out of the car. I began to challenge the officers, telling them they had become a huge disgrace to the badge and to the uniform. "How can you, with a clean conscience, pretend that this is a random check stop?" I encouraged them to admit they were there because some corrupt politicians had asked them to harass and intimidate law-abiding citizens. We were people who came to peacefully express our dissatisfaction with this government's overreach. It was a very intense moment. They were not happy with what I was saying.

At the same time, my brother had to blow into a breathalyzer. "What are you doing?" I asked them. "More and more, you look like the Gestapo of old. Think people! Is your salary or your pension worth doing this to your own neighbors?"

It seems like they have a dislike for thinking and just want to follow orders. To them, it was obvious: One of their own—the "SS-Gruppenführer" (SS-Group leader)—needed support, and they were more than glad to give it to him. They were ready to hurt the innocent to please their masters. My trying to reason with them meant absolutely nothing. To them, it did not matter that Copping and the rest of his party had been destroying us for the past two years. It was the never-ending story of one law for them, the elites, and one law for the rest of us, the slaves.

Eventually, Dawid was asked to drive away, so I went back inside the vehicle, and we took off. "Can you believe this?" I said to my son and my brother. "What a bunch of liars."

The only purpose of this charade was to check the driver's licenses of everyone attending and to intimidate those who dared to come. It was totally the "Crown shirts" of Kenney" government. We had been driving for around five minutes when I suddenly saw flashing lights in our rearview mirror. *Here we go again,* I thought to myself. There were a few police cruisers behind us. Under a bridge, we parked our car alongside a hectic road that merges with the highway.

An officer approached Dawid's window, still holding his telephone and talking to someone on the other line. When the officer was done, he asked my brother to step out of the vehicle; Dawid obeyed the order. I stepped out of the car as well with the camera, recording everything that was happening. Nathaniel was also recording the incident on his telephone.

Nathaniel asked the officer as they were escorting his uncle to the cruiser, "Why is he being arrested? What are you arresting him for?" He repeated it again.

With a puzzled look, the officer said, "Suspicion of breach." Wow! They were told to arrest us, but they had no idea why! It was apparent that the order was coming from the politicians. Possibly the very one whose house we were protesting at. Obviously, we had struck a chord.

When corrupt authorities feel that they might be exposed, their natural instinct is to strike as hard as they can. They cannot help it. Just like a cornered rat will bite, it is just in their DNA. Their biggest fear is being revealed for who they truly are.

The officer on my side was also talking with someone on his radio. He stopped talking, listened for a while, and asked, "Him too?" while pointing to me. I could tell he received his instructions by the look on his face while waiting for a response. It became clear I was to be arrested as well. He moved towards me and declared, "You are under arrest!" Two more officers approached me.

Abundant snowfall and persistent cold temperatures in Calgary marked January 1st, 2022. We were all standing in deep snow in the ditch on the side of a busy road. I had repeatedly informed the police that they could contact my lawyers if they wished to arrest me, and I would willingly surrender. There was absolutely no need for these theatrics and the enormous use of unnecessary force. My thoughts were: *Call us and I will walk into the police station, and we will deal with the issues. But if you insist on this craziness with excessive force, with a S.W.A.T.-team-style takedown, you will have to carry me to the car! I have zero record of any violence, but if you want to do it the Nazi way, then you will have to go all the way!*

One had to wonder what they were accomplishing by doing it this way. Was it scare tactics? Shock effect? Were they sending a message to the rest of the population that said, "Look what we can do with those who disagree with us?" Perhaps.

I can't understand why the local Police Department would be willing to take part in such an injustice. Supposedly, all those arrests, tickets, and court proceedings were carried out for our own protection. However, safety meant nothing to them. This arrest was done in a very unsafe way. In the middle of the highway with speeding cars, by a merging road, and in the middle of the snow. Does this sound safe to you? It had the look of a theatre right out of Nazi Germany's early 30s. Someone must have been studying the tactics of those old boys.

Dawid was already handcuffed and placed in a police car, and now it was my turn. I thought to myself, *You want drama? I'll give you drama. Do you want visual effects? Well, here it comes*, and I went to my knees, dropping deep into the snow. Once again, the officers were caught off guard. The arrest was not going according to their plan.

One officer raised his hands up and dropped them down in a melodramatic gesture of resignation. His partner became enraged and forcefully grabbed my hands, intending to handcuff them from behind. He did this so aggressively that he pushed my entire body straight into the snow. That day, I was wearing a heavy winter jacket that my wife had reminded me to put on just before I left the house. Laying on my stomach in the snow, the hood of the jacket fell all the way forward, covering my entire head. It looked like my whole head and face was in the middle of the pile of snow, which I'm sure was quite comical to onlookers.

I heard the officers on either side of me talking. "What do we do now?" one of them asked.

"You want to arrest me? Then you'll have to carry me!" I made it clear to them that I was determined to maintain peaceful non-compliance and complete non-cooperation throughout the arrest.

They tried their best to carry me through the snow, but my 100 kilograms of weight was a bit too much for one of them. He released his grip on me and toppled onto the snow, right by my side. This infuriated them even more. The poor fella covered with snow finally stood up again and, determined to finish the job, dragged me to the police cruiser.

One looked at the other and said, "Now, what do we do? We will need to wait for the van to come and pick him up." The one who had some anger issues would have none of that idea. He was very determined to squeeze me into his little cruiser. He grabbed my jacket with the force of a madman and yanked me away from the door. They joined forces to forcefully stuff me into the police car after opening the door. Naturally, I was experiencing significant pain since I was handcuffed, and I knew that if I did not help them out, they would break either my hand, arm, or leg. The anger completely blinded one of those officers. He was pushing me inside the car with such force and hate that it was just a matter of time until he did something stupid!

With my assistance, I successfully maneuvered my limbs into the small space, narrowly avoiding having the car doors slam on my head and legs. *My goodness,* I thought, *he would actually break my legs if I was not fast enough to move them aside.*

Once inside the car, the officers began to repeatedly ask me questions—which I refused to answer. In Canada, if you're arrested, you have the right to stay silent, and anything you say can be used against you in court. I chose to remain silent until I could consult with my lawyer. That angered the angry officer even more. He looked at his partner and said, "Let's put another charge on him: obstruction of justice!"

What a perverted situation, I thought. The officers, who should represent the public, pretend to enforce the law but have no issue breaking it by cooking up charges and making stuff up! That was not a big deal to them. After all, they were the law, right? So, let's just throw another charge. Why not? Why not bring kidnapping or drug trafficking while we are at it? How could making stuff up be referred to as law "enforcement?"

Ultimately, I was charged with mischief, obstruction of justice, and a breach of the Rooke order. And off we went to the Spyhill Detention Centre. By now, this had become the story of my life. Things happen to me that do not happen to others. There, I was searched thoroughly and with extreme dedication. The officer behind the Processing counter confiscated my personal belongings, sealed them in a bag, and processed me again.

When I was done, I was taken to my designated cell for the night. It was totally concrete (floor and bench) with a sink and an attached toilet. I felt thankful for being appropriately dressed in warm socks and insulated pants. As I entered the cell, the heavy metal door slammed with a loud bang behind me.

I knew that Dawid was probably going through the same ordeal somewhere nearby. I was allowed to make my phone call to the lawyer, and then I waited for the bail hearing. Some time passed, and I was taken to the fingerprinting room, where my fingerprints were placed on yet another piece of paper. *How many sets of fingerprints do these people need?* I thought. Yet another mug shot was taken and off I went back to my dungeon. Several hours later, both Dawid and I were led to a room with a computer screen for our bail hearing.

We were eventually released, but with conditions that prohibited us from going to the Minister's house and required us to "keep the peace and be of good behavior," whatever that meant. It turned out that the charge of obstruction of justice had *miraculously* disappeared. I'm guessing it was just part of the game of pure intimidation—piling up charges to scare me.

There was no worry; we had no intention of going back to that guy's house, anyway. We were not the organizers of the protest, and we had gone to ensure it remained lawful and peaceful. And to try and prevent something that might backfire on the entire movement. Over the following weeks, life went back to normal with preaching, Street Church, feeding the hungry, etc.

A COLD, COLD CHRISTMAS 2021

When I was asked to speak at the "Worldwide Rally," I used the platform to introduce the term "Solidarity" and its 21 demands to the Canadian audience. Despite the freezing temperatures, thousands of people gathered in Calgary's Millennium Park, demonstrating their resilience and passion.

The event organizer introduced me by saying, "This man requires no introduction. He has worked tirelessly and without compromise to awaken the lions in Canada and around the world. Please give a welcome to Pastor Art the Lion Pawlowski. It was an amazing experience to see and hear the outpouring of support from thousands of Canadians for Freedom.

As I thanked everyone for coming, I said, "I know it is cold. But after all, this is Canada!" Then I began my speech, which went like this:

I mean, if you want your rights back. If you want your freedom back, you have to fight for it as hard as you can. Here is what our Prime Minister once said because the one that we have right now is not our Prime Minister. Here is what a real Prime Minister, John G. Diefenbaker, said: "You can't stand up for Canada with a banana for a backbone." We have been lied to for too long!

All truth passes through three stages, according to Arthur Schopenhauer. First, it is ridiculed. Second, it is violently opposed. Third, it is accepted as being self-evident.

We have been intimidated and harassed for too long! We have been excluded from the decisions that are impacting and affecting our lives and the lives of our loved ones for too long!

We have been treated without justice and the rule of law for too long! We have been cheated and robbed for too long! We want our resources, our lives, and our freedoms! We are done asking for permission on how we are to live our lives! We want Canada back! We demand our country back!

Some say to me: Why are you involving yourself in the fight for freedom? Why not just stick with the Gospel and the Church? Here is my answer, which comes from the Bible:

> *Learn to do good; seek justice, correct oppression; bring justice to the fatherless; plead the widow's cause.*
>
> ISAIAH 1:17

As Christians, we can do no other! When we see evil, injustice, abuse of power, and lawlessness. We have to speak! We have to act! This is our Christian duty! Coming to the rallies, I have heard hundreds of you asking me a simple question! What now? What is the next step?

The politicians have betrayed us! The clergymen have abandoned us! The media is manipulating us, and the professors and teachers have been brainwashing us! We have corrupted courts, and the elections have been stolen from us! Medical personnel want to hurt us and our children! The whole system is rotten and rigged!

What can we, the free Canadians, do? What are we to do? We will create our own system outside their corrupt agenda—a movement that will not be controlled by the globalist devils—grassroots! Our own government of the people, by the people, for the people, and God in the middle!

With His law and order! With His justice, we will not lose!

We want our voice back! We are nobody's slaves! We are Canadians! We want servants in the Parliament and legislatures and city halls, NOT tyrants! Tyrants need to GO!

> *I am Canadian, a free Canadian, free to speak without*
> *fear, free to worship God in my own way, free to stand*
> *for what I think right, free to oppose what I believe*
> *wrong, free to choose those who govern my country.*
> *This heritage of freedom I pledge to uphold for myself*
> *and all mankind.*
>
> JOHN DIEFENBAKER, CANADIAN HOUSE OF COMMONS
> DEBATES, JULY 1, 1960

People cheered, clapped, and loved the message. A few men grabbed the banner that Marta had painted by hand, and we presented that to the people! It was like the roar of a thousand lions! It was beautiful! I continued to explain what solidarity meant:

Here, today I present to you, our own Canadian Solidarity Movement! I grew up under the boots of the Soviets, behind the Iron Curtain, and I am telling you that in 1981, when people said, "We are not in this together with the corrupted government officials; we are in Solidarity!" [I pointed to the thousands of people gathered in the park together as people cheered even more!]

And it is time! It is time to create our own society outside of their corrupted system! Where we will work with each other. Where we will hire and support each other.

Here is the list of the 21 demands that we want from our servants/politicians who have apparently forgotten why they have been hired by us!

1. No unlegislated or unconstitutional mandates or laws.
2. No compelled, coerced, forced, or uniformed medical procedures.
3. No lockdowns or mandated public measures.

4. No censorship or de-platforming of free speech is imposed by any platform or government.

5. No government-owned or government-funded media. All media should be independently owned and operated away from government influence.

6. Democratically elected judges separate from the government.

7. Referendums on key issues.

8. The right to recall politicians and judges. No lifetime appointments.

9. Audited paper ballot elections using picture identification to verify voter eligibility without mail-in ballots or electronic tabulators.

10. Local police leadership selection with a right to recall.

11. Open public debate without censorship.

12. No taxation without representation. Transparent audits of taxation funds and allocations.

13. Education reform.

14. Recognize parental authority in ALL matters and in particular matters of education and medical treatment. Reform government overreach into the family sphere.

15. Sovereignty over environmental regulations. Reform environmental policies toward actionable and measurable results.

16. Sovereignty over firearms rights. Reform gun control to respect the use and ownership of firearms, including the symbolic deterrence from both foreign and domestic threats.

17. Sovereign local tax collection that stimulates both corporate and private growth.

18. Restitution or monetary compensation for those who have been subjected to illegal COVID mandates.

19. No citizen should be restricted from any place, activity, education, or livelihood because of government-imposed restrictions or medical mandates that may be imposed on them or their families.
20. We want amendments to the Constitution of Canada to prevent the future abuse of power by elected and non-elected individuals.
21. Pastors, clergy, and religious leaders should be free to perform their duties free from government interference.

We have to unite. We have to stand up and stand warm!

People began to yell, "Solidarity! Solidarity! Solidarity!" And it felt good to hear so many excited about taking back their country from the hands of the communists! The movement was growing slowly. Each day, the number of people signing up for memberships kept growing.

Following our example, Australia started its own solidarity movement, and the United States wanted to join, as well. Once again, the force that brought down communism in the 1980s was emerging in Western countries. A growing number of individuals acknowledged that we're confronting a sick combination of communism/socialism and fascism.

JANUARY 8, 2022, CITY HALL SPEECH, CALGARY!

Every week, we gathered to oppose the regime and to educate the public about the truth behind what was going on. We were no longer just a few. We were now in the thousands strong. Here is what I said:

Time to push as hard as we can! Lions, do not break the line! They, the evil politicians murdering doctors and lying propaganda media, have been destroying our families, businesses, our education, and our way of life for two years now! It is time to push back!

The same lies! The same fear! The same Nazi/Communist tactics. No real science! No Facts! Truth is not allowed! Propaganda chasing propaganda! They say that the problem and the risk are so huge that they have to remind us about it every single hour! A virus so deadly that if it was not for their fear-mongering, no one would even notice that the problem even exists! Two years of abuse of power! Two years of hypocrisy! One law for them and one law for us! Segregation, discrimination, and lawlessness! Two years of destruction and lack of accountability! Terror and misinformation! Punishment for those who ask questions and dare to challenge the government's lie!

Why? Because they know that there is no real pandemic, no real emergency, and the jab has caused more health issues than all the cases of flu combined! By now, everyone with a brain knows that! Their canceling our ability to provide for our loved ones is an open attack against Canadian citizens!

Forcing their deadly agenda on the rest of us is simply treason! They all should be charged with crimes against humanity! Nuremberg Trials are needed more than ever!

Here is what Benjamin B. Ferencz, who served as both investigator and prosecutor during the Nuremberg War Crimes trials, said: "Nuremberg taught me that creating a world of tolerance and compassion would be a long and arduous task. And I also learned that if we did not devote ourselves to developing effective world law, the same cruel mentality that made the Holocaust possible might one day destroy the entire human race."

We are witnessing a repetition of history! Today's psychopaths like Jason Kenney, Deena Hinshaw, Justin Trudeau, Doug Ford, or Teresa Tam are just following their heroes of the past!

Here is what one of them, their hero, Hermann Goring, second in command after Hitler, said during the Nuremberg trials:

> *Why, of course, the people don't want war...But after all, it's the leaders of the country who determine the policy, and it's always a simple matter to drag the people along whether it's a democracy, a fascist dictatorship, or a parliament, or a communist dictatorship. Voice or no voice, the people can always be brought to the bidding of the leaders. That is easy. All you have to do is tell them they are being attacked, and denounce the pacifists for lack of patriotism, and exposing the country to greater danger. It works the same in any country.*
> HERMANN GORING, *GERMANY REBORN*

Goring also wrote, "Education is dangerous - every educated person is a future enemy."

By attacking our humanity, love, charity, faith, and families, they have proven to be unfit to govern us free Canadians, and they immediately should be removed from power!

Therefore, every order that comes from those traitors' mouths should be ignored, opposed, challenged, and fought against to the fullest of the Law! They, the elected and unelected villains and traitors, should be brought before a people's tribunal charged with treason! They should never again be able to run for public office. They have to resign!

However, until then, it is our duty as true Canadians to stay strong in our beliefs! To be faithful to the Canadian Constitution and to our own Charter of Rights and Freedoms! True to our convictions! Free to worship our God in our own way! Free to stand up against this great evil that we see today! Free to oppose those who have elevated themselves above those who elected them!

Keep our right to live without fear and free from lies implemented by those corrupted, so-called representatives!

We make this pledge, so help us, God Almighty!

This is our heritage! This is our country! This is our land!

Those are our children! Canadian children are worth fighting for!

Be blessed, Canadian lions!

LEDUC AND THE NEXT ARREST!

For the past few years, if I was available, I had been attending many rallies, protests, and vigils. I always did my best to attend and support the local freedom fighters all over our beautiful nation. So, when I was invited to participate in the rally in Leduc, I did not hesitate. My wife and I packed our van with solidarity banners, T-shirts, and hoodies and went to Leduc. The three-hour drive from Calgary to the rally was uneventful. I was asked to come and address the crowd that gathered to hear us speak.

God had deposited a few things on my heart into my spirit. After the speeches, we had a great time with the people from that city and surrounding areas. It was so good to be with the people who loved their nation. People from the rural areas were so different and down-to-earth in comparison to the city folk.

Shortly after we left, I noticed a police vehicle flashing its lights behind us. This time, it was an RCMP cruiser. Initially, I thought I might be going too fast, but the speedometer proved otherwise. I turned to my wife and asked, "Did I take a wrong turn?"

She looked as puzzled as I was. I said, "Start recording; this doesn't look right."

Two officers stepped out, and one went to my right on the passenger side and another one approached my window. For precautionary measures, I began recording as well and opened the window. The officer informed me that I had a warrant out for my arrest, and to step out of the vehicle.

Here we go again, I thought and handed my cell phone to my wife. I stepped out of the van, but to my shock, the officer was actually very respectful and polite. I was expecting him to put handcuffs on me, but he did not. He asked me to go to the police cruiser. He was not pushing me around or treating me like a terrorist. There was no "walk faster" power trip attitude. That was a big difference from the treatment I would have generally experienced from the Calgary police.

I must confess, this was a new experience for me, but I enjoyed it. No drama, no theatrical show of power. Those guys were the real police officers not just the muscle for the government mafia. I walked to the car where I was searched. The officer opened the door, and I stepped inside the cruiser.

The officers explained that there was a warrant for my arrest from December 20th, 2021, for "disturbing the peace" and two other undisclosed charges. They were unable to explain the other charges when I asked them. Additionally, I questioned why they chose not to handcuff me and simply guided me to the car. "What for?" one of them answered. "You're not running away! The charges are not dangerous. They are minor, and there was no need for the cuffs."

Wow, I thought. *I think I just met some genuine peace officers, not some kind of robot individuals obsessed with power.* It was obvious that the Calgary RoboCop's had a personal agenda. There was a vengeance that they were determined to implement. Someone was telling them to treat me in such a hostile way. I had a feeling that sooner or later, we would find out who was behind this abuse of power. And also we would come to know who was wasting taxpayer money on their own personal war against me.

But for the time being, I was locked inside an RCMP police car. The officers phoned for instructions on how to proceed with me, and were advised to fill out a "promise to appear" document for the court and then release me. Twenty minutes later, I was back on my way to Calgary. All along the way home, I tried to remember what I had done on December 20, 2021, which would warrant three charges and *another* court trial.

Marzena called Dawid to check my social media page and see what happened that day. BINGO! He found it. I was genuinely surprised when he revealed that it was the day I went to retrieve a registered letter from a Canada Post Office. I could not believe it! That was the day *I* was discriminated against. Even though they were the culprits who stole my mail and wouldn't give it back, I was now being portrayed as guilty?

It turned out I had been charged with a criminal offense of disturbing the peace, trespassing, and not wearing a mask. The trespass notice was actually given to me on the 21st, not the 20th, but it seems like they disregarded that small detail. Evidently, they found three charges to be more appealing than two.

A friend of mine, who was an ex-police officer, watched the video of the post office incident and said, "Art, I was a police officer for many years, and this is not disrupting the peace. It's far from it. They are making this stuff up, plus they know that you have a medical exemption and you do not have to wear a mask. There is no other way to put what is happening. This is a clear case of police harassment. Someone simply wants to silence you and is using the court system to achieve that."

We didn't get home until it was very late. In just a few hours, we had a church service scheduled and, after that, a big rally. On Sunday, I was invited to speak at a rally in Okotoks. Then, in the evening, I had a meeting with a few politicians who were concerned about what was going on in our province, just like me. It looked like it was going to be a busy weekend.

Then came the Great Canadian Awakening: The truck convoy!

Be strong and courageous. Do
not be afraid or terrified
because of them, for the Lord
your God goes with you; he
will never leave you nor
forsake you.

Deuteronomy 31:6

CHAPTER SIXTEEN
A COSTLY SPEECH

IN 2022, the organizer of the Alberta Convoy contacted me, requesting that I provide food for the convoy as it made its way from various locations in British Columbia and Alberta to Ottawa. He also asked me if I could perform a church service with an official blessing. The convoy was scheduled to arrive around 9-10 p.m. on Sunday night.

It was a very busy Sunday. First, we cooked food for the homeless at Street Church. People loaded the trucks and fed them in front of Calgary City Hall. Then, the preparation, cooking, and loading started for the truckers. I was so thankful for the amazing volunteers that God had provided. They were truly the best of the best. Marzena made an amazing chili and hot tea for our Canadian heroes. On top of that, we had tons of other items for them to take on their journey. We arrived a little after 8:00 p.m., and there was already a big crowd waiting in anticipation of the trucker's arrival. The air was electric; people were so excited to welcome their heroes. Hope had entered their hearts.

The truckers were heading to Ottawa to fight against the medical tyranny. The support for this freedom convoy was demonstrated by thousands of people. There was food and singing. People were so encouraged, and many came to thank us for what we were doing.

The day ended very late. I was back at home very late in the night and just a few hours later, we went back for the church service and a benediction to send off the truckers on their way to Ottawa. Early in the morning, we were greeted by a parade of trucks, RV's and other cars. They drove with their vehicles decked out with freedom signs, Canadian flags, and other symbols of freedom. It was wonderful!

Hundreds of people were standing with their flags and signs on the side of the road. Some were on the grass, and others on the sidewalks. Anyone with eyes could clearly see that this had united the hearts of Canadians. I gave the people gathered my blessings and prayed with them.

As the convoy was driving away to Ottawa, many were crying with tears of joy that someone was willing to fight for them and their loved ones. Many of my friends there were going with them. It was indeed a family on the move. All were going to the capital to remind the politicians that they were supposed to work for us and protect our rights.

Everyone could feel the momentum building, including the corrupt politicians. Thousands of Canadians, in solidarity, were rising up for the future of their children. Of course, the wannabe tyrant

Justin Trudeau started his own campaign of smears and lies. He was already calling the truckers anti-Semites, racists, and homophobes.

Trudeau referred to this group as a "small fringe minority" that must be stopped because they do not represent "real Canadians." In his opinion, these diligent Canadians were classified as terrorists. The convoy went to Ottawa, and we, in solidarity with them, had the biggest rally in Calgary. About 20,000 people came to stand together against tyranny.

WE MUST NOT BOW TO EVIL

People often ask why not simply bow before the Pharaohs of today. Why stir the pot? It would be a lot easier to just obey and be done with it. You may remember the story from the Book of Esther, where Haman was elevated to the highest position in the Kingdom of Persia. The orders from the king were very clear. Everyone was commanded to bow before that man; Haman and everyone did because they thought, *why risk our lives and provoke the evil to anger? Let's just remain in the shadow of conformity and blind obedience. Hopefully, the evil will go away and leave us be.*

The problem with this thinking is that **evil never goes away.** It simply cannot because that's not the nature of evil! Just like a hungry bear or a pack of wolves, it will come back after it tastes human flesh. Once it smells and tastes the sweetness of blood, it will always thirst for more. It will keep hunting humans unless someone stops it. There's absolutely no other way.

Evil is like a cancer that spreads everywhere. First, it starts small. Then it gets a taste of men's flesh, then moves on to the other parts of the body until it devours everything, eventually killing the very one that is feeding it. Just like we are observing today, where the politicians and the bureaucrats are literally murdering and destroying the very people who have elected them and pay their salaries.

They need to be stopped—with non-compliance, peaceful resistance to something or someone that is evil, just like Mordecai did. The orders from the king were unambiguous; they were supposed to bow before Haman. And everyone did. But Mordecai chose not to follow the King's command, which contradicted his values. He would not bow before the devil or his minions. The good and righteous never submit to evil and corruption.

Yes, Mordecai was risking his life by disobeying King Ahasuerus' command. However, Mordecai knew that his chances of survival were better by remaining clean in God's sight than by obeying mere men—even those as powerful as the sin-contaminated king. Haman represented perversion and wickedness, i.e., the devil.

Good men do not worship the devil and definitely do not bow to him. The heart of an evil man is filled with hate, and one cannot bargain with hate. You cannot make a deal with cancer. Haman's heart was filled with hate towards the children of God. He was thirsty for blood and filled with greed and power-hungry. Nothing could hide or even change his desire. He was hunting to kill.

God was hunting for someone, looking for someone who would stand up against wickedness. Someone who loved God more than they feared for their own life. Later in the passage, Mordecai says to Esther:

> *For if you remain silent at this time, relief and deliverance for the Jews will arise from another place, but you and your father's family will perish. And who*

> *knows but that you have come to your royal position for such a time as this?*
>
> ESTHER 4:14

In other words, if you do not do what is right, God will raise another, but you will miss your blessings.

One time, God spoke to me when I was struggling with my own fears. The attack was very heavy; I had no more money to fight the corrupt officials. Evil surrounded me on all sides, and I had moments of doubt. I was almost ready to throw in the towel—to quit.

While feeding thousands of poor people on the streets of our cities, I had to work in construction just to earn enough to pay for utilities. One trial after another, the bills kept piling up on me like a relentless wave. During that time, God gave me a vision.

I saw a man hiding in a cave and knew immediately who he was. This was Elijah from the story in 1 Kings, chapter 19. He was hiding and terrified. I could see the fear in this man. His fate was sealed.

Then God spoke to me: "When you start running in fear, you will be running for the rest of your life, and I will not be able to use you. I will have to replace you with another, and he will do what I ask him to do."

The fear of those words entered my heart so that I could feel it in my entire being. I was shaken. God's words shook me like never before and never since in my entire life. I said to the one who spoke to me, "Please do not replace me with another. I will continue to fight! I will not quit. Just give me the strength to keep going."

It was at that moment I understood nothing was sadder than a man missing his destiny. I always knew in my heart that this was my true calling; I just had to persevere and not give up. After all, in our ministry at Street Church, we had a motto: "Quitters never win.

Winners never quit!" I reminded myself that my enemies don't control my destiny; it's my God's guidance that matters. I decided that in my life, He would always have the final say!

ANOTHER RALLY, ANOTHER ADDRESS TO THE PEOPLE

In Calgary, we had another big rally. Thousands of patriotic Canadians came with their families and friends in an open act of defiance against the lawlessness in the land. I was able to address the crowd. Here are some of the things I said:

I've never seen a bigger pride of lions than the one I am seeing right now! We have been plowing for two years! We have been removing the stones for two years! We have been putting the seeds of freedom into the ground and it was hard. Sometimes, it was just a few of us, but now the lions have been awakened! And now, do not dare quit! We have the momentum! We have the wind in our sails! This is our time!

We have a straightforward message to the villains! Those wanna-be tyrants. To Trudeau! To Kenney! Here is the message: Back off or else! There has come a time when the men and women—the lions and lionesses—will take back what is rightfully theirs! This is our nation! This is our country!

[While pointing to the children by the platform] These are our children! Those are Canadian children! When they came for our little ones, when they came for our food supply, they crossed the line. Now we remember that it was them that did this to us! Do not

forget their names! There will come a time when, in Solidarity together, we will gain the power back.

We must remember the Kenneys of today! We have to remember the Hinshaws of today! We have to remember the Chiefs of Police of today. And say to them: Now it is your turn to go to jail! Now, it is your turn to sleep on concrete! Now, it is your turn to be criminally charged for what you have done to us... But the traitors hate that!

We are being treated like the Jews during the Nazi era! Like the blacks during the Civil Rights Movement! They arrest us and ticket us! Harass us and prosecute us! You know what that tells me? That tells me that they are scared! That tells me that we are winning! That tells me that the hyaenas are on the run! Because there is the biggest pride of Lions that is coming after them! So, my Canadian Lions, keep roaring! And don't you dare stop! Because we have already won! Be blessed!

People were cheering and clapping! It was great to witness such a passionate gathering of Canadians! We were encouraged, and we marched through downtown with the solidarity banners leading the way. At the end of the march, there was a dancing party on the streets that lasted for about 20 minutes. It was truly a good day, and it ended without any problems. Throughout the entire gathering, the police were very accommodating, leading the march and securing the roads.

The next rally was as big as the one the week before. Canada was getting its momentum. The eyes of the world were on the truckers in Ottawa, and it was putting pressure on the politicians. Trudeau was hiding in an undisclosed location.

He was elected only because of his father's name and money, with no substance of his own. After insulting Canadians and threatening them with the use of force, he hid himself somewhere, terrified to talk to his own citizens.

The convoy had triggered other countries to rise; about 40 of them had joined the Canadian fight for freedom. A few politicians yielded to the collective pressure of Canadians standing together. The Premier of Saskatchewan declared he was going to relax the mandates. Alberta's Premier stated his intention to possibly follow suit. We began to see the light in this very dark tunnel.

THE SPEECH THAT PUT ME IN PRISON!

The Freedom Convoy was created to protest vaccine mandates for truckers crossing the United States border and traveling across Canada. But it later evolved into a protest about COVID-19 mandates in general. Beginning in January 2022, thousands of vehicles formed convoys from several points and traversed Canadian provinces before converging on Ottawa on January 29, 2022, with a rally at Parliament Hill.

Tens of thousands of pedestrian protesters joined the convoys. It was beautiful to see so many true Patriots coming together in Solidarity with each other! For a very long time, I had been waiting for Canadians to rise up and revive the notion of patriotism in their hearts and so it felt amazing! I was proud once again to call myself Canadian!

The protest called for the end of vaccine mandates in Canada during the ongoing COVID-19 so-called "pandemic." The people in Ottawa were putting pressure on the corrupted, lying politicians there, and we were doing what we could here, locally. On January 29, the date that the Freedom Convoy arrived in Ottawa, a group of truckers formed a protest at the Sweetgrass–Coutts Border Crossing, which connects Sweet Grass, Montana, via U.S. Interstate 15 with the town of Coutts, Alberta, via Alberta Highway 4.

Alberta Premier Jason Kenney called the blockade illegal and threatened that protesters would face penalties under the province's Critical Infrastructure Defence Act and could face criminal charges. Due to the continuous pressure, the farmers and truckers requested that I hold a church service for them at a local establishment called The Smuggler's Saloon. I agreed and packed up supplies and food, and headed to the Alberta/Montana border.

We took Nathaniel's car because our vehicles were so old that I was afraid we might get stuck somewhere if they broke down along the way. Nathaniel's BMW was not new (it was 11 years old); however, it was in very good condition. He had dedicated his entire summer to doing construction work so he could purchase this $9000 car. As expected, the car was later described by the crown prosecutor as a "luxury car" when he convinced the judge to deny me bail.

We brought along speakers, banners, and a team including Nathaniel, Larry Heather, a worship singer, who led the way to Milk River, approximately 20 kilometers from Coutts. During the three-hour drive, I did a one-hour interview on television that was being broadcast to around 60 other radio stations across the U.S. Millions of people around the U.S. were monitoring what was happening in Canada! All eyes were on Coutts, filled with hope that this movement would restore sanity to our nations. When we arrived at Milk River, there were hundreds of trucks and cars parked on both sides of the highway, some in the middle of the ditch.

THE REAL STORY OF WHAT HAPPENED IN COUTTS, ALBERTA

There was turmoil at the border, and I received several calls from the people at the border telling me they felt discouraged and depressed. There were police officers dressed in black, in full gear, with machine guns watching closely as the children were playing street hockey. I was invited to conduct a church service with the purpose of instilling hope, peace, and sanity. I went there for the sole purpose of delivering a church service and Holy Communion.

Americans were also there, cheering us on. Upon arrival at Milk River, a police barricade completely blocked the road to Coutts. Cars, trucks, and some farming equipment were parked along the road and in the ditches on both sides. Several people who identified themselves as "leaders" approached me and said that the Royal Canadian Mounted Police were working with them to keep the peace and ensure everyone was safe.

I was told: "They are super friendly today. And some of them are on our side." I was instructed to avoid mentioning the police for the same reason because they said, "We want to keep this friendly relationship with the police."

At Milk River, there were families, parents, and peaceful Canadians who were tired of the government's overreach, which had gone on for two years. It was a suppression of their liberties. It was a very cold day, so people brought firewood and fire pits to surround them just to keep warm. For the entire time that I was there, not one officer or anyone came to me saying that this was an unlawful or illegal gathering.

Contrary to that, I had multiple discussions with RCMP officers to inform them of my intention to speak. I asked if they could redirect traffic to a lane 30 feet away from the individuals. My concerns were that when I began the Church service, especially during Holy Communion, some people might try to come closer to receive the symbols. They might step in the middle of the road to get them.

I was given the flat deck of a semi-truck as a stage, and the people were separated by the road and me. For safety issues, it made sense to use the second lane. The officers went to the RCMP Command Centre to talk with their superiors. The two individuals who identified themselves as leaders also talked to the RCMP officers.

They relayed to them that I was about to initiate the service and expressed worries about traffic and safety. Both were in their late 20s or early 30s and said that they were waiting for the answer from the command post. Finally, the answer came. I was told by the uniformed RCMP officer that the command centre had declined the plan to divert traffic further away for safety concerns.

The two leaders came to confirm what I had already heard; we were all told the same. This plan was straightforward and wouldn't involve moving a single police vehicle. It was unclear why they didn't allow it unless they wanted a dramatic incident to justify a harsher crackdown on the protesters.

But because they rejected the suggestion, I assigned a few men to keep an eye on the people and the traffic during the service—just in case! I also asked the other protesters to help me with the safe distribution of the Holy Communion. The service went without any problems. Larry sang a few songs, we all sang the Canadian National Anthem, and I delivered the sermon.

At this point, I did not know if I would be allowed to go on to Coutts. Again, the road was blocked entirely by police vehicles. During my sermon and communion, the RCMP officers were recording the entire service and taking photos. After Larry finished leading the songs, we decided to travel to the border to cheer the people up there.

As we were leaving, an officer asked where we were going, and he looked multiple times inside the car. Nathaniel told him that we were going to Coutts because we had some supplies for the people and wanted to perform a church service there. The officer peeked inside once more and then let us cross the barricade. Police removed their vehicles, and we drove through—uninterrupted.

The distance from Milk River to Coutts is about 20 kilometers (close to 12 and 1/2 miles). Along the way, there were multiple police vehicles, and they were also parked by the road when we arrived in Coutts. Once again, both sides of the road had farming equipment, big semi-trucks, pickup trucks, and regular vehicles parked all along. There were already several people waiting for us; everybody knew that I was coming.

I attempted to listen to various people who clearly held positions of leadership in this particular area. Some suggested that to catch the politicians' attention, a different approach might be necessary over what we had been doing thus far. When we came out of the meeting, Larry had set up the speakers for the service. All of a sudden, three or four people who were clearly leaders grabbed the microphone and said that they had decided to take this whole thing "to the next level."

I could see the people were frustrated, and many of them wanted to do more. They were sick of waiting for the government to acknowledge the legitimacy of the protest. The people at the microphone announced that they were going to bring the trucks and farming equipment to the Capital, paralyzing the entire city of Edmonton. I thought to myself, *This is going to be a disaster*. The eyes of the world were on this tiny sliver of land. The people there had a great relationship with the police, and everything was peaceful. *Why change that?* I thought to myself.

People from the crowd started yelling. *What? Who decided that?* Whose behavior were they discussing? The crowd was as surprised as I was by this announcement. As we were, the whole room was stirred. Some were yelling, "You do not represent us. You do not speak in our name. We are not going."

The tension was very visible, and it was hard to hear anything over the crazy sound of multiple voices. It was paralyzing. The Capital was not a good next step, knowing that the Ottawa police had been confiscating protesters' resources, And the tensions were growing.

I could imagine what a totalitarian regime like Kenney's government would do to those peaceful families. It could turn very ugly very quickly. People like Kenney are cowardly and extremely weak. Weak people do stupid things when they feel threatened. I feared that he might do something that would hurt people in a way we had never seen before.

They might use this to crack down on the protesters and destroy the movement. They would feel within their rights to do as they pleased. We had already seen the politicians and the propaganda that the so-called mainstream media had painted of peaceful Canadians simply defending their rights. They had been labeled as terrorists and racist homophobes, antisemitic, dangerous, and completely un-Canadian.

Every time I heard rhetoric like this coming from the corrupt government, I knew they were looking for a justification to hammer the peaceful protesters. When you create drama and control the narrative, it becomes a perfect reason for them to start arresting people. I suspect there were operatives in the crowd from either CSIS (Canadian Security Intelligence Service) or RCMP attempting to create dangerous situations to justify forceful and brutal actions against the people.

Someone obviously had a plan: take the peaceful people from here and move them to Edmonton. Then, create chaos and arrest as many as possible, just as was done in Calgary. That would "clean" the problem.

Usually, I would agree this plan could work. However, I knew in just a few hours, thousands of people were going to come to Coutts. Diverting so many people and thousands of cars, semi-trucks, and farm equipment would truly paralyze the Capital. I was afraid of Kenney's reaction; he was already panicking and looked scared.

He lied so many times on television about what was really happening. He was manufacturing stories. He was about to unleash hell on his own people.

Here in Milk River and in Coutts, the situation was controlled and incredibly peaceful. Police were not interfering with the people's rights to peacefully protest, and from what I was told, they had no intention or command to change that. So why abandon something that is working and risk moving everything to Edmonton? It could truly become a disaster—potentially a violent one!

Another thing came to my mind: the recent crackdown on the peaceful protesters with the natives and their teepees at the legislature grounds. The government had no problem violently removing people exercising their God-given rights with the use of force. They confiscated private property, and without warrants or mercy, they broke almost every law in the land. I sensed that this could be one of those occasions. While hearing people in the crowd openly declaring their decision to stay put, I took hold of the microphone.

I shared with the people what I had experienced growing up under the tyranny of communism. I emphasized the importance of unity and peaceful solidarity for us to achieve victory. Below are excerpts from the transcript of my speech to the truckers that got me imprisoned!

The eyes of the world are fixed right here on you guys. You are the heroes of the solidarity movement. Don't you dare break the line? The whole world is watching you. They're afraid of us. Do not lose your momentum. You have been waiting two years for something like this. Now they're scared. They're afraid. Now we have a moment in the history of our beloved country finally to deal with the Trudeau Castros and traitors Kenneys.

It's about time for Canadians to rise up and start roaring. And I'm talking about — I'm talking about peaceful resolution. I'm not talking about guns and swords. This is our province. This is our nation. I did not immigrate here for my children to be enslaved again. Look at this girl here. Look at her eyes. What kind of nation is she going to have in a few years? That's up to you, every one of you. You are deciding today what kind of Canada is going to be for her.

This is our time. For two years we have been dancing a polka with them. For two years, we have been trying our best to reason with the villains. But I know villains. See, a bully will never stop bullying. He will keep stealing from you all the time. They have — they have big appetites, those greedy dogs. You have power now.

Don't give it away. The eyes of the world again are here on this little border. And the world is watching you. Will you give in? Will you stop fighting? Will you stop defending the rights of the free Canadians?

Polish people did it the right way. They said, "We shall not cooperate with the villains. We do not work for the KGB and Russians. We will not work for you anymore." They walked out of their jobs. Albertans, walk out of your jobs in solidarity with the truckers.

Say to your employers, "You're implementing those mandates. I will not give you my money, and I will not work for you." If every man and every woman would do that, within a week, all the mandates would be gone. That's power. We need our country back.

How are you going to get your country back if you're not going to stand up? Stand up. And thousands are coming to help you to stand up. Be blessed!"

When I finished about 20 minutes later, you could feel the fire among the people. So we had Holy Communion, and Larry took over singing while I mingled with everyone.

There was a lot of food and piles of cleaning supplies, including toothbrushes, pastes, and shampoos. The support that Albertans showed the protesters was truly remarkable. The tyranny had brought unity in the hearts of Canadians that I hadn't witnessed before.

THE CONTRAST BETWEEN AMERICAN PATRIOTISM AND CANADIAN MULTICULTURALISM

The open display of American patriotism has always inspired me. Every time I visit the States, I am deeply touched by seeing the American flags everywhere and watching Americans sing patriotic songs expressing their pride in being an American, like Lee Greenwood's "God Bless the U.S.A." It is also deeply touching to me when people cry with their hands over their hearts.

During those moments, I have often wished to be an American. America is a symbol—a dream about a better world without persecution and hate. It is a place where a man can work hard and achieve something beautiful for his family that he can then pass on to his children.

While I was imprisoned, Americans called the switchboard in Calgary, demanding that the government release me. Thousands of calls came into the system, and operators nicknamed the line the "Artur Pawlowski switchboard." Eventually, the calls overloaded their phone system, and they had to move the switchboard to another city.

I was told that operators were frustrated by answering calls from American citizens all the time. They would ask, "Why do you care about a Canadian citizen?" The response was, "We care because he is one of us—a Christian."

Americans were also organizing protests all over their country, just outside of Canadian embassies. Prayer groups and meetings with politicians were organized, and I believe God used Americans to ultimately set me free.

Canada had unfortunately lost that in this huge mixture of multiculturalism. We were hearing that being patriotic is considered "un-Canadian" by some. That being proud of one's heritage is racist and extremely dangerous. In Canadian schools, we had stopped teaching children about history and the heroes of old that came before us hoping to build a better tomorrow.

History was being substituted with indoctrination and propaganda. Patriotism was replaced with an open hate toward the very heritage that established this nation in the first place. A confused generation had been bombarded with the notion that the past was terrible and the future was no place for individualism.

Ultimately, everyone who has a brain knows that a tree without roots cannot survive. The winds of life will, sooner or later, topple the tree down. It's true that the founding fathers of the Confederation were not perfect; the fact is that no one is. They did some good things and some not-so-good things.

But willfully erasing the heritage left the population wiggling, and anything could trip them to the ground. If you do not know where you came from, you do not know where you are going. As a builder, I knew how important the foundation was. If it is weak and non-existent or rotten to the core, it doesn't matter what you put on top of it. It would be just a matter of time before the whole building would come crumbling down.

This nation was built on freedom in the Bible. Here are some fascinating facts about how Canada was formed. Everywhere you look, you see faith, God, and the Bible. Those things are mentioned on our buildings, in our national anthem, and in the historical facts of those who came here before us. To erase that is destroying the foundation.

Look how far Canada had fallen from the original plan. It is so different today that it might as well be called by a totally new name, like Chinada. At first, they went after the children by exploiting a law created to restrict freedom; prayer was removed from schools, and abortion was legalized. Then, they attacked Bibles in public places. And then prayers were removed from the government buildings.

Then, next was the removal of the Ten Commandments from our courts and the legalization of sexual perversion. And there was punishment for those who disagreed. With the grooming of the children, it was a total secularization of society. And there was only one God—not the God who formed us, but the government.

From that moment on, it was effortless to subdue the nation. With their new idol—the government and its false prophets, the mainstream media—lying came naturally to them. They were very loud and in your face.

And the people? Well, the people were eating it up. The churches ultimately gave up their power to influence society. They have since exchanged the salt for silver and the light for gold. The church has become unimportant and irrelevant—and, in the words of our oppressors, "unessential." As mentioned previously, marijuana stores, liquor stores, abortion clinics, Walmart, and IKEA were declared essential. But assembling in the church was unlawful.

BACK TO THE TASKS AT HAND

When driving back to Milk River, no one stopped us. In fact, the crowd had grown from when we had left a few hours before. In this unconventional field of camaraderie, fire pits were lit, food was being served, and people were smiling. The cars were decked with the words "Freedom," and Canadian flags were displayed everywhere.

It felt good to be a Canadian. The RCMP kept the blockade shut, with their marked vehicles staying away from the people. Every minute, another protester joined our group. I was right in saying to the people in the saloon that thousands of people were coming. Later, I learned that over 10,000 people had joined the Milk River protests that day.

This church service and communion became an ongoing practice that gained momentum. I spent my Fridays catching up with emails and texts and preparing my sermon for Saturday. Then, we would attend the rallies, and every week, they got bigger and bigger.

Central Park was filled with thousands of Canadians of every color. People united in solidarity from every background to peacefully oppose this government's tyranny. People stopped me for a hug or a selfie. In just a few hours, I must have been hugged by at least a thousand people. About 17,000 to 20,000 people walked together along 17th Avenue, expressing their disapproval of what this corrupt government was doing to them.

People were dancing, singing, and enjoying themselves, causing no trouble for the police. In fact, the police closed the roads and let them parade all the way. Not once was anyone told that this was an illegal gathering. The rally ended without any interference from the authorities. For about another hour, I tried to make my way to the car. However, every step of the way, someone would stop me and thank me for all we had been doing or for a picture. It was truly incredible.

Typically, on Sundays, I was with the people in the Street Church, helping to feed the most vulnerable in our society. Typically, I would deliver a 20-minute sermon, and Larry would sing some songs. Sometimes, we would have a person sharing testimony.

However, this Sunday, I was invited to speak at the Okotoks rally. The turnout was amazing. People came from all over. We even had cowboys who came with their horses and wagons. Can you believe it? It was Alberta at its best—the true spirit of the West.

I loved every minute of it. Several speakers, including some children, were lined up before me, and I was scheduled to speak last. The Plaza was packed, and many cars were driving back and forth, honking in solidarity.

There were families with children, young and old, and of every color. It felt so genuine and patriotic, like real Canadians. A bunch of children were talking before me, and as always, I was deeply touched by their plea.

They asked the adults to stop the segregation. "We don't want masks," they said. "Let us play with other children. Let us be children."

And then there was my turn to speak. I remember asking the people the same thing I had been asking for the past few years. Stand up, rise up. If you don't want to do it for yourselves, then do it for these children.

I asked them to please remember the names of the villains. In the future, when God shows us mercy and empowers us, we will address past injustices and ensure that those responsible face the consequences. I told them to remember their names because one day, justice would be served. The response from the people was phenomenal, as always. Everyone was waiting for the end of the craziness. Everyone just wanted to live their lives in peace.

The park was packed! Cowboys came with their horses and wagons, and a truck convoy circled around the park. The energy was fiery, and people were in high spirits! The truck convoy had pumped everybody up in Canada and beyond!

I pointed at the crowd and said, "Remember their names! We need justice to be served! We need accountability! If we do not make them accountable, they are going to come back again, and they are going to do this to us again! In the Bible, there is a portion of scripture that says that cowards will not inherit the Kingdom of God. This is not a time for cowards. This is time for the men and women of Canada to rise up, to stand up. And if you do not want to do it for yourself, do it for them." Pointing at children, I repeated, "Do it for the children!"

"Can you trust a greedy politician? Of course not! Sooner or later, he will betray you and will sell you for a slightly bigger bowl of soup!"

The following message came to me there; it is how God described the corrupted politicians of that time! And let me add that not much has changed!

> Ezekiel 34:1-5 (ESV) The word of the Lord came to me: "Son of man, prophesy against the shepherds of Israel; prophesy, and say to them, even to the shepherds, Thus says the Lord God: Ah, shepherds of Israel who have been feeding yourselves! Should not shepherds feed the sheep? You eat the fat, you clothe yourselves with the wool, you slaughter the fat ones, but you do not feed the sheep. The weak you have not strengthened, the sick you have not healed, the injured you have not bound up, the strayed you have not brought back, the lost you have not sought, and with force and harshness, you have ruled them. So they were scattered because there was no shepherd, and they became food for all the wild beasts."

We have elected them to represent our business and to work for us! To protect our loved ones and to govern our resources so we can all prosper and be protected! In return, we have been robbed, attacked, hurt, and enslaved by the very people that swore to take care of us!

Betrayed and abandoned by the traitors, we have to once again rise up and say to them: No More and Get Out!

The time has come for Justin Trudeau, Jason Kenney, John Horgan, Heather Stefanson, Doug Ford, and the rest of the pile of snakes, vipers, and scorpions to resign! Go and never come back!

In our beloved Canada, there is no place for tyrants and traitors like them! Canada was built on the idea of freedom—a dream of a new beginning—a place without persecution or prosecution—a place where you can work hard, build your home, raise your children, believe in your God, and live your life in peace!

They, the political snakes, have forgotten what Canada is! And it is not them! Canada is us! We Are Canada! We are Canadians, free Canadians.

We are free to speak without fear, free to worship God in our own way, free to stand for what we think is right, free to oppose what we believe is wrong, and free to choose those who govern our country.

And today, we free Canadians are saying to you, corrupted politicians! Resign!

We, free Canadians, are telling you tyrants: take your filthy hands away from our children!

We, free Canadians, are telling you: take your hands away from our places of worship, our restaurants, city halls, and schools!

We, free Canadians, demand your resignation!

"I am Canadian" invokes strong sentiments based on the understanding that Canadian law acknowledges the equality of all citizens.

The same Law for all! Not one law for the elites and another one for the rest of us! The law must be applied equally, or there is no law at all!

Isaiah 10:1 NASB Woe to those who enact evil statutes and to those who constantly record unjust decisions,

Proverbs 29:2 NASB When the righteous increase, the people rejoice; but when a wicked man rules, the people groan.

Psalm 125:3 NASB For the scepter of wickedness shall not rest upon the land of the righteous so that the righteous will not put forth their hands to do wrong.

Proverbs 28:15 NASB Like a roaring lion and a rushing bear Is a wicked ruler over a poor people.

Micah 7:3 NASB Concerning evil, both hands do it well. The prince asks, also the judge, for a bribe, and a great man speaks the desire of his soul; So they weave it together.

Isaiah 1:23 NASB Your rulers are rebels and companions of thieves; everyone loves a bribe and chases after rewards. They do not defend the orphan, nor does the widow's plea come before them.

Ezekiel 22:27 Her princes within her are like wolves tearing the prey, shedding blood, and destroying lives in order to get dishonest gain.

Isaiah 56:10-12 Israel's watchmen are blind, they all lack knowledge (they are all ignorant); they are all mute dogs (they are all dumb dogs), they cannot bark; they lie around and dream, they love to sleep (loving to slumber). They are dogs with mighty appetites; they never have enough (they are greedy dogs that can never be satisfied). They are shepherds who lack understanding; they all turn to their own way, and they seek their own gain. (Each one to his unlawful gain, without exception.) "Come," each one cries, "let me get wine! Let us drink our fill of beer (strong drink)! And tomorrow will be like today, or even far better."

It sounds like our political arena right now: All of them are after their own gain, after their own belly!

Here is how God wants rulers to behave! Proverbs 16:12 It is an abomination to kings to do evil, for the throne is established by righteousness.

There is always a choice for everyone! You can be a rat, or you can be a king! The choice is yours!"

After the Okotoks rally, we met with some businesspeople and former politicians. Several people were already waiting for us. We talked for hours, and in the end, I decided to go back to Coutts with two friendly politicians to see how we could try to hammer out a deal with Kenney's regime.

We wanted to start negotiations with the government, just like during the Solidarity movement in Poland, when politicians would sit down with the protesters, legitimizing the protest itself. It was very important to be able to present the grievances to the government. The idea was to open a dialogue with the representatives from Kenney's office.

Tension was building in Ottawa, and we were trying to prevent something crazy from happening here in Alberta. If this would, in fact, happen, Kenney would have to acknowledge that the protesters were also Canadians with rights and the right to be heard. I was proposing that the Premier send someone from his cabinet. I believed that would happen, and most people would reasonably start to negotiate and talk about how we could end this problem.

Now, everyone was so angry with the government that it seemed they did not care about what they had to say. We put down a list of proposals and points that needed to be addressed with the mutual understanding that both parties came from totally different spectrums.

When the dialogue is open, anything and everything can happen. Of course, calling good Canadians, fathers, mothers, and children terrorists, racists, and Jew-haters was not helping. We wanted to ask the government to stop throwing slogans like this towards the people. The plan was set, and we were supposed to go there Tuesday morning.

IT DIDN'T GO AS PLANNED

Ultimately, this series of events and my ongoing encouragement to the people to go all the way and take a stand is what landed me in prison. I wanted our homeland, Canada, to become unified and patriotic, as I had observed in other countries. I wanted the people and the government to work things out together.

Although I had been arrested many times before, this experience was something I never could have imagined. I knew God was with me. And I knew that I had planted seeds in the minds of the people at that last rally. But the prison guards' manipulation and hours on end in solitary confinement would test my faith like never before.

CHAPTER SEVENTEEN

THE WAVES OF THE ENEMY'S ATTACKS

[DAY 31]

HAVE YOU EVER NOTICED that the enemy attacks in waves, combining attacks of discouragement, fear, confusion, and hopelessness? Even when I talked with the inmates, they testified to the same thing. The attacks came like a flood, and if you fell for that, they lasted much longer. But if you resisted, they disappeared pretty quickly.

So, the idea was to withstand the attack. Patience and determination are embodied in faith. We had to consider who was bigger: Our adversary? Or our God? Who had the real power over our lives? God? Or the Devil and his minions? That was the battle that every man had to go through.

I was supposed to be taken to court, but of course, the usual, or should I say, the *unusual*, happened. The guard informed me the day before and the lawyer confirmed I would be brought to court. So I was ready for the transport, waiting to be picked up by the guards.

However, that did not happen. Even the morning guard was confused. Instead, I was given a telephone to listen to the counselors and the judge. They ultimately put aside everything until the following week.

The lawyer went to a different courtroom, and I was taken back to my cell. Well, it seemed the fight would continue.

> *Get angry, Lord God. Do something. Attack my furious enemies. See that justice is done.*
>
> PSALM 7:6 CEV

The Bible says that an evil person is like a woman about to give birth to a hateful, deceitful, and rebellious child. Such people dig a deep hole and then fall into it themselves. The trouble they cause comes back to them, and their heads are crushed by their own evil deeds. The reward comes from the one you submit to. If you submit to God, you will live and be victorious. If you submit to the evil one, you will be miserable and eventually die.

After three weeks of waiting, the lawyers finally received transcripts. Now, they could start working on the bail review. During my time out, I did my best to minister to the boys. If I only had more time with them, I could help straighten their path. They all needed direction. Like wounded sheep, they went on wounding others because they did not know how to live any other way.

For the few minutes that I had with them every day, even the toughest criminals stopped talking about their violent stories. They stopped cursing and prayed with me, with their heads bowed down. It really was something else, I must admit. During our church "services," when we sat at the tables before lockdown, even the hardest men had tears in their eyes.

God could not be stopped by the bars or the concrete walls. His spirit moved freely through the barbed wires and the steel doors. One thing was for sure: He loved us all. I was there; they were there. God had some plan for this unusual match. Here is my public statement for Day 31:

The past two years have shown us we no longer live in a democracy. We have lost our freedoms and rights. Our legal protection has disappeared, and our beloved Canada has become a police state where pastors are imprisoned for simply opening their churches or giving speeches.

The Prime Minister acts like a dictator, and elected officials no longer serve the interests of the people but rather the state. Kenney came to Alberta labeled as a savior, but has proven to be a traitor. Traitor to Alberta! Traitor to the Constitution. A traitor to Freedom. The past two months have shown that this was never about keeping us safe and protecting our loved ones. The Covid era has clearly demonstrated that this crisis was used to rob free citizens of their protected rights. To control and oppress all and any opposition against their greed for power. This is truly a very sad time for law-abiding citizens and freedom-loving Canadians.

[DAY 32]

For the past few days, I have had specific thoughts that come back to me. The Bible says that when the Spirit of the Lord took over, people knew what to do. They had the wisdom to do the right thing. Also, they *dared* to do the right thing. And what's even more fascinating to me is that they actually went and did it.

Over the years, I've met many people who knew what to do and how to do it but were too lazy or too cowardly to obey the leading of the Word of God. When the Spirit of the Lord took over and took control, everything changed, and amazing things followed. Enemies trembled and were defeated. Sometimes, it is hard to know what to do, and so my prayer is always this: "God, may Your spirit take over. Not my will, but Yours."

I did not like being in this crazy place, but I enjoyed my morning Bible studies. There was very little distraction in prison; most of the inmates were still asleep, tired because they were talking, banging on things, or yelling during a sizeable portion of the night. So, the mornings were quiet—just me, my thoughts, and my God.

Another enormous benefit of being there was that I did not have to rush. There was nowhere to go, and the three steps to the door were usually a quick journey back and forth within a few seconds. No need to worry about my coffee getting cold—it was cold to begin with. We hardly ever got hot water in the morning, so I drank mine cold. It wasn't very pleasant, but it was coffee! And after a month, I was slowly getting used to it. Probably after a year it might have become my preferred favorite drink.

Sometimes, I wondered how my life would have looked if I had kept my mouth shut or ignored the evil like everyone else had for years. If I had just said, like most Christians, "Well, it is what it is. There is nothing we can do here. God said that it was going to be bad. Now we see it. What can we do?"

That is still an excellent question. What can a man do against overwhelming evil? What actions could I have taken regarding the man who sent armed officers and the Alberta Health Services (AHS) to attack our church illegally and unjustly label me as a criminal for doing good? He arrested me, charged me, and penalized me for over two years.

Or what can we do against people like Tyler Shandro, the new Minister of Justice, who purposefully kept me in prison? He was the very man who broke his own mandates and yet quickly penalized those who dared to do the same. How can we hold people accountable for abusing their power? That man viciously attacked, like a mad dog, anyone who cried out, "This is illegal. This is hypocrisy."

How do you deal with corrupted men like him? Can you be silent? Does God want good people to remain silent? Are we to see and know but do nothing? Did Jesus come down, leave his throne, sit down under a tree, and do nothing? Did the Prophets of old keep their mouths shut? Did the heroes of old prefer comfort rather than doing what was right?

What about the apostles? Did they negotiate with evil to achieve peace so they could feed their wives and children? Did they ever say for the sake of their work, rent, or mortgage, "We have to do what we are told. We know it is wrong, but we are just following orders."

What does God want us to do when we face evil? Pretend it is not there? After all, it is not my problem; it is God's problem. What are we to do when we hear the cry of a woman being attacked on the street or next door? Are we to say, "Thank God that this is not my daughter or my wife? Thank you, Lord, that this is not happening to me!"

So, one day in Poland, I was arriving back from school in a town called Gliwice. There, I witnessed two grown men attacking a young girl who was maybe seventeen or eighteen years old. Those men wanted to harm her in the obscure ally street with no one there to help her.

I was sixteen, and they were big men, but I had no choice. At least for me, there was no choice. I could have said, "It is not my fight. This is not my problem. I am not looking for trouble. Art, just keep walking. Do not look in that direction. Pretend this is not happening. Just keep walking." But I did look. I knew exactly what they wanted to do to this young girl and there was no one else that could help her but me.

I went and told them to stop. Their vicious, animalistic aggression immediately turned on me. The girl was on the ground, scrambling to pick herself up. She was shaken and crying her eyes out.

The moment I engaged in the scene, I knew it was going to be ugly. However, I did not hesitate because I knew what needed to be done. I had to stop these bullies from hurting this young girl. There was no other alternative for me.

The blows were sharp; fists were flying back and forth. They kicked me multiple times, but I kept fighting them both. The men were huge and strong; I was fast, but small and skinny. The pure weight of those men was causing me trouble. My blows were more rapid than theirs, but were not causing enough damage.

Next to us, the girl was picking her stuff up from the ground. I was trying to protect the vital parts of my body. Just as I got another kick, the girl started running—she was free at last. The villain's entire concentration was now on me.

They did not even notice her leaving. She was free, and for me, that was what mattered the most. I was not stronger than them, but fast enough to make them realize they would not take me down; they were already tired. Finally, the men turned and walked away from me, disappearing into the alley. I picked up my things—a few books from school.

It made me a little angry that the girl did not even thank me for what I had done for her. I risked my life to save her. At the time, she was so scared and in shock that all she could think about was running away from those wild animals.

And me? If I were to do it again, I would not even hesitate. But that's just me, and that's why I had ended up here, in solitary confinement for over a month now, reading the story of Samson and getting hit by God's words once again. During that story, God was looking for a man who would fight the injustice all around. He was picking a fight with the corrupt people of the land. He was stirring trouble for them, and He needed someone willing to go, someone willing to stand up.

The Bible discusses how God is always looking for someone who would obey and do the right thing. It says:

> And I sought for a man among them, that should make up the hedge, and stand in the gap before me for the land, that I should not destroy it.
>
> EZEKIEL 22:30 KJV

Over the years, countless individuals have advised me to take it easy. "Stop stirring. Stop rocking the boat. Do not push the envelope. Just relax," they said.

Just relax and do what? I thought. Watch as the wicked men raped our country, destroyed our resources and our economy, robbed us of all rights and freedoms, stole our children, and destroyed their future? I could not then, and I will not now!

Just like all those years ago, I could not just keep walking, pretending that I saw nothing, or that I heard nothing. Did I make a mistake helping that battered girl those many years ago? I do not think so. I'm sure she did not think so. For her, it made all the difference. One act. One decision. One life changed.

How many lives did we miss? How many girls have we left in the claws of evildoers? And how many more must die and suffer before God's Church does what needs to be done: to stand up and fight the good fight of faith?

I did what I had to do, and for that, I got many blows. Yet, I do not regret even one of them. Today, I did what I had to, and for that, I am still getting blows. God wired me that way and created me for such a time as this. When I see evil, I call it out.

In our country, many girls and boys are under attack. Who will stand up and defend them against the workers of iniquity? I pray the Lord's Spirit takes over and guides me like before so I can do His will.

When a man is no longer angry with the evil in the land, he must ask himself this very simple question: Why not? God is an honest judge. He is angry with the wicked every day.

> *For the wrath of God is revealed from heaven against all ungodliness and unrighteousness of men, who by their unrighteousness suppress the truth. They know the truth about God because he has made it obvious to them. For ever since the world was created, people have seen the earth and sky. Through everything God made, they can clearly see his invisible qualities—his eternal power and divine nature. So they have no excuse for not knowing God.*
>
> ROMANS 1:18-20 ESV

God is very clear. He does not muddy the waters. Faith reflects poorly on the cowardly and faithless. Sometimes, I do not know who hates me more: the corrupted so-called church or the corrupted political system. I guess they're two sides of the same coin, much like Herod and Pilate or the Pharisees and Sadducees. They're the same devil, a double-headed snake. I think cowards are the worst of them all.

Samson did what God wanted him to do. He entered his destiny in the Lord. What was his destiny? He was to begin the process of setting Israel free from their oppressors, the Philistines. Who was upset with Samson when he was doing what the Lord wanted him to do?

It was the Philistines and the cowards. The Philistines loved to oppress, and they were not willing to let go of that power. The oppressed were too cowardly to oppose them and risk the very little that their masters gave them. In their minds, it was easier to kill one troublemaker than to stand up like men and put an end to the oppression. In Judges 15, verse 11, we see how fear ruled over the men of Judah and blinded them. Their enemy was huge, and their God was very small in their eyes. In verse 12, they tie Samson up and turn him over to the Philistines.

When I was young, I'd see my mom cleaning. Every Saturday, there was a mandatory thorough cleaning time in our house. I couldn't make sense of why she was doing this. Instead of cleaning and making everything look better, it appeared that she made everything worse. She flipped things, pushed sofas away, removed sheets from our beds, and threw stuff here and there. She made a huge mess, and the effect, to me, was horrifying. I enjoyed shopping, and that's exactly what my mom would make me do. Standing in never-ending lineups for a loaf of bread was easier for me than watching the horror of flipping the house upside down.

After buying all the groceries, I would come home, put it all into the fridge, and run to the local flea market to buy vegetables. Halfway into the day, my mom was not even close to finishing. The house still looked like a few grenades had been thrown in the middle of the kitchen and the living room.

When I finally returned from the market with flowers for the coming week, I was shocked at the transformation. The floor was so clean you could literally eat food from it. The rooms were shining. The sheets were done and smelled terrific. Just touching them made you want to go to bed.

When the house was clean, Mom started cooking the Saturday dinner, which was always fresh chicken. Father got one leg; I got the second. Mom got the chicken breast, and Dawid got some leftovers.

Dawid was always a super picky eater, and it was a war to get him to eat. He did not like this; he did not like that. To tell you the truth, I do not know how he survived, but somehow, he lived to see another day. I will cherish those memories for the rest of my life. The super clean house, the smell of fresh flowers, and the taste of that Saturday dinner.

When I was young, I couldn't figure out why you had to make a big mess to see a good result. It took me many years, but now I understand. To do a good cleanup, you must remove everything. Nothing can be overlooked. You can't sweep dirt under the carpet; you must move things around.

You have to push the envelope, rock the boat of comfort, and get rid of indifference and laziness. This process is a must in order to see the difference. Go to places where you usually do not go. Look into the corners of spiders and their webs.

At first, it feels chaotic, disorganized, and messy. Only later, you can see it had to be done. My mom knew that. She was then, and still is today, the best of the best. She knows that sweeping dirt under the carpet will not do the trick; sooner or later, the smell will be unbearable, and the job of cleaning the place will be even harder.

The longer you wait, the worse it becomes, and the dirt that surrounds you will not let go so easily.

Ultimately, God is the best at cleaning. His blood cleanses the stuff that nothing else can: all the stains, all the dirt in our souls. Nothing but the blood of Jesus can wash away our sins. The devil tells us, "Sweep it under the carpet. It is not so bad. Others have even more dirt than you. You're still okay."

But the problem is that without Jesus, you stink, and wherever you go, you contaminate others. Like the Black Plague, sin is deadly and highly contagious. God wants to flip the tables, roll the carpets, and move the couches in our lives to show us what is hiding in the corners and shadows. Underneath what is visible, it is not pleasant. It looks messy, and it is very hard work to make it clean.

However, when it's all done, when the purification is finished, when you have finally given up all the secret places where you hid your personal garbage, you can marvel at the finished job and say, "Wow, if I had known before, I would have done it sooner."

When you put your head on those clean, nice-smelling pillows and sheets, it feels like a purified aroma for your soul—like a cleansed body, the house, the temple of God. When you feel His presence and peace, knowing that all the evil is gone and all the spiders have been chased away, you are ready to have the best dinner with your family in the cleanest place on earth: in the house of your Father God.

The men of Judah wanted to put the dirt under the carpet, and Samson wanted to clean up the ongoing problem of contamination that he despised. So, the never-ending struggle between those who desired relative peace and immediate compensation triggered conflict with those who wanted freedom and God's blessing.

More often than we care to admit, it sometimes seems easier to remove the so-called troublemakers who want to deal with the enemy than it is to deal with the enemy itself. Today is no different. So many have chosen to live a life of slavery in their dirty and impoverished homes. It breaks my heart knowing that God is more than ready to help them deal with the evil if they would only be willing to receive that help.

In the story of Samson, truth and right and wrong didn't matter one bit. Cowards do not like to be disturbed. Samson exposed the problem, the occupiers, the Philistines. The problem did not appreciate the exposure. The people who were living in the slums in the middle of the dump were too terrified to change. They were comfortable knowing where all their garbage was lying.

Samson needed to go. He dared to stir the dirt. If they allowed him to continue, they would have to be forced to clean it, and that is something they were not willing to do.

When we who are willing get tired and weary of cleaning the dirt of the world and fighting God's enemies, we can always call upon His name and say, "Lord, please help us win a battle against evil and do not allow us to die of thirst. Give us fresh water, even if it must come from a rock, so that we can feel strong again."

When I looked outside my window, I saw a poorly maintained little yard there. It wasn't a big one, maybe 40' by 30', with barbed wire on the top and bottom of the fence. I thought it would be nice to use it for a little garden. Not here. Such a crazy idea probably never crossed their minds. To give people here something to do, something positive, would be too good, too generous.

If you found yourself here, you were already guilty and punished. In comparison, dogs and cats in this country are treated better than humans. The other day, I read an article about animal cruelty. It said that cruelty against animals is never right. However, it is considered perfectly acceptable to be cruel to those who have been charged with a crime but not yet convicted.

I knew things were going to happen to the people of Canada. It had already begun. Their selfishness and indifference towards those who were hurting, the poor, and the abused were being judged. I had been prophesying about this since 2005. God showed me the striking down of their idols, their money, and their pride. If only people would be smarter, but they were not. We grow immune to the lessons of history and make the same mistakes repeatedly. We're no different from the Israelites in that regard.

The doors opened to my cell, and an officer walked in. He looked around, checked what I had on my shelves, and said, "Very clean. I like it."

Almost every day, I heard comments like that. I had to lead by example, not just spiritually but physically as well. Some of the inmates made such a mess that I did not know how they could stay and sleep there. I thought to myself, *We are humans. Let's at least act like it.*

Samson's story ended with tragedy. Betrayed, alone, mocked, humbled, and blind, he prayed one last time to finish the race. He started his journey with God's anointing, and he wanted to finish the same way. God granted him his last wish. He restored his power, and ultimately, Samson crushed more enemies than during his entire lifetime. God is a God of second chances.

The man across from me, who was brought in a few days ago, was having a hard time. Today, when they served food, and the guard opened the door of his cell, I noticed the man was crying. I overheard them talking. He said that he had had enough. Locked up and left with no tangible or meaningful support, people started breaking.

When I spoke to the guard, I offered my services to the inmates. I said that someone should be able to comfort them and that they just need someone to talk to. The guard was very appreciative; however, even though he felt this man's pain, there was nothing he could do. The orders, he said, were coming from the top.

So I filled out a request to go to the Chapel with the boys, and if we couldn't go there, I said I could hold a church service in the common area for anyone who wanted to come. The director politely declined. I did not know why they had stripped us of our rights. What was the purpose of denying the church service? Were they afraid of too much positive impact? Perhaps Christianity was a threat to their drug trafficking enterprise, since real Christians do not take drugs. When you looked at this from that perspective, it made perfect sense and answered the "why?"

It turned out that the man from across the cell remembered me from the Drop-In shelter years before. I was there, across the street from that shelter, taking hundreds of people off the streets, baptizing, and feeding tens of thousands of people in need. We talked a bit about that experience. It looked like the conversation cheered him up.

When Nathaniel showed up with Dawid outside the prison with the rest of the people, his mind completely changed. He smiled and even made a little placard for his window that said, "Jesus is Lord." The support group made his day! Praise God. Another guy from the cell next to him also watched the outdoor service and gave me a "thumbs-up." At least they could see and hear what was going on in the parking lot of the Remand Centre. The boys looked so happy, clapping their hands and dancing. They came to the door every few minutes to smile and update me on what was going on at their side of the unit.

Through my little window, I could see just a little sliver of what was going on outside. I think that was the purpose: the administration did not want me to be encouraged in any way, shape, or form. That was why they moved me twice to this cell. It was part of my punishment.

However, I was extremely happy for my new friend. From tears in the afternoon to laughter, clapping, and dancing in the evening, I did not know who was making a bigger impact: me on the inside or the church on the outside. One by one, the prisoners came to me and said, "Wow. People love you, man. This is awesome!" Later on, they let me out alone again—with no one around me. It looked like our little prayer group bothered them immensely, but we prayed through the doors anyway.

Today's support group outside was at least twice as big. We could all hear the bullhorns and the chanting, "Free Pastor Art." It was loud, and it was amazing. They would not let me out with the boys, so I had some extra time. I called Marzena and learned God has a sense of humor. She immediately put me on the speakers, and I was able to talk to the protesters outside who gathered in my support, and I shared with all of them. I thanked them very much for coming and told them about the impact that they were having on this side of the fence. We could all feel the difference in the spiritual atmosphere. Something was being broken. The heavy oppression of darkness was lifted.

The villains must have been listening because our phone call was suddenly cut off. I asked another inmate to dial the number for me using his Orca number. He did, and I continued the conversation. It was unbelievable. It felt great to talk to the people and hear them cheering—it was out of this world.

Someone told me that the protesters' children built a snow fort by the trees outside and were playing with each other and having a great time. While the parents were fighting for their rights and the rights of all Canadians, kids were being kids. This was absolutely unacceptable to the sheriffs! They viciously destroyed the kids' entire fort because they would allow nothing positive to come from these interactions.

What the sheriffs did not expect was that those kids were the children of freedom fighters, and they immediately rebuilt what the villains destroyed. Week after week, the officers demolished what the kids built, but the kids faithfully rebuilt what the enemy destroyed. What a fascinating lesson came from these youngsters, the next generation of warriors for truth. My political statement for today was:

> When people unite under one banner, Freedom, the villains become powerless. They know that the time is coming when they will have to give an account for all the evil they have done. Sooner or later, justice must be served. Look at Hitler, Ceausescu, or Hussain. With the powerful resistance against this tyranny, one day, we will once again see justice served, the rule of law restored, and freedom for our loved ones and the next generation. Stay strong and hold the line.

Jesus said:

> *Peace I leave with you; my peace I give you. I do not give to you as the world gives. Do not let your hearts be troubled, and do not be afraid.*
>
> JOHN 14:27

Daniel told me he was glad that I was there, not in the sense that I was in prison, but because I was helping a lot of people there. He knew everything happened for a reason. He said, "Now I know Christ, and I am turning my life around."

A few days later, he came to me and spoke again and said, "Something good is going to come out of this. I know it. I heard you a few days ago, and the moment I heard you, I knew. That the light is here. I could not talk to you then, but I knew. The light is here."

CHAPTER EIGHTEEN

HOURS TURN TO DAYS, DAYS TURN TO WEEKS

[DAY 33]

I WAS LET OUT of my cell around 11:25 a.m. and walked to the phones, but they were all taken. This gave me only 20 to 25 minutes to get to the phone and call the church. If this was to work, it had to be done at a precise time. If I could get to the phone, I could give a sermon to the church straight from jail.

Not many can say they did this. For over a month, they opened the doors for me at random times only known to them. I never knew when they would come and get me. Sometimes, it was in the middle of the day, sometimes in the evening, and still other times, it was in the morning.

My window of opportunity to call the church, when services were being held, was from 11:00 a.m. to 12:00 p.m., which only gave us an hour. It would take a miracle to pull something like this off. In other words, the odds were against us. Only God could do the impossible and make that happen.

This morning, I felt sure that it was not going to happen. There was some kind of commotion with the other inmates. And the clock in the common area was still not fixed, so we did not even know what time it was. From my end, there was absolutely nothing that I could do but just wait. If it was God's will for me to talk to the church and to the parishioners, then He would make a way.

I had just finished studying the story of Ruth and Naomi. I was reading about their struggles, and Ruth's faithfulness and dedication. Her bold, filled-with-faith statement was, "I will go where you go; I will live where you live. Your people will be my people; your God will be my God. I will die where you die and be buried beside you."

While reading this, I began to weep. This was a Moabite woman with so much faith and trust that nothing else mattered to her. All the way, no shortcuts and no cutting corners. For her, it was everything or nothing. Life or death. That level of faith was very hard to find then, and it is especially hard to find now, so it was deeply touching to read of a young foreign woman being so strong and powerful.

Then came Boaz, a relative of Naomi, who showed such kindness to someone that he did not even know. He helped her with his generosity and treated her like one of his own family. I cried even harder. I couldn't stop. Oh, to have the faith and dedication of Ruth and the compassion and mercy of Boaz.

I prayed, "Lord, let me always remember the poor and the broken. Let me always be generous to those seeking my help. Give me the faith that trusts you all the way, even to the death." While wiping my tears away, I said, "Lord, I will go where you want me to go. I will live where you want me to live. Your people are my people, and I want you to be my God until the day I die."

And miraculously, a few minutes later, we were let out. The phones were all taken, but Ray was waiting to give me his phone. It was about 11:30 a.m. and was perfect timing. While sharing with the church, I heard the trumpets going, the cheering, and the excitement.

How many pastors have preached from jail, locked in the medical unit where people are held 23 hours a day in solitary confinement? I was sure that few could say that. I talked about the book of Judges that I just finished studying, reminding everyone that when the Israelites were faithful, God protected them. But the moment they went after idols and walked away from God, He allowed the enemy to have the upper hand.

God used the enemy to bring the nation back to Himself. When they cried out to God and turned away from their evil ways, God always forgave them. He came to their rescue.

"Stay close to God, my friends," I said. As I was talking to the parishioners, several inmates listened to my mini-sermon with great interest.

I decided to do something extra special and put one of the inmates on the call. Danny shared how blessed he was to see the supporters outside the prison every day. He thanked them for that. I put another prisoner on, then another, then another. They all shared a little with the church. It was outstanding. Afterward, an inmate told me, "I have never done something like this before, and it felt so good."

All of us prayed together as we gathered around the table. I blessed everyone there with peace and the Holy Spirit and prayed for God's perfect will in their lives. Then, we all prayed for the guards and for our many enemies. "God forgive them and lead them to you."

Among us was a young man who had already spent seven years in prison. He was just released a few months ago and got arrested again. He was the one responsible for the shooting near our church. His family ran a drug trafficking business, and only God knows what else.

This young man was deeply touched. For over a week, he had been the hardest to crack, but that day, he was listening and praying with the rest of us. He said he used to be Baptist but then totally walked away from God. Danny shared the gospel with the young man and told him that only God—only Jesus—could set him free.

"You need Jesus," Danny told him. "He's the only one that can turn your life around."

What a day! What a powerful testimony that we all witnessed in that time. Ruth was the great-grandmother of King David and an ancestor of King Jesus. God honored this woman with such a blessing.

They locked us back up and so I continued my study of the Book of Job. Here was a man facing horrible, unthinkable circumstances. He lost his wealth, and then he lost his health. At first, his friends came to comfort him but later accused him of wrongdoing. Now, an innocent man who was simply being tested by God had to defend himself from his own friends.

Almost the entire book of Job is about him trying to understand all the "whys." Why is this happening to me? What have I done to deserve this? Why Lord? He tries to defend himself from the accusers, but to no avail. In their eyes, he must be guilty. Otherwise, he would not be here in this situation. I could relate to that part of the story. My so-called friends accused me of wrongdoing just because we had money problems.

I was also being hammered by the enemy, the devil. But to be attacked by your own troops is always the most difficult. However, that's always part of the test, and Job passed it with honors. Eventually, God healed Job and restored what the locusts had eaten. Job's friends learn their lesson through correction, and God gets the glory. Now, generations are being blessed by reading this man's story. It made me think, *God, let me also see the victory in my life and force the enemy to give back sevenfold what had been stolen from me.*

At around 3:00 p.m., after the guard's shifts changed, I had an unpleasant visitation. It was by an officer from last night's shift who told me he had been "grilled" by the boss. I think it was the Director who gave him a hard time because the officer had let me out of my cell yesterday. For that, this officer had received a grilling and was now grilling *me!*

As you remember, I was able to talk to the people and encourage them to stand strong. The prison staff were extremely upset that I spoke to the people outside of the prison. The officer also passed along a message from the boss that this was not a proper place to conduct such a protest.

Whenever the protesters came, some guards would fire at me, "They should not be here, but rather at the Court House!" They would try to persuade me to change the location.

I disagreed and would reply to them, "They are here because I am here. They are here to support my being locked up like a dog in a cage." They never liked my answer.

This officer in front of me looked shaken. They must have given him a hard time. Then he asked me this question, "What would you do if you were in my shoes?"

"Well…" I paused, "…If I was in your shoes, I would quit. I would not work for an organization that locks people up like dogs and keeps humans without trial in cages. That is inhumane."

He wasn't happy with that answer, and I knew I was in for some kind of punishment. It was always a never-ending story. The darkness is terrified of the light. They did not want me to talk to the public or expose what was really happening in jail.

My buddy across from my cell was happy again. I could see that he was looking through his window, watching the ongoing rally. He yelled to me from his cell, "I think I see your brother." Then he went back to his window, lifted his hands, and danced to the rally music. That side of the jail had some fun and could be encouraged by the preaching and the music.

I was thinking about what that officer said to me and wondering if he'd keep his mouth shut if he was in the same position, an innocent man being targeted by some seriously messed up government officials. Wouldn't he want to communicate to the entire world what was happening to him? I think he'd do whatever it took to let everyone know about the injustice done to him.

This constant cliché that so many are using, "I am just doing my job," will not cut it when they stand before the living God. If every good man opposed the evil in the land, the evil would have no option but to retreat. But to be attacked by your own troops is always the most difficult.

I felt like a trapped lion, caged and overpowered by evil hyenas. Walking back and forth, sizing up the bars, looking at the locks, not being able to do anything. How long would the wicked keep me bound? How long would He allow the corruption to keep his servant trapped? Would they always be able to say that God could not rescue me from their snares? How long would they say that my God was not strong enough or was not powerful enough? The enemy was laughing while I was counting the days.

They said to my face, "He was trusting the Lord, and the Lord has abandoned him." But I knew God was with me; I could feel him, sense his presence. God had never left me or abandoned me. In Him, I put my entire trust.

So that day, I let them laugh because I would be celebrating soon. I prayed God would let me go through this test with my head held high and with my eyes fixed on him. My tongue proclaimed:

> He is my strong tower. He is my deliverer. In him, I put all of my trust. Lord, you always have perfect timing for everything. Every day for me is like the scourging of whips. Every day, I look for a sliver of hope. I believe that you remember and that you have not forgotten. The hours have turned to days, and the days have turned to weeks. I still wait for you to come and pull me out from the claws of the hyenas. Their teeth are sharp and slowly tear my flesh. Even though I am surrounded by so many of them, I will always choose to say, "One day, my Lord and my King will rescue me. One day, those who have done this to me will receive what is due to them."

Good men stop following evil orders. There comes a time when you have to say, "No more!"

My friend across from my cell yelled through the door, "I would never imagine sitting here with you in jail. Not in a million years. It is hard to be good these days." He smiled.

"I know," I replied, "but we have to be."

"Yes," he said. "We have to."

When the people started to go home from the rally outside, he yelled through the door again. "When I get out, I want to be part of this."

> *For I know the plans I have for you, declares the Lord.*
> *Plans to prosper you and not to harm you, plans to give*
> *you hope and a future.*
>
> JEREMIAH 29:11 NIV

My previous feelings were eventually confirmed. I was punished by the Director's order and not allowed to leave my cell. This punishment was designed to correct my unacceptable behavior of talking to my parishioners. According to the Director, when I got out of jail, I would become a better man.

Twenty-three hours in a small box definitely forces people to think about the Canadian justice system. I guess it was a lesson well learned, and I would do my best to remember. Every day, my statements were recorded and broadcast by my son. My statement for today was:

I am in solitary confinement in prison because, according to the corrupt government, I have committed a crime. What was my crime? I stood for the people against tyrannical mandates that have caused many to die. Restrictions that destroyed countless lives. I stood for the people who lost everything. Some lost their loved ones. Some lost their jobs, and others lost everything.

My job as a pastor is to stand, to be with the hurting, with the broken. To stand with them in solidarity against evil in the world. The evil that we see all around us. The evil that claims that we are in this together and at the same time gives itself more, while others lose more and more. The evil that says one law for me and another for thee. This evil has a name. Its name is Kenney's government, with its corrupt bureaucrats. A pastor's job is to fend off such evil wolves, and I wish that more clergy would peacefully join me in this fight against this evil.

[DAY 34]

Another morning had come, and another theater with the nurses. I was still in solitary confinement. Every morning, a nurse came in with the guard. He would open the door, and the nurse would always ask the same question, "Are there any concerns?"

If you said "No," she marked something in her notebook and happily moved on to another cell. They came every day and asked the same questions, expecting the same blunt responses. People were half asleep after the nightly yelling contests and being awakened by the slamming of metal doors. Most people just wanted to sleep and be left alone.

It was perfect timing, and they expected a perfect response from you. A simple "No" was good enough for them. Well, on this particular day, I decided to change that this time. I heard the usual questions uttered, "Are there any concerns?"

I said, "Yes." Her eyes grew big. That is not how you are to respond. I continued. "Why are we kept in cells for almost an entire day, like dogs in cages? Why are there no activities done with the inmates."

She interrupted me and said, "I am only interested in your health."

I replied, "I *am* talking about health. People here are going crazy staring at the walls, screaming, yelling, walking in a circle, and crying."

The guard got very uncomfortable and slammed the door in my face. The nurse wasn't supposed to hear what was really happening here. The last thing I asked before the doors closed was, "Why are we not allowed to go to the Chapel?"

But no one cared to listen anymore. I heard the next cell being opened, and I could hear the same question asked again, "Are there any concerns?" They kept repeating the question like a broken record, and most didn't even bother responding.

Many of the inmates had been here for a long time, and they knew better. They were expecting you to say "no concerns" so they could check it off in their small notebook and proceed. It was part of the business. If you dared to say anything contrary to the party line, well, not only would the door be slammed in your face, but you were risking additional punishment.

I know because it happened to me many times. People were afraid because there was no justice—just cruelty and lawlessness. And on top of that, there was absolutely nothing you could do about it. Individuals without criminal records experienced unimaginable abuse of power, something I never thought possible in a civilized nation.

Section 12 of the *Canadian Charter of Rights and Freedoms* clearly states that "Everyone has the right not to be subjected to any cruel and unusual treatment or punishment." Torture is inherently cruel and unusual under section 12. As the Supreme Court wrote in *Suresh vs. Canada (Minister of Citizenship and Immigration) (2002),* torture is "so inherently repugnant that it could never be an appropriate punishment, however egregious the offense."

The Court noted that the "prospect of torture induces fear, and its consequences may be devastating, irreversible, and indeed, fatal."

This view of torture goes back to *R. vs. Smith (Edward Dewey),* in which Justice Lamer said, "Some punishments or treatments will always be grossly disproportionate and will always outrage our standards of decency: for example, the infliction of corporal punishment." Besides violating section 12, in *Suresh vs. Canada*

(Minister of Citizenship and Immigration) 2002, it was found that torture violates the rights to liberty and security of persons under section 7 and shocks the conscience.

There it was! What was happening to us under their supervision was nothing short of torture. The purpose, without a doubt, was to create a situation in which an inmate would plead guilty or accept the offer, a deal with the Crown, to escape the ongoing cruelty that they could no longer endure.

Quite ingenious, I have to admit. Drugging people up and creating unbearable circumstances secured a perpetual clientele. Broken people forced to take a plea bargain, hooked on heavy drugs, who one day would be released upon society only to re-offend. Since there was absolutely no effort being made to ensure their previous behavior was corrected or addressed in any way, shape, or form, this outcome was inevitable.

The Canadian government had become a totalitarian regime, and the nation was starting to follow the examples of Russia, North Korea, and China. Over there, of course, this kind of treatment is neither unusual nor cruel. The abuse of power by tyrants is as prevalent as the air we breathe.

I continued the story of Job in chapter 30, verse 1. This was a hard book to read. I had read this portion of the scripture many times before, but being there, locked inside solitary confinement, it had a totally new meaning to me. Surrounded by misery, seeing the suffering of others and myself, the story of this good man, Job, profoundly touched me.

In the last cell on the block, there was a man in a wheelchair with a partially amputated foot; his image was disconcerting. Every day, his cell was flooded with water. The small cell had a bed, a table screwed to the wall, a seat screwed to the floor, and a toilet with a sink. You could tell that this man was not 100% sane.

He was scared and slept most of the time. The guards and nurses were very intimidating to him. Most of the time, he just lay on his bed or sat in his wheelchair, staring at the wall.

Every time he used his toilet, it flooded his cell. I would hear the guards coming and yelling at him, calling him nasty names. After a few days of such harassment and insults coming from left and right, he just wanted them to stop. Terrified by the intimidators, he stopped flushing his toilet. The stench was hard to endure. The poor man did not know what to do. He did not want to be yelled at anymore.

The prisoners next to his cell tried to advocate for him. They notified the guards about the plumbing problems, but to no avail. The plumbing issues caused flooding. There was feces on the ground, and his amputated foot was exposed to the filth and became infected. The nurses came to see what was going on, but the battered man was snapping at them. He was like a cornered dog, baring his teeth after enduring days of cursing and yelling.

This craziness went on for about a week. I watched this drama unfold in horror. Eventually, the plumbers were called, and they successfully fixed the system. The man cleaned himself up and remained locked in his cell for days. Then, one day, he emerged from his cell, showered himself, put aside his shame, and joined us for those few minutes in the common area that we had between phone calls.

The man was very timid, but there was no sign of aggression in him. He just wanted to be treated like a human being, that's all. There was an unspoken rule: Do not stir trouble. Keep your mouth shut, and maybe we will give you a bone. Several cells were empty, and they could have easily moved him to another one until the problem was fixed. But the officials purposefully kept him there in his own mess as some kind of twisted punishment.

Job's plea was simple: he just wanted to be understood and shown compassion. Instead, he received accusations and rejection. He was insulted, and his closest friends were quick to judge him, claiming that all that was happening to him was his fault. They were to him like salt on an open wound. He was broken, hurt, and waiting for justice.

Justice, however, did not come for a very long time as he pleaded his case and asked, "Lord, why?" It was one thing to be charged. It was a different story to be arrested, sentenced, and executed without the ability to defend yourself. I'm not even trying to compare my situation to the one that Job was in, but I know a little about how he felt facing injustice.

My fellow inmate in the wheelchair was in a situation that he could not deliver himself from. He needed help, not lashes. Job needed encouragement, not some smart comments or accusations. When you're hurting or being ripped to shreds by the enemy, the last thing you want or need are self-righteous so-called friends telling you that you are the problem.

Even after over a month, the air conditioning was still not working. It was crazy hot inside, sweating hot. We walked around half-naked, but it gave us some relief from the heat. We had to find the positive in the little things. They released us from our boxes around 12:30 p.m.; by then, I had been in my cell for over 24 hours straight. I talked to the boys, and they told me the same story. The game of punishment continued, I guess.

The boys were swift to tell me what happened yesterday. I had a very limited view of what was going on in the parking lot outside; they had an unobstructed view. One after another, they would come to me with the stories. One said, "As I was watching the people yesterday, I started to cry and could not stop. I do not even know why, but I was crying and crying."

Another man came to me and said, "It was so beautiful I did not sleep all night thinking about what I saw. The tears were coming on their own. I could not stop them."

Another man told me, "It was so encouraging to see so many people that actually care."

I think that was the precise point that touched all those inmates one by one. Someone *did* care about what happened to them. God cared, and His people also cared.

While talking to them, I commented that we were in "the pen," meaning the penitentiary. However, I was quickly corrected. The pen is apparently outstanding in comparison to our facility, which was hell. A few others jumped into the conversation to educate me.

"In the pen, we had over one hundred television channels, video games, a gym, and a basketball court. We were allowed to play badminton. There were all kinds of meetings held, Chapel and Bible studies. The only time you had to be inside during the day was for the countdown."

As you all know, I was a rookie in my knowledge of this criminal lifestyle in prison. I thought that there was a lot worse than this. No, they all eagerly confirmed, explaining that it was quite the opposite. So, no one really understood why they treated us the way they did. It did not make any sense.

I analyzed it. What if this place was treated as a business running around the clock? They were doing everything they could to break people psychologically with the use of torture just to plead guilty. It was a never-ending stream of money, a revolving door. Client after client and many more to come. They just needed us to be so sick and tired of the solitary confinement, isolation, and mental torture that we would plead guilty and go to a nicer facility where we could at least interact with others.

Everything made sense. Most of the people there were in limbo waiting for their court hearings, charged but not convicted yet. Forcing them to plead guilty would ensure the clients and the money flowed like a river. Many there pleaded guilty to escape the worst place in this business.

There is an old Polish saying, "If you do not know what the whole thing is all about. it is always about money." Canadian citizens who have not been convicted of any crime were subjected to an unexplainable horror. I called my wife with my revelations. She said that they would pass this on to others.

When I was done with my phone calls, we all sat down and prayed. More and more people were joining us daily for prayer. The guard came out, shaking his head. He was very unhappy with what he saw. We all ignored him, trying to finish our prayer meeting. Then he yelled, "That's it. Go to your cells."

The inmates gathered around me, and those sitting at the table in the common area ignored him as well. Heads down, some had their hands stretched out as if waiting for a gift, and we all kept praying. When we were done, I said, "Amen," and we went back to our cells. It was another victorious day in that hellish, evil place. My prayer that evening was:

Please, Lord Jesus, give us more. Lord Jesus, I also ask you to not allow me to forget about these people here who are subjected to such cruelty. Let me remember their pain and speak on their behalf. I know, my holy God, that they are not perfect, far from it. But You have created them also in your image, and you hate corruption and abuse of power. It says that you are mighty and you care about everyone. You make fair decisions. It says in your word that the wicked will be cut down, and those who were wronged will receive justice. Place me in a position of power and honor, and allow me to straighten this crooked path.

I continued my study of the Book of Job, which ended with restoration. God is God, and no one has the power to challenge him and succeed. Job is reminded that God has the ultimate wisdom, not him. His friends are corrected and humbled. The man of pain and sorrow again becomes a man of blessings and prosperity.

In the end, God knows all the "whys." Because one good man refused to curse God, his story touches and changes millions of people around the world to this day. If only Job knew what a testimony he would become.

During my imprisonment, I learned something very interesting. First, the Calgary Remand Centre is privately owned and is one of the most sued institutions in the world. Later, I discovered from a seasoned "professional criminal" who has been in various facilities that it ranks as the third most severe maximum-security prison in the developed world. The first one was in Russia, called the Black Dolphin followed by a maximum-security prison in Texas.

In British Columbia, Canada, the practice of solitary confinement, also known as segregation, was ruled illegal. However, that did not stop the Alberta prison system from still practicing this form of torture.

The support group was outside, but the sheriffs and correctional officers decided to block the parking lot that people were using to come to the rally—a total blockade. People were forced to turn around, so they parked their vehicles in a retail parking lot down the road and came to the location on foot. So much for the right to protest!

One prisoner told me through the window, he saw the S.W.A.T. team practicing in full riot gear. Can you imagine? How evil and twisted those people were to put this kind of show of force with a total willingness to attack Christian women and children for the "crime" of peacefully assembling. Shame on them all. I do not know how they slept at night. How could they? To paraphrase Psalm 3:1, I have a lot of enemies. Many fight against me and say, "God won't rescue you."

I reminded myself, *God, you are my shield, and you give me victory and great honor. I sleep and wake up refreshed because you, O Lord, protect me.*

There were about fifty officers in uniform, some undercover cops, and a helicopter in this team practice. That is how much the corrupt are afraid of the righteous. God let their plans bring their downfall. Fear is a real thing. If you bow to it, it will own you and turn you into a slave.

My thoughts went back to a church where I was invited to speak. I spoke about faith and courageous men and women of old and did my best to let the people know that God is greater than any virus on Earth. When I invited people to come up for prayer and healing, I closed my eyes, waiting for people to come, and many did.

When I opened my eyes, I was shocked. People stood in front of me, including the pastors of the church, all masked up. Looking at me with their wide, scared eyes, they would not dare to take the muzzle off.

You can't have it both ways. You cannot say that you serve God Almighty and, at the same time, bow to His enemy. He won't listen to such a hypocritical prayer. Make up your mind. Serve the Lord and trust Him, or serve the devil and follow his commandments. But you must choose who your master is.

CHAPTER NINETEEN

GROWING CLOSER TO MY FELLOW INMATES

[Day 35]

IT WAS A Monday. I was looking out the window and saw geese. Two pairs and one alone. The field adjacent to the trees was of considerable size. However, for them, it was obviously too small. Or at least the two pairs must have decided that it was not big enough to accommodate them and the single one.

They attacked the single one consistently and steadily. I could tell they were saying something in their own language and were visibly upset. I could almost understand what they were saying to the single one. According to the others, this single goose was an intruder, and they were telling it, "Get out of here! You're not part of our group. You're not welcome here."

The lone goose was moving with as much dignity as it could muster and kept ignoring them but keeping a safe distance. This one was not looking for trouble. It was just minding its own business. The field was big enough for hundreds of them.

However, for whatever reason, the two pairs believed it was theirs and only theirs. They thought they could control it and prohibit others from benefiting from it. So, they kept attacking the lonely goose repeatedly—from one side, one pair, then a minute later, the other pair from the other side. Eventually, tired of the hate and such unwelcoming behavior from the others, the lonely goose spread its wings and flew away.

The two pairs were the kings of the jungle. Instead of celebrating and rejoicing, they spread their wings and flew away, leaving the conquered ground unoccupied. They flew to a little triangle field by my window on my side of the fence, flying above the chains and the barbed wire. I could not believe it. They went through all this trouble chasing the single one out, only to abandon the ground that they fought for and fly into a self-inflicted jail ground.

Now, it was me and the self-made prisoners on the other side of the wall looking into the park through barbed wire and a fence. I could not help but draw a parallel between what I was witnessing and humans. This was just like people who fight for something that they genuinely think that they need or want. They will even hurt others and do horrible things for it.

When they finally have what they were fighting about, what they were chasing brings them straight into a self-made prison. So many will step on the shoulders of others. They will lie, cheat, steal, and even murder for the "big field" that could accommodate everyone. Do you want to be the king of an empty castle, a broken castle?

Evil men are never satisfied. They pillage, and they take. They chase others away, and they are stuck with a big fat nothing, so they move on to destroy other places. They become prisoners of their own selfishness and greed and slaves to their own ambitions. For them, swift justice awaits. Sooner or later, they will be accused, judged, and sentenced, and it will not be pretty.

Why can't we share and live in peace with each other? Why do some want everything to the extent that others will suffer? One day, the God that owns everything will make things right again. Oh, how I am looking forward to that glorious day.

People are constantly chasing and never satisfied. Oh, wretched men that we are, who will save us from ourselves? Why is it so hard for us to understand that unity and support for each other are the true power? Cutting the branch that you are sitting on will always have the same outcome. Keep cutting, and eventually, you will end up on the ground.

God gave me great favor there with the inmates. Even the mean-looking ones were very warm towards me. First, they sized me up, kind of intrigued by my presence there. They would give me a look that said, "And who are you exactly? What on earth are you doing here?" Of course, their choice of words was slightly different, if you know what I mean. A day or two later, I would be praying with them and receiving a fist bump or a hug from them.

It was obvious to me that God was there, making the way and opening the doors of human hearts. Only He could do that. For a strange reason, I had become close to them. In a weird way, they were my buddies on this unbelievable journey. One day at a time. As time went by, many faces changed and new people would occupy different cells, but that created another opportunity to sew a seed in the hearts of more.

> *The Son of Man came eating and drinking, and they say, "Here is a glutton and a drunkard, a friend of tax collectors and sinners." But wisdom is proved right by her deeds.*
>
> MATTHEW 11:19 NIV

A new man with tattoos all over his body, including his face, came to our unit. He was the very one who was attacked with a machete by the son of a police officer in Calgary. The story was all over the news during that time. The guy went on a rampage, killing and chopping everyone that he could find. Our new friend almost lost his arm and his head. A sizeable portion of his face was slashed with a huge scar.

At first, he was very reluctant to join our group. However, every time we prayed, his hostility melted away. Later, he came to us saying, "Every time you guys prayed, I was being touched in a very profound way." Hearing the words of hope impacted him from the inside out. He added, "It felt so good."

We continued our church meetings on the inside, and Nathaniel and the group continued meeting on the outside. I was worried about them. There was so much hate coming from the authorities, which made me anxious. The Director was a very evil and corrupt individual. He hated this unwanted exposure and was determined to stop it. My prayer was the opposite, "God, stop him before he can stop anything that you have ordained."

They moved my friend from across the hall to the general population—to a better and more free environment. His departure meant to me that I was losing my "eyes on the battlefield." My vision was restricted, but I was certain they were outside.

This was becoming the longest, nonstop protest in the history of Canadian penitentiary centres. For thirty-four days, many remarkable people gathered to bring awareness to what was happening inside our jails. Rob, who is now our worship leader, along with his children, led worship every day. What is interesting is that Rob went from a life of alcohol, abuse, and singing in bars to risking his life as he sang for a pastor facing strong opposition.

And there was Ray, a prophetic voice in our church, along with others, was preaching and prophesying God's will in this situation.

A few months before my final arrest, God spoke to Ray and told him that the pastor was going to be arrested for a longer period and that it was his responsibility to be outside prison every single day until his release. And that's exactly what happened.

Once, Ray was even arrested for doing this! While being detained, he posed a thought-provoking and somewhat humorous question to the authorities, "Do you really want *another* pastor in your jail?" Realizing that I had been more than enough for them to handle, they quickly released Ray.

There were many others, like Lana with her shofar, who came every day and miracles eventually did happen. (I walked out of that place a free man!)

I find it fascinating that those who claimed to be anointed and equipped, the so-called Christians, were nowhere to be found in a time of trial. God raised others. My son Nathaniel had to step up as a man to fight for his father's life. A bar singer became a worshiper and was now leading worship in the church. A businessman brought his eight children every single day to fight for a man that he did not even know well.

They must have been striking a chord, since the corrupt mainstream propaganda had chosen not to even cover it once. The media's complete sellout and corruption were clearly demonstrated by this fact.

Daniel was becoming an amazing light in this place. I started to call him "Deacon" and hoped that Jesus would grant him the strength to keep going for the Kingdom of God. Daniel now had a mission. He made his way around, providing help and support to anyone and everyone he encountered. He was talking to them, comforting them, and praying for them, a true disciple of our Lord. To see that was beautiful and made my heart rejoice. Here is my public statement given for Day 35:

I am a very privileged man to feel the presence of my God right here with me during this difficult time. I can't imagine experiencing life's difficulties without the loving care of Jesus Christ. It must be terrifying. Please pray for all of those who are hurting but do not know him yet. Pray that they will embrace His love, mercy, and grace.

As I was praying today, I felt the Lord telling me to forgive those who are prosecuting me and to leave them in His hands. So that is what I am going to do. I am releasing those who have done this evil to me into the hands of the living, merciful, and just God, in the name of Jesus Christ of Nazareth. From now on, they are in his hands.

I want to thank all of those who are standing with us, praying for us, and supporting us in this time of trial. I can feel the prayers. They keep me strong. God allows me to be here as a witness to the entire world of what happens when you kick God out of your nation. Lawlessness, injustice, abuse of power, and corruption creep in. I am also here to be a witness to the prisoners. I have visited them on a personal level. I have become one of them. Because of that, I have been blessed every day with an opportunity to tell them about Jesus. In the end, to be able to do that is all worth it.

[DAY 36]

From time to time, when a new guard came, the attack on my medical exemption started again. Some were very determined to muzzle me at all costs. For some reason, they wanted me to wear that stupid mask, even though we were all in isolation. They would pressure me; I would resist, and life in prison continued. Thankfully, it never escalated to something more. The whole issue was so ridiculous.

When the guards were hiding in their "den" behind the doors, their masks came down. It was only when they were visible that the game of pretense and hypocrisy continued. I had caught the guards many times, not wearing them. Most inmates wore them under their chins only because of the potential repercussions that might come if they refused to have them visible. It was truly a sick show.

Another man had cracked under the pressure of isolation. He was sobbing, then we could hear his loud crying. People would break down emotionally from time to time, not being able to withstand the torture of isolation and segregation. I had been fighting this for the past two years. To triumph over evil, one must confront it head-on.

This reminded me of an analogy that I had been sharing during my sermons. A good doctor, one who actually cares and loves you, does a thorough examination of your body. If he notices something off about you and genuinely cares, he'll let you know what's going on and what needs to be done. If he finds cancer, he won't keep it from you and think to himself, *I better not break the bad news to my patient. This news will probably make him and his family sad and worried. Let's just keep the conversation positive. I will save him from the emotional hardship. Hopefully, everything is going to be just fine.*

Imagine a doctor who, instead of telling you the truth, is playing with your life with a game of political correctness. "I do not want to offend your feelings. Let's pretend that everything is wonderful!" He could look into your eyes and say, "You are a walking pinnacle of health and in perfect condition. Go home and be merry." Would you like such a doctor?

A real doctor—the one who truly cares for you—will say, "There is a problem, and it is serious. If we do not do something about it, you might die. As shocking and unpleasant as this might be for you, this announcement is for your own good."

You *need* to know. You must know. The doctor gets you mentally ready before the operation. The cancer needs to be cut out. He will take you to an operating table and put you to sleep. He will take the sharpest scalpel there is and will cut you open.

Blood will flow from your body all over, but he will continue. He will look for the enemy. When he finds it, he will show no mercy. He will cut it out, all of it—every piece that infringed on your well-being will be removed. A good doctor will not toy with it or debate with it. For this is not a time for a conversation. The killer, the destroyer, must be eliminated.

The doctor understands that the cancer is spreading. It will never stop until the victim is dead. It must go. The work of a surgeon is extremely bloody. The patient will be hurting. There will be scars forever. Part of the body is being cut out, but it must be done. When it is all finished, the cancer, the filth, and the evil are thrown away. The would-be killer ends up in the trash. The wound is sewn back together.

When the patient awakes at first, he is numb. Medications and drugs are keeping him temporarily from pain. He will, however, feel the impact of the operation soon. The pain will hit with its full force. "Doc, what have you done to me?" The patient might say. It is so painful but good. A real doctor will look at him and remind him, "I just saved your life. I cut the enemy out. Now you will be free."

We all have cancer in our lives, and it is killing us slowly. Day by day, it spreads more and more. Sometimes it takes many years to finish us off. For some, it will be like a wildfire, and they will be gone quickly. The sickness that we all are dealing with is called sin. The sin that needs to be dealt with. It must be cut out if we are to survive. We have to recognize that we have it. That is the very job of the good shepherd of God. It is up to him to diagnose the problem and then move into the bloody business of cutting it out. There is simply no other way.

The Remand Centre has a profitable gig taking place. It is privately owned, so money is the foundation of its endeavor. There, if you want some extra time or extra food, then you work for the guards. You can become a cleaner and wash the floors or clean the cells, and for that, you will get extra incentives.

What a brilliant form of servitude. First, wear them down, then inflict cruelty, the hardship of segregation, and isolation, and then use them as your personal slaves. Ingenious. The enslaved are willing to work for some extra freedom and food. The rest of us who were unwilling to bow were stuck in the hole. On the flip side, the organization managed to save a massive sum of money, comparable to an unstoppable flow of dough.

The AC system was still broken. We had to walk around half-naked. In the common area, it was slightly better, but we did not get to enjoy it for too long. Maybe they thought sweating was good for our health?

> *This is the fate of those who trust in themselves, and of*
> *their followers, who approve their sayings. They are like*
> *sheep and are destined to die; death will be their*
> *shepherd (but the upright will prevail over them in the*
> *morning). Their forms will decay in the grave, far from*
> *their princely mansions.*
>
> PSALM 49:13-14 NIV

Benny, a fellow inmate, was run over by a car, and since then, he had some significant problems with his ability to walk. While I was in his cell for that one night when the truck convoy arrived, I took the chance to pray for him and his leg. Here is what happened.

A few weeks had passed, and he was sent to see the doctor preparing for an operation. The doctor checked his leg and did an x-ray and, to her surprise, found out that the bones that were separated had come together on their own and that the operation was no longer needed. She said that she had never seen something like this before. She called it a "miracle." Ben was so happy to share this story with all of us. Even in a place like that, God was showing up with His miracles and His mercy.

That day, the prisoners were extra excited. Apparently, I was all over the news. The fifteen thousand people who gathered on the streets protesting the lockdowns declared their demands: to get rid of the restrictions, including the travel bans, and to release Pastor Artur Pawlowski from prison. Praise God! People have such enormous power. They just needed to exercise that power.

The transcript from the court finally arrived, and the lawyers moved to prepare for the bail hearing. I was told that maybe within ten days, we would have another opportunity to present our case before the Queen's Bench judge. I scheduled a meeting with the lawyer for tomorrow so we could discuss some of the upcoming trials. We still did not have a trial date or a bail date, and not knowing when it would be was like torture on its own.

How long? It could be a few weeks, a few months, or even more. Quite often, I prayed for God to give me the strength to endure this. There's something unique and profound when men suffer together—when they go through hardship. Whether it's their actions or the actions of others, being in the same boat in the middle of the ocean, battered by storms and lightning, unites and connects people. Stricken by similar circumstances, the pain and difficulty of being there brought camaraderie.

After a while, some disappear from the place of your mutual suffering, and you simply miss them. It is a bizarre feeling. You do not really know them and yet, they become close to you. I remember all their faces and their unique behaviors. Some are either out or have been moved to a different unit or facility. They were gone from my life, and I missed them. Like frightened sheep surrounded by wolves, they were finding comfort in the closeness of each other. There, under the circumstances, even the toughest wolves could become the most timid sheep. Loneliness breaks everyone and brings people together.

The system only gave so it could take more, but it was never theirs to give. It was always yours to have. As I watched this young man sweating, cleaning the cells, and mopping the floors for an extra bowl of soup or some extra time out of his cell, I thought, *this is how it must have looked like during the Nazi era.*

CHAPTER TWENTY

LESSONS LEARNED FROM THE GEESE

[Day 37]

THE GEESE were back today with no competition in sight. All alone. They briefly walked through the big park and just moved on. There is no one else to fight with, so why bother, I guess? Through a small window in the cell opposite to mine across the hall, I saw a man outside in the parking lot wearing his useless blue mask. It has been two years, but I still marvel at the foolishness of men.

How is it possible that some, even quite highly educated people from a civilized and advanced country, would fall for something like this? This behavior does not make sense. It was God who allowed those arrogant and proud individuals to fall into a severe delusion.

The Bible teaches that God completely turned the wisdom of sinners into stupidity.

> *Where is the wise man? Where is the scribe? Where is the philosopher of this age? Has not God made foolish the wisdom of the world?*
>
> 1 CORINTHIANS 1:20 BSB

> *...because they refused the love of the truth that would have saved them. For this reason God will send them a powerful delusion so that they believe the lie, in order that judgment may come upon all who have disbelieved the truth and delighted in wickedness.*
>
> 2 THESSALONIANS 2:10-12 NASB

It is almost like God said, "If you want to be stupid and do foolish evil things, fine. Have it your way; so be it." They go to the slaughterhouse blind and muzzled, their blinders up.

I finally found out what that blind man was in here for. His name is Jason, and nine years ago, he was shot in the head by the police. He survived but lost his eyes.

Jason is still suing the police department and because of that, according to his story, he is being constantly targeted by the authorities. He claims that the man who was the only witness to the incident was arrested before he could testify and overdosed on fentanyl, here inside the Remand Centre.

Since Jason lost his eyesight, he has been arrested multiple times. His assertion is that the guards attacked him and, just to taunt him, they confined him in the exact same cell where his buddy was murdered. On this occasion, his arrest was for the alleged mistreatment of his service dog. The mystery was finally resolved.

I had been slowly going through the Psalms. I completed my morning workout and was informed about a visitor coming at 1 p.m. who may be my lawyer. The study of Psalms was very enjoyable. Some of my favorite passages are listed below:

- **Psalms 68:6 NASB** God makes a home for the lonely; He leads out the prisoners into prosperity.

- **Psalm 72 1-2, 4, 8, 12** Endow the king with your justice, O God, the royal son with your righteousness. 2 May he judge your people in righteousness, your afflicted ones with justice. 4 May he defend the afflicted among the people and save the children of the needy; may he crush the oppressor. 8 May he rule from sea to sea and from the river to the ends of the earth. 12 For he will deliver the needy who cry out, the afflicted who have no one to help.

- **Psalm 73 2-20** But as for me, my feet had almost slipped; I had nearly lost my foothold. For I envied the arrogant when I saw the prosperity of the wicked. They have no struggles; their bodies are healthy and strong. They are free from common human burdens; they are not plagued by human ills. Therefore, pride is their necklace; they clothe themselves with violence. From their callous hearts comes iniquity; their evil imaginations have no limits. They scoff and speak with malice; with arrogance, they threaten oppression. Their mouths lay claim to heaven, and their tongues take possession of the earth. Therefore, their people turn to them and drink water in abundance. They say, "How would God know? Does the Most High know anything?" This is what the wicked are like— always free of care, they go on amassing wealth. Surely, in vain, I have kept my heart pure and have washed my hands in innocence. All day long, I have been afflicted, and every morning brings new punishments. If I had spoken out like that, I would have betrayed your children. When I tried to understand all this, it troubled me deeply till I entered the sanctuary of God; then I understood their final destiny. Surely you place them on slippery ground; you cast them down to ruin. How suddenly are they destroyed, completely swept away by terrors! They are like a dream when one awakes; when you arise, Lord, you will despise them as fantasies.

Today, after over three weeks of fighting with the administration, my lawyer, Sarah Miller, was allowed to come and see me in person. It had been almost a month since I had talked to her, and that was over a telephone booth where the conversation was listened to and recorded. The next few meetings were on the telephone or video screen. For weeks, she wanted to come and go over certain things but kept being denied. When she was calling to make an appointment with me, they would put her on hold for an hour. In the end, no one would answer.

They played this game for over three weeks. Despite having important documents to give Sarah, nobody bothered to care. One time, even the judge told them to make sure that I had access to my lawyer, but they ignored her request. Finally, today, after a month, I was able to pass my handwritten confidential documents over to my lawyer. I had included all the details I could recall about the cases I'm being tried for and accused of. She took the documents with her, which list the locations, the names... everything.

In addition, I found out today that the guards told Colton to beat me up. Thank God he refused! The inmates themselves acknowledged that this entire situation was not right and such an abuse of power. After learning that officers wanted to hurt me using the hands of the prisoners, I was on edge.

Sometimes, I would have anxious thoughts, imagining that officers stormed into my cell and beat me up. Here in this unit, there are no cameras inside the cells. They could easily say it was *me* who attacked *them.* I have heard multiple stories from several inmates with similar concerns. They said that if the guards want to hurt you, they will push you sometimes into the shower (no cameras in there), and they will beat you up. In the end, it's your word against theirs.

There was an unusual surprise today; they let us out for *two* hours. When we were finished phoning, we sat down at the tables. It felt so good. There was no rushing, no running, just being able to sit and talk to each other and listen to the other inmates' stories.

For the first time, I conducted a little Bible study, talking about God and His Word. We prayed, and it was amazing. The boys were all moved. This is exactly what they needed: hope and a positive message.

I also received an offer from the Crown's Office. If I pleaded guilty to mischief, all the other serious charges would be dropped, and I could probably walk out of here as a free man. When Sarah shared this offer with me during our meeting, she anxiously awaited my response.

"I cannot plead guilty to any of these charges. I cannot take this deal. I have done nothing wrong." I told her.

If I accepted the deal, the prosecutor would give me a significantly reduced sentence. If not, they would be asking for more. I looked at Sarah and I said, "How can I say I am guilty? I delivered a speech to desperate and hurting people. People who were fighting for the future of our children. For the future of Canada. It would be a total betrayal to say now, after two years of standing up, that I was sorry and wrong—that I did not really mean it. That I had been pinched, and I now needed to escape the pain. It would be like making a deal with the devil. I cannot take such a deal."

She replied, "I was hoping you would say that. I had to ask; I am glad you stand by your conviction."

You see, this situation was no longer about me or my family. This struggle, this resistance, was on behalf of the millions who suffered due to the falsehood and insanity of COVID-19. The eyes of many men and women were fixed on this story. How could I sell them for a better deal with the liars? I could not, and I would not.

We talked some more and strategized our next steps. Once we finished, she went her own way while I was led back to my small cell. The thought of going home and being with my family was very appealing. I wanted to go home and get out of this crazy place!

But I was not willing to sell my soul to achieve that. When the prisoners heard about it, they came and gave me hugs. They thanked me for standing up, not compromising, and for not giving up. Due to our influence, Colton enrolled in a rehab program for the first time in his life. God was winning another soul into his kingdom.

I have received feedback from others affirming that I was there for them. They spoke kind words like, "God is using you to save us," and "Thank you for being here."

Gradually, my presence there began to make sense, with my loved ones outside praying, declaring, prophesying, and revealing. God was cleaning this place. Nathaniel told me that the day before, they laid their hands on the prison building. The correctional officers freaked out and told them that they could not do that. However, my supporters kept praying and ignored them. God was on the move, and there was nothing they could do about it.

Today, there was a full moon, and since my window was on the south side, I could see the big bright circle with all its gray spots. Every month in the Old Testament, God instructed the Israelites to observe the full moon festival because there was something very powerful that happened during that time. And like then, today, we could all feel it.

There was some kind of excitement in the air, as if something was about to happen—something good. The moon was big and perfectly round, a majestic sight. It felt so close, like it was at the tips of my fingers. I could just reach out and grab it. It was just like my freedom—so close and yet so far away. It was an impossible task without the God of the impossible.

> *Sound the ram's horn at the New Moon and when the moon is full on the day of our festival; this is a decree for Israel, an ordinance of the God of Jacob. When God went out against Egypt, he established it as a statute for Joseph.*
>
> PSALM 81: 3-5

My statement for today was:

I have been locked in this place for over a month now. There is no trial date. The presumption of innocence is gone. The rule of law is ignored. This is Kenney's Alberta. He replaced one crook, Kaycee Madu, with another under investigation, Tyler Shandro, as Minister of Justice. That's how big the corruption is in Kenney's totalitarian state.

Here is how things looked here. Inmates are treated like animals logged in cells for 22 to 23 hours a day. There are no activities being done here, no counseling. There is nothing to do. No effort to change the behavior of prisoners. A correctional centre that corrects nothing. In fact, quite the opposite.

It damages people even more and then sends them back into society. The treatment creates crazy people, mentally disturbed. They are being punished before they are proven guilty.

I have seen people here so depressed because they are locked up for so many hours in their cells that they are sitting and staring at the wall or walking in circles. I have seen inmates crying to go out of their cells just to talk to someone, and they were told no. You are to sit here like a dog in a doghouse and do nothing. No Chapel allowed. No church gathering was approved. Director's orders. The same director that was kicked out from Edmonton for corruption.

This is Kenney's and Shandro's New Alberta. The tactics of Putin. Arrest and imprison any voice of opposition. Remember, that's the same Premiere who said that the COVID passport is not going to be implemented in Alberta. How can you trust a perpetual liar and a cheat? Those types of tyrants will tell you everything just to keep their power over you. They need to go. They need to be replaced.

[Day 38]

What a fantastic day. They let us out for one and a half hours, and we had enough time for a Bible study. I could minister to an inmate who was a gun for hire and had murdered people for money. During our conversation, he expressed doubt about God's willingness to forgive him for his past actions. He wanted to change his entire life, but would God accept him?

I talked about Saul, who was a murderer who arrested and imprisoned Christians. God struck him down, blinded him, and changed his entire life. The old was forgiven; it was now gone, and the new came.

Saul became Paul, a man who eventually greatly suffered for the kingdom of God. Paul gave us a sizeable portion of the New Testament. I shared the story with the group and also laid my hands on the "hired gun" and prayed for him.

His whole body started to shake! I prayed that God would change him completely and fill him with his Holy Spirit. Those moments are worth living for. The entire atmosphere is changing in this place. The boys are super friendly and hungry for the truth. The harvest is ripe and ready to be taken to the storehouse. Thank you, Jesus, for the amazing opportunity to be the light in this darkness.

The geese are back, and so is the fight. Who is the king in the castle? The empty park is still empty. The two pairs of geese, for whatever reason, cannot live together. The notion that somebody else could use the park as well was unthinkable to them. So, the war continues. They flap their wings, feathers flying, bills and beaks forward, ready to strike. A couple of minutes later, one of the pairs won.

It was all theirs: the desolate empire with no one in it now completely belongs to them. After the fight, the winning pair went to the side of the field and lay down satisfied. Humans act the same way, just like animals, or perhaps the animals act like humans. Selfish and, like my brother says, kings of a broken castle, alone and miserable.

This is not how it is supposed to be. We have been called to something a lot bigger than dust and dirt. We have been created to live as the crown of God's creation, not just merely flesh focused on flesh.

Today, I shared with the boys the story of the girl who lost her parents in the arena.

352 - Artur Pawlowski

When you get to Heaven, what will your story be? Imagine you have just died, and you get into heaven and are seated at a large table with many people sitting around it. You look around and see some of the great people of God, like Paul, Matthew, Elisha, Peter, and John.

They are all going around telling their stories. They talk about the mighty things that God did in their lives and how they were used for His kingdom. They talk about the suffering and persecution they all endured for their faith. And sitting right beside you at the table is this little girl, and it comes time for her to share.

Her story goes like this: "I was taken by the Romans with my whole family and thrown into the Colosseum. The Romans demanded that my parents and brother deny Christ. They were told if they did not deny Jesus, then they would be ripped apart by lions. My parents and brother refused to deny Him and were all killed by lions right in front of me.

"When it came to my turn, they said I must deny Jesus Christ, and then I could go free. I told them I cannot deny my Savior. He gave me life, and if I deny him in front of people, He will deny me. So they threw me into the arena, and the lions killed me."

So now, my friends, it's your turn to tell *your* story. What is your story?

When I finished telling them about the girl who lost her parents, I looked at every one of them and asked these questions:

One day, you will see God face to face, and you will have to give an account of everything you said and everything you did.
- What is going to be your story?

- When you see and hear the great heroes of old with their incredible adventures and exploits for the Kingdom of God, what are you going to say?
- Will you have your own stories? Or you will simply say: I lived. I robbed and murdered. I lived a selfish life, and then I died. I have wasted my opportunity. I have wasted my life.

I cautioned them to remember that the wages of sin, even one sin, is death. And I told them that God had so much more for them. They must " Live and not die."

Today, I also called to find out if there was a date for my bail hearing review. It was almost 4:00 p.m., and we had heard nothing yet. They were doing everything possible to postpone the dates. It was incredible that they could keep someone in prison for so long without any consequences coming their way.

I returned to the boys and planted more seeds of faith in their hearts. We started talking, and I heard from them again that this place had the worst reputation of all the correctional centres in the country. And it has the greatest number of murders committed.

> *To the church of the Thessalonians in God our Father and the Lord Jesus Christ: Grace and peace to you from God the Father and the Lord Jesus Christ. We pray this so that the name of our Lord Jesus may be glorified in you, and you in Him, according to the grace of our God and Lord Jesus Christ.*
>
> 2 THESSALONIANS 1:1, 2:12

People from all over sent me numerous letters today. It was very touching, and I was grateful that someone stood with me and my family throughout this trial.

Members of our church were outside the prison—praying and worshipping. For the previous two days, I had felt some kind of excitement. It's hard to describe, but it felt like something was about to happen. Actually, it felt like something *was* happening. I don't know what, but we will wait and see.

We had already won; it was just that the enemy was slow to realize that. I could see my friends outside praying and lifting their hands. I couldn't hear them, but I could feel the Spirit.

God is good. I will praise Him, even if it means from my little prison cell because He is worthy to be praised. I could also hear the inmates singing, *Jesus loves me, this I know*. Obviously, they could hear what was being sung outside. I started to smile. Someone was having fun.

The hardest part of being there was the unknown—not knowing when or for how long was the toughest thing to endure. People came and went from there, but I can still see them in my mind— sometimes the nameless faces of those who were once locked in there with me. I can recall the conversations and the words of encouragement given to them: "Hold on. Stick with God, and everything is going to be okay."

[Day 39]

The morning guard walked in that day, and, like every day, I said, "Good morning."

He replied, "Good morning, Pastor." Not all the guards were evil.

Today, an inmate told me about a discussion he had with another guard concerning me. The inmate said that I was helping him to focus on good, on God, on the positive, and to change his ways from a lifestyle of crime and violence. The guard responded to him by saying, "Stay close to the pastor. It is good that he is here helping you."

Wow! There are still decent people everywhere. My prayer was that God would replace the evil, wicked ones in the places of authority with good women and men who value life, honesty, and truth.

> Justice and fairness will go hand in hand, and all who do right will follow along.
>
> PSALM 94:15 CEV

Verse 20 of the passage above teaches that God is opposed to dishonest lawmakers who gang up to murder innocent victims. Every totalitarian regime enacts its own laws. The Romans, the Persians, the Ottoman Empire, and all those who had more swords and more power dictated what was legal and what was not.

That's how it was, and that's how it is going to be until Jesus comes back. Human nature is selfish and sinful and wants it all. Control over other people has always been the signature of tyrants.

In the Nazi era, when Poland was invaded and its soldiers fought back, the Nazi regime referred to them as "bandits." When you opposed fascism, *you* were the bad guy, and *they* (the aggressors) were the good guys. During the time of my childhood, under communism, everyone who fought with them was called a "terrorist."

Today, I had a Zoom meeting with Sarah. The bail hearing has no date yet, but it might happen next week. We shall see!

The geese came back to the inner prison side of the fence. It looks like they like this side of the fence. Maybe God gave me Noah's power to attract all kinds of animals.

Also, I heard that a guard named "Freeman" left his work at the Remand Centre because of how the prisoners were being treated. Apparently, he got himself a job in a maximum-security prison, which I found very interesting. An inmate overheard this guard verbally fighting with another guard. Psalm 101:6-8 CEV says, "*I will find trustworthy people to serve as my advisors, and only an honest person will serve as an official. No one who cheats or lies will have a position in my Royal Court. Each morning, I will silence any lawbreakers I find in the countryside or in the city of the Lord.*"

Would there ever be a day when Canada would have a ruler like this one? If so, the nation would be completely transformed. Instead, at least for now, we had corruption that placed its roots everywhere. Liars that were choosing liars. But in the end, they will fall into their own pits.

> *...until what he foretold came to pass, till the word of the LORD proved him true.*
>
> PSALM 105:19

Joseph remained a slave until his own words had come true and the Lord had finished testing him. Then, the king of Egypt set Joseph free and put him in charge of everything that he owned. Joseph was in command of all the officials, and he taught the leaders how to use wisdom.

In the Kingdom of God, testing is a must; it has to come, and it is given. Before the iron can be sharpened, it has to be created or forged. And that takes time. You need the right material—actually, a combination of materials. Then you need fire and water, like drowning and an inferno.

According to the website *Making 101: How to Forge A Sword | The Crucible*, these are the steps needed to create a useful, powerful weapon:

- Step #1: You need material. High carbon or Damascus steel. Only certain steels can be hardened. You can get a good idea of what kind of steel it is based on the sparks produced. High-carbon steel will produce sparks that separate into several branches. You also need tools to make that tool: A hammer, anvil, tongs, a vise, forge, chisels, punches, drifts, sandpaper, magnet, quenching oil in a metal storage container, and a belt sander.

- Step #2: You need a design. What are you dreaming about? What are you going to use this weapon for? Will it be a traditional design, unique, or specialty?
- Step #3: Heat until red/yellow. Grip the steel with a pair of tongs and heat in a forge until the steel's color turns red/yellow. The material will have reached temperatures between 2,100 and 2,200 degrees Fahrenheit. The heat may be uncomfortable and dangerous, but it's necessary for success.
- Step #4: Shape the Material. Once it has reached temperature, remove the steel from the forge. Set the stock flat on your anvil, and using a hammer, shape the corner into the shape of a sword. Make sure to taper both sides of the steel evenly.
- Step #5: Flatten the Sword Blade. Bevel the edges of your steel with a hammer to create a cutting edge on either side of the sword. Once you have hammered one side, flip the sword on the anvil and hammer the other side until both are even. Sweat and repetition are needed! It is not an easy fix. It takes time.
- Step #6: Heat and cool. Heat treatment. This is a crucial step. This changes a sharpened shard of metal into a brilliant weapon. Once you have the shape of your sword established, reheat it to normalize the steel. Grip the steel with your tongs and bring it up to a non-magnetic temperature (about 1420

degrees Fahrenheit). Let it cool off at room temperature. Once all the red color has left the steel, place it back in the forge and repeat this process three times. When heating the piece up, make sure not to overheat it. Start with a low temperature and bring it up gradually. Make certain that the blade is evenly heated, paying special focus to the tip and edges. After quenching, comes tempering. The quench makes the steel brittle, and tempering brings back the toughness of the metal.

- Step #7: Sanding. As soon as you eliminate the deep scratches, move to hand sanding. The process takes a long time, but the results are worth it. Sand the sword to smooth out the edges.

- Step #8: Strengthen and sharpen. Once the sword has been beveled, normalized, and sanded, reheat it and dip it in oil until it reaches room temperature. This process is known as quenching, and it hardens the steel to strengthen your sword. Make sure you transfer the blade from the fire to the quenching as quickly as possible. If you are too slow, the sword blade will not harden properly.

- Step #9: Reheat. Slowly reheat your quenched sword in a forge to a lower temperature. This will relax the brittleness and stress induced by the quenching process.

- Step #10: Create the hilt. The hilt is another word for a sword handle. It is usually made from leather, wire, or wood and is fastened to the blade to provide ease while holding the sword. The pommel is a large fitting at the top of the hilt and is usually made of metal. It ensures that the sword will not slip out of your hand and also provides a weighted equilibrium. Then comes the cross-guard, which has a few crucial functions. The first is to prevent an enemy sword from sliding down your own blade into your hand. Without this, a blade will cling, clash, and slice. The other crucial function is to stop one's own hand from sliding up into the blade, unlikely but possible.

- Step #11: Sharpen. With a fine file and whetstone, carefully sharpen your sword blade until you are satisfied.

Constructing a weapon that is also a practical tool is a difficult process. It can be painful for the maker (God), and it is definitely painful for the material (you and me)! God is not interested in just any scrap of metal. When He decides to work on you, He aims for perfection in His job! He wants a holy one just like He is holy!

Only a few will submit themselves to go all the way from the fire to the water and back to the fire without quitting or breaking. That is why there are not that many heroes around us these days. Everyone would like glory, but not many are willing to pay the price for that title!

> I baptize you with water for repentance. But after me comes one who is more powerful than I [mightier than I, KJV], whose sandals I am not worthy to carry. He will baptize you with the Holy Spirit and fire.
>
> MATTHEW 3:11

To become what God wants you to be, you need both the water and the fire! When the Master is done with you, He will put you to the test! There will be many tests in our lives. When it is done, and only then, you can sharpen each other and conquer more territory for God.

A man/sword in the hands of the King sharpening another sword/man is the most difficult test to pass—iron sharpening iron—because it will cost you everything. Sometimes, you will have to give things up to get what you need. You will have to walk away from things you want or like. The desires of your own flesh need to be sacrificed. There is always a price attached to the forging and the testing, such as your ambitions or plans.

If you desire to serve God, you must be willing to submit to the test. When the hammer hits, the sparks will start flying, and only the best, the real ones, the strongest, those who are willing to die for the King, are going to pass it. Fire and water will reveal who you really are! What kind of steel are you made of? God's children are not only to be tough but also sharp. To sharpen a sword requires something strong.

> *As iron sharpens iron, so one person sharpens another.*
> PROVERBS 27:17

AN INTERESTING OBSERVATION ABOUT A PERPETUAL HABIT

Every day, I was observing and learning something new about the way of life in prisons. Today, the lesson was about how the trafficking business functions in this place. The security here is tight. If the guards and administration wanted to keep the drugs out of this place, there was absolutely nothing that the inmates could do. Simply put: There would be no drugs in jails.

However, that was not the case; it's quite the opposite. The drug business flourishes under the supervision and watchful eye of the administration and the nurses. For weeks, I had been closely watching the guards and nurses as they worked together seamlessly, distributing various substances to the inmates.

I understand that this may come as a shock to you, but trust me, I was equally surprised. Instead of fixing the problem, they drugged the problem, and violence resulted from that. They facilitated, encouraged, and provided the very thing that brought people into this trouble initially. That is so evil!

Every day, at least twice a day, they would come with their little table on wheels and, on it, a variety of drugs. The nurse, along with the assistance of a uniformed guard, created a really weird image, like in a movie straight from Russia. I watched the same scenario repeatedly.

The guard would visit and open your cell, and the so-called "nurse" would inquire if you required anything. I noticed that almost always, the inmates desperately needed something. Later, I found out that it was the drugs that they were waiting for.

Since I am a very lousy criminal and do not take drugs or drink alcohol, I needed to educate myself through the inmates who knew what the whole thing was all about. And believe me, some of the people that I spent time with were experts on the subject!

The majority of these experts had ended up here because of drugs, either because they were taking them or trafficking them. As you remember, during my first three weeks, I was not allowed to have any physical face-to-face interactions with other inmates. When I was let out of my cell, the other prisoners were commanded to go in.

But now, I was able to interact with others. So naturally, I talked to them about my observations. Pills. Pills. Pills. Changing hands all throughout the day. First, the nurse, assisted by the guard, helps the inmate get his pill. Sometimes the inmate *pretends* that he is taking it but then sells it to somebody else. When all the "clients" are taken care of, the nurse takes her little business to the next unit.

That's how the constant flow of dope, dough, and clients ensures the never-ending cycle. It's a river of revenue with a revolving door. The government claims to combat drugs, but paradoxically they supply them to the individuals who end up in prison for involvement with those substances. These drugs are freely being given to them right there behind the iron bars.

That's quite a system, I must say. The difference is that the drugs being pushed there were "legal" and a bit cleaner than the ones being sold on the streets. However, the result was the same: addiction, crime, and ultimately, death!

Since I was unfamiliar with the game, I had to consult my inmate friends to learn the names of the drugs being distributed. It is also very interesting to note that I put all the names of the substances on a piece of paper with a clear note: "For my lawyer only." But when I spoke to my attorney later, the guards confiscated the note from me. Of course, confiscating such documents is illegal, but since law and order were out the window, they truly believed they could do whatever they wanted.

However, I was able to give one piece of evidence to my lawyer when we met. So, what kind of narcotics are we talking about? First off, Suboxone is an opioid known for its severe side effects mentioned below:

Headache, insomnia, sweating, swelling in arms and legs, nausea, vomiting, constipation, mouth or tongue numbness, burning, and redness if you use the orally dissolvable film, low blood pressure when you stand up, impaired liver function, adrenal changes, sleep-related breathing issues, allergic reactions, back pain, abuse and dependence, breathing problems, coma, hormone problems (adrenal insufficiency), liver damage, severe withdrawal symptoms, depression.

Headaches are a common side effect of Suboxone. In one study, about 36 percent of people taking it experienced headaches.

And yet this narcotic was handed out freely in prison.

A big problem resulting from the regular use of Suboxone begins when an inmate is released. The withdrawal symptoms include nausea, diarrhea, headache, muscle aches, insomnia (trouble sleeping), anxiety, irritability, drug cravings, and excessive sweating. It is evident that people who quit this highly addictive drug may attempt to maintain their addiction on the streets, potentially leading to criminal behavior and re-imprisonment.

The next drug, routinely administered in prison, is called Wellbutrin, which has many adverse reactions, as well, including tremors, dizziness, excessive sweating, blurred vision, tachycardia, confusion, and cardiac arrhythmia. Not to mention auditory disturbances, aggressiveness, agitation, chest pain, confusion, and hallucinations. The list goes on and on, addressing side effects such as depression and suicidal tendencies.

Some users describe the "high" from Wellbutrin as similar to cocaine or methamphetamine, highly addictive but with less intensity. It has also been aptly named the "Poor Man's Cocaine" because it elicits stimulant effects like cocaine and crack, but it is much cheaper.

I was routinely offered Methadone, a synthetic opioid that was created by German doctors during World War II. Once again, the side effects take a full page to mention, and the drug itself is highly addictive. How about Vyvanse, a stimulant that may cause serious side effects, including cardiac, mental, and psychotic symptoms?

Along with Adderall, Vyvanse is among the two most abused prescription drugs among adolescents and young adults.

There we so many more. So much for rehabilitating addicts to get off their addiction, right? They stay hooked and are later released to the outdoor world. It's just a matter of time before they will come back to this professional drug-pushing facility.

So, the government makes tons of money while taxpayers fund the bill for narcotics distribution in prison—and no questions asked. One just says that they want it, and Voila, they get it. What a business with perpetual clients and a well that never dries.

It appeared like everyone was happy. The corrupt institutions were making tons of gold, and the inmates had the opportunity to resell what they obtained or just become hooked on it themselves. The only person who didn't know what was going on was the taxpayer. He was struggling to pay his bills and buy lifesaving prescriptions that he needed to survive but couldn't afford, and the elected officials were saying that there was no money in the coffers.

Right in front of my eyes, the pills circulated from one hand to another, and the legal government-approved business now became illegal. The product remained the same; the people did not change. The environment was identical. There was only one thing missing. Now, it wasn't the government pushing the substance; it was the inmates doing this by themselves.

The guards were happy now that they didn't have to do much. The inmates were in heaven. Since there was nothing to do there, why not take drugs offered to them to kill the time? It was like a death in installments—one day closer to the departure.

Since jails were full, that ensured a fresh batch of addicts for life. It's a very clever setup, don't you think? When the nurses came to my door asking if there was anything I needed. But what they were really saying was, "Do you need your daily fix? We can hook you up. Just say the magic word, 'yes. '"

Silly me. While I was talking about us being locked inside here like dogs in cages for 23 hours a day, losing our minds, they were not interested. That was not why they were there. I was not a drug addict, and I did not want to become one, so I was a waste of time to them. There was no money to be made with me. Shut the door and move on to the next cell.

They didn't want to be occupied with trivial things like segregation or isolation. Take the pill, and everything will be fine. You and your imaginary friends will have an amazing trip!

WE SHALL NOT BE MOVED!

It was about 8:00 p.m. that evening, and supporters were outside the prison. Suddenly, the prisoners started to chant, "Free Pastor Art! Free Pastor Art!" It bounced off the metal and the concrete. The guards were not happy. The whole unit was punished by having no lights in the cells. We were to sit in darkness.

It was a small price to pay for freedom. It is a very beautiful night with a full moon again. I thought about the festivals that God commanded us to observe during the full moon. It would be nice to eat something good again and to hear some worship music. It would be great to dance to the tune of "*We Shall Not Be Moved*." Instead, for now, I had to imagine dancing, singing, and eating.

There, the time went so slow. I was asking God to please speed it up somehow. As I looked through the window, staring at the bright round ball in the sky, the fence, and the barbed wire, this verse came to mind:

> *I don't care if they curse me as long as you bless me.*
> PSALM 109:28A CEV

The moon was so bright and intense that it reminded me of a holiday that our government had canceled: Canada Day.

REFLECTING BACK ON A MISSED CHANCE FOR CANADIAN PATRIOTISM

One day in 2020, I received an invitation to speak at Parliament Hill for Canada Day. For over a century, Dominion Day, an occasion commemorating Canada's federation, had been celebrated on July 1st. However, during the administration of Pierre Trudeau, the holiday was changed into Canada Day. The 2020 event was to take place on a hill between Parliament and the Centennial Fire. Canadians nationwide were to convene at this major event to show solidarity and oppose the politicians' illegal actions.

It was also supposed to be a good trip to spend some time with our family, including my brother Dawid. In Ottawa, we met with some of our friends and prepared for the big day. The weather was scorching at that time of year, and it didn't help that the parliament had no shade whatsoever.

I was one of the first speakers. About 5,000 people came to stand together for their freedom and their families. God had blessed me with two speeches, and I was conflicted about which one to deliver. I selected the one I thought the top boss wanted me to share with Canadians. As I spoke, the atmosphere was electrifying. Thousands of people clapped and were on fire as the words came from my mouth.

Together with my wife, we hoped to remind Canadians about our fascinating heritage. For example, the symbolism behind the colors of the flag, the message placed on the walls of the parliament itself, and the words that had been chosen by the forefathers for the Canadian National anthem. It was a good feeling to remember our origins.

When the people of a nation don't know where they came from, they won't know where they are heading. Knowing the heritage and history of the past is very important to the survival of any society. While speaking, the receptivity to the message was overwhelming. They absolutely loved it. In my heart, I felt that God once again was warning and telling Canadians how far they had fallen from the original plan. He alerted us to the precarious situation our nation was in. And if we did not change our ways, we would be facing the consequences of our rebellion.

We spent two days on the hill. The first was with all the Patriots, doing speeches and interviews. The second, we came to worship our God by the Centennial Fire and to pray. As usual, Larry did a great job leading us into some old hymns filled with so much wisdom and the word of God. We also had the opportunity to meet some new freedom fighters and their families, and thanks to their generosity, we enjoyed a great barbecue in their home.

God desired us to confront the greed and perversion in our nation on Dominion Day 2020. Particularly the sin of homosexuality, which was in our faces everywhere we turned: in the windows of the banks and stores, on the billboards, and next to the national flags. Even as we walked the streets of Ottawa, we would see the symbols of sexual perversion on their sidewalks and crosswalks/crossroads.

The entire nation seemed to have lost its pride in being Canadian. Secular/sexual preferences became the only thing that mattered, while everything else became unimportant. As we walked and observed all of that in our capital city, I knew deep inside that God had no option but to judge Canada. If He had not done it, Sodom and Gomorrah would have had a right to appeal. Just as before, God would make his presence known and be heard by all. He would say, "I am not pleased, and I am coming with my judgment."

Looking back, I marvel at how merciful and patient God is. He had been warning and knocking at the door of the nation and at the hearts of the Canadian men and women, repeatedly saying, "Come back to me! Repent and turn away from all your evil ways."

But there had been no answer. Everyone did and continued to do what was right in their own eyes and minds. I wished every city, every town, and every village would take this fight for freedom to their streets.

CHAPTER TWENTY-ONE

THE GROWING SUPPORT OF THE INMATES

[Day 40] Shabbat

THIS DAY began with around ten correctional officers storming the unit. We were told to walk out of our cells; everyone was commanded to leave his cell, including the guy in a wheelchair.

"Put your masks on," the command was given.

I said, "No."

The officers talked among themselves and determined that I had a medical exemption. The guy in the wheelchair, the one with the plumbing issues and mental problems, was grumpy. You could tell he was not 100% and probably should never have been locked up here. He should have been treated by medical professionals who dealt with mental issues.

As they rushed him from his cell, he was told to put the mask on his face and keep his bed sheets and clothing with him. He struggled with the clothes and, being frustrated, threw them on the ground. The most aggressive female guard, who was also the most vocal, picked his stuff up and threw it on his head.

After that, we were told to walk all the way to Admission. They put all of us in a little cell and, in groups of three and four, took us all to get new coveralls and towels. How weird! There were so many officers there that it felt like a freak parade and was totally unnecessary. Every week, they just opened the doors and gave us fresh, clean stuff, and it was not a big deal. But this time, it was.

My fellow inmate, Jay, said that not long ago, the officers had forced them to do the same walk, but completely naked—just for fun. So, imagine a dozen or more inmates walking through the hallways naked in front of other guards, male and female alike. Because some twisted, perverted mind decided that it was completely acceptable in Canada to humiliate other human beings in such a way. Well, I guess I should consider myself lucky.

> *I am your servant! How long must I suffer? When will you punish those troublemakers?*
>
> PSALM 119:84 CEV

Those proud people had rejected God's teaching, and they dug pits. I couldn't help but think, *God, please let them fall into their own devices.*

One guard yelled, "Put your shoes on. Where are your shoes?"

I looked at this insanity and wanted to say something, but the guy in the wheelchair just rolled himself away from the crazy woman. One of his legs was missing, and his other foot was partially severed. The man could not put their stupid orange boots on, so it was clearly a psychotic power trip. Perhaps the officer was taking the same pills that the prison staff had been so eagerly promoting to the inmates. You never know.

We were finally locked back up in our cells. Laying down on the very uncomfortable mattress made my body ache. So, I moved around and tried to change positions. Finally, I had had enough, so I stood up. Tried to move a little, but there was nowhere to go.

I took two or three steps, and it was over; I was at the door. Frustration was beginning to surface again. I looked through the window; there wasn't much to see. The barbed wire and fence painfully reminded me that I was, in fact, in prison.

Being restless or impatient was futile because there was nothing I could do. From time to time, I would hear the banging on the walls or the doors, which was another clear sign that a frustrated inmate was going nuts. Sometimes, I would hear yelling or cursing accompanied by banging: "Let me out. I want to get out of this f###ing place. Let us do something."

Finally, there was quiet. I guess another one realized that there was absolutely nothing he could do about his circumstances and that he was stuck. According to one guard, he would allow us to be out of our cells all day if he had the choice. He said he did not understand why we were being locked up for such a long period of time because it did not make any sense to him.

He was right, and it definitely did not make any sense to us. There were no fights in our unit; everyone got along. The inmates cleaned the place every day for incentives and for more freedom. So why not let us socialize and play some chess or checkers? It seemed no one had an answer to that question.

Today, the inmates made a petition that everybody signed. In the petition, they asked a very simple question: Why were the other units permitted to be out of their cells all day long, and we were kept in our cells 22 to 23 hours a day? The petition demanded that we be let out into the common area, or there would be a problem.

One day, when I was going to see my lawyer, I witnessed other units being allowed to play chess and other activities. In our unit, it was a struggle to have a normal telephone conversation without running out of time. Then we only had time to run to the shower, and it was all over and time to go back into our small cage—back to the doghouse.

Be a good doggie; take your pill and have your trip. If you were not an addict, well, I guess you should become one. Life in this unit could be a bit more bearable. If you could not or would not, well then, you would suffer. After all, it was our own choice, right?

Today, numerous people came to support me as they gathered outside the Remand Centre. There was also a large group of police officers, correctional officers, and sheriffs. The crowd moved to the front of the building, and I could only see a little through a small window in the cell across from mine.

A SIGN FROM GOD?

About ten minutes had passed, and while peering through the window, I saw two beautiful mule deer. They were big and mature, right there about 150 yards away. They were unbelievable and simply beautiful. The deer were eating and minding their own business.

When they brought me here, I saw this magnificent white wolf walking in the middle of the field, also about 150 yards away. This time, I saw those deer. It was like they had come from out of nowhere. In my heart, I knew it had to be a sign.

When I talked to my wife, she said that she felt in her heart that I was coming home; it was just a matter of time. She described it as the same feeling that she had when I came home from an extended mission trip.

I was enjoying watching the deer when suddenly they began moving their tails. Their ears went up, and their heads turned to the left. Having seen this type of behavior before, I knew this meant someone was approaching. At first, I thought perhaps there were police cars coming. A half-hour before, I had seen the police cruisers going in that direction behind the building.

To my surprise, it was not the police. It was my wife, Marzena! She was walking there all by herself in her red coat! *Wow!* I thought. *Why is she venturing around this evil place surrounded by so many officers?*

Then, suddenly, from around the corner, others emerged—a lot of them. I could not believe it. The Church was actually conducting a Jericho March all around the prison. It was incredible! I'm confident that no one has ever done this before. God was breaking spiritual walls. The Spirit was moving. People were marching. Fear was crushed, and something changed! What a Church! What a family!

Everyone did what needed to be done. I did my part; the family stood strong, the Church was unmoved, and the community came together in times of trouble. In the end, eventually, God gave us victory!

I saw familiar faces but also people that I did not know. There in the crowd, I saw my father with my sons, Nathaniel and Gabriel.

This was something else. They came straight to the fence. Some grabbed it with their fingers; others chanted. They waved and smiled. My father pointed in my direction. I think he could see me.

I was waving back. It was truly a remarkable view. People filled the entire fence line in my view and were smiling, chanting, and pointing at me. I was so happy!

Then suddenly, the doors of my cell opened. A guard stood there, visibly disturbed. He told me to pull my coveralls up and follow him. I thought to myself, *I guess it's time to suffer.*

Several guards took me to the door leading out of the unit. Colton was there. We hugged. And the boys shouted, "We stand with Pastor Art." Colton and I were escorted out of the unit. He was saying something, but I could not hear him well.

I just repeated, "We are winning. We are winning."

I was led through the hallway all the way to the Admission Office. There were a lot of guards there and a lot of prisoners. When they opened the doors, I saw hundreds of prisoners crammed into all those little cells, all dressed in blue, sitting next to each other. It looked kind of funny and reminded me of blue Smurfs all staring at me with intensity.

I was a bit worried that they might just throw me with them and say, "Now finish him off." Thank God that did not happen. Some higher-up officer looked at us and suddenly started to yell. "Not here. Take him from here. Get him out of here."

So again. The door was opened, and I was taken out of Admission. As we were walking out, maybe 15 or 20 inmates were being escorted in a single file into the Admission Office. I was being escorted by multiple officers on the right side of the hallway. There were officers in front of and behind me. This whole craziness made me feel like some kind of Al Capone or El Chapo of Calgary—the most wanted and feared in all of Canada. The most dangerous Pastor!

The boys were escorted to the left. As we passed them, I said, "Do not lose hope. Do not give up. Guys, do not lose faith."

The officer in charge was very unhappy and told me to keep walking. He turned to me and said, "We're going to add more charges on you—a lot of them—including inciting." I think what he meant was inciting a riot.

It looked like they were thinking of piling up some more made-up charges against me just for the fun of it. Honestly, I wasn't surprised because it had happened to me many times. They had no problem lying under oath, making stuff up, and fabricating documents. Yeah, they were simply not good people, but those who lied, cheated, manipulated, and cooked up stuff.

I looked at him and said, "Sure, bring it on. All of it! Everything. Bring it all on, as many charges as you want."

He looked surprised that I wasn't scared. We kept walking until they opened the door, and I was taken to a little cell.

THE CONCRETE TREATMENT

The new cell was approximately one-third the size of my usual one. There was a little bench. But there was no sink, no water, and no washroom. I braced myself for a long night on the hard bench. This cell was so small that I devised a plan just in case someone would try to walk in to hurt me.

If an inmate tried to come to beat me up, I would brace myself with stretched legs, preventing them from opening the door. I was very confident that I could keep the door closed while in a lying position. If the guards came, then I guess it would be game over.

I am completely unaware of the length of time I was confined in that cell. Finally, the doors were opened, and I was escorted back to my unit by a nice guard who I had gotten to know. All of that craziness was absolutely for nothing. Taking me out of my solitary cell, parading me in front of other inmates, and then locking me in a smaller cell all by myself. All of that only took me back to my original cell, and for what?

It was another form of intimidation to mess with my head. But whatever their reason, I was safe and back in my cell. Afterward, fellow inmates filled me in on what had gone on during my absence. They saw supporters out their windows who had banners, placards, pictures, and signs that read, "Free Pastor Art."

A number of the inmates repeatedly said that this was the most beautiful thing that they had ever seen. The people. The families. Holding the barbed wire fence. Chanting for my freedom and singing. To them, it was absolutely amazing!

One man came to me, crying. They were deeply touched. By the time I was brought back to my cell, the family and the supporters had already left. It was very touching to hear the inmates describe the events and tell me what had happened after I was taken away. They really thought that I would be beaten by the guards.

This man told me that they prayed that this would not happen. So, God granted their prayers. I glanced out the window and noticed a paper heart attached to the fence. My heart melted. Thank you, Jesus, for all those wonderful people. Thank you for your hope.

My 40th day in prison ended with a splash. It truly was a powerful full moon festival, and the extraordinary Shabbat day ended. Of course, preaching to the church from prison by phone was an accomplishment that I am sure not many can attest to. I have to admit, the last few hours kept me in suspense and gave me an adrenaline rush. (*With a lifestyle like mine, who needs drugs, right?*)

As I was lying in bed, I heard something familiar. I jumped up and came closer to the door; someone was reading the Bible out loud. By pressing my ear against the door, I could clearly decipher parts of the scripture being read. Although I could not see the person, their voice was coming from the common area.

I thought to myself, *it must be the young man. I'll have to ask him tomorrow.* His voice was steadily reading along. *How fascinating,* I thought as he moved through the scripture!

When I looked out of my window, the little heart was gone. Some guard, or, as my daughter would describe it, some "meanie," had taken it down. I guess the love symbol must have been bothering the Director.

It was getting late, and I was not allowed to leave my cell as a punishment because of the supporters and my family daring to protest around the prison. Well, at least others were allowed to enjoy at least a bit of freedom. If the evil was so disturbed, it must have been working.

I often told Marzena and Nathaniel on many occasions, "Do not stop. This is a very corrupt place, and its wickedness must be exposed. I will manage. God will give me the strength." Suffering for doing good is a privilege and a blessing, even though it didn't feel like it at that moment.

[Day 41]

Our buddy, Justin, had become collateral damage. Just a few days before, he got the cleaning job. After staying in a box for months, he was thrilled that he had "advanced" in the eyes of the oppressors. And Justin did a great job of cleaning what needed to be cleaned and even what did not need to be cleaned.

He went the extra mile just to keep that little privilege of being out of the cell a bit longer than the rest of us. He was doing more than was required of him because it meant that he could be out of his cell. He could watch TV and make as many phone calls as he wanted. Justin would walk from cell to cell, asking if anyone needed some hot water. The cells contained only cold water. To enjoy a hot soup, we had to retrieve it from the common area. And, of course, being locked inside the cell, that was impossible.

For a couple of days, the guards had been fuming with hatred. Given the international scrutiny, they were unwilling to personally inflict physical harm on me. Therefore, they were trying to hurt me by hurting all of us locked in our unit. They would keep me locked longer while others were allowed to come out of their cells. But I guess that was not good enough for them. So they lashed out at Justin.

So far, he had done the best job of anyone since I had been there. There was someone banging on the wall and doors. Donnie brought Benny and Colten along and shared that Justin was losing it after being dismissed as a cleaner by the guards. Justin was understandably quite upset.

I told the boys that we needed to help him out. If we all stayed together and refused to take this job, they would give it back to Justin because they would have no choice. This idea went all over the unit, and every inmate agreed to the plan except one.

First, they would not tell me which one. They were also shocked and said that soon I would see it for myself. Well, sure enough, I got my answer. The only inmate who refused to stand in solidarity with all of us was Ray.

It was a very hard blow. Ray always looked so solid, like someone who understood the concept of sticking together in prison. He displayed tattoos everywhere on his big muscles. It felt like such a betrayal.

This particular morning, I saw him cleaning the floors. He came to my door, and I asked him what was going on. He said that he just could not stay in the cell for that long anymore; he had to get out. Well, that's exactly how the establishment wins; that is exactly how the "kapos" in the Nazi prison camps were made. To explain what a "kapo" is, read this excerpt from online:

> They [kapos] were also called "prisoners by self-administration." The prisoner functionary system minimized costs by allowing camps to function with fewer of Hitler's paramilitary (SS) personnel. The system aimed to turn victim against victim by pitting prisoner functionaries against their fellow prisoners to maintain the favor of their SS overseers.
>
> If they neglected their duties, they would be demoted to ordinary prisoners and be subject to other kapos. Many prisoner functionaries were recruited from the ranks of violent criminal gangs rather than from the more numerous political, religious, and racial prisoners; such criminal convicts were known for their brutality toward other prisoners.
>
> This brutality was tolerated by the SS and was an integral part of the camp system. Prisoner functionaries were spared physical abuse and hard labor, provided they performed their duties to the satisfaction of the SS functionaries. They also had access to certain privileges, such as civilian clothes and a private room. Prisoner functionaries were often hated by other prisoners and spat upon as Nazi henchmen. (*https://en.wikipedia.org/wiki/Kapo*)

So, instead of uniting together and doing what was right, we witnessed, once again, the weak human nature. He was selfish, egotistic, and focused on me, myself, and I.

Ray's thinking was, *As long as I have it easier, well, who cares about others?* You can talk the talk, but in the end, the test reveals the truth—what you're really made of?

While everybody said, "No," Ray took the opportunity to please the very beast that was doing this to him in the first place. It was so sad. People like him are like a bird that sees the bait but ignores the trap.

As I explained earlier, when I was arrested, I immediately began fasting. For me, it was a "standard operating procedure." God was the only one who could help us. After fasting for 14 days, my wife took over. Yesterday, we reached 40 days of fasting combined as a couple.

So today, Marzena began eating, and I took over fasting once again. This decision made the young man from the nearby cell very happy because I promised him today's meal. Apparently, he was always hungry, so I was glad to make at least someone happy.

I looked out and could clearly see the pair of geese on the roof. Once more, everything was blanketed in snow, pure white. The geese were just sitting there and looking down, checking out an entirely empty empire.

It appeared that they had managed to drive out the competition, at least for today. The world outside was cold and windy, but inside the jail, it was like a tropical island—extremely hot and sweaty. The intense heat shifted my mind to the wonderful time we had experienced once in the Caribbean. Oh, how I wished to be there now to minister, relax, swim, and enjoy God's amazing creation!

RECOLLECTIONS OF MINISTRY TO THE PEOPLE OF BARBADOS

Once, our friend Kelly informed me that a lady we knew would be coming to Calgary. The lady had been greatly used in a realm of prophecy, and our friend thought we might like to have her at the church. I agreed without hesitation because I enjoy guest speakers when they are real servants of God. They always brought something fresh and new to the congregation. A change of speed and style was good for the people. If they had the same person speak week after week, it often became predictable and boring.

The lady's name was Marguerite. She was from Barbados, and I looked forward to her visit. The services she conducted were great, and they were ministered on the streets for the homeless. When her time was done, she said, "Come visit us in Barbados. Bring your family; we will take care of you." I told Marguerite that if it was God's will, we would see each other again.

Some time passed, and Marguerite called to say that they were organizing a "March for Jesus" in Barbados, so we decided to go. Someone assisted us with the purchase of plane tickets, and Marguerite arranged for us to stay in a house owned by the Minister of Justice in a beautiful beachfront area with a coral reef.

It was absolutely beautiful. I could literally jump from the deck and swim with fish of every color one could imagine. The staff cooked for us daily, and we were able to minister. Their church was in a poorer neighborhood, and the old building needed some work. But it had a touching character that took you back to the time of the English. Barbados was a former slave colony before receiving its independence.

Outside the church, barefoot children played soccer. Barbados had beautiful, naturally rich soil, but the country was struggling with poverty. Marguerite put us to work every day. I was either going to do some interviews with the media, or we were preaching in the churches. I was invited to talk at the only government-owned TV station, which was a real treat.

I invited people to join the March, which was scheduled to happen in one week. We also invited numerous radio stations and were featured in a nationwide newspaper. We shared our story of how miraculously Jesus healed Nathaniel and changed our entire lives. Interestingly, there was also a ceremony for the graduate prisoners inside their state's maximum penitentiary. It was a big deal, and I was invited to be the keynote speaker during that ceremony.

After going through a heavy security check, we finally reached the area where the ceremony was to take place. The room was very hot and filled with thousands of inmates waiting with anticipation to hear and see the pastors who were there to speak. One by one, the names were called, and the graduates would come to receive their certificates.

After everyone received their documents, I spoke. I began by explaining that the true prisoner or slave is not the person behind bars, but the one without a king to grant them freedom. True freedom comes from within, and it's a gift that only God can give.

"You can be out there," I said while pointing to the window, "living in palaces and having fancy things, but the truth is that a man without God in his life is the poorest and the most miserable man on earth. When you come to Jesus, you must leave the past behind, the things you have done, and the things that were done to you, and move forward with Him, the giver of life. You'll receive freedom that no man can take away from you."

The inmates clapped, visibly stirred. I shared a little about my past and explained that we were called to be lions, not hyenas. They should not settle for the crumbs at the devil's table but should dine with God. At His table, there were plenty of good things for everyone. It was amazing to share with them and to encourage them with hope.

Between the speaking engagements, media interviews, and church gatherings, we found time to swim in the absolutely beautiful waters of the Caribbean Sea with the coral fish and blue turtles. That was breathtakingly beautiful, and God had created it for us to explore and enjoy. We went sightseeing around the island. We saw the famous caves and went to a pristine beach to swim with the big turtles.

One day, we went to see the surfers riding on the waves. Our son, Gabriel, had always wanted to do that and used every opportunity to practice at the local swimming pools in Alberta. He really wanted to try surfing in the open sea.

We found a man who was willing to take him for his first-ever lesson of surfing—first on the ground, or a "dry lesson," as the teacher called it. When he was somewhat satisfied, they went to the water. The task was not that easy; the waves weren't huge but big enough, and there were rocks that they had to watch for.

But after a few attempts—wow! Gabriel was surfing on the water. He and the teacher would go back and forth to catch another wave. It looked like a lot of fun, but I could tell that Gabriel was becoming exhausted. When he came back to shore, he could barely stand up.

The teacher, a professional surfer, came and said that he had never had a better student than Gabriel. He gave him a high five and said that he was amazing. Some people are born with the ability to do certain things. Well, surfing was definitely one of my son's gifts, and we were so proud of him.

The time for the March for Jesus in Barbados had come. We brought banners from Calgary: the big one with the "March for Jesus" wording on the front and smaller ones featuring the Ten Commandments and the Word of God. We passed out gospel tracks and gave balloons to the children to carry.

At Marguerite's encouragement, the speakers made a few stops along the route for praying, worshiping, and dancing. We stopped at the parliament to pray, declare, and prophesy the will of God over not just Barbados, but the entire Caribbean. This region desperately needed a move of God. People stopped and clapped with us; some even joined the parade. We had such a great time.

The kids and the youth did a fantastic job dancing through the entire event. We ended the march throughout downtown, and while holding hands, we worshipped and prayed again for God's perfect will in the nation. It always deeply moves me to witness countless people openly celebrating the Lord and unapologetically embracing the name of Jesus.

Before we left Barbados, Marguerite had a special surprise prepared for us. With a beautiful ceremony, we were dressed in special garments for the ordination, as we had been appointed as pastors of their denomination. It was a very beautiful way of thanking us for coming and spending this time with them. Part of my heart will always remain there in the Caribbean.

After returning home, we stayed in touch with Marguerite. Sometimes, she would call with insights from the Lord. Sometimes, I would call her and ask, "When are we holding another March for Jesus in the Caribbean?" We were planning another one in Jamaica. But for now, God had different plans for me.

CHAPTER TWENTY-TWO
BACK TO REALITY

JUST AS I remembered that story, I realized I was confined in a solitary cell. Recounting that day reminded me that God had allowed me to bring them a sliver of hope. There I was, a man telling the church in Barbados that there was a better tomorrow if they would only be willing to receive it. And now, back in Calgary, no one was allowed to come to our unit to bring the light. There were no activities, no church services, no gymnasium—nothing. We were just a bunch of people locked in cells left to waste the rest of our lives.

If these prisoners were encouraged to press on toward something, they would have gladly done it. But what was killing them and making them even more angry at the world? Sitting and looking at the same spot all day.

We were all here to be punished by spending hours upon hours lying down, wasting resources, and throwing away opportunities. And supposedly, this was being done for the *benefit* of society. It was hard to grasp the concept that this thing called "justice" had anything to do with justice. The system focused on one thing: dehumanizing an individual caught by those who loved power over others. Yet there was no way that those who tasted this kind of abuse would become better humans. No way!

When they are released from here, their attitude becomes bitter, angry, unforgiving, and ruthless, with a specific goal in mind: They will not get caught the next time. There is no talk about resocialization and changing their ways, even though some have been locked up for years. Once they complete the treatment, they would be likened to a dog that had repeatedly been kicked—growling, barking, and biting.

During my time in prison, I observed inmates snapping and talking back to guards, only to face further punishment without any empathy or attempt to comprehend their situation. Their books would be taken away from them, or, as they did with me, their Bibles would be snatched. No more reading positive messages for you. You sit like a dog in a doghouse, and don't you dare complain, or we will think of a worse thing for you to endure.

The sweat coming from my eyebrows brought me back to reality. I washed my face and dried it. The heating system was broken and was obviously not a priority for the administration. If it wasn't bothering the Director, then who cared, right? To paraphrase Proverbs 3:3-4 (CEV), "Let love and loyalty always show like a necklace. Write them in your mind. God and people will like you and consider you a success."

I had another prisoner come to me, telling me an interesting story. Upon his arrival at this unit, one of the guards approached him and informed him of their intention to "accidentally" leave my cell door open. They wanted him and another black guy from a different cell to attack me. If they were willing to do that, then the guards would give them extra time outside of their cells. The inmate replied to the guard, "Why do you want us to beat this guy up? Because he's not wearing his mask and because he thinks that he is some kind of Messiah and prays and stuff?"

He continued to the guard, "I would never do that. Why would I beat up a clergyman? I will never do it."

Can you imagine the level of hate that they have against me? Even now, after so many days, they would keep fishing for someone, anyone that would, for a little incentive, agree to hurt me. Wow, what sick people!

Today, I discovered the name of another drug that was offered to us—Gabapentin, also known by the brand name Neurontin and known on the street as "gabbys." They are anticonvulsants used for seizure disorders, as well as certain neuropathic pain conditions. Gabbys are most commonly used to treat epilepsy, restless leg syndrome, hot flashes, and neuropathic pain. They are often used as a less addictive alternative to Opioids; however, Gabapentin addiction and abuse still occur in many patients. In addition to its potentially addictive nature, Gabapentin can cause suicidal thoughts, mood swings, and abrupt changes in a user's behavior. It can also cause elevated blood pressure, fever, sleep problems, appetite changes, and chest pain.)

In the box, you have a lot of time to think about what's important—i.e., what's *really* important. Your thoughts turn to what you would do if you were able to get out. Most people cannot wait to get out to talk to their kids, wives, parents, or friends and to be with those who love them.

These strong, tough men had caused so much suffering to others, and yet at the mention of their wife or mom, tears would start coming to their eyes. Today I saw a man writing a beautiful letter to his wife. On every second page, there was some kind of drawing done by him. He would put red hearts or some kind of picture that represented what was dear to him and to her.

The man writing the letter shouted out to me with a smile because he was proud of his work. He painstakingly took his time while writing, page after page. There were words mixed with drawings. He wanted to put as much there as he could. This man was a fully grown-up man, covered with tattoos, playing tough. But with his girl and for his girl, he was just another kid desperate for love and acceptance.

The more time I spent with the inmates, the more it confirmed my theory that most of them joined some kind of organization simply to belong and to be part of a bigger group. They wanted to feel stronger and accepted. It's unfortunate that the Church overlooks such a significant chance to connect with them and inspire them to join what is good. To invite them to the winning team—the pride of lions.

> Wise friends make you wise. But you hurt yourself by going around with fools.
>
> PROVERBS 13:20 (CEV)

I just finished writing this down when an officer opened the door and told me to follow him.

"Where are we going?" I asked.

"I was told to take you to Visiting."

I looked at him. "Do I have a meeting with my lawyer?"

"I do not know," he answered.

As we walked through the corridors, I realized there was no visitor waiting for me when the final door opened. They were locking me in a "tank," as the inmates called it—all by myself.

When the officer locked me up, I knew that they just wanted me here during the period when the supporters were coming outside the prison. *Well, I guess I have a few hours to kill on a hard bench,* I thought. Looks like the evil always finds ways to torment those who are children of God. Who would even imagine that a pastor in Canada would be treated in such a shameful way? In the "Land of the Free." Sorry, I guess they meant "oppressed."

This was pure psychological torture. The tank was strictly concrete, with no water or washroom. It had no furnishings. The presence of guards waiting to harm me caused great concern.

This little cell was also extremely cold, which I don't get. In our unit, inside our cells, it was always crazy hot. We had to take our tops off, and we were still sweating.

Here, in this one, it was the opposite. I was shivering. Of course, not having socks didn't help. If they had only told me where and why I was being taken from my cell, I would have at least taken my Bible and some socks with me!

The fan blowing cold air was working overtime. But maybe that was the plan. Part of the punishment? People outside were praying right while their pastor was simultaneously receiving this "special" treatment.

As I was sitting there thinking about my new accommodation, a guard opened the door and did something that immediately caught my attention. He did not close the door behind him; I stood up. By now, I had heard multiple stories of guards using inmates who would beat people up.

But this was strange; I had never seen a guard not closing the door behind him. I was listening to every sound. Ready for a fight, I braced myself against the door. All kinds of strategies were going through my head. If anyone barged in, I decided that if this was to happen, I would fight like a madman.

About five minutes later, the guard came back again and looked at me, noticing that I was ready for a fight. He walked through the same door and disappeared. Thank God nothing happened. Sometime later, a high-ranking officer showed up and escorted me back to the unit. The boys welcomed me with cheering. They spoke to me and reassured me that this was simply a scare tactic.

"They're messing with you." My fellow inmates shared. "They're just messing with your head. That's what they do. They mess with your mind."

I was not looking for a fight. But if the fight would come, I wanted to at least be ready.

[Day 42] Monday

The morning arrived, and I couldn't stop thinking about yesterday. The guards intentionally left the door open twice, and I had heard multiple inmates' stories of being beaten up by guards. One man told me how, one day, they walked him to the shower. He knew the game and said, "No."

"There are no cameras in the shower and washrooms, you see," as he continued his story. "If they want to hurt you, they will take you through the hallways and suddenly will tell you to go to the bathroom. Or they will say. 'You need to take a shower,' and they will wait. Do not do it. That's your clue. They're planning something."

He was in a similar situation where he was asked to go to the shower while being escorted, but he refused. However, they pushed him violently into the washroom, and the fight began. They punched, and he punched back. "They do that," he said, "just to mess with you."

In the process, they broke his arm and said that *he* attacked *them*. He spent four days in the tank with a broken arm. He is currently taking legal action against the institution.

Another inmate recalled a very similar story. Yet another said that for him, they used other inmates.

"Here is how it works," he said. "The guards will take you somewhere that they know there are no cameras and leave the door open. Suddenly, there are other inmates storming your place and you have no choice but to fight."

This man was a big fella and a professional athlete, so he beat them up and pushed them out of the cell. But so many others were not that lucky. This was wrong on so many levels. I had to watch my back. This was particularly significant given that I had already received testimonies from at least four inmates who were offered similar incentives by the guards to harm me.

They paraded me in front of so many other prisoners. They effectively declared that this was the guy that needed to be hurt. This was the villain. I was the reason why they were on lockdown.

But I was thankful to God because "so far, so good." I was still healthy and alive despite their best efforts and determination to do something to me. My God is my shield and a strong tower. He has the final say in everything.

> *To humans belong the plans of the heart, but from the*
> *Lord comes the proper answer of the tongue...*
>
> PROVERBS 16:1 NIV

There had been a tangible change in our unit. We could all feel it. This was probably the most peaceful place in the entire jail. There were no fights here. People got along. We prayed together, and we read the Bible together. Something had been broken.

Nathaniel told me the same thing; there was the same feeling from the outside. He said that after the heavy crackdown last week, the officers were more relaxed and friendly now. I would not trust them anyway, but it was a welcomed change.

We finished our day with a corporate prayer. A female guard was watching us; she was absolutely shocked. She stopped like in the middle of the air and did not know what to do. It was kind of funny. I bet they do not see the whole unit praying together very often, if even ever before.

I blessed the prisoners and prayed for God's perfect will in their lives. We also prayed for the guards—that they would come to Jesus. We released our enemies into the hands of the living God, the Judge of Judges. The guard was visibly moved. After we finished saying our "Amens," she immediately returned to her previous activities.

It was time for the countdown. It was easy for her since all the inmates were sitting at the tables praying. I was tired, and very quickly, I fell asleep. The rush of adrenaline of the past few hours helped. I was definitely being tested.

> *Silver and gold are tested by flames of fire; our thoughts*
> *are tested by the Lord.*
>
> PROVERBS 17:3 CEV

A nurse came again in the morning. She opened the door and asked if I would like to be swabbed, to be tested for covid. This was getting ridiculous. I said, "No!"

The nurse replied, "I didn't think so, but my job is to ask again."

She left, and I stared at the door. It had been 42 days on the inside of this institution, and they were still trying to play the game. By now they should know that I was not playing! Also, I heard that Jason Kenney was lying about me to the media again.

> *Eloquent words are unfit for a fool; how much worse are lying lips to a ruler!*
>
> PROVERBS 17:7 CEV

For the first time today, I was allowed to use the machine in the small exercise room. It felt so good. There was only one machine, but it had four different weight systems. Under the circumstances, I was happy with anything. We were given an extra half an hour so I could spend it with the inmates. It was a good day.

> *Favoring the wicked isn't good; it denies justice to the righteous.*
>
> PROVERBS 18:5 BSB

> *There is no wisdom and no understanding and no counsel against the LORD. The horse is prepared for the day of battle, but victory belongs to the LORD.*
>
> PROVERBS 21:30-31 NASB

The geese were back and, of course, yelling at each other. One pair was on the prison side of the fence, and the other was on the opposite side. The big field was left empty.

I guess history was teaching us that territorial disputes will continue until everyone is dead and gone. Some geese and people just do not change. Go, you foolish creatures! Now you can have that whole park for yourselves.

No! They prefer to yap from behind the barbed wire. Their own satisfaction depended on harassing others and making their lives anything but enjoyable. *You will not have it. We will not have it. We were all going to be miserable,* I thought!

My bail hearing review in Lethbridge was scheduled for the next day. The weird thing was I had to stay there and watch it on the computer screen while my wife and Nathaniel drove there and attended the hearing in person. Marzena and my son were told that Zoom was more than enough for me and my lawyer.

What crazy times we were living in. Why were they required to be physically present while my lawyers and I were expected to communicate with the judge through a computer screen? We will see how that plays out tomorrow at 1:00 PM.

> *Remove the wicked from the king's presence, and his throne will be established in righteousness.*
>
> PROVERBS 25:5 CSB

It was my second day of fasting once again. Marzena had completed an amazing 26 days straight, which was quite an accomplishment. Since I took over, I felt okay. With fasting, the first few days are always the hardest.

We knew that our hope was in God. He was the only one who could save me from those corrupt people. The next day, a judge would decide whether I would be allowed to go home to see my family— my wife, kids, parents, and friends.

I learned that my brother Dawid had been driving a trailer around with my picture on it. He had built a billboard and was now driving around the city with massive images of two of the Nazi-style arrests. There was also a write-up about it, with the caption, "Free Pastor Art."

I was told that the reactions to his mobile billboard had been very positive. People were honking and giving a "thumbs-up." *Good for him. My little brother is fighting like a lion.* I missed them. It was time to go home, and it had been too long. We were so close and yet so far away. When you are far from home, you feel like a bird without a nest.

> *Like a bird that goes away from her nest, so is a man who goes away from his home.*
>
> PROVERBS 27:8 NLV

A guard walked in. He said that I had to eat because I had lost a lot of weight. He looked really concerned. I guess there are still good people in the system. I assured him that everything was fine, that this was not a hunger strike but a fast.

I told him, "I am a Christian, and we fast from time to time."

He replied, "I know who you are, and I know your story." He looked genuine, which really touched my heart. I felt goodness coming from him, not evil, and I had to remind myself that God has His people everywhere. Even in this wicked, evil place, there were people who were shining. *God bless this man with your mercy and favor. Reward him for his kindness,* I thought.

They let us out together, so I spent an hour counseling, preaching, and sharing with the boys. We prayed for a kid who had some problems with homosexuality and with drugs. He received Jesus as his Lord and asked God to clean his life. Today he also got accepted to the treatment centre. Praise God. One step at a time. Thank you, Jesus, for allowing me to minister to them in such a place as this.

Through the window across from my cell, I saw Nathaniel and the supporters who gathered to pray and stand in solidarity with me and with those locked in here. I was so proud of my boy; he was a young lion following in his father's footsteps. It was a touching moment.

I peeked through the window just to look at them. The faithful warriors were breaking the power of darkness in this evil place. I went back to the tables and shared with them the story of my son's birth. He was the miracle "star baby" who was featured in a documentary called *Street Advocate*.

Our conversation was interrupted as the guard came and said that he had received the order to move me to "Visiting." I followed the guard and felt no evil from him. He was a good man.

As we walked down the corridor, he said, "You are fighting the good fight of faith. You're doing the right thing." I could see that he was both a friend and a brother.

After my time on the concrete, I was let out. When the supporters were walking around the building, I had my mandatory time in the Visiting Area without any visitors. The boys were in lockdown in their cells. Eventually, they were let out, but I received the "special" treatment.

When I got back, the boys greeted me warmly, and we continued our Bible stories. I have to admit: this was one of the most amazing evenings I have spent in this place so far. I shared some testimonies about my walk with Christ and about our shortcomings.

Then, the entire unit prayed. Some were sitting at the tables; others were standing around us. It was so powerful and beautiful. Some prisoners asked me to come to their cells and cast out some demons that had been manifesting there at night. They could not sleep and were tormented.

I went there and prayed over their cells in the name of Jesus. In just a few hours, I was asked to do that again for the second time. God was winning their hearts. They were coming to me, saying that they were drawn to me. They had a strong urge to be close to me and to pay attention.

The Holy Spirit was luring them to His freedom and His life. Lord Jesus, save them all. Save them for now and for eternity. You are an amazing God. It was fascinating to watch a Muslim man come to a Christian pastor, asking him for prayer and to cast out the demons from his cell. I must admit, it was remarkable.

> *So Jehoshaphat lived in Jerusalem and went out again among the people from Beersheba to the hill country of Ephraim and brought them back to the LORD, the God of their fathers.*
>
> 2 CHRONICLES 19:4-5 NASB

> *The bloodthirsty hate a person of integrity and seek to kill the upright.*
>
> PROVERBS 29:10

CHAPTER TWENTY-THREE

POWERFUL PRAYERS, POWERFUL ANSWERS

[Day 43] Tuesday

TODAY, THERE was a breathtaking sunrise with a multitude of colors in the sky. I knew it was going to be a gorgeous day. Of course, the geese were by the fence—the usual suspects—two couples next to each other.

However, there was no drama, no flapping of wings or attacking each other. Well, that was progress; hopefully, it meant that the war was over. Maybe the geese had come to the same conclusion: That there was, in fact, enough that God had created for all of them.

The Lord is powerful and faithful. Why were we fighting with each other, anyway? We need to conserve our energy for the actual issues we face. The geese were lying down close to each other, and I thought they might be tired. Or perhaps it was too early in the morning to start a fight.

Was this a temporary truce? I hoped not. I prayed that all God's creatures would find peace that surpasses all understanding. I especially prayed for the people on this side of the fence; the inmates and the guards who desperately needed the peace of God in their lives.

My wife and Nathaniel were alone at the courthouse in Lethbridge. The judge, the Crown, the lawyers, and the accused—me—were all going to attend by video. The only people required to attend in person were my wife and son.

They had scheduled a discussion about my release for 2:00 p.m. Would I continue to be confined in prison or given house arrest? Waiting for the hearing, I had a visitor for the first time in 43 days. A chaplain came to talk to me.

I shared the exciting things happening with the boys here. I told him how hungry the inmates were for the Truth and how ripe they were for the harvest. They just needed someone to lead them in the right direction.

I let him know that there was nothing at all done with the inmates here. There were no games, no chess, no checkers, nothing. There was absolutely nothing to do here, and I asked if he could help those boys. I let him know that I would buy the games and could get someone to bring Christian books for them.

If somehow, he would be allowed to get them to this unit. He thanked me for the information, of course, while wearing the mask and an additional shield on his face. I provided him with my cell number and offered assistance to inmates through my church. He ended the conversation with a brief prayer, and he left. Even now, I haven't heard back from him.

While working out, a few guys joined me in a discussion about eagles. Why does God talk so much about eagles? We talked about how they fly, how they teach their youngsters, and how they renew their strength. We also talked about lions and their majesty.

"You have to know who your God is, and you have to know who you are in God," I said to them. "We are the sons of God. We are the sons of the King of kings and the Lord of Lords. And this will never change. They can lock us here, but we are still the sons of the king. We can be at our lowest and poor, but we never cease to be the heirs to the throne. Our Father is the King, and no one can change that. We are the lions that go for the best, fresh meat. We're not hyenas satisfied with the leftovers. Know who you are. Know who your father is. Keep your eyes on the prize. Keep your eyes on freedom."

The bail hearing went well. My wife and son testified, and the Crown cross-examined them. Tomorrow, the Director of the Remand Centre would testify. I believed that by now, they had reached Calgary.

While I was reading in my cell, an officer walked in and said, "You're going to Visiting again." So, I am back in a little familiar concrete room—all by myself. There is no water, no washroom, and it is still cold, very cold.

My hope was that they would not keep me there for too long. As hours passed, I was freezing like crazy. Again, it reminded me of the forging of swords, from the hot cell to the cold one. What a test! I thought to myself, *God must have something very special for this "criminal" sitting here.*

The stories from the communist era are still fresh in my memory—the hate and the terror. They absolutely despised any man of the cloth, and so there was a lot of persecution and arrests for the clergymen. I would never imagine that one day I would be locked up in a freezing little cell that measured only 1 ½' by 2 ½' for simply being a pastor. For giving a passionate speech about keeping faith and standing for our rights. For simply being Canadians.

I had gone from a businessman to a pastor to a prisoner. It was a story that would be very hard to find anywhere else. Sure, I had watched a few movies and read some books about crazy stories like this one. But now it looked and felt so surreal to play the lead role. This was absolutely strange.

Sitting there made me realize again how evil those people are. Just evil. Every time I heard a reporter from the mainstream media, I realized how disgusted they were acting toward anyone who dared to stand up for their rights. They were offended by anyone who demanded protection from the overreach of the government. They hated it. People who wanted freedom were despised by them. To them they were worse than murderers.

Murderers and rapists get out on bail. The thieves and the gangsters were treated better than people who stood up for freedom. They could not tolerate anyone who was willing to give people hope. Just like 2000 years ago, instead of embracing the Giver of life, they shouted, "Give us Barabbas!"

The people were evil, and they wanted an evil man. They hated what was good and anyone who was good. Good reflects badly on evil; therefore, a villain is closer to their hearts. They are made of the same corrupted clay. They are part of the same gang. They stick together. They must. Or the House of Cards will start crumbling down.

It made me wonder if that was how Bonhoeffer, Paul, Peter, and John must have felt.

> There is no way to peace along the way of safety. For peace must be dared. It is itself the great venture and

> *can never be safe. Peace is the opposite of security. To demand guarantees is to want to protect oneself. Peace means giving oneself completely to God's commandment. Wanting no security, but in faith and obedience laying the destiny of the nations in the hand of almighty God. Not trying to direct it for selfish purposes. Battles are won not with weapons, but with God. They are won when the way leads to the cross.*
> DEITRICH BONHOEFFER

Finally, I could now somewhat comprehend their emotions and what they were going through. Perhaps what their thoughts were.

Again, time was dragging its feet. On the corner of that little "visiting" cell, there was a camera. I always wondered if someone was watching and evaluating if the suffering was enough.

Or perhaps more was required. Would he break? Would he take the deal? Have we crushed him to the point of him saying, "I have enough, I quit. I give up! No more, please."

Who knows what they were thinking? One thing was for sure: I was there for no other reason except some kind of punishment, and the camera was watching me. But it was comforting to know that one more person was watching. God saw it all. Every one of them would one day receive their just reward.

At this point, I had been confined in cells of various sizes—small, medium, and large. Every time I was taken to a different one, I was shocked at how dirty it was—absolutely filthy. Sometimes, I saw guards or inmates walk around and spray the doors with disinfectants. They would wipe the surface and move on to a different cell, but the rest of the cell remained untouched.

I would be amazed when I saw them walking around in their gowns and masks, playing this twisted game of *Pretend*. It required a special kind of stupid or extremely brainwashed to participate in this evil social experiment. Perhaps they were bought? They had sold their moral standards and common sense for a pension and a paycheck. That would explain a lot. It hurt to even observe this tragic comedy.

> *There is something else meaningless that occurs on earth: the righteous who get what the wicked deserve, and the wicked who get what the righteous deserve. This too, I say, is meaningless.*
>
> ECCLESIASTES 8:14 NIV

[Day 44] Wednesday

After hours of special treatment in the "tank" cell, I was brought back to the unit. I asked the officer escorting me why I was being kept in the tank for hours. "If I had committed a crime, then charge me," I said. If not, then why?"

The answer surprised me. "That is the country that we are living in," the guard spoke back.

The amount of corruption and power trips was staggering. When we reached the unit, the boys were still out enjoying their recently won freedom of an extra hour in the evening. Maybe the signed petition helped, or the Director wanted to look good before the judge since he was to testify tomorrow.

One thing was for sure, I didn't trust them. I had seen too much. They had no problem lying under oath. They were manipulating and manufacturing documents; making stuff up was something so normal that I don't even think that they thought of it as a crime. If it was not for our own evidence and the video recordings, I would probably never leave jail.

I remember this one officer named Bissett. He was a supervisor for the bylaw services in the City of Calgary. One time, he manufactured a document of an incident that never took place. This was the only document given to the judge. He swore that this was the truth and an accurate description of what happened.

Thank God that we had video evidence contrary to what he was saying. We dealt with some pathological liars and very evil individuals. One day, they will face the Judge of judges. When Bissett was confronted with the video evidence, our lawyer asked him a simple question: "Are you not concerned that what you put in a document was not what really happened?"

He looked straight at my lawyer and said without hesitation, "No, it does not concern me." Such evil to the core. Everyone, including the judge, was shocked. His brazen admission of guilt, showing complete disregard for law and justice, exemplified our decline from the rule of law.

After that trial, he was promoted to a higher position within the City of Calgary. Evil always protects and supports evil, at least for a time. There is no shame in their game. I wondered what kind of lies the Director was going to tell the judge.

Before we were confined to our cells, I had the chance to tell the story of the golden image that Shadrach, Meshach, and Abednego refused to worship. The boys listened to every word I said. The guards were watching, and one of them made some stupid comment. However, we just ignored him.

Once I finished speaking, Daniel led us into a powerful prayer. He was doing so well. I hoped that God would continue purifying Daniel into His precious diamond. Alongside another individual, he provided testimony to our lawyer about our treatment there. I hoped that their testimony would shed some light on this whole mess.

In order to get rid of the darkness, you must bring the light. One of the boys told me about a conversation that he overheard. Someone higher up was yelling at one of the guards, telling him, "I told you to watch him all the time and to listen to every word he says. He was badmouthing us on the phone. I want you to watch him all the time and listen to everything he says."

Now I understood why my phone was not working; they were blocking it. They were so terrified of what I might say about what I had witnessed there. They didn't want it exposed and for people to know what was really happening behind closed doors.

Every time I picked up the phone to call, it was disconnected. They were watching me on the camera. I tried multiple times and was always cut off. Thank God that already a few of the prisoners had been able to talk to my lawyer and testify about our treatment. I guess as a punishment, the boys and the cells were searched.

The Director testified with the typical phrases like "Everything is fine. Everything is good. There is nothing to see here." The judge reserved her decision until Friday. I also learned that even if this judge released me with conditions, I would have more charges coming from the Crown, so I would have to remain in jail no matter what. So, it appeared that I was officially stuck there, and who knows for how long.

> *I will repay you for the years the locusts have eaten...You will have plenty to eat, until you are full, and you will praise the name of the Lord your God, who has worked wonders for you; never again will my people be shamed.*
> JOEL 2:25-26 NIV

One officer came and apologized for not allowing us to finish our prayer the day before. Well, that was nice. No one is beyond redemption.

Those in charge were extremely committed to keeping me in this place. I realized more than ever that only God could rescue me from their grip. I had to have total reliance on God. No more clever arguments, lawyers, and Crown prosecutors. Just Him. I had to wait on Him. After all, it was God who had allowed the enemy to lock me here. And it would be God to say when it was enough.

As I was being escorted to the Visiting cell, I said to the officer, "There's not much *visiting* in Visiting."

He chuckled from behind his blue mask. Well, at least someone had a good laugh at the situation. I was not laughing. I was back in the tank, and this time, it was a little bigger one. The time went very slowly there.

After being brought back, the boys had already been out for more than an hour. I called Marzena and thankfully, the phone worked this time. I visited with both her and Nathaniel. Someone from the United States had managed to put up a huge billboard in Times Square, NY, with my picture on it. It read, "Free Pastor Artur Pawlowski." Americans are so incredible!

The evening ended with me preaching from the book of Amos. Daniel finished with a prayer. Overall, it was a good day. Souls were touched, God received His glory, and my life was still in His hands, not in the hands of my enemies. At the end of the day, He would have the final say. God, it's not my will, but yours be done. Just give me the strength to endure the hardship.

[Day 45]

In the Bible, Joseph had a destiny prepared for him by God himself. He received the promises when he was a young man. However, jealousy, pride, and betrayal put events into motion, and those threw Joseph right into the hands of the slave owners. The man with a great God and amazing promises became a slave.

I'm sure he was heartbroken when that happened to him. He took it one day at a time, one hour at a time. Under the circumstances, he decided to work hard and keep his faith. He didn't know if his situation would ever change. Maybe God has abandoned him. Maybe he didn't care anymore.

But God was there with Joseph in his suffering. He was there when Joseph's closest relatives sold him into slavery. He was there watching when Joseph worked hard and kept his faith, integrity, honesty, waiting, and believed that one day things would change. God was molding him into someone who one day could be completely trusted.

How can you test loyalty and dedication? How can you know if the man in front of you is the right one? Well, it's quite simple. You put that man into the fire. Into the pit. You pinch him as hard as you can and wait for the reaction. You tell hard truths that are not nice. You make the circumstances painful. You allow the difficulties and challenges to come, and then you simply watch.

Will the person snap at you? Will he attack you? Will he bite? When we go through tough times, we have the tendency to blame mostly others and often God himself. Our misfortune becomes His doing. It is always somebody else's fault, right?

Our unpleasant circumstances are part of the test. Will you come out of the fiery furnace victoriously, or will you perish there in the middle of your bitterness, unforgiveness, or hatred? And the truth is, whether you make it is totally up to you. God always stands for you. He is cheering you on. Even if you walk through the valley of the shadow of death, He is there with you.

Joseph was undoubtedly shocked by what he believed to be the ultimate betrayal of his own brothers—being sold to the enemy for just a few pieces of silver. And then he was sold again to the Egyptian official. Confused and caught by surprise, Joseph suffered greatly. I cannot even imagine the pain of being betrayed by those he trusted the most.

But he had no choice. He could give up and die, or he could rise up and use what God has given him for God's glory. So, he worked hard, as hard as he could, despite the circumstances. And then we read that the Lord was with Joseph and helped him with everything he did.

At the end of the day, that is what mattered. That God was with him. Soon, Joseph's work was rewarded. He became the right hand of Potiphar, who was the captain of Pharaoh's guard, and he was placed in charge of his house and all of his property.

Today started early for me. The noise from a broken radio was very loud and annoying. It woke me up several times during the night. The switch was not working. I reported it to the guard. He tried to shut it off from his booth, but it was not working.

They said they'd send someone to repair it. For the time being, it was loud, and there was nothing I could do about it. A few weeks ago, I asked for earplugs, but the request was denied. I guess after 40 days, I should get used to it, but I could not. The buzzing noise was everywhere.

During my break from solitary confinement, I learned why the boys were searched and their cells raided. The guards said that it was because of Daniel. They did not like that he was becoming more like a preacher than an inmate. Daniel has become very close to me. And apparently, this was not good for the guards.

I talked to Daniel today, and I explained to him that when the light shines brighter, it spreads everywhere, and the darkness hates it. "You are becoming a powerful witness here, Daniel. And those who are evil do not like it. The enemy is terrified. Now, it is not just one preacher locked in here, but two. Soon, others will join. And that is exactly how revival starts."

Continuing my instructions to Daniel, I said, "Remember how tough it was to talk about God to them at the beginning? They were at first resisting the gospel, but now we have the whole unit praying and listening to the sermons every day. They come and sit here of their free will. That is exactly what the light does. It takes over. It is like when a person walks into a dark room and then switches the lights on."

"Suddenly, the darkness is no more. It has no choice but to go. It becomes defeated. The devil hates the light and fights it. As long as you do not compromise and stay in the light, you will prevail," I said as I finished my teaching for Daniel.

Daniel made it known that he would rather I stayed here for a little longer. "There is so much I need to learn from you," he said. "Before you go. I need you to stay here until I am ready to be what God wants me to become."

I told him, "Even if I go, you are never alone. God is and will always be with you. He will never leave you or forsake you. Also, now he has you here, so you can spread it. Didn't He say, 'Go into all the world and make disciples of all the nations?' Now you go and make disciples here. Multiply yourself and the good news of God here in this place."

It made me realize that I was there for that particular moment, and I wanted God's will to be manifested. God knew what He was doing. He knows all the "whys" and "where's." Joseph didn't have a choice. His life was snatched from under him by a very sinister plot.

Joseph could scream and kick his heels. But that wouldn't get him anywhere. He was stuck in the reality of his situation. He was a slave working for an Egyptian. That was the fact.

He had to deal with that because God had allowed it. So Joseph dusted his feet off and went to work. He said to himself, "If I am stuck here, let me at least do my best." And then he went and did it! Friends, accept whatever God has in store for you, and you will succeed.

THE DAY OF THE KIDNAPPING!

That morning, I saw my friends, the geese, and noticed that one of them had some major problems with his leg. There was blood on his feathers, and he was visibly hurt. He could barely walk!

I have no idea what happened to him, but it was disturbing. Somehow it managed to fly above the fence and the barbed wires and was lying down just under my window. It probably felt like me: wounded, bleeding, and hurting.

When we were out of our cells. I sat at the table, visiting with one of the inmates. An officer walked in, looked straight at me, and said, "Pawlowski, come."

I got up and walked towards him. He said, "You have a visitor," and immediately started to escort me from the unit. I was surprised to have a visitor, thinking that perhaps Nathaniel had decided to come or the lawyer wanted to see me. I had no time to even say "Bye" to the boys at the table.

As I followed the officer, I could do nothing. When we reached the Admissions area, I knew that something was up. The officer had lied to me, and several officers and sheriffs were waiting there for me.

They walked me to the Search area, and I thought that maybe they will do just that: search me for some crazy reason. However, they told me to keep walking. At the counter, they brought my clothes that I was arrested in and told me to put them on. I did, and I had to sign a document confirming that I indeed received them.

Then I was placed in the tank. The sheriffs finished their paperwork, and the guards delivered my belongings from the cell. "You are being transferred," I was told.

"May I know where?" I asked.

They looked at each other, and one of the sheriffs said, "To Red Deer." Then, with the other officers, they said, "To Edmonton." Edmonton had its own Remand Centre which was nearly 304 km (approx. 200 miles) away.

I was shocked. It was only one day before my bail verdict, and I was being moved hundreds of kilometers away. But why? A pair of handcuffs and the leg bracelet followed, and I was led to a van and put in the little box in the back. Then off we went.

At the Red Deer police station, two sheriffs were already waiting for us. They changed my handcuffs, and I was taken to Edmonton. Ironically, on the way, I saw a billboard that Rebel News had placed directly near the highway. The sign featured three photos of Alberta pastors, including me, who had been arrested by this regime. The sign included the writing "SaveArtur.com."

Finally, we arrived at Edmonton's Remand Centre, and I was strip-searched. My clothes were thrown into the bin, and I received an orange suit and orange slippers and was taken to sign some papers. First, I demanded an opportunity to call my lawyer and say that I was not signing anything until I got the okay from them.

"Fine," they said. Then, I was taken to a three-story unit. This was a totally different ball game. I knew that this one was for special prisoners. It was called Unit MX-D-U-1.

Metal was everywhere, and bulletproof glass covered everything. I was told to go to Cell #1 on the third floor. I was taken aback when I entered. The room lacked windows and a pillow, but had a camera in the corner, monitoring everything. The belongings I was promised never arrived. Instead, an officer showed up and handed me a document from Placement.

The document was a notice of administrative placement and restriction, which stated that my sudden move was because I was considered "unsafe to the centre and to the staff." The reason was also in the description, along with these instructions: "Placed on administrative segregation as per senior management. House and exercise alone." There was that word again: alone! I was being punished without a trial.

The document reported that they could keep me there for 15 days. And I was allowed only one hour out of the cell with no interaction with other human beings.

In my new "Max Pod" it was crazy cold, as if someone had intentionally cranked down the air conditioning. Through the intercom, I messaged a request for a guard to come to my cell. And when he did, I told him how cold it was in my cell and I asked for an extra blanket.

The guard began laughing, telling me that at least I had fresh air, and then he walked away. To keep myself warm, I paced back and forth, thinking about the boys in Calgary. *How was Daniel holding down the fort? Are they doing okay? Will the geese make it?* I had spent weeks with those inmates and had really become fond of them.

That first night was brutal. It was so cold, and I was awakened multiple times while shivering. I received a blanket full of holes, similar to your grandma's handiwork, but it didn't suffice. Without a pillow, it was hard to fall asleep. And the crazy noise coming from the fan was so loud it sounded like a car parked next to your bed.

They considered me "extremely dangerous," and therefore, I was not allowed to have a pen or any books. And certainly not a Bible. It was hard to sit in this small, confined, and extremely cold place doing absolutely nothing.

I was still fasting, so I passed on the food tray. A nurse came to see how I was feeling. I said "terrible. This feels more like Russia."

She looked at me and said, "I don't understand."

"Well," I said, "I am locked here alone, cold and shivering. I am not convicted, and yet I am already punished, just like in Russia."

"Okay," she commented. "But sorry, there is nothing I can do about it. So, how are you feeling?"

"Sad," I said.

"Okay," came the reply. "Do you hear any voices?"

I came close to jumping, prepared to state that all I heard was the never-ending noise from that fan. It was like a loud tractor next to my bed. But instead, I bit my tongue. I thought to myself, *I don't need more enemies. I've got plenty.*

I asked her for some paper and a pencil, my belongings from Calgary, and, at the very least, a blanket and a pillow. She said she would see what she could do. Later, a guard arrived and gave me a blanket. I also received some paper and a pencil, so at least I could begin writing again.

I have to admit, this was one of the most depressing moments during this whole ordeal. Being in this horrible place—alone—and separated from my family and church. Having been removed from my friends in Calgary in such a cunning way was difficult.

That day, I recalled the story of Joseph and how much he had endured. His hurt was so severe that even years after his release, he named his first-born son Manasseh. For he said, "God has made me forget all my troubles." Joseph endured thirteen grueling years of hardship, slavery, and imprisonment, questioning his circumstances with a constant, "Why? What have I done to deserve this?"

While we understand he had some arrogance and cockiness in his youth, 13 years of slavery is hard to fathom. There were moments when he questioned the accuracy of his recollection of God's dreams. How was he going to become someone so important that his father, mother, and all his brothers would one day bow before him? That was an impossibility for a slave in Egypt.

In the meantime, he did his best to survive and honor his God. He worked hard and was elevated. When everything started going well for him, the blow came with false accusations and charges of rape.

Everything changed again in an instant. He thought he had already made it and had finally turned his life around. Now, he ended up with nothing, once again. Furthermore, his situation worsened as he was deprived of all possessions and sentenced to prison as a Hebrew slave and an accused rapist.

Wow! He was completely knocked off his feet. Everything was working against him. In human eyes, he was done for—game over. The only thing left was to await execution. I bet he was crying, and I bet he was losing his mind. He probably thought, *what is going on, God? Why is this happening to me? Please, Lord, answer me. Where are you when I need you? Please, Lord, I beg you, speak to me. Answer my prayers. Say something.*

This is how I felt, too. I pleaded with God and thought more about the Bible. When I had the opportunity to call my lawyer, I also called Marzena. She asked me how I was doing. "Are you holding on?"

No, I was not holding on. I was in big trouble, in the hands of a beast system that wanted to finish me off. I was very far from being okay; I just wanted to cry. And finally, I just let go of all the emotions and cried.

After experiencing the brutal conditions of my newest accommodations, I was sure that I would not come out of this alive. When I read the document that they could keep me here indefinitely, I was heartbroken. I was losing my strength. The knowledge about the guards trying to bribe the inmates into hurting me was adding to the stress. I never knew when or who would storm my cell and finish me off.

So, I said my goodbyes. "I don't think that I am coming back," I said to my wife. "They will try to keep me here as long as they can, and I think this is too much for me. So, if I don't see you on this side of eternity, I will see you on the other side."

My wife understood that I had reached my lowest. She immediately contacted our lawyers, explaining what was happening, and contacted everyone she could to pray and pressure the government to stop this insanity!

And it worked. The lawyer sent a letter to the judge. The judge was shocked, and as you know, I was transferred.

I want you to understand that if it were not for my wife, my family, and the support we were receiving from so many people on the outside, I am sure that I would not have made it. Little by little, I was losing the strength I once had.

Every man and woman must know that it is just a matter of time before you hit rock bottom, and then what is most important is God, family, and the community. Without that, you will not make it!

Marzena's job was to lift me up when I fell low. She was my window to the outside world, informing me of what was happening and doing so constantly so that I did not feel alone. There were also multitudes of people standing with us, praying and cheering for the victory! This kept me strong and focused so I would not give up.

My wife was my lifeline, encouraging me to keep going forward. That was her mission, and she accomplished that perfectly! She had the power to crush me or to lift me up, to give me another dose of hope or take that away.

When men are paying the price (fighting for freedom and providing for the family), the wives must stay and support their husbands. I have met so many men who were not on the same page with their spouses and who actually hindered them from doing what was right. So many couples even split and divorced because one of them was not willing to pay the price. You must stand together. You must be in unity or the house will crumble.

I was so grateful that my wife was different. She not only stood by what I was doing, but she was a part of everything that I was doing. God truly had given me the right soulmate, my lioness.

Only yesterday, I had an entire unit on my side. We held Bible studies and prayer meetings and had favor with many of the guards. They brutally took away all of that from me—without mercy. I felt a little like Joseph, in an unfamiliar environment, all alone. I had to start all over again.

But to do that, I needed God's strength. My wife began talking about random things, and her voice calmed me down. The lawyer sent a letter to the judge telling her what had happened to me and this relieved my mind somewhat. I finished the conversation surrounded by metal glass in a ghost-like unit for terrorists and gangsters that could house at least one hundred inmates. I was there by myself, watched by three guards.

Unreal, I thought to myself and went back to my cell. This was one of the lowest moments I had experienced in the time I had been here. It dawned on me that I may never be allowed to leave.

[Day 46] The Bail Hearing

The bail hearing lasted hours. An officer sat in front of me, listening to the proceedings. He was told to report everything that the judge said. He told me that what they were doing to me was making an example of me. He was an older man, and he was not wearing a mask.

Halfway through the proceedings, he was replaced with a younger one. He was a mouthful, for sure. He very vocally referred to the politicians in a way that I cannot repeat. "We have become a totalitarian regime," he said. I also learned from him that they placed me in segregation because I was high profile and there was media attention. Imagine that. Punished from every angle.

When I left the room after the hearing, I was approached by a female officer. She was saying something with her mask on. I could not understand a word she was mumbling from behind her muzzle. I came a little bit closer to hear what she was saying. She freaked out. "Stay away! Six feet!" she said, stretching out her arms. I'll repeat it: "What. A. Gong. Show."

Then she repeated some information she was told. She said that I was forbidden to harass the Crown prosecutor, and I had to stop calling him. "What?!" I was totally puzzled.

"You have to stop calling the prosecutor's office immediately!" she shouted.

What kind of mind games are they playing? I thought to myself. What is this new tactic? What kind of cruel punishment are they going to inflict on me this time? Our phone calls were all recorded and monitored by the guards. It was effortless for them to find out if I made any calls from jail or not. I repeated multiple times to her that I had not been calling the Crown's office, but she absolutely did not care.

At that moment, I thought that I had become some sort of subject in a psychological experiment or something. They wanted to break my mind. Maybe they were waiting for me to snap and do something stupid. Maybe to bring me to the point of giving up? "Take the deal, and you can be free. Bow, and we will let you live again. Keep resisting, and we will keep hammering you with everything we've got...with every nonsense we can muster." I was told to go to my cell, where I picked up my Bible and read.

Suddenly, a voice from the intercom brought me back to reality. An officer informed me I was to be moved again to a different unit. *Wow again?* I thought to myself. There was never a dull moment. I was to pack my stuff and wait. So I did.

Sitting on the bunk bed, I heard the intercom instruct me to leave my solitary cell on the third floor. Downstairs, an officer was already waiting, and I was told to follow him. Soon, we were joined by several other high-ranking officers, and we walked through several doors and corridors to a very special unit. How special? Well, I was about to find out.

I spotted people in orange suits from a distance through the window. My first thought was that this was good because at least I would not be by myself. We entered through a metal door, and I saw about three dozen inmates.

Their behavior, however, was bizarre. Some of them were jumping up and down. Some were walking in a circle. Several officers were positioned on the left. I turned to them and asked: "Where am I?"

They laughed. "You are in the wild, wild west."

"What does that mean?" I asked.

"You are in the psych ward."

"Wow," I replied. "How wonderful." I was instructed to go to Cell #24. Inside the cell was a young guy who was asleep. I put my stuff on the upper bunk without waking him up.

I had been "officially" admitted to a unit for the mentally challenged—the insane. Can you believe it? Well, I guess I would have much work here to accomplish and a lot of prayers to pray. Just perfect; I have moved from one trouble to another, from the frying pan into the fire.

I took a seat in the common area and began observing the people confined in this space. Many of them were visibly disturbed. People were stuck in a perpetual cycle, endlessly walking in circles. I informed Marzena about the situation over the phone. I have to admit it had been a difficult day for me.

Marzena informed me that a guard punched Kevin, the African-American guy from my unit at Calgary Remand, and placed him in solitary confinement for supporting me and sacrificing his phone time. The boys from Calgary Remand had called my wife, and Daniel had also called Marzena. She mentioned that everyone was praying for me and wanted to remind me about the fire, explaining that God was purifying me through it.

While listening to what she was saying, I wondered why this fire had to be so freezing. Once again, it was freezing in this new unit. It was disheartening to see the boys in Calgary punished, not for illegal behavior, but for their loyalty to their pastor. They were suffering for doing good. Obviously, doing good in a correctional centre was not welcomed. I went back to my cell and introduced myself to my roommate, whose name was Ray.

Ray was a young fellow who was there because he had murdered his own brother. In fact, he chopped him up with a macheté. *Excellent,* I thought. *God, please watch over me and protect me.*

In the common area, there were tables, chairs, and a TV. And there was also a separate room with another TV. I went to the common area, trying to figure out how I was going to survive this ordeal. I observed a couple of guys doing some paperwork, so I sat next to them.

The older guy looked at me and then looked at the papers on the table. Then he said, "Aren't you that pastor that ends up always in trouble?"

I replied, "Guilty as charged."

He jumped up, grinning from ear to ear, and in a voice that was almost yelling, he said, "You are my hero! I absolutely adore you. You have no idea how happy I am to meet you. What an honor!"

At least in this asylum, I had one fan. We talked some more, and then I went to explore the rest of the unit. There was a concrete basketball court with balls lying around. However, it was way too cold to play outside. I walked back in and went to explore the other TV room. Some inmates were watching a movie.

Cool, I thought. I have not seen a movie for almost two months. Joining them to watch TV, it was only about ten minutes into the film when another fella who was lying on the ground jumped up like someone put a fire under him. He went to the TV and switched the channel; no one dared to move.

As I waited to see what would unfold, it became apparent that this man would get up and switch the channel once more, consistently at the ten-minute mark of every show. No one said a word or even moved. Everyone in the room just began watching whatever was on the *next* channel. I exited and revisited the room several times, and the modus operandi remained the same each time. After about ten minutes, the program would be switched abruptly, and a new one would be watched.

I guess that's how you watch movies in a mental institution. I walked out and played chess with a couple of inmates; I won! At 10:00 p.m., we were told to go back to the cells, which were insanely cold. Despite using two blankets, I kept waking up multiple times at night because of the cold.

CHAPTER TWENTY-FOUR

POSSIBLE LIGHT AT THE END OF THIS TUNNEL

[DAY 47] Saturday

I HEARD A KNOCK on the door, but I ignored it. However, whoever was there was very persistent. Finally, on the fourth knock, I peeked from under the blanket to see who it was.

There was an officer on the other side of the door, gesturing for me to come to the door. I jumped from my bed and walked to the door, leaning closer to the window. The officer said, "I had this very heavy on my heart to tell you that God loves you. God loves you very much."

He reminded me that God loved me and had not forgotten about me. I thanked him and he left to get back to his rounds. When we were let out, I called Marzena and discovered that there was a possibility that they would let me out on Monday; this was also confirmed when I talked to my lawyer. Not letting my emotions get the best of me, I thought, *we will see what happens on Monday.*

Later in the day, I called my wife again during service to address the church. She put me on the speakers, and I recounted what had happened to me in the past few days. I told them where I was, and I shared with the church the story of Joseph. I talked about the hardship of betrayal but then the ultimate victory. What the enemy meant for evil, God turned around for good. "Do not lose hope," I said. "In the end, we know who wins." I could hear the cheers and the clapping.

God has blessed me with good people. I could hear them praying for me. May God's will prevail in my life. No matter what, God is good all the time. The people who walked before us were not perfect people, but they did their best. Sometimes, they failed; sometimes, they succeeded.

The God of Abraham, Isaac, and Jacob was, however, a perfect God to very imperfect people. Recognizing our own vulnerability and dependency is the first step toward triumph. An arrogant person filled with pride does not need God. He thinks he can do it on his own. Our society is in a sorry state with so many people like that around us. We are in a mess, with dirt in every corner and under every carpet.

Joseph's story was fascinating also because it led this man to the end of himself. When he was in jail, he was still waiting for men to help him. He said to the Pharaoh's Chief Cupbearer, "Please remember me and do me a favor when things go well with you. Mention me to the Pharaoh so he might let me out of this place. For I was kidnapped from my homeland, the land of the Hebrews, and now I am here in prison, but I did nothing to deserve it."

You see, humans have a tendency to seek help from other people or things. Perhaps we will find it in wealth or power. However, God wants to bring us to the end of ourselves. We must go to our knees and say, "God, if not you, then no one. If you will not come to the rescue, then I am as good as dead."

Joseph, like so many of us, was holding on to the earthly methods, and I didn't blame him at all. I have also done that many times. Pharaoh's official had forgotten about Joseph. He moved on with his life. Joseph was just a memory from the past.

Like many others, people today are hoping to leave behind the events of the past few years. Joseph was just an unpleasant memory. Unfortunately, that's our nature. When things go sour, we look for each other's company, and we seek God. When the hardship passes, we forget. Since it no longer has an impact on us, it is no longer our concern. Human nature is so predictable and so selfish.

Two years later, abandoned and forgotten, Joseph was ready to die if need be. Then Pharaoh had a dream, and no one could interpret it. No one had the answers. Then, the chief cupbearer remembered the Hebrew slave who was a prisoner who had God on his side.

Finally, Joseph stood before the king, but now as a changed man who was ready to die. Considered a God, anyone who challenged the Pharaoh's divinity was met with a fatal consequence. When the king asked Joseph to interpret the dreams, Joseph's reply was fascinating. He put everything on the line: life or death with nothing in between.

Joseph told Pharaoh, "It is beyond my power to interpret the dreams, but God can tell you what it means."

What he said was so powerful. In front of others, he straightforwardly told Pharaoh, the most powerful man at the time, that he was not God. In fact, the real one would reveal the dreams to him. What a bold and powerful statement. Right there, Joseph was risking his life, but he did it with humbleness and total trust in his Savior. And God came through.

God interpreted the dreams and gave Joseph such a wisdom that Pharaoh and his officials were totally impressed. Joseph quickly rose to the second-highest position in the kingdom, just below the king's throne. Later, he became responsible for saving countless lives and was called "the savior of nations."

Yesterday, I came to that place where it was everything or nothing, life or death, for God. "Into thy hands, I submit myself. You are my only deliverer. You can come and rescue me if that is your will."

> *Many are the plans in the mind of a man, but it is the purpose of the Lord that will stand.*
>
> PROVERBS 19:21

Today was my seventh day of fasting this time around. I felt great, and my roommate felt even greater. This young guy was always hungry, so he was definitely thrilled when he got my lunch today. I hope he will do everything in his power to keep me alive, if for nothing else but the extra food.

I had a great conversation with the guard. He claimed to be a born-again believer and assured me that my story would be remembered. He told me that there were people there that are searching for God, and he was doing everything he could to bring them to God. Praise Jesus!

God's light was everywhere. I prayed that God would give that guard wisdom like he did for Joseph so he could change lives in that horrible place. I asked the guard for a pillow and a blanket, and he responded with "no problem."

He went and got them for me and as we walked to my cell, he shared with me that he had a dream about telling me that Jesus loved me and had my back. The guard had been scheduled to work in the Max Pod. But when he arrived at work, it turned out that he was moved to the unit right where I was. First, he was upset because he wanted to share his dream with me and knew that I was supposed to be locked in the Max Pod.

However, he was pleasantly surprised when he learned that I had been transferred to the very place that he was going to be working at. This is how God works. What are the chances? None. The guard was 100% sure that he was going to see me in the Max Pod. And yet, I was transferred at the same time that morning to where he had also been transferred.

This all happened by God to cheer me up and to deliver a message of hope straight from God to me. *Thank you, Jesus, that you brought this man to show me your favor.* Later on, the guard brought me an extra blanket and a bed sheet and also encouraged me to stay strong.

"Your stand has encouraged so many people," he said. He continued, "You are inspiring so many. You cannot give up. God has your back, and no one can touch you." He mentioned that he had read Isaiah while on his break. "Remember what happens with God's enemies," he added.

I needed that spiritual boost and those words of encouragement. *Thank you, Jesus, for this man and for your faithfulness.* The guard told me that tonight there was going to be a prayer meeting at his church. He promised me that they would all pray for me, including his pastors. When he left, I was in awe. What an amazing God we serve.

Later, I was reading the story of Isaac and Esau. I was intrigued by how little Esau valued his own birthright; he sold it for a bowl of soup. When faced with challenges or struggles, many people are quick to avoid them. Esau was very hungry and wanted to eat. You can't blame him, really. Every man needs to eat.

However, his contempt for his birthright was unbelievable. It exposed his character, which was evident in his selfishness and self-centeredness. "I need to satisfy my temporary needs, and who cares about higher things? Give me what I want now, or I will die."

Esau played the drama queen and thought that was supposed to give him what he wanted right then! He made a deal, but that deal had consequences that would follow not only him but also the next several generations to come. The stew—the temporary satisfaction—cost him everything.

It is a very sad story. So many people were making the same mistake. Do not sell what God has given or promised to you; that is betrayal. Jacob, of course, was not righteous either, and for that, later, he gets corrected by facing his own hardship. My prayer is that I would never sell what is rightfully mine, especially for something that is so cheap that it eventually turns into dust.

Tonight, I started my first Bible study since being transferred to this unit. Two students came. In Calgary, it took weeks for the boys to warm up to the idea. Now I know, because they had called Marzena again, that they were standing strong and praying for me. *Father God, let this seed that has been planted produce a mighty harvest that would multiply and touch multitudes. Let the light shine and let the fire which had started there continue to burn.*

Today, a man who worked for Alberta Health Services visited me. He was perplexed as to why I was in that unit and asked, "Mr. Pawlowski, what are you doing here?"

"That is a good question," I replied. "I have no idea."

He said, "No one should be here without a Doctor's evaluation and the approval and knowledge of Alberta Health Services."

"And yet, here I am," I responded.

He looked at me and said, "I have no idea why or who gave the order for your transfer here." He continued, "The administration is not allowed to do things like that."

I told him, "In comparison, it's a lot better than in Max Pod in the freezing conditions and total isolation." I thanked him for his consideration.

He said, "It is not about you. We cannot allow sane people to be housed with people with mental issues. The sane people would be able to take advantage of the insane people. That's the policy and I have no idea why you have been placed here. That is unacceptable. I will look into it."

As he was walking away, I thought to myself, *He is more worried about the well-being of criminals who are locked up here than the innocent man who has been placed in this crazy place for simply delivering a sermon to people.* Honestly, everything was upside down.

[Day 48] March 27th

The unit that I was locked in had three floors; I was on the bottom floor. The inmates on the bottom floor got the most free time out of all the others. The second floor had a few more regulations and was a little stricter. The third floor had a rubber room, and the inmates were not allowed to interact with the rest.

People on the third floor were visibly disturbed and challenged. Banging on the walls and doors there was normal. In the common area, which is in the middle, they had a few tables that were screwed to the floor with permanently attached stools. There were several telephones available for the inmates to use for calls. Some inmates watched TV all day long when they were allowed to leave their cells. Some walked around in circles, while others sat and talked to each other.

Sometimes I would see someone just staring at something that only they can see. I had numerous conversations with different individuals. One was trying to convince me that he had a big family of at least 30,000 members and that they owned corporations that were on the market worth billions of dollars. I was also told that the big stones that we could see outside of our windows by the fence, especially the red ones, were worth millions of dollars.

If I wanted to be rich, I should consider collecting those stones and selling them to the Chinese. *Okay then. Interesting theory.* One fellow worked every day, nonstop, on his business proposal. I was told that he was in the restaurant business, and he was working on a total takeover of the fast-food chains. He was convinced that his proposition was going to eliminate the competition entirely.

The man even showed me his new plans. Now, it had eight restaurants with a tower and balconies. I must admit that he had impressive talent, and his drawings were of high quality. There was not much to do in this place!

The bizarre quirk of watching multiple channels on television did not change, either. There was this self-appointed fellow who believed that it was his duty to abruptly stand up and change the channel every ten minutes. Initially, it was kind of hilarious, but I am sure that in the long run, this would become an issue.

We also had some transgender people there, but up to that point, I had not heard even one sentence from them that was not related to naked men or something along those lines. *My God, these people are so messed up.*

It was very interesting to observe humans with such broken minds all around me. They had complete faith in all the stories they were telling me. They were in their own world, outside of the sphere of reality. My roommate slept most of the time. When he wasn't asleep, he would discuss his numerous children and adventures.

According to him, he had over 30 children and several wives. Apparently, some of his kids were almost as old as he was. I did not even attempt to ask him how he thought that this was even possible.

For the time being, I decided to observe and listen. I prayed over some of them, and when I saw that they were stressed, I would talk to try to calm them down. There was a basketball court there, but it was still too extremely cold outside to play. I tried a few times with some of them, but it was hard for them to concentrate, so it made the game somewhat difficult.

Finally, the banging and yelling ceased for the time being, so this was a good time for me to read the Bible. I plowed with them through the story of Jacob. God appeared to him at the Bethel. He promised to be by Jacob's side and protect him, no matter where he went.

And that's exactly what happened; however, Jacob's life was not excluded from hardship and hard work. Quite the contrary. There were times when Jacob was repeatedly cheated. He had to outsmart the position and work out the waves of circumstances piled up against him.

We often mistakenly believe that having God by our side or receiving promises from Him means we won't face any hardships in our lives or households. We must always remember that the enemy never stops plotting against God's people. The devil uses people just like God uses his servants. The devil comes to steal, kill, and destroy. His mission never ceases.

On top of that, the enemy is very determined and focused. That is why it is so important to keep the faith and not give up. My life did not belong to the Crown prosecutors, the Premier, the mainstream media, the lawyers, the jailers or the judges. My life belonged to God.

And I had received many promises from Him. Many of them had not yet been fulfilled. However, in the end, the war was fought for our destiny and the destiny of those whom God intended to impact through us and our testimony. I had been told by tens of thousands of people in the past two years that my story was such an inspiration. Multitudes of people were being greatly impacted because of my suffering.

But the truth is that as much as I was very grateful that God had chosen me and my family to touch so many, it was extremely difficult to endure the level of hate thrown at me from what seemed like every direction. I was hurting. My heart was crying. I wanted to go home to my family, friends, and church.

I was not a criminal who should be locked up in a maximum security facility. Nevertheless, here I was. My Father, who was in Heaven, had allowed for reasons only known to Him, to hand me into the hands of my enemies for a bigger plan. He knew my beginning, and He knew my end. God knew my pain, and that I missed my wife, children, and extended family.

I was looking through a little window and could see the road far away. Freedom had been taken from me by very corrupt and evil men. Freedom seems to be so close and yet so far away.

The showers were on the same level as my unit. They had a door that covered only a portion of your body. The bottom was open, and the top was open. But at least the water was nice and hot.

In just a few minutes, they would be letting us out again, and I would call Marzena. Those phone calls kept me from breaking down.

I was very grateful to talk to my family and hear about their daily lives that I had been deprived of. I had to take it one day at a time, one hour at a time. There was nothing else that I could do but wait. One day, my God would say, "Enough. I am setting you free again!"

I saw a young man playing alone on the court with a ball. It was cold, but I decided to go and play with him. He was a very nice, polite man who, I found out, had asthma. We played a little soccer and then some basketball. It felt good to move around a little. The young man quickly got tired because of his asthma, so we went inside and played checkers.

He told me his story. When he was 16, he was hit in the head multiple times, and since then, he had mental problems. I told him about Jesus and about healing. "You know," I said, "there is God, and He can heal you."

He replied, "I believe that. I know that Jesus can heal me." Then he asked me if I would like to receive a gift, a cross that his roommate in a different unit made.

"Sure," I said. He guided me to his cell and presented me with a meticulously crafted handmade cross necklace.

I thanked him and asked if he needed anything. "Can I give you something?"

He replied, "No. I do not want anything."

"How about coffee or sugar? Would you like some coffee?" I asked.

"Sure," he replied.

I brought what I had, some coffee, sugar, syrup, and butter. Due to my continued fasting, I had an excess of things in my room. I had some extra stuff stacked on my bench.

THE CROSS

I prayed that this young man's gift of making those crosses would touch many. The cross is a symbol of victory. Since tomorrow was my birthday, I viewed his gift as a gift for my birthday. Tomorrow, I would turn 49 years old. I hoped that God would also give me a gift tomorrow, and I would be able to walk out of that place and be reunited with my family.

Following dinner (Well, for my roommate, *it was a double dinner!*) I was entertained by my roommate and the stories of his family. According to him, his family owned the CPP, which he said was wrongly labeled. The proper name was "RL" a rail of the family name, Lavallee. Evidently, his family also owned the Red Wood trees in British Columbia. It was truly fascinating to listen to him. He shared his stories with such a conviction that I am sure that he really believed in every word that he was saying.

[DAY 49]

This was my birthday. What a coincidence that I had just finished 49 years, and I had been in jail for 49 days. What a way to spend a birthday! I must admit it was the most unusual birthday celebration so far, at least for me. It had been 49 days on a rollercoaster—up and down, never knowing what they would hit me with.

Not knowing what kind of twisted attempt they would use to punish me for daring to expose their corruption. Almost two months of not eating properly and fasting had taken its toll on my body for sure. I felt dizzy and very weak.

Today was the 9th day of my new fast, and my body was starting to say, "No more!" I guess everyone has their limits, physically and

434 - Artur Pawlowski

psychologically. When I talked to the man from the mental
department of Health Alberta Services, he said the same thing:
keeping people in segregation damages them.

I didn't understand it. Instead of moving forward in Canada, if it
came to human rights, we moved backward. We went straight to the
times of the British Empire, where every form of torture was
acceptable. It feels like the spirit of the Brits has resurfaced.

Lawlessness has always been particularly hard on those who serve
the Lord. It is extremely difficult to talk about righteousness when
you are surrounded by such wickedness. But God wants us to go and
warn people about the consequences of sin.

Of course, not many want to go. Our flesh, in particular, screams,
"No way. I do not want to be hurt!" Human logic says, "Why would I
risk my life for them who do evil?" The human spirit is very weak
and has a hard time standing up in the ongoing war between the
will of men and the commandments of the living God.

Jonah knew that perfectly. He was commanded to go and tell the
people in the great city of Nineveh, the wicked city, that God was
bringing judgment on them. He was given clear instructions. He
wanted to go and give this clear message: God was not pleased, and
judgment was coming.

Jonah, however, went in the totally opposite direction. He simply
ran, terrified and scared. Preaching the word of God in an evil city
carried the risk of punishment, beatings, imprisonment, or even
death. It was not a small thing.

And it's no different today. Doing what is right requires courage,
but not just that. It requires a willingness to pay the price for doing
good. Not many people around us are willing to go all the way. Most
want to be quiet and maintain a low profile.

We like to pretend that we don't see the problems. I hear nothing. I see nothing. Therefore, I will not say or do anything. Jonah ran.

But you see, God had different plans for Jonah. God's love for the people of Nineveh was bigger than any inconvenience or potential hardship for any individual. Jonah ended up in the ocean, in the belly of a big fish, for three days, which was enough time to reflect on his life.

Jonah admitted his disobedience and vowed to obey his Lord. When we encounter powerful, evil people, we sometimes forget that our God is more powerful than all the wicked combined together in the entire world. Jonah pledged to keep his vows and stated what we should never forget.

He declared that his salvation came from the Lord alone. Jonah had truly reached his end. He was finally and totally dependent on the will of God. Now he could be used. Now he was ready to change the lives of many.

Nineveh heard the message. The truth penetrated their hearts, producing tangible change. Their souls were touched. The power of repentance entered the city, and the people asked God to forgive their sins. From the king to the lowest of the lows, they all turned away from their evil ways.

And that humility and humbleness changed the mind of God and as a result, He did not destroy the city. My friends, there are many cities like Nineveh out there, and there are many Jonahs running away from responsibility. We must remember that we were called to be the light in the darkness. We were called to be the salt of the earth.

Who will fight for the Ninevehs of today? God feels sorry for all the countless lives living in spiritual darkness. He wants to save them, spare them from the horrors of hell. If we are truly followers of God, we would also have compassion for them all.

I talked with my criminal lawyer, who informed me that I would have to spend a few more days in this place. The Crown Prosecutor was causing more trouble. For the breach of probation, he wanted additional money, and the hearing was scheduled for the coming Wednesday. It looked like God wanted me there for an additional few days. Happy birthday to me!

MY POSSESSIONS ARE BACK

My things from the Calgary Remand Centre were returned to me. It only took them a week to bring them. It looked like everything was there except my newspaper clips and *McLean's Magazine*. For whatever reason known only to them, they took that periodical away from me. Too bad, because there was a very good article on the corruption of Kenney in there. Maybe that was the reason? Who knows? I was surrounded by very interesting humans, both guards and inmates.

When I talked to Nathaniel today, he said that yesterday hundreds of people showed up for the protest outside of the facility. They were singing songs and praying for me and my family. It was nice to know that there were some who cared about what was happening to me.

Today, for my birthday, Nathaniel, Dawid, Marta, and a few others came to Edmonton from Calgary to pray and worship. When I called Nathaniel, I wished him a Happy Birthday, as well, because we were born on the same day—March 28th. The protesters sang a Happy Birthday to me outside the prison. It was nice they came to wish me a happy birthday in the bitter cold, even though they had to sing it outside a barbed wire fence.

Marzena had to take over the fast since I was beginning to feel very weak. Having a meal for both lunch and dinner made me feel instantly better. Since my arrest, I was told multiple times that my being in prison had some grander meaning. That people were being inspired and some great things would come from all of this.

As I lay down on my very uncomfortable prison bench, I wondered what good would come from that misery. I was locked in a cell with a young man who had murdered his own brother with a macheté. What good was there in that?

Today, I had a visit from the chaplain, whose name was Les. We talked for about an hour. He seemed like a great man. I introduced him to some of the inmates, and together, we shared the gospel with them.

Les was the same one who had visited Pastor James Coates, who had been locked in this facility the previous year. Pastor Coates was arrested and imprisoned because he refused to shut down his church. Eventually, his church was fenced off and seized by the government for three months. The pastor spent 35 days in the Edmonton Remand Centre.

I thoroughly enjoyed my visit with Chaplain Les. We talked and ministered, and in the end, he prayed for me, and I prayed for him. It was a significant change in this horrible environment.

At 8:00 p.m. I held the Bible study; this time, multiple guys joined me. We discussed the story of Jonah, and we talked about the blind beggar. After I prayed for all of them, I spent some extra time with a young black man named Bernard.

Bernard was very quiet, just sitting at the table with his Bible. I ask him, "If Jesus was sitting here at this table, what would you want him to do for you?"

He replied. "That he would lead my path."

And that is exactly what we prayed for. I have to admit that my 49th birthday was the most unique one ever. We all agreed to do this again tomorrow.

[DAY 50]

I never crossed paths with any of the individuals from the Edmonton Remand Centre again. Shortly past 4:00 a.m. I was awakened by an intercom in our cell. "Pawlowski? Pawlowski?" the voice repeated.

I replied, "Yes?"

"Wake up," the voice said. "You are being transferred." I was told to pack all of my stuff and wait. At around 4:45 a.m., I was told to follow an officer. We went to the area where I had to strip and change into my own clothing. I was instructed to remove all my clothes in front of a female officer and a group of others.

Once I was dressed, I was escorted to the tank cell where I waited for almost five hours. This concrete business had hurt my body. My back was hurting almost all the time by now and once again, it was extremely cold. Everything you touched was cold.

When I left the cell, at least I was able to say "Goodbye" to my roommate, Ryan. He wished me luck. And I left him the two additional blankets that the guard had given me previously. I also left him some coffee, sugar, and milk. In jail, those things were like gold.

I was disappointed about not having the chance to say goodbye to my new friends or to pray for them one last time. So I just prayed that God's spirit would deliver them all—guards and inmates alike.

When the sheriffs finally arrived, I was freezing. They put shackles on my feet and handcuffs on my wrists, and the Penguin March began again. I had to sign a few things and then off we went to another holding cell. They went to pick up my private property and all of my documents that I was writing for the lawyer. I had been doing my best to document everything that was happening *to* me and *around* me since the time I had been arrested.

When the door opened and I was escorted to the sheriff's cruiser, they were already a few guys inside. I was placed in a little cage and as I looked inside there was a bigger cage that held two other inmates. We drove back to Red Deer, the same police station that I had "visited" on the way to Edmonton.

After switching cars and ditching one guy to a different van, off we went to Calgary. The ride wasn't that bad, although it was hard on my bottom after sitting on concrete for two months. Overall, it was an uneventful ride.

The guys in the front recognized me from the news. They asked numerous questions about what I did and how I got arrested. It was quite fascinating to hear criminals being so sympathetic to the freedom of speech and religion. To their disbelief, a pastor, in the same restraints as them, was accompanying them on their journey. And I wasn't there for stealing, murdering, or beating someone. No, I was there for simply encouraging people to stand up for their rights. The others in the van kept shaking their heads repeatedly. "This is so messed up," they said. *What is happening to our nation?*

Our conversation was suddenly interrupted when we turned to Bowden, a medium-security institution in Alberta. I grew silent. As we waited for the doors to open, I began to consider the possibility of a change in plans, leaving me behind. The guards were talking to the boys in a box, and I heard them say they were definitely headed to Calgary. That left only me. Once they opened my door, I knew I would be spending the night in Bowden.

Bowden had a very terrible reputation with drugs, violence, and abuse of power. We waited. A few minutes later, a couple of officers brought another fellow and placed him into the box to my left. To my relief, all four of us started our final leg of the journey to Calgary Remand Centre. As the van began to move, our conversation shifted to the pastors, the truckers, and the overall state of Canada. I did not know if I would be placed in the same unit in Calgary or not, but I was glad that I wasn't being left in Bowden!

When we arrived, I was placed in a separate cell, away from other inmates. Then after a while I was taken to the change room. And the routine started. First, they stripped me and conducted a search, then I was given my familiar blue coverall with a black pocket. I got my blanket, fresh underwear, bedding and off I was escorted towards the unit. To my surprise, I was placed in the same unit as before. I was greatly greeted by my friends.

An inmate named Justin yelled when he saw me, "Free Pastor Art. Free Pastor Art." It was so awesome. Again, I was not allowed to be out with them for whatever smart reason, so I went to every door to talk to them. I shared with all of them what had happened to me since I left Calgary. When I was done I asked. "And how was it here?"

"Different," they said. "The guards became stricter, and Kevin was punched multiple times in the face and placed on administrative segregation."

"Why?" I asked. "They punched him for supporting you and for telling your family what was going on with you on the phone." Kevin had received 14 days of punishment and a few punches in the head! He paid a price for standing up for what was right. May God greatly reward him for all the kindness that he has shown me.

Daniel was doing great and was still strong in faith. He still had a lot to learn, but he was doing awesome. The prayers were still going. His father was not doing well, and that greatly disturbed him. He needed a lot of prayers. Colton, Ray, and others were very happy to see me. I guess not all inmates are bad; not all guards are evil.

During this time, I met some amazing, compassionate guards and some great inmates. As the saying goes, People are people wherever you go. It was definitely a blessing to see everyone; it was like a family that I hadn't seen for a long time.

There I was, back in my old cell with the doors locked. And I was alone once again. The slowness of time was overwhelming behind the four walls. *Maybe it feels different in the general population.* Perhaps there are more things to do there because here, time was truly dragging its feet. Confinement for only an hour was cruelty, and for the entire day became torture.

They let the boys out, but they kept me locked. Once again, I was not allowed to interact with them. So, we talked through the glass. I'm so impressed with Daniel. He was asking the right questions and focusing on the right things. I believed that if he kept his eyes on Jesus (and I prayed that he would) God will accomplish amazing things in and through him.

It was already dark, and I had no opportunity to call my wife or the lawyer yet. I was positive they were wondering what was happening with me right then. I gazed out the window, unable to utter a word. There was a bold eagle with its majestic white head, flying about 100 yards from where I was. What a view and what a gift. He flew along the entire length of the window. What an amazing creature; truly the king of the skies.

I was denied the ability to contact my lawyer or call home. Every time I asked, an officer replied to me, "I will ask my supervisor," or "It is not up to me. I have to ask."

And, of course, the answer always came back as "No!" Such tyrannical logic was baffling.

They also told me that because I had been "transferred and then returned back," I would have to be segregated from the rest for 14 days. Why? Because I might spread something! I had the chance to interact with the cleaner, hug him, and spend time together, but not with anyone else.

Once again, I found myself spending 23 hours in segregation, with only one hour of freedom from solitary confinement. The cleaner is someone who was out pretty much all the time with me, along with the rest of the inmates. Yet somehow this made sense to the authorities.

It was evident that the true intention behind all of this was not about science or ensuring people's health and safety. It was about control, manipulation, and lies. Marzena was always reminding me, "You're trying to find logic in what the devil is doing. There is no logic there. He knows he's a liar, a thief, and a murderer. He knows he is a deceiver."

She was correct because, in the end, no matter what kind of deal you will make with the devil, he will always rob you. That's what he does.

CHAPTER TWENTY-FIVE

I'M READY TO BE FREE AT LAST

[DAY 51] My Last Day in Prison

I HAD JUST finished reading the fascinating story of Nahum. The God of mercy and love had declared, "I wish that none should perish," but He also has limits. Justice demands action, and if you keep pushing, God will eventually push back. He gave Nineveh a second chance. How did the big city repay him for His mercy? With contempt and evil.

I believe that Canada had been receiving God's patience for a very long time, and God was pleading, warning, and knocking at the hearts of men. They were just not interested. In 2008, God revealed to me that the streets of our cities would be filled with blood. People were laughing at me about that idea.

But today, Calgary and Edmonton were filled with murder, guns, and violence that occurred daily. They had kicked the God of life from their cities, and the devil remained. Instead of honoring preachers of love and freedom, they were arresting and imprisoning them.

What we see today we had seen before. Nothing is new under the sun. When light is suppressed, the darkness has free rein. Nineveh had its chance. They couldn't say, "We didn't know, " because they had already been warned. And for a while, they acted accordingly and were spared.

However, later, they became even worse. Finally, they faced the full force of justice.

> I will make your grave, for you are worthless.
> NAHUM 1:14B CEB

> Look! I am against you, proclaims the LORD of heavenly forces.
> NAHUM 2:13 CEB

> Fire will consume you there; the sword will cut you down; like the locust, it will consume you.
> NAHUM 3:15-16 CEB

In the book of Nahum, God warns, "There will be no escape. It's game over. Great city of Nineveh, you have played with fire, and fire will finish you off." Sooner or later, evil will be consumed by the fire of God's judgment.

The geese were back today and congregated just outside of my window. They could be seen on one side of the fence and then on the other. A pair of them were on the other side of the barbed wire, sleeping peacefully a few yards from each other. Had they made a truce, perhaps? Was there peace, after all? Was that even possible? I guess, for today, it was. I hoped it would last. While I was still thinking about it, the door opened and I was allowed to go out for a while.

While showering, around ten guards stormed into our common area. I finished dressing and walked out of the shower area to find that the rest of the inmates were being searched with their faces against the wall. I went back into my cell but was asked by an officer to come out as well. I had no idea what was going on.

He searched me, and then the guards marched us together to the Administration area. I mean *all* of us, including those of us from the so-called "quarantine" unit, who were normally kept segregated. So much for keeping the spread of the virus in check within the facility!

Like I have said so many times before, this whole charade had nothing to do with keeping us safe or healthy. This was merely a chance to exploit us, deprive us of our rights, and continue to mistreat us without repercussions. We were placed in a tank. And then, two-by-two, we were stripped naked and searched. Once that was completed, off we went to another tank.

A NON-SENSICAL SITUATION

It wasn't until our bizarre encounter in the common area that I fully learned the significance of the situation. Apparently, a few days after I had been transferred to Edmonton, two of my inmate friends had "visits" from two guards. The taller inmate was asked to leave the Visiting cell, leaving my friend Kevin behind. Once the officer was alone with him, the beatings started on Kevin. Punches were coming to his head and chest, although Kevin did not return the punches because of his broken hand.

When the officer was done, he jumped on Kevin's cast, causing the cast to break. After that, the officer left. My friend suffered those beatings because he assisted me with phone calls and testified to the lawyer about my situation.

While they were sitting in the cell together, one of the inmates said to the guard, "You're not allowed to treat us like this; we have our rights."

The officer smiled, turned to us, and spoke. "No, you do not. Not here. You are in jail."

However, the inmate insisted, "Yes, we do have rights."

The officer abruptly finished him off, "Not according to our rules."

And that was the end of the conversation. The door was shut; end of the story. Why? Because they said so. Apparently, my friend's cast that the officer crushed had "disappeared." What actually happened is that the officer took the cast and disposed of the evidence.

Kevin called his lawyers and reported the incident. The officer got scared and discarded the cast. Kevin's cell was searched multiple times, but there was no sign of the cast.

A few days later, Kevin received a Letter of Disciplinary Action against him. No explanation was given for his placement in administrative segregation, nor were any other details provided. Shortly after receiving the disciplinary letter, the guard who had beaten Kevin came to his cell and said, "Okay, I won't file anything. And you do not say anything about what happened, and we are cool." This is how things are done in the Wild West.

A LONG-AWAITED MOMENT FINALLY COMES

While reorganizing my cell after the common area incident, my cell intercom squawked, "Pawlowski? Pawlowski?"

"Yes?" I answered.

"Pack your stuff and be ready. Okay?"

I took all my things, a pen, glasses, a few pieces of paper and walked out. I hugged the inmates and said my goodbyes as we shook hands. Then I was marched *back* to the Administration area. I retrieved my clothes and got dressed, made a phone call, contacted my wife, and was subsequently returned to the tank cell.

Eventually, the judge ordered my release on very strict conditions: house arrest, curfew, sureties, a big monetary bond, and a few other things. However, because they placed additional charges on me while I was already in jail, I was to remain here until another bail hearing took place for those charges. High-ranking officers from the Remand Centre came to pick me up from the Admission Office while I was waiting, already dressed in my own clothing.

Surprisingly, I was not taken directly out, but I was escorted through a kitchen with multiple officers wearing stars. One of them looked at me and said, "Art, don't come back here; you don't belong here."

What a sight it was as I saw the gates while stepping out! Marzena was there, waiting for me. We exchanged hugs and kisses while a crowd a few hundred yards away cheered. I learned afterward that they were told they were not allowed to come near the entrance, or I would be arrested immediately. I waved at the people and got into the car, where my son Nathaniel was waiting.

Although I had prepared a statement, I was not allowed to deliver it. So, I leave you with it here:

STATEMENT PREPARED FOR DAY 51!

I have tasted their justice system, and I am telling you it has nothing to do with justice. However, it has everything to do with a totalitarian regime. There is a great need for a major reformation. We need new leaders that will stand for the people, that will come from the people and that will be chosen by the people. Not chosen and appointed by the corrupt, lying media and their rotten masters, the elites. It is time for equalization and fairness. One law for all Canadians!

We need to bring accountability to our beloved Canada. Starting with the politicians, courts, and policing and ending with the healthcare system, education, and the media. All levels of the government are rotten to the core.

Imprisoning me was a very poor attempt to silence me and others who dared to expose the level and the depths of corruption in our society. It did not work. I have seen, and I know too much, to be quiet. I know how evil those people are.

I vow to you I will keep exposing the real villains, and as long as I live, I will keep defending the rights of all Canadians to speak their minds, and, if need be, I will peacefully protest and oppose those who have forgotten who they are working for! People are inspired by the actions of courageous men. But they themselves quite often are not courageous themselves. They admire strength, but they are extremely weak. To do extraordinary things requires choice. To be a lion, you have to choose to be one. Criminals don't know what justice means, but all who respect the Lord understand completely. Proverbs 28:5.

I have no intention of stopping my efforts to bring justice back to our nation. My kidnapping by the agents of the corrupted political regime just strengthened me even more in my determination to stand against it and to keep exposing it. At the end of the day, what those villains like Trudeau or Kenney fear the most is a man that speaks the truth. Truth is a weapon that the liars cannot and will not prevail against. Arresting preachers and peaceful protesters just proves how terrified they are of us.

The lie is crumbling before our eyes. May God give us strength to keep on course for Freedom.

MY RELEASE

NOTE: *I want you to understand that a significant part of this book was written from memory after I was released. Many of the pages I had penned in jail were illegally confiscated. In jail, I had to rewrite numerous things constantly because they were continuously taken away. The pages I wrote about corruption, including officer names, guard names, and drugs given to inmates, were all seized. Thanks to my lawyer, the pages with the names of medicines and specific things were smuggled out before they could be taken.*

When they set me free, we left slowly in the car with open windows, expressing gratitude and waving to those who had come. The officers warned me multiple times that they would arrest me if I said even one word to the crowd. They realized they had hurt us by taking me to the Edmonton Remand.

They wanted to stop the weekly protests, and I did not want to cause additional harm to my family. Even after we left the Remand courtyard, there were people on the side of the road waving at us. We were being followed by an undercover police truck, and a few kilometers later, we noticed a helicopter.

Once we arrived home, my brother Dawid and my father were waiting. We hugged and went inside, where I hugged the kids. Right away, Adam Soos from Rebel News wanted to interview me, and I understood that since everything was fresh, it would be a good idea.

Also, I ate steak for the first time in months! I was informed that my bail restrictions were so strict that I would be re-arrested if I were to even step on the sidewalk. I was under house arrest and had to remain at home. My lawyers and the Crown Prosecutor were confused for weeks, as they were unaware of my release conditions until the judge clarified in writing.

The confusion was about if I was under house arrest and under a curfew or if it was just one or the other. We were under the impression that both were applicable for weeks, but that was later clarified. At that time, I had two options: 1) Shut up and fly under the radar, hoping that the government would forget about me, or 2) I could become louder than ever and keep pounding on their corruption. My family and I chose to be as loud as possible!

So, I began exposing the corruption in the prison system, relating stories about the abuse of power. And I kept reminding people who it was that was doing this to us—the very people we had elected to serve and protect.

I did many interviews and started typing my book, which included the things I had written in jail. The release conditions stipulated that I had to contact the probation officer assigned to me every two weeks. I had to call, and every month or so, I had to see her personally. I kept going to church, but according to the conditions of my release, I was not allowed to attend Street Church.

STREET CHURCH

In addition to the regular church, I have pastored and fed the homeless at Street Church since 2005. The goal is to bring the church to those who aren't accepted as they are. Although I have been criticized greatly at times for this, I figured that Jesus hung out with sinners, and it was important for me to do so, as well.

Years ago, many people approached us, claiming that the shelters were not providing them with food. The people said, "Pastor, you talk about love and Jesus, but we are hungry." So we started doing BBQs because we wanted to *show* God's love, not just *talk* about it. Once we started feeding them, hundreds started showing up every day we were there.

After my release, the Crown Prosecutor did everything they could to keep me away from my people; to prevent me from going to Street Church. They want it to cripple me in every way by taking away my ability to preach, inspire, heal the broken and oppressed.

Following my release from prison in the summer, I was approached by certain individuals with a request. My friend Bob and his wife were instrumental in this decision, along with the interim leader Vicky. Over the weeks and months, I had visits from politicians, media personnel, regular individuals, and influential figures. Bear in mind that I was still on a curfew/house arrest, so people would mainly come to see me at my home. I accomplished everything they tried to stop me from doing.

One of my recollections from spending time incarcerated was a time when I was sitting in my cell and began pacing back and forth in deep thought. I thought to myself, *if they won't allow me to be just a pastor, I'll become a pastor politician. That which was chasing me yesterday, I will be chasing tomorrow.*

ENTERING THE POLITICAL ARENA

When those individuals approached me, they offered me the opportunity to become the leader of the Independence Party of Alberta. The idea of becoming a politician made me laugh due to their corruption. My initial response was to say, "No way." *What do they think? That it says "fool" on my forehead?* I thought.

But then God reminded me of that moment I had experienced while in solidarity confinement. So, I asked for three days to consult with my family and church before I gave them my decision. To address this corruption, my family and church decided that confronting the problem directly was the only solution. Exposing it was not enough; we needed to hold them accountable. So, I accepted the offer to run for the leader of the party.

I remembered the Independence Party from the freedom rallies during the COVID mandates. I didn't exactly like their logo, colors, or tables and viewed them as a bunch of people trying to do something that would never happen. However, I was friendly with them because I believed taking action was better than doing nothing, so I appreciated their effort.

And I didn't even know their political platform. But it's a platform—a political vehicle—and it was better than walking. Yeah, the bus was broken and old and needed to be fixed. But it still had four wheels. We decided to get on that bus and make adjustments as we moved along.

Running against me was a lawyer named Katherine; we had five debates all over the province, including one in Grand Prairie. I loved the debates because they gave me an opportunity to communicate with people. When I began my political campaign, the government initially made it challenging for me to debate, gather, and meet because I was still under house arrest. I needed special permission from my probation officer, which I managed to secure to attend events across Alberta.

Town halls, meetings, and rallies were now allowed for me because it's one thing to attack a pastor but a totally different thing to deprive a citizen of running for office. I had caught them off guard. Through a series of debates, The Independence Party grew exponentially, and I emerged as the leader.

Throughout all the debates and town hall meetings, including private meetings with the board of directors, I always told them, "I'm a pastor and have no intention of stopping being a pastor. If you want just a politician, don't even bother. I believe that only God can help us fix this mess. I will maintain my voice as a pastor and speak the truth because, without God, we're finished."

This was my speech to the Church when I ran for office:

I have an announcement to make! After months of prayers and waiting on God's confirmation, we, as a family, have decided to throw ourselves into the hands of destiny! We can no longer avoid the calling of responsibility!

I will be running in the upcoming leadership race for the Independence Party of Alberta and, later on, for the position of Member of the Legislative Assembly in the Province of Alberta! I have come to this realization that they, the corrupted politicians, will not let me live my life in peace and will not allow me to be a Pastor, which I am called and love to be. Therefore, I will become a Pastor/Politician, and the evil that was chasing me yesterday, I will chase tomorrow!

The past few years have shown us that the level of lawlessness and corruption has reached new heights, and it will require someone who has the spine and the willingness to get the biggest plunger in Alberta and drain the swamp that has pillaged and contaminated our beloved Alberta for far too long!

I have been avoiding this moment for a long time; however, I believe that I heard the voice of the Lord saying, "Whom shall I send? And who will go for us? I could no longer pretend that He was not calling me, and finally, I said, "Here am I. Send me!" (quoting Isaiah 6:8)

If not us, then who? And if not now, then when? If not here, then where?' We have to start somewhere! I say, let's start here, in our beloved Alberta!

We have to go and remind people that there is a living God, that He loves them, and that it is not His will that they should perish! We have to remind this land that God is calling us back to Him and wants to make this Land once again Glorious and Free!

Freedom and Prosperity will come back to us when we decide to come back to God, who established this land for us that we proudly call Home!

I will do my best to walk in the footsteps of legends from the past, like William Aberhart, the seventh premier of Alberta from 1935 to 1943. The Premier was known as "Bible Bill" for his outspoken Christian views. An estimated three hundred thousand people in and near Alberta tuned in to "Bible Bill" every Sunday as he preached his weekly sermons. The Bible Hour had a higher Hooper rating in Alberta than Jack Benny, whose program followed.

I will do my best to follow in the footsteps of Ernest Charles Manning, best remembered as Alberta's premier from 1943 to 1968—the longest-serving premier in the Commonwealth—and as the host of Canada's National Bible Hour for nearly half a century. These dual roles exemplify his practice of integrating Christianity with every area of his life. I will do my best to follow in their footsteps!

Here are a few things that I will follow learning from his life: 25 consecutive years as Premier, Ernest Manning was defined by strong social conservatism and fiscal conservatism. He was an outspoken critic of government involvement in society. Constantly publicly denouncing socialism and communism before, while, and after becoming premier, Manning remained a staunch anti-communist all his life.

Instead, he encouraged strong religious, individual, and corporate initiatives in addressing and solving social issues. Manning believed that the "government was there to motivate and give direction, not to intervene and carry the load."

On his radio broadcasts, Manning emphasized the individual side of faith. It was thus consistent for him to stress less government and more individual responsibility. His emphasis was on the life-changing effect of a commitment to Jesus Christ. And he wanted his listeners to understand that their parents, church or good works could not make them Christians. As individuals, they were responsible for their own spiritual condition and destiny.

Being a Pastor and a politician, I promise you this: I will continue preaching the Truth, and I will always stand for people's rights to choose their own path!

Ernest Manning's radio preaching—which spanned forty-six years—blended evangelical pietism with an emphasis on the messages of the Bible's prophetic books. He spoke often of the need for national spiritual revival and urged Christians to live in the light of Jesus' imminent return. It was his radio work that gave him a national profile, particularly with respect to his Christian faith. At its peak, the National Bible Hour was estimated to have six hundred thousand listeners from across Canada each week. It is time to go back to Alberta's roots that made this land so amazing and prosperous!

In addition, Manning was a founder of the Fundamental Baptist Church in Edmonton. He was also active in such Christian organizations as the Gideons (a service group whose members distribute Bibles in hotels, hospitals, schools, and prisons) and the Evangelical Fellowship of Canada.

If elected, I will also do my best to honor my God, Jesus Christ, and to serve people with honesty, accountability, and integrity! I believe that it is time to stop the insanity of voting for the lesser evil and doing over and over again the mistake of the "revolving door"! Different name, different party, the same swamp!

We can do better! We should do better and vote for a grassroots party that is outside of the entitled old boys' club that has been destroying our beloved Alberta for a very long time!

Do not vote out of Fear! Vote with your conviction! Never again vote for evil! From now on, only vote for GOOD!

By now, everyone who does not have blinders on can see that they are all the same: the wannabe Tyrants! Spoiled, tyrannical destroyers of our future and the future of our loved ones! Pathological liars are only interested in the people during the time of elections. Like monkeys that will go to bed with any creature if that creature would promise them their vote!

Isaiah 56:11 puts it this way; they are greedy dogs Which never have enough. And they are shepherds Who cannot understand; They all look to their own way, Everyone for his own gain, From his own territory. They seek their own personal gain.

Uninterested in real people and their problems, professional politicians have betrayed the trust, they have committed treason, and instead of serving those who have elected them, they use them only to enslave them! This must stop! I will do my best to expose them and to stop them!

It is time for the people to get their voice back! I will give you that voice! As a victim of their corruption, I will restore the checks and balances, accountability, and the sacred task of being the servant of the people—for the people that they have forgotten about!

Let's, together, you and I, remind them what it means and what it looks like to serve and protect those that God has entrusted to us. What it means to be a real representative of the government of the people, for the people, and by the people!

I do not know what the future holds, but I do know who holds it! It is not them, the political snakes, the vipers, and the scorpions, but our God, who is bigger than all of them combined!

Here are the words of a man you may have heard of: President Donald Trump. "A lot of people want me to run for things, for a lot of high offices. The polls always show that I win any election that I'm in. But I don't have any real interest in running for office. I'm more interested in supporting people."

I echo his words. I don't have any real interest in running for office. I love being a Pastor. I love feeding the poor! I love ministering to the people. Politics is like a human manure in the sewer canal! You jump in, you stink. You get too close; you get splashed, you stink. You need a shower after every encounter! If it was not for God and His clear will in my life to pursue this avenue, I would never throw my name into the hat!

Nevertheless, not my will, but thine my God be done! So today, I once again submit my life into His hands and will do my best to serve Him and the Canadian people to the best of my ability, so help me God!

So, remember, you will not lose your pastor to politics. You will have a politician and a Pastor in One! Be blessed, and stay strong!

WORDS FROM MY VICTORY SPEECH - THE CULMINATION OF A JOURNEY

When I was last in Bowden, I found myself in the back of an Alberta Sheriff's prison transport van heading to Calgary from Edmonton's prison, all for opposing unconstitutional mandates. The sting of those memories remained fresh in my mind. From the bustling streets of Calgary to the cold confines of a prison cell, I'd seen it all.

So it was with a deep reverence that I told the crowd, "I want to thank God for his blessing and inspiration. Through every step of my journey and every battle I faced, it was His guidance that became my bedrock."

Turning to the wisdom of scripture to highlight the challenges of our times, I voiced, "Ezekiel 34:1-8 The word of the Lord came to me... And to me, these verses weren't just ancient words; they were a mirror to our current leaders, a call for them to serve, not exploit."

With heartfelt passion, I told everyone there, "In our beloved Alberta, there is no place for tyrants and traitors like them! I've always believed in Alberta's spirit, its promise of freedom and opportunity. And seeing that spirit threatened? It lit a fire in me."

Emphasizing the core principle of justice, I declared, "I've always believed in the equality of all citizens. The law should be a shield for everyone, not a tool for the powerful. There must be an equal application of the Law, or there's no Law at all! How can we trust leaders who bend the rules for their gain?"

I concluded, driven by a mixture of hope and determination, "Alberta's spirit, its very essence, is unbreakable. And I, along with countless others, will stand tall, ensuring that our voices are heard and that justice prevails."

There were around one hundred people present, and you could tell that hope had returned to the crowd by their standing ovation. Amid claps and cheers, countless people came to congratulate me. It was remarkable to see so many cheering us on, willing to build something beautiful with us.

I was understanding God's plan more clearly in my life. It was just as God had promised in His Word when He asked His disciples to gather the leftovers after the feeding of five thousand. I knew now that God had taken the broken remnants of my life—my 51 miserable days in prison—and he was going to make something good come from them. Because that's what God always does.

> *Gather up the fragments that remain, that nothing should be lost.*
>
> JOHN 6:12 ESV

EPILOGUE

THE REAL WORK BEGINS

THROUGH A combination of church activities, helping the homeless, frequent meetings, and press conferences, our numbers grew, and our name became well-known in the mainstream. More and more people were able to see that there was an actual, tangible option for the upcoming provincial election. Town hall meetings were absolutely incredible. I went on a tour with Bob Blayone and his wife, and everywhere we went, there were hundreds of hungry Albertans seeking an escape from this swamp.

From Grand Prairie to Camrose and High River, there were packed houses of excited people who came to listen to a real option. As the party grew, I started to have very interesting visitors.

BRIBERY

First a few meetings with some people who came to me at my house, claiming to be sent by the Alberta government, and then by some claiming to represent Danielle Smith, the front runner for office. They came with a proposal that if I were to back her up and her party, I would be offered a job for $250K a year to become the chair of the public inquiry at a panel of experts regarding Alberta's Covid response, although one stipulation attached to the offer, that I must not run for political office.

My question to those who brought me the offer was, "If I find something that was done wrong during COVID-19, will I have the power to deal with that?"

The response was, "None."We will have to report to the government and leave it at their hands."

I realized the government wanted me to become their puppet to eliminate me from the race; during that time, the story was getting bigger and bigger and bigger. We were becoming more popular, and the establishment started to take notice.

DANIELLE SMITH-THE NEW RULER/PREMIER OF ALBERTA

There was a by-election in Brooks-Medicine Hat, and we decided to have our own candidate as an opportunity to bring exposure to the party; Bob Blayone decided to run against Danielle Smith.

Already during this time, experts had been sounding the alarm about side effects or adverse reactions to the COVID-19 vaccines, and it had become a hot topic in the public. By that time, pretty much everyone knew that vaccines were harming people. The "sudden deaths" and "mysterious deaths" were not unknown anymore. This by-election opened our eyes to what sort of a woman Smith was. By that time, she was actually elected to be the United Conservative Party of Alberta.

Bob Blayone was attending a number of debates, trying to bring to the forefront the knowledge surrounding the damaging consequences of the mandates and vaccines. During one of the meetings, he had a private conversation with Danielle Smith, telling her that right now, in our province, people are dying because of the vaccine injuries, and she grabbed his hand and said, "I know, Bob; I know people are dying because of the vaccines," she is aware, she knows, and yet a few months later she rolled out the vaccines for 6-month-old babies.

She got elected, and she won the seat on the promise to bring an amnesty bill for those who were attacked, ticketed, and arrested by the government for opposing the mandates. Smith promised to bring back justice and the rule of law to our province. She went on public to apologize for the mandates and the prosecution the unvaccinated citizens faced, and here is a shocker: she actually went on television in front of the reporters and stated that she has never seen more "persecuted people in her life than the unvaccinated," we were really presently surprised, "wow, perhaps we were wrong? Perhaps she did really change."

The backlash of the left mainstream propaganda machine that is bought and paid for by the federal government was too much for Danielle Smith, the new premier of Alberta, and revealed again who she really was. Under pressure, she caves in and apologizes for calling the unvaccinated the most persecuted. Her entire campaign was based on freedom, and she claimed that pastors deserve apologies and re-compensation for the wrong that the government did to them.

I witnessed the same betrayal and flip-flopping before in another party called The Wildrose, which had colossal momentum and tens of thousands of people within it. Our chance to become the ruling party in Alberta was ruined when Danielle Smith made an unexpected move—she made a backdoor deal and crossed the floor with a few other MLAs, enticed by the offer to become the deputy premier. She abandoned the party, effectively destroying it. We were left without a leader and without most of the MLAs.

Fun fact: *She did not get what she was promised. Not only did she not get what she was promised, but she also lost her seat because people became disgusted by her treachery.*

But if you think her career was destroyed, think again. It seems that in the current era, the more corrupted you become the more rewarded you will be. A radio station called QR77 came to her rescue after she lost her seat; she was offered one of the most popular jobs as a radio host. I remember that time because I was shocked; I thought her career was done because of what she did, yet she was promoted in a way with a considerable salary. She worked there for years like nothing happened.

During the mandates and restrictions, she did not come to the rallies or protests, standing with the hurting people. And yet, during her campaign, pretty much all you heard from her was "freedom, standing up against the oppressors. " It's like she hijacked our plea; I knew right away what she was doing.

She was riding on our suffering to promote herself as the new hero of freedom. Since freedom and conservatism became more popular again, she hopped on the bandwagon. By the way, that's exactly what Pierre Poilievre (running to become the Prime Minister of Canada) has been doing in the federal Conservative Party. We have been surrounded by traitors, liars, and cheaters. In the end, no apology or re-compensation came to any of us.

Smith ran on the policy that she'd bring amnesty to all those prosecuted for COVID-19 mandates. During the election, we held a Town Hall at her riding, and about 600 people showed up to listen. This number was actually surprising to see. The vibe, energy, and appreciation were there. I think the United Conservative Party (UCP) government realized we were becoming a real and renderable threat with our growing popularity, so the bribers revisited me.

They offered to work to drop the charges against me if I stopped exposing the UCP. I replied that first, I had to be freed from house arrest, and my charges must be dropped; then, we could start talking. They were not happy with my answers.

The party kept growing, and momentum was building; the enemy was scrambling. Then, the announcement came that the election was happening in spring. And surprise, surprise, another visitor came knocking at my door.

This time, I was told that an offer was on the table. If I were to cross the floor like Smith did years before, the ruling government party would offer me a guaranteed seat in the legislature. My name would be placed on the ballot in a historical area where people always vote conservative. I was offered to have a place at the government table, but I had to abandon the people and cross the floor.

At that time, I lost it. I told the messengers, "Who do you think I am? I'm a Christian Pastor; I don't abandon people for incentives." They were not very happy, to say the least. "I'm not a whore of Babylon," I added.

They left the meeting disappointed, and the new year kicked off. My trial was scheduled for February 2023. Running a church, feeding thousands of people on the streets of Calgary, and being a political leader under stringent restrictions and house arrest was not easy. However, we managed.

On February 2nd, 2023, I stood in front of the judge, Gordon Krinke, accused of inciting mischief, interfering with crucial infrastructure under the defense act (eco-terrorism), and a breach of release order. The crown prosecutor, Steven Johnston, maintained the accusation that I caused the Canadian economy hundreds of millions of dollars in damages for my 19-minute speech and that I incited people to commit crimes.

The trial was strictly based on my speech. No witnesses were called; everything was based on my words. The transcript of my speech was given, and they went sentence by sentence and word by word, talking with the judge about what I meant when I said certain things. This has never been done in Canada's history. We have ventured into the realm of a totalitarian regime.

The crown prosecutor went utterly insane and used a case comparing my speech to the Rwanda genocide, trying to somehow allude that my words were triggering violence. He compared my sermon to someone inciting murder on people. To top it up, he implied that my political party, "The Solidarity Movement of Alberta," was more like a coup attempt.

Don't forget, when I spoke to the truckers, I was wearing a hoodie that had "Solidarity" and "With God We Win" printed on it. Apparently, that was proof enough for him that we were trying to valiantly topple the government. It was an absolute disaster.

The judge reserved his decision for a later date. On May 2nd, when he rendered his judgment, I became the first Canadian ever to be found guilty of this new legislation, eco-terrorism, and for inciting mischief. But first, we need to go back to March. That is when I received a phone call from the Premier herself, Danielle Smith, ahead of the elections.

The conversation was recorded based on the advice I received from my lawyers. Every time I talk to high-profile government people, I must always be prepared that they might lie about the conversation and try to entrap me in something—the conversation was recorded for my own protection.

Premier Smith was playing the political game. She thanked me for my work and promised that she was working in the background with the Crown prosecutors trying to fix this problem.

I forwarded the conversation to my own legal team just in case I'd be accused of saying something that I could be liable for.

The team was split. Some believed that it should be forwarded to the public, thinking that it could benefit my case because of political interference since, in their opinion, I don't stand a chance due to negative publicity. Whereas the other lawyers thought that it was unneeded, and under the legal analysis we would win since I haven't committed any crime. The other opinion is that it would hurt my case. I agreed, and we left it at that.

For months, we were very active with the Independence Party, exposing the corruption of the government. We also hosted more town halls to come together with our people, and to hear them.

Here's a shocker! The board of directors I inherited when I was elected the leader of the party, which I became a part of once I was elected, to my surprise, was opposing everything that was common sense, like building the party, getting memberships, and raising funds were all being shot down by the board. The job of a board is to support the leader, and from this board we were receiving nothing but opposition. At that time, I did not know that they were told (offered something perhaps) to torpedo the party since we were getting too powerful and popular.

We were told multiple times that they don't want us to mention God in our town meetings, to "tone it down," and to be more secular. Do not talk about the grooming of the children or pedophilia that was rampant in Alberta. We do not want you to even mention controversial things.

In one of the board meetings, we were openly told that the town hall meetings were a waste of time. "Don't talk about the WEF, the mandates, the vaccines, don't bring the doctors to the town halls educating the public about the harms of the vaccines and mandates." This was going on for months. I, of course, did not listen to the board and continued doing what I knew to be right.

After multiple attacks that we started to receive from our own board, we realized that something sinister was happening. They were either bought and paid for, or they were trying to replace us with someone else. Board member and former rival Katherine was attacking me publicly. She didn't take it lightly the fact that she lost the leadership to me.

On March 28, my birthday and exactly one year later from having celebrated my birthday in prison, without contacting me at all, they publicly announced that I'd been removed as the leader of the Independence Party. They voted me out. Effectively meaning that nine people went against the will of thousands of people, undermining the whole idea of democracy.

The mainstream media picked up the story. They were happy to do everything they could to embarrass me across the country. The board torpedoed the party two months before the provincial election. I was fired three days before the general AGM.

On the day of the AGM, the electors revolted, disgusted at what the nine members of the board did to me, and voted every single one of them out. However, the damage was already done.

We have this Polish saying, an old saying: "You don't enter the same water twice." I was done with that party. The new board didn't reinstate me since the committee that became the new board was hired by them, and then that board resigned as well. The party basically became irrelevant. It was done. Smith accomplished what she wanted!

On the 29th of March, the conversation with the Premier was sent to CBC and to the NDP. The recording has become probably one of the longest ongoing political scandals in the history of Alberta's politics. The story received coverage for months non-stop; it was unbelievable.

The conversation proved to the whole world that Danielle Smith still cannot be trusted and that she's a flip-flopping liar. She is a manipulator who would do anything to advance her political ambitions. Flipping it each time, she changed the same story four times.

There were many angry Albertans. The biggest shocker to me was that the public's anger was not directed at the one who betrayed our trust, the liar, the one who walked away from the election promises she publicly gave to us. Still, the anger was directed at me, even though I was the victim of this story.

I was viciously attacked and called a traitor, NDP supporter, and government operative working for Soros, Russia. They went as far as to claim that I work directly with the Liberal Party! And again, my "crime" was exposing a liar. The video was not released by me since we decided the video would only hurt the case. The only people who had access to the video were the legal team. It turned out (allegedly) that the video was leaked from the criminal lawyer's office.

In January, I held a press conference to challenge Danielle Smith after she walked away from her promise of amnesty, which gave her an opportunity to do the right thing. "Just do what you promised because what you promised is what got you elected. Keep the promise that got you elected, or resign." Today's politicians find this idea too unfamiliar to grasp.

Eventually I decided to do another press conference at the legislature to expose the briberies. From the moment the media obtained that leaked recording, which was done without my approval by a former lawyer, it created a massive backlash and caused problems for both me and my family. He breached confidentiality and was fired.

The mainstream propaganda machine relentlessly pressured me for months to discuss my conversations with the premier. I refrained from fueling the controversy, but the story grew too large, and the attacks turned vicious. Therefore, I felt compelled to share the entire story with the people, particularly before the election.

When I made my announcement that I was going to reveal the background story of the encounters I had with the UCP government, I didn't know I was unleashing another Pandora's box. The anger and the hatred directed at me was unbelievable. People were calling me, texting, and emailing, demanding that I do not dare to tell the public what really happened.

"You're going to damage her reputation," I was told. "You're going to weaken the party, and the NDP will take advantage of that," I was told. "It's better to have the *known* evil rather than the communists. Don't do it. Don't do it," the voices echoed.

I was shocked that these types of rhetoric were coming from people I considered "freedom fighters," people that I marched with and bled with, and people who faced tickets, arrests, and harassment under the boots of the government during COVID-19. I could not believe how quickly the tide was changing. Somehow, the villains that were responsible for destroying lives and destruction of our economy were somehow appealing to them as long as a bigger villain would not come and take the reins.

Once again, we were facing the lesser of two evils dilemma, the same dilemma that got us into this trouble in the first place. I even got calls from people I considered friends asking me the same thing: to stand down. I have to admit, my heart was torn in half. But deep inside, I knew I had to do the right thing, and that was to tell the people the entire story.

Even driving to the legislature, I had people calling me non-stop. Trying everything to persuade me, not to expose the lies of the premiere. And when we arrived at the legislature, the media was already there. I don't think I've ever seen a more significant gathering of snakes in one place.

The cameras were like bazookas, ready to fire. I did my thing. I told the people the whole truth; I believed that people deserve to know who is leading them, and maybe today, not many appreciate that. Still, I believe their eyes and ears will be opened one day. They will understand what I was trying to tell them. But, until then, it is what it is; everyone will face the judge of judges and be responsible for everything they did and everything they said.

It was a complete and utter circus. A 15-minute long announcement turned into a three-hour standoff with the media. They were vicious.

When everything was said and done, the premier made her press announcement, the NDP and the wicked Notley, the leader of the opposition, took their swing at the situation, and the story lived on for days and weeks until the day of the election.

In May, since we were without a party, we were only allowed to start campaigning and submitting documents after the date of the election was dropped. Honestly, right now, I believed my involvement in the election was over.

I have to admit, part of me was glad. That's the truth. In a way, I was subconsciously looking for a way out because I hated politics, but when they kicked me out, I felt free because, at the end of the day, my heart was being a pastor, and that's what I love doing. Politics is like a cesspool of constant manipulation and dealing with con artists who never mean what they say, and it's very tiring to keep an environment like that.

I was surrounded by absolutely amazing people, and it was them who came to me to not quit and keep going. People like Nick and his wife and Bob and his wife and my brother Dawid were the only reason I could keep going and trying for office.

During one of the meetings with the independent candidates, because we all decided to run as independents after the purge from the Independence Party, a man told us there was a way to form a political entity without the thousands of needed signatures. During election time, if you have more than half of the ridings full of candidates running in the provincial elections, you automatically form a political party.

My jaw dropped, my eyes opened, and I said, "Are you serious? Why didn't you tell us before?" I thought we were done.

And he smiled, "Well, that's another way of forming a political party; I thought you knew about that," he said.

"No, I didn't."

Believe it or not, Nick and others were all hands on deck, and within ten days, more than half the candidates had signed the papers for elections Alberta to run in this provincial election under the name of The Solidarity Movement of Alberta.

In this weird twist of events, we were given a gift from heaven: our own uncorrupted, un-infiltrated political party. Our hopes were restored. It was a miracle of God, for sure.

We understood that we had run out of time and did not have the resources or time to conduct a proper campaign. However, the purpose of running candidates was to establish a political party, and now it's time to build it up. We had a little social presence, a few billboards, and so on.

Meanwhile, I was still dealing with house arrest, being under the boots of the totalitarian government, and facing 12 years in prison. During the election, our little, brand-new political entity managed to have over 40 candidates. And, because of that, we effectively were able to remove from power Alberta Minister of Justice Tyler Shandro and Jason Copping, the Minister of Health. Deena Hinshaw, under extreme pressure, was removed as chief medical officer of health. Finance Minister Travis Toews did not run for re-election. And as you already know, Jason Kenney was removed from power.

THE POLITICAL FIXERS

Between the verdict and the sentencing, I started to receive weird phone calls from people who identified themselves as "fixers." The fixers were claiming that they had a meeting with former Conservative Prime Minister of Canada Stephen Harper, Former premier of Alberta Jason Kenny, and the potential prime minister of Canada Pierre Poilievre.

I have to admit I was taken off guard by those phone calls. I'd understand why Jason Kenny and Stephen Harper would be interested in destroying me since I was exposing their government's corruption, but what was Pierre Poilievre doing in this?

I was told that it was quite simple: My exposure of the corruption within the provincial Conservative Party was potentially damaging the federal Conservative Party. Today's leader, Pierre Poilievre, was worried that when the federal election kicked in, he might lose some votes because of me telling people who those corrupt politicians are.

The man on the other line... if I told you his name, your hair would stand up. We are talking about one of the most powerful men, a well-connected millionaire, the deep state. When the government has a problem, they go to these people to "fix" the issue in the shadows. The meetings are secret, and they are not recorded.

The conversations were straight from a Hollywood espionage movie; I truly felt like I was dealing with some spies in the Cold War era. I was told that they wanted me to be just a pastor and keep doing what I love to do; they said, "You love feeding the people, right? And that's what you pretty much want to do? We are going to give you that opportunity; the judge is bought and paid for, and the conservative government has decided to eliminate you from the board (the game). You must withdraw yourself from politics."

I was told multiple times to stop talking on the shows and on podcasts. They warned, "You have to stop talking about politicians at least for the next two years, and you must give $100,000 to us, plus a $50,000 donation to a charity of our choice."

They continued, "As a penalty for the trouble you are costing us." So, if I agreed to these terms, then they would "fix" my problem. We owed the judge, I was told, and this judge was from Medicine Hat. Interestingly enough, he was from the Premier Smiths riding himself.

I endured the phone calls for a few months, and when they realized that Artur Pawlowski was not for sale and terrified of their threats, they stopped calling. In the last conversation I had with them, I was told to pack my bag and take my toothbrush. They intimated, "You are going to prison, and I might not come out (meaning I might get assassinated there)."

And just like they said, the judge agreed with the lying prosecutor, Johnston, and found me guilty on all charges, including eco-terrorism. On top of that, he concluded that everyone who participated in that protest (Freedom Convoy) was also a criminal. I've never seen a judge more nervous and shaking than this guy. He could not articulate a sentence without sipping water and was not making eye contact with me at all.

You could tell that he was uncomfortable, and he completely looked different from during the trial. During the trail, he was very sympathetic and asked the right questions. The sentencing was reserved for a later day. I was guilty of "inciting mischief," a criminal offense, and breaching my release conditions. The "interfering with crucial infrastructure" (eco-terrorism) charge was later, almost a month after the verdict stayed by the crown.

Upon leaving the courtroom, I made it clear to everyone that the battle was far from over, and I would persist in my fight against this oppression regardless of the circumstances. The pressure was mounting. Political friends, mainstream media, and even political commentators analyzed this situation and came to one conclusion: I was going back to prison; there was no other way.

According to them, I embarrassed the government to such a degree that they had to make me an example of what not to do. I contacted my friends around the world to put more pressure on my enemies, and I did hundreds of media interviews during that time span to raise awareness of what was going on.

I guess it worked. For August 9th (the scheduled day for sentencing), there was a convoy being organized from BC, Saskatchewan, and Alberta to come and put political pressure on hundreds, potentially thousands of trucks rolling to the court. It seems like the government got a hold of the idea, and my sentencing was moved from August 9th to September 18th. The time for my life started ticking.

My lawyer advised me that the pressure is so great and the political vendetta against me and my family so incredible that I must prepare myself for what might happen. Sarah, my lawyer, called me and told me that I might not come out of the courthouse and might be arrested right there and then sent back to the very place where I was exposing corruption at the Remand Centre.

Obviously, this worried us since it was there that we had learned that the guards were giving incentives to prisoners to murder me. It was also there where I had been kept in metal cages, solidarity confinement, and ultimately in a max pod for the most dangerous inmates in Alberta. I was eventually placed in a Psych Ward without evaluation or even the knowledge of doctors and professionals. The prospect of going back to such a corrupted environment was becoming very real and very dangerous. I was told that I could be potentially kept there for weeks or even a year if the stay for the appeal would be denied.

Needless to say, the pressure was enormous. I put my house in order, got my finances checked, and gave my wife everything she needed to go on without me. I guess the worst thing in such circumstances is always not knowing what might happen, but there was nothing much we could do about it. We did everything in our power. Now, it was in the hands of God and God alone.

During that time, our Church stood shoulder to shoulder with us, praying and supporting us. Quite interestingly, people from around the world called us or emailed us about the visions and dreams they had regarding this affair, and every single one of them said this: God would not allow the enemy to put me back in prison. Soon, we were to find out if those prophecies were true or not.

NATHANIEL IN EU

Because of my troubling restrictions, I was not allowed to leave the country; when the opportunity arose, my wife would travel with my son to testify. The meeting took place in the EU Parliament in Belgium and was about the erosion and attacks on our liberties in Canada.

Marzena and Nathaniel met with some of the government's most influential people, such as MP Christine Anderson, who was fighting against lockdowns and mandates. There were all kinds of people who stood against tyranny. Nathaniel gave a speech testifying about what was happening in Canada. He sat on a panel in the European Union Parliament and addressed the members present, as well as many others in attendance. This is what he said:

> Thank you for having me. My name is Nathaniel Pawlowski from Canada. I'm going to speak about the consequences of abuse of power under the guise of health—set out by The WHO framework that local governments take upon themselves to implement. I'm the son of pastor Artur Pawlowski, who you will hear in just a minute.
>
> I am here today in desperation, a cry for help. I would like to stand here and tell you all the things about freedom and democracy that I like, but I no longer know those things. They have been taken away from us Canadians. Canada has fallen. We no longer have freedom of religion, freedom of speech, or the right to protest or assemble, associate or express ourselves, have free media, or

disagree with the government. Anyone who does so is arrested, charged, and jailed as a political dissident.

My father was just found guilty of inciting mischief for giving a sermon to the truckers when they went and stood for rights in 2022. A Christian sermon that referenced the solidarity movement was criminal in our government's size. The charge carries a penalty of up to ten years in prison. This case sets a precedent for all Canadians and the world.

If you allow this to happen, then anybody, including politicians and media, does not have the freedom to say or express what they have in their hearts for fear that what they say is mischief and could be liable to prison. I myself have been charged for preaching and reading the Bible publicly because the government claims the Bible isn't inclusive and is hateful.

This is what the Canadian government is doing to us. In my father's case, the Crown Prosecutor (and I believe in naming names because our oppressors do not get to get away with this without being named and shamed) so the Crown Prosecutor Steven Johnston and Judge Gordon Krinke claimed that when Pastor Artur, my father, referenced the solidarity movement in his 19-minute sermon it was an act of mischief against the government.

The very solidarity movement that this parliament reveres and has placards about all over the building, the peaceful movement that broke the Iron Curtain and repelled the communist hold on Europe. The movement the Canadian government condemns and says is unacceptable.

So I ask you, the rest of the free world, to intercede on Canada's behalf and pressure the Canadian tyrants to stop persecuting law-abiding free Canadians, especially clergy. They simply did their duty and gave hope.

My father told the truckers to stand for the rights solidarity style and to do so peacefully. His sentencing is this August 9th, 2023, and if he goes down, we are all lost as Canadians. If a pastor goes to prison, what can they do to the rest of us? [arresting] For giving a sermon in Canada, they are no better than the tyrants of old.

So please, I ask you for help and to pressure Canada on this matter and to help us deal with our oppressors who act like modern-day "Caligula's." Trudeau is a modern-day Caligula. We cannot allow these mad emperors to… well, run mad. And remember, all of this is being done under the guise of health safety and protecting us by stripping our rights and ushering in tyranny.

We must not allow Canada to treat its citizens, especially clergy, this way. Who has structured a way to take away our rights, and our local governments are doing that.

Now you will hear my father. He will speak via video, so this is Pastor Artur Pawlowski, a political prisoner. Thank you.

That speech opened the political arena's doors to my son, as his speech echoed from house to house all across the world. I was also able to speak via video. Later, my wife would testify that the people gathered there, including the parliamentarians and the guests, stood up and cried. My wife said, "Everyone was crying." It was a profound supernatural moment in that place. The video spread like wildfire and reached tens of millions of views in a very short time, and the Canadian government was not happy.

Upon arrival from Belgium, Nathaniel was temporarily detained, and was told that he had a warrant for his arrest. Later on, we found out that it was related to the protest outside of the public library that Nathaniel attended and was charged with illegal participation in a protest, and because he read the Bible out loud was charged with the crime of harassment. Ultimately, he was let go, and we had to hire a new lawyer to defend him.

JUST BEFORE MY TRIAL

The day before the trial, I visited my sick mom (during my imprisonment, she had open heart surgery, and I did not know if I would ever see her again). We spent time together, had dinner, hugged, and the next day, took our entire family, kids, and even our dog Simba to Lethbridge on the 17th. Many people from the church came down with us as well.

In the evening, the Church did a Jericho March—singing, praying, and marching around the building seven times. During the night hours, I had a dream, and I pretty much never dream or forget when I wake up, but this one was like an open vision. I saw myself standing by the ocean; the beach was dirty, and you could see debris and footprints on the sand. Suddenly, a big wave came and washed all the dirt away, smoothing the sand and removing the footprints, and I heard a voice say, "There will not be even a trace," and I then woke up. This dream coincided with what other prophets have said.

I went downstairs to check out of the rooms. A hotel employee I didn't recognize stopped me and thanked me for my actions.

So we went to the court, people were already gathered, and Rob was already worshipping. We had decided that every time we were dragged to the courts, we would bring the church and do a service. This would happen before each trial, and that's precisely what we did this time!

The court was packed. Inside and outside were people praying and worshiping. Here is what I said to those gathered:

> *We are not to simply bandage the wounds of victims beneath the wheels of injustice, we are to drive a spoke into the wheel itself.*
> DIETRICH BONHOEFFER

The Truck Convoy, the peaceful protests, rallies did just that; we drove a spoke into the wheel of injustice itself, and it scared the tyrants! Truth always scares the liars!

> *Freedom is never voluntarily given by the oppressor; it must be demanded by the oppressed.*
> MARTIN LUTHER KING, JR.

We have never seen the level of corruption coming from politicians, mainstream propaganda, and the so-called justice system than the one that we are seeing now!

And again, the words of Edmund Burke hit home once more, The greater the power, the more dangerous the abuse.

Martin Luther King, Jr., leader of one of the greatest examples of civil rights movements recorded in history, speaks from the past warning us today.

A man dies when he refuses to stand up for that which is right. A man dies when he refuses to stand up for justice. A man dies when he refuses to take a stand for that which is true.

> *We cannot defend freedom abroad by deserting it at home.*
> EDWARD R. MURROW

We must engage! We must speak up! We are Christians! We are Canadians!

Are you dead to the cry of the victims?

Are you dead to the pleas of injustice?

Are you dead to the abuse of power and the screams of Truth?

I hope not!

> Those who deny freedom to others, deserve it not for themselves.
>
> ABRAHAM LINCOLN

John Diefenbaker, our great Prime Minister, said in the House of Commons on July 1, 1960, "I am Canadian, a free Canadian, free to speak without fear, free to worship God in my own way, free to stand for what I think right, free to oppose what I believe wrong, free to choose those who govern my country. This heritage of freedom I pledge to uphold for myself and all mankind."

I am about to be sentenced today by a corrupt core political entity! For almost two years, they tried to bribe me, scare me, manipulate me. They have arrested me, imprisoned me, and taken me through the wringer, demanding my surrender!

Here is my answer! Never! No surrender! No Retreat! No deals with the wicked! No bowing before the hyaenas! We are lions following the Lion from the Tribe of Judah, the One and Only Living God!

> *Success is not final; failure is not fatal; it is the courage to continue that counts.*
>
> WINSTON CHURCHILL

Churchill also cautioned us by saying:

> *All the great things are simple, and many can be expressed in a single word: freedom, justice, honor, duty, mercy, hope.*
> WINSTON CHURCHILL

Proverbs 26:24-27 says: Enemies disguise themselves with their lips, but in their hearts they harbor deceit. Though their speech is charming, do not believe them, for seven abominations fill their hearts. Their malice may be concealed by deception, but their wickedness will be exposed in the assembly. Whoever digs a pit will fall into it; if someone rolls a stone, it will roll back on them.

Our children are worth fighting for! Hold the Line! We are Canadians, Christians, and we have already won; the enemy just doesn't know it yet!

The words echoed, bouncing from the concrete walls of the courthouse. People cheered, and some cried. I hugged my children and wife and walked into the court. It was my Red Sea moment. Politically speaking, there was no way out of this situation. The enemy was behind me, the mountains on my left and right, and the Red Sea in front of me—an impossible situation. The room was packed as the judge entered, and the lawyers began talking.

NOTE: You're the accused, and they're talking about your life. Either it will be destroyed, or you're a free man, but you're not allowed to say anything as you listen to outrageous lies from the government. "This is a show trial," I said.

We knew that the government was really bent on putting me behind bars. The crown prosecutor is demanding a minimum of 1 year to imprison me; he also informed my lawyer that he's not happy with my speeches and videos, especially the ones where I am referencing him and his lies and his manipulations during the proceedings. He tried to influence my lawyers to tell me to stop talking about him. Well, I didn't, and I had no intention of stopping; people deserve to know the agents who are working for the corrupted politicians.

I was told that I might walk into the court, and when the judge pronounces his sentence that includes imprisonment, I might be handcuffed and taken from the court immediately. I was informed that I may be looking at a maximum of 12 years in prison— ten years for inciting mischief and two years for violating a release order.

Since hundreds of people showed up, they brought extra police and sheriffs; they had to livestream the proceedings from a TV just outside of the courtroom. Distant cheers and boos would breach the walls from time to time, depending on the direction of the proceeding.

The family was there, and lots of people were concerned as to what might happen. The common theme of the Crown Prosecutor's arguments was that I was unrepentant. He believed that my lack of remorse justified additional punishment.

The precedents they were referring to were so weak and out of context to what happened in Coutts that it was apparent they were pulling straws. Here are some things that were said.

"Probation would serve no useful purpose as the accused does not believe he did anything wrong. He is not remorseful for the harm he has caused," Krinke, with the Alberta Court of Justice, said in his decision. During the trial, prosecutors said Pawlowski's impassioned speech to truckers fanned the flames of unrest and convinced them to stay longer.

"This case is not about freedom of religion, and it is not about free speech. This case is a straightforward criminal case," said Prosecutor Steven Johnston.

"In this case, the accused comes before the court with no sense of remorse. The lack of remorse, the lack of introspection is important in this case because of the fact he is likely a high risk to redo this," he said.

Ultimately, after a back-and-forth between the lawyers and the judge, we heard something that I'd never heard before in my entire *criminal* career. The judge said he had to take a break and "discuss the sentencing with others." The whole room was shocked.

Who were the "others?' Who was waiting in that other room? Who was he consulting with? Politicians? Other judges? Government representatives? Who was there? Maybe we will never know.

When the judge returned to the room, he sentenced me to 61 days in prison. I had already spent 50 days in prison and was released on the 51, so I had already served 51 days. Since that time was mainly in solitary confinement and in Remand, it counted as time and a half. I was told the time counted as time served, and I was allowed to walk out of the room into a cheering, clapping, happy crowd. I was free!

More than 200 supporters waited outside the courthouse, with some chanting, "Hold the line."

As I stepped out of the court building holding the hand of my wife, Marzena, a friend, Bob, gave me a shepherd's staff and said that God told him that we were entering a new season—a season of open doors, symbolizing a new season of authority! I grabbed the microphone and spoke.

. "I hope that my oppressors are listening because this is not over. This is just the beginning. For the past 18 months they've done everything in their power to force me to say that I am guilty, that I am sorry. They were forcing me to apologize, but I have nothing to apologize for."

I encouraged the backers to support the Solidarity Movement of Alberta party in the upcoming provincial election, referring to Crown Prosecutors, judges, and politicians as "political traitors."

"They should live every day in shame for what they're doing to us free Canadians, " I told the crowd. People were touched, and they cheered. The buzz of freedom was tangible. People hugged me with tears going down their cheeks, expressing how grateful they were that I was free. It was something else.

From that moment on, house arrest, probation, and restrictions were gone. I was unleashed. Freedom was mine.

A couple weeks later, we filed an appeal, and I hired a new set of lawyers to go after the villains. To go after everyone involved in this injustice. We decided to sue all of the involved parties that tried their best to destroy me, our church, and our family.

It was time to push forward with the offensive! It was time to go after the villains! Here is the short version of the press release:

Artur Pawlowski and Dawid Pawlowski v His Majesty the King In Right Of Alberta and others | Court Action 2301-16154 |

PRESS RELEASE AND FORTHCOMING STATEMENT

Artur Pawlowski and his brother, Dawid, have filed a Statement of Claim against the Alberta Government, the Attorney General of

Canada, Alberta Health Services, the Calgary Police, the RCMP, the Prison, Canada Post, and additional presently unknown parties in relation to allegations that over the past three years and beyond, these Government agencies engaged in malicious prosecution, abuse of process, false imprisonment, unlawful discrimination, battery and assault, cruel and unusual punishment, infringement of Charter rights, breaches of the principles of procedural fairness and natural justice and other unlawful behavior stemming from the alleged systematic harassment, investigation, and prosecution of Artur Pawlowski and his brother Dawid, who have been outspoken opponents of the Government's COVID-19 mandates, among other things.

We have decided to push hard! Since the house arrest ended, I could travel outside of Canada again. I was invited to join my American family in Florida, and my family received an invitation from the Ohio House of Representatives as well. We were honored in their House during their session and given a standing ovation.

While I was receiving a standing ovation, Trudeau and Zelensky and the entire parliament were giving a standing ovation to a Nazi, one of the worst embarrassments in Canadian history.

(134th General Assembly) (House Resolution Number 194)
The resolution, introduced by Republican state Reps. Reggie Stoltzfus and Timothy Ginter, was cosponsored by 11 of their colleagues and appealed to the historic legacy of religious liberty in Canada, the United States, and Ohio as the basis for their condemnation of how Canadian clergy have recently been treated by authorities.

A RESOLUTION

To urge the United States Commission on International Religious Freedom to take whatever action is necessary to address and rectify the situation described in this resolution, and consider adding Canada to the Special Watch List of countries where the government engages in violations of religious freedom.

RESOLVED That we, the members of the House of Representatives of the 134th General Assembly of the State of Ohio, urge the United States Commission on International Religious Freedom to take whatever action is necessary to address and rectify the situation described in this resolution and consider adding Canada to the Special Watch List

The fight was on! I was busy between traveling, speaking, Church, and feeding the poor. The momentum was growing again. Although Albertans have currently opted for the lesser of two evils and haven't entertained the idea of us forming the government, I have faith that one day they will see the truth, and justice will prevail in our province once more.

AN HONORED INVITATION

At the start of 2024, Donald J. Trump invited me to his house as a guest speaker. Wow, the prophecy from the prison to the palace was slowly being fulfilled. The event was incredible, and my address was live-streamed for hundreds of thousands of people to hear. God was elevating us and promoting me and my wife, giving us more and more opportunities to speak and to encourage people to stand. Here is what I said:

My Speech at Mar-a-Lago

It is a great honor for me and my wife to be here. Thank you for inviting us. Ladies and Gentlemen, today I speak to you on behalf of our preachers who are being prosecuted and persecuted simply because they believe in the Word of God.

I am standing here on behalf of the journalists who are being arrested for nothing more than just doing their job!

I am here on behalf of millions of Canadian Christians, truckers, and farmers who are being denied their right to worship their God and to live their lives in peace!

We must understand that when Religious Liberty goes, all the other Rights will follow! There cannot be Freedom without the Freedom to Worship!

America belongs to God! There will be no Free America without the God of Freedom!

I have faced over 120 court cases. I received over 340 citations, and I have been imprisoned almost 20 times. I was kept in metal cages and solitary confinement. Threatened and abused, charged, and attacked without mercy. My Crime? I am a Clergyman.

And yet here I am, standing in front of you. Not moved and not shaken! For I am the son of the Living God!

I am willing to pay even a higher price, but I cannot do it alone. We, the Canadian Christians, need our American brothers and sisters to stand in solidarity with us. (We witness Solidarity in Poland! The power-people)

When we stand together in unity, Protestants, Catholics, and of every color, with our God, we will truly become unstoppable and unbeatable! With God's Truth, we cannot and will not lose! We have already Won! Where the Spirit of the Lord is, there is Liberty!

When God shows up, it is over for our enemies! America, bring God Back to America! The Cross and the Flag married together in the holy matrimony of Freedom! Benjamin Franklin once said, "Fear God and your enemies will fear you."

Some time ago, I watched the movie *The Patriot*. There is a scene in that movie that I could never shake off. A young girl speaks to the churchgoers, and here is what she says:

"Will you now—when you are needed most—stop at only words? Is that the sort of man you are? I ask only that you act upon beliefs of which you have so strongly spoken and in which you so strongly believe."

I have the same question for all of those who claim to be Christians! Are we not the servants of the Most High God, the Creator of the heavens and the earth, the King of kings, and the Lord of lords? The Alfa and Omega, the beginning and the end, the Giver of Life?

Do we not believe in the World of God, the Truth itself? The One that said, stand for what is right?

There comes a time when a real man, especially a man of God, must say: "A Shepherd must tend his flock. And at times, fight off the wolves."

A man of God does not shut down the Church! A man of God keeps it OPEN!

When injustice is done to one of us, it is done to the rest of us! When one hurts, we all hurt!

Martin Luther King Jr. once said, "The ultimate tragedy is not the oppression and cruelty by the bad people but the silence over that by the good people."

It is Time for the Great American Eagle to Flap its Wings once again! It is Time for the Land of the Free and the Home of the Brave to Roar, for the entire world to hear!

Let them say that in America, the Church is a Force to be reckoned with! We are the Church! We shall never Surrender! We are the Lions of God!

We are the messengers of Hope! This word desperately needs Hope! We must give it to them!

Ladies and gentlemen, let's not just make our Beloved America Great Again! Let's Make America *Blessed* Again!

In Jesus Christ's Name! Thank you!

We felt that God was not done yet, and a standing ovation sealed that feeling. There are more incredible things in store. He intended to use us and our story for a much larger purpose than we anticipated.

While we traveled and spoke everywhere possible, our son Nathaniel was fighting his own battles. Because of what we were doing, the Canadian government denied him access to universities across the land (he applied everywhere for two years). Thanks to our U.S. friends, he got accepted to study Law at Virginia's Liberty University, the top Christian university.

In the meantime, Nathaniel became engaged to a girl from our church, Tobyn Friesen. You may remember our friend Ray, who was arrested for coming to the prison protests with his children. Tobin was Ray's daughter. She and Nathaniel were married in the summer of 2024 and moved to Virginia for him to begin his law studies.

Did our son ever consider that the girl protesting outside the Remand Centre would become his wife two years later? I doubt it. God works in mysterious ways! His ways and thoughts are higher than ours, that's for sure!

Nathaniel still gets arrested (briefly detained) every time he crosses the Canadian border. Apparently, there is an error in the system that the border authorities don't know how to "fix." It's not a big deal, I guess. By now, our son is very well known among the customs officers, who smile every time they see him.

Since my release from prison, I have traveled to many places, and everywhere I have gone, people have wanted me to share my story. Countless individuals would constantly approach me, asking if I could write a book. "Yes, yes," I would reply.

But how? I have always been swamped. After finishing one thing, I was immediately chased by another thing. This was in my life's never-ending revolving door. One task finished, the next immediately waiting on the burner. To write a book requires time, time that I did not have.

Sometimes, I would tell people, "If I could only find some time, please pray for me." Well, God answers those prayers. So, it took prison, solitary confinement, and the craziness of COVID-19 to finally accomplish that. All the Glory goes to the Living God!

To take off from an aircraft carrier, a jet plane needs 54 kilometers per hour of wind. To reach this steady breeze, the captain turns his ship into the wind. The jets must fly into the wind. This is the only way to achieve the lift. Facing the wind becomes your advantage.

To achieve a great victory, you need two things: 1) courage and 2) strength. And you need a powerful enemy/challenge. Putting your trust in God will always lift you up, especially when the wind blows in your face. Do not turn to the left or the right. Keep your eyes on the Lord, and you will soar like eagles.

Deep inside me, I always knew that this was going to happen. I felt it inside my cells, in my bones. Of course, my wife was always a lot more accurate—like a barometer. She felt it. She told me it was coming.

A few days before, she came to me multiple times and spoke. Typically I have the same feeling, particularly during significant things that happen to us. I know something big is about to happen.

On the day before my arrest, Marzena said, "You are going to be arrested. And this time, they will keep you longer—a lot longer. But this must happen. This has to happen for something a lot bigger." And it did!

Needless to say, there were countless other scenarios, encounters, occasions, and extraordinary individuals who were by our side during this madness but didn't make it into this book. Sheila Zilinsky was part of the "Call to Repentance" in Edmonton at the Legislature. There was also the memorable church service held on the steps of the Supreme Court in British Columbia with Laura-Lynn Tyler Thompson.

In addition, countless church meetings and town hall talks were held, along with the unforgettable court rally in Manitoba, where Tobias Tissen and his extraordinary family were present. The memorable experience with German Parliamentarian Christina Anderson, who we gave a "white hat" welcome in Calgary, is still fresh in our minds.

The details of these events and circumstances showcase the power of God in our lives. Nevertheless, we had to trim it down to maintain the story's narrative. So many things happened! Perhaps those stories will make it in the next book; God knows.

Thank you all for your willingness to journey through this with us. May God richly bless you!

As I near the completion of this book (September 2024), my lawyers are currently delivering their presentation before a panel of three judges in Alberta's Court of Appeal. It'll take some time, possibly a few months, before we learn what their decision is. No matter what. God has already won. The victory is ours. Lions do not bow before the hyenas. We eat them for breakfast!

ABOUT THE AUTHOR

Artur Pawlowski's religious journey began in the streets of Calgary, where he became the pastor of the Cave of Adullam congregation, a role that allowed him to touch many lives. But he didn't confine his calling to church walls. He ventured out, leading the Kings Glory Fellowship (KGF) and founding the Street Church Ministries. This was more than just a religious initiative; it was a mission to reach the lost, broken, and downtrodden. Through his street preaching, Artur has brought hope to many, reminding them of God's love and grace.

As his religious pursuits thrived, Artur felt drawn to a new realm: politics. In September 2022, he took the reins of the Independence Party of Alberta. Though his tenure was short-lived, ending in March 2023, it was a testament to his leadership capabilities. Not to be deterred, Artur focused his energy on founding the Solidarity Movement of Alberta in 2023. This party became a platform advocating for causes close to his heart, particularly freedom of speech and religious rights.

In 2012, the Magen David Adom honored Artur Pawlowski with the honorary chaplain position in the province of Alberta. This recognition wasn't just for his religious endeavors but also for his unwavering support for Israel. Artur's humanitarian efforts in Africa also earned him an honorary ordination in 2011, a testament to his commitment to serving beyond borders. The Progressive Group for Independent Business also awarded him the "Free Speech Award" in 2012.

Artur believes in standing up for one's convictions, even in the face of adversity. He has been a vocal opponent of abortion, advocating the sanctity of life. Even when his views on traditional family values have put him at odds with mainstream thought, he has never shied away from expressing them.

Through religious and moral activism, he has been actively involved in protests and rallies, championing the foundational beliefs he supports. Whether supporting a Calgary Transit bus driver or leading the way for the tyrannical efforts imposed during COVID-19, Artur remains on the front lines, leading by example.

Artur Pawlowski and his wife, Marzena, currently live in Alberta, where they continue their valiant work to serve as a beacon of life for others. They have three children, Nathaniel, Gabriel, and Maya Grace, who support their father's work and serve the Lord gladly. Artur's unwavering faith and commitment to justice and freedom make him a role model in a world where compromise is easy. He serves as a reminder of the power of conviction.